The Dissertation

The Dissertation
An Architecture Student's Handbook
Second Edition

Iain Borden and Katerina Rüedi Ray

ELSEVIER

AMSTERDAM BOSTON HEIDELBERG LONDON NEWYORK OXFORD
PARIS SAN DIEGO SAN FRANCISCO SINGAPORE SYDNEY TOKYO
Architectural Press is an imprint of Elsevier

Architectural
Press

Architectural Press is an imprint of Elsevier
Linacre House, Jordan Hill, Oxford OX2 8DP
30 Corporate Drive, Suite 400, Burlington, MA 01803

First published 2000
Reprinted 2001, 2003, 2004, 2005
Second edition 2006

British Library Cataloguing in Publication Data
A catalogue record for this book is available from the British Library

Library of Congress Cataloguing in Publication Data
A catalogue record for this book is available from the Library of Congress

ISBN-13: 978-0-7506-6825-5
ISBN-10: 0-7506-6825-3

For information on all Architectural Press publications
visit our website at www.architecturalpress.com

Printed and bound in Great Britain

06 07 08 09 10   10 9 8 7 6 5 4 3 2 1

Contents

Acknowledgements

Katerina Rüedi Ray offers her sincere thanks to Assistant Professor Deborah Fausch for her extensive help and encouragement, and to Assistant Professor Pamela Franco for her advice, both of the School of Art History at the University of Illinois at Chicago. Thanks also to Sherry Bates for his role in developing the agenda of the Image/Text dissertation group at The Bartlett, to Alex Zambelli for his role as a teaching colleague, and to Peter Cook and Stephen Gage for their support for the programme.

Iain Borden wishes to thank all of the various tutors who have worked in the History & Theory and PhD areas of the Bartlett School of Architecture, UCL. Similar thanks are also due to the many students on the Diploma Architecture, Masters in Architectural History, PhD Architecture and PhD by Architectural Design programmes at the Bartlett, and particularly for doing things differently.

We wish to acknowledge Katherine MacInnes at Butterworth-Heinemann, whose original suggestion it was to produce the first edition of this book, as well as Miranda Housden, Leonie Milliner and Nancy West at the RIBA. Ian Latham and Katherine Shonfield also played a part. Special thanks are due to Ruth Kamen, former Director of the British Architectural Library at the RIBA, who generously supplied much of the information regarding internet research in Chapter 3.

And of course our particular gratitude to all those who have graciously allowed us to reproduce extracts from their dissertation: Susannah Bach, Megha Chand, Nic Coetzer, Kathryn Ewing, Alvin Foo Tze Yang, Alexander Franklin, Paul Gardiner, Olivia Gordon, Robert Holford, Michael Levey, Yeoryia Manolopoulou, Anna Radcliffe, Edward Taylor and Huw Williams.

1 Introduction

Why Write a Dissertation?

As a student of architecture, the major part of your education is always going to be the design of buildings as executed through drawings, models and other kinds of visual representation. Together with the work space of the architectural studio, the presentation of designs followed by a challenging crit or jury, and the submission of a carefully wrought portfolio – these are undoubtedly the main elements of an architectural education.

Yet as anyone who has ever tried to explain architecture quickly realises, architecture is not only about images and models. Words, too, are an integrated part of what architecture is all about. Architecture is textual as well as visual and spatial. Most obviously, words are a necessary explanation of what kind of architecture is referred to in drawings and models, and if you don't believe that words are essential, try explaining your designs at a crit without speaking at all. Words are also a way of exploring new territories, new ideas, new kinds of architecture – from the Roman architectural theorist Vitruvius to the modern Robert Venturi some of the most important and influential works of architecture have been books and other kinds of writing.[1] Indeed, without these words there would be no buildings, no architects and no architectural study.

A dissertation is (wordy) architecture made of words. It is a way of conceiving and producing architecture through sentences, paragraphs and considered argument. It is an arena in which to alternatively explain, explore, challenge, theorise or imagine architecture. A dissertation can therefore be about many different kinds of subjects, from the study of the *oeuvre* of a single architect to tentative speculation about the relation, for example, between shoe design and architectural culture. Most importantly, though, it is a place where, just as in your architectural designs, you have the opportunity not only to learn about architecture but also make a contribution to what we all think about it; the architectural dissertation is your chance to explore what you believe and aspire to, and to present those thoughts to others.

One other thing. A dissertation is a common requirement of many architectural courses worldwide. In the United Kingdom, universities also often require you to pass your dissertation independently of your design and other architectural studies – no dissertation, no degree! The dissertation is also, therefore, often a part of the requirement for all those seeking accreditation or licensing from or membership of their appropriate professional body, such as the National Council of Architectural Registration Boards (NCARB) and the American Institute of Architects (AIA) in the USA, or the Architects Registration Board (ARB) and the Royal Institute of British Architects (RIBA) in the UK, or the Royal Australian Institute of Architects (RAIA) in Australia. If no dissertation means no degree, then it can also mean no professional qualification. For those wanting to be professional architects, doing the dissertation is in many countries not a matter of choice.

The Handbook

This handbook provides a guide to the whole process of starting, writing, preparing and submitting a dissertation. It also offers some advice on what to do after the dissertation. It explains carefully what to do, how to do it, when to do it, and what the major pitfalls are to avoid. Each university and architectural programme does, of course, have its own rules and requirements, and you are strongly advised to check everything said here with what your own institution expects. Nonetheless, if you follow the guidance in this book, and if you add to it your own intelligent and rigorous efforts, you should go on to produce a dissertation of the best possible standard.

The book, following this introduction, is divided into six more chapters. These follow the general chronological procedure by which a dissertation is normally undertaken.

Chapter 2 (*Starting*) describes what to do when first beginning to work on a dissertation. It explains what kind of study a dissertation is, how to select and assess a potential dissertation subject and how to choose a supervisor to work with. It also explains the importance of writing a proposal.

Chapter 3 (*Researching*) identifies what research is, and briefly outlines some of the main kinds of approach that architectural historians and theorists have adopted in order to work within the discipline. On a more practical note, this chapter also explains what you actually have to do in order to research an architectural dissertation: research techniques, working methods, libraries and archives are all covered. A special section, extended in this edition, deals with the internet, which offers particular opportunities and challenges for the architectural student.

Chapter 4 (*Preparing*) deals with (the arcane mysteries of) writing a dissertation, and how to go from the blank sheet of paper or bare screen to a complete first draft. Advice on how to organise and structure a dissertation (including what to include in an 'Introduction' and 'Conclusion') is complemented with tips on working methods, illustrations, referencing, bibliographies, how to avoid plagiarism, submitting a draft, and the use of computers. This chapter also suggests how you might change the format of a dissertation into a multimedia or other non-conventional form of submission – indeed, these are kinds of dissertation which have recently been the subject of much discussion, development and innovation.

Chapter 5 (*Presenting*) covers the important process of finishing off, printing and binding a dissertation, and generally making sure that it looks as good as possible while meeting all scholarly requirements. This chapter also explains how tutors commonly assess dissertations.

Chapter 6 (*Afterwards*) moves into the future, when the dissertation has been submitted and assessed. If you have done very well, you may want to consider further study or research in this field, and some suggestions are made about the kinds of courses which you might consider. You may also want to prepare your dissertation for publication, and similar suggestions are made as to how you could do this. This chapter also offers some 'troubleshooting' advice if you are faced with serious difficulties during the production of your dissertation or if you disagree with the result that you have been given.

In Chapter 7 (*Dissertations*) you will also find numerous examples of prize-winning dissertations previously completed by architecture students, many of which have been submitted to the RIBA in London for their international President's Medals Students Awards competition (www.presidentsmedals.com). You will therefore find in this book not only pertinent advice but also instances of how architectural students have tackled the dissertation with extremely successful results.

Reference

1   Vitruvius, *The Ten Books on Architecture* (New York: Dover, 1960); Robert Venturi, *Complexity and Contradiction in Architecture* (New York: Museum of Modern Art, 1966); Robert Venturi, Denise Scott Brown and Stephen Izenour, *Learning from Las Vegas* (Cambridge, MA: MIT, 1972); and Robert Venturi, *Iconography and Electronics Upon a Generic Architecture: a View from the Drafting Room* (Cambridge, MA: MIT, 1996).

2 Starting

What is a Dissertation?

The first thing you need to know about a dissertation is what it is not. Unless you are undertaking a PhD, your dissertation is not going to be like a book, for reasons of time as much as anything else. Consider for one moment that a typical book is commonly something about 80 000 to 100 000 words in length, and can easily take 3 years or more to write and produce – a PhD is about the same. By contrast, a thesis for an MPhil is typically around 40 000 words, and takes 2 years to complete, while a dissertation for a graduate architectural course in the USA or a postgraduate architectural course in the UK can be anything from 5 000 to 25 000 words. In practice, an architectural dissertation is often only around 10 000 words (as with most of the details in this book, you should always check the specific requirements of your own institution), and has normally to be completed within one academic year, or 9 months. Many students therefore have about the same space and time available as a more experienced author would have to write a single book chapter, or a long article in an academic journal. This situation is even more complex in that many universities will now also accept dissertations that make extensive use of visual material, with some appropriate amendments then being made to the overall number of words.

The dissertation is not, therefore, the appropriate place to try to sum up everything that you have ever thought or believed about architecture – you simply have neither the time, nor the number of words, nor the number of images at your disposal to cram everything in. Instead, the dissertation is a place in which to enquire into an architectural subject which is of interest to yourself. It is a conscious and deliberate attempt to identify, define, explore and articulate a subject of some relevance both to the architectural discourse and to your own development as an architectural designer and thinker.

A dissertation is, then, a kind of staging post – an opportunity to step outside of the studio, or to straddle between studio and other areas of architectural exploration, and to focus for a relatively short period of time on a particular aspect of architecture that appeals to you, and which you think would be of benefit when thinking about what architecture is now and might become in the future.

Selecting a Dissertation Subject

One of the biggest problems facing any architecture student when starting off on a dissertation is what subject they should choose to study. Some schools of architecture have specific guidance on this matter, such as the stipulation that the dissertation must be about a single building by a well-known architect. However, such requirements are quite unusual, and nowadays most architecture schools will allow just about any subject as long as it has some bearing on architecture. Quite what that bearing is for you to propose and to discuss with your supervisor.

To begin with, then, you have to locate a subject which you want to explore, and which you can begin to talk about. The first thing you need to realise here is that, unlike many other essay assignments that you may have been given, your tutor is not going to tell you what to do. Rather, the whole point of the dissertation is that you yourself should come up with a topic.

Where, then, might you locate that subject? There are several places where you might look:

- *Yourself.* What are your interests in architecture? One of the common mistakes that people make about architecture is that they assume that what they are interested in is also what interests everyone else. Consequently they assume that what they know about architecture is already understood by everyone else, and thus that they cannot write a dissertation about it. This is rarely the case. Indeed, one of the great joys about architecture is that it is capable of being thought about in a near-infinite number of ways. So have faith in the fact that what you are interested in will no doubt be shared by some but not all others, and this is your opportunity to convince everyone else of its importance to architecture. The dissertation is, after all, a place of individual work, so give vent to your own obsessions and preoccupations.

    How, then, can you identify your own interests? One of the simplest things you can do is to try writing down a few key interests: The way buildings weather over time? The idea of memory? The different kinds of people who inhabit architecture? Advanced-technological systems? Political meanings of buildings? The inter-relation between word and images? A particular architect's life and work? Have a kind of brainstorming session with yourself and see what you come up with. Or (if you are brave enough) talk to some friends in the same position and ask them to tell you what they think you are interested in, and vice versa.

- *Your portfolio.* The portfolio you have produced in the design studio over the years is in many ways a record of yourself, your architectural thoughts and how they have developed. Dig out those old designs, and ask what the key themes are within them. Alternatively, what is absent from these projects but which you might like to spend some time thinking about?

  One particular question that you may want to bear in mind is the connection between your design work and your dissertation subject. For some students, the dissertation is an opportunity to take a theme from their designs and to explore this in great depth in the dissertation. For others, the reverse is true, and the dissertation is seen as an opportunity to do something entirely divorced from the studio which may only later inform design work, or may remain entirely independent of it. For most, it is probably somewhere in between these two extremes: pick something related to your architectural design interests, but don't make it a slave to studio projects. By the way, although most architecture schools have very broad definitions of an acceptable dissertation, the one kind of subject that many do entirely ban is the dissertation about yourself: writing directly solely about your own design work is not normally acceptable. On the other hand, some of the developments in those dissertation which artfully blend both design-based and word-based work may relate very strongly indeed to the student's own studio work. The essential thing to bear in mind here is that the word-based work should not be a commentary on the design-based work, and nor should the design-based work be simply the supporting visual evidence for the word-based work. Rather words and designs should be used as equivalent and inter-related ways of exploring the same subject matter.

- *Other work.* You will probably have already completed a number of different history and theory essays, and maybe even a previous dissertation. As with your portfolio, look at this work and ask what the issues are that you have discussed previously, and what this tells you about your preoccupations. Alternatively, what have you already covered and what you might like to move away from? If you have already written about, for example, contemporary architecture, perhaps it would be a good time to explore something older, such as Victorian Gothic architecture, or perhaps something outside of the immediate architectural profession, such as the way architecture has been represented in theatre design (and vice versa).

- *Books.* What are the books you already own, and which are most attractive to you in the school's library? What kinds of subject do they tend to focus on? Also, what kind of thing have you always wanted to read about but never been able to find? One good trick is to deliberately attempt a kind of parallel study of a chapter you like.

For example, if you are impressed with Alice T. Friedman's analysis of the role of the female client in the design of the Schröder House,[1] how might a different building be subjected to the same kind of analysis? Or how might one consider the vernacular architecture of your local city in a similar way that Mirjana Lozanovska has treated the migrant house in multicultural Australia?[2]

- *Magazines and periodicals*. These are particularly useful for two reasons. First, browsing through the most recent issues will confirm to you what are the most up-to-date debates and issues under discussion, and you may want to take an active position within debates on, for example, the body in architecture, the culture of immersive environments, or rethinking the work of Cedric Price. Of course, just because there are suddenly lots of articles on, for example, parametric surfaces and architecture does not mean that you should do the same – indeed, these things can often help you decide *against* as much towards choosing a particular subject.

  Second, many extended journal articles are about 6 000–8 000 words (sometimes shorter), and so are often not too different from the kind of 10 000-word dissertation that many students undertake. For those undertaking a longer study, the magazine or journal article is about the same length as a typical section or chapter. With these comparisons in mind, take some time to note the range and organisation of the argument, the kind of depth that you will need to go into, and the types of evidence and documentation referred to.

- *Everyday life*. Architecture does not exist only in the studio and architectural school, but is also out there in the city, on the streets, on the roads, in the suburbs, in the landscape. In addition, it has a virtual, mediated existence in the specialist architectural press, on television, in movies, on the internet and on the radio. Here the scope of subjects you might find is truly vast, ranging from how architecture is photographed in different professional magazines, to its role in public spaces or private ways of life, to how it is represented in films or on the World Wide Web. If you are short of a subject, take a stroll down the nearest busy street, or drive across an unknown landscape …

- *Other people*. Talk to other students in your programme, and with your friends and family. Make yourself unpopular for a short while, and make them listen to what you are thinking about. It may not even matter what they say in response – simply saying something out loud a few times will often make you realise more clearly what you are working towards. Listen to their response if it seems at all useful – it may make you see issues you may not have thought about.

- *Seminars, lectures, conferences*. As you will discover when researching your dissertation (see Chapter 3), most of the information you will need is not contained in books in the library – for the simple reason that these contain work that has already been completed and published. By contrast, seminars, lectures and conferences are places where architectural thinkers often talk about work in progress, about tentative proposals and strange ideas that are in development. So you can often get clues as to new concepts and lines of thinking from these less formal, more speculative arenas. They are also places where people sometimes talk about exactly how it was that they came to arrive at a subject, how they are developing it, and what problems have arisen on the way.

- *Tutors*. The people that actually oversee your dissertation can also be enormously helpful at this stage. Don't be afraid to go along with your initial thoughts, and ask their advice. One useful thing that you can do is to come up with a number of different proposals, say three or four, and quickly run through the merits of each in turn. Above all, remember that the initial ideas should always come from you, so that your tutor has something to respond to and make suggestions about.

  It is also sometimes a good idea, if you have the opportunity, to talk to more than one tutor or professor about your ideas. Even if a particular tutor is not formally part of the dissertation programme, if you think someone might be useful you can always ask her or his advice – most will be flattered to be asked, so don't be shy. You can also ask your tutor whether there is anyone else that they recommend you talk to. Contrary to what you might think, your tutor will not be upset if you ask someone else's opinion about your dissertation.

Assessing a Dissertation Subject

Rather than just thinking of one topic and launching straight into it, you should aim to identify, say, three to five potential subjects for your dissertation, even if some of them seem hardly feasible. You are then in a position to assess each one of these proposed subjects in turn. Doing this will help you understand the range of different studies that you might undertake, and hence pick the one most appropriate to your own interests and situation.

Going through this process may also be of some help at a later stage in the dissertation, when mid-way through the research and writing process you begin – as everyone does at some point – to have a few doubts about whether you are studying the right thing. If you have carefully assessed the subject early on, you can then remind yourself of this fact, and press on with relative confidence that, yes, you are indeed doing the right thing.

In evaluating a potential dissertation subject, try to identify four things:

- *Objects of study*. What are the particular objects that you are going to look at? A dissertation may be highly philosophical or it may be highly empirical, but it will always have to be *about* something. So what exactly are you going to study: what buildings and architects, books and other media, specific events and historical periods, ideas and concepts? What exactly are you going to talk about and refer to?

- *Interpretative possibilities.* Not only do you have to find something to study, but you also have to know that there is something to say about it. What can you say about architecture in relation to the Casa Malaparte, billboards in Madrid, or the idea of ornament in Indian temples? In general, small objects can have large questions asked of them, while big objects need to have much more precise lines of enquiry: for example, you might be able to study the life of a single architect, such as the Californian modernist Ralph Rapson, but not of a whole city like Beijing. Alternatively, you might be able to explore the idea of spatial diagramming in the layout of colonial cities in Latin America, but that might prove too constraining for a study of a single building. In short you need to know:
  1 What kinds of issues and questions you want to investigate
  2 How these issues relate to your chosen objects of study
  3 How much, or how little, this will give you to discuss.
- *Nature of the investigation.* One of the things you need to know early on is what kind of study you want to produce: descriptive or explanatory history? Critical history or interpretation? Speculative theory or philosophical musings? Chapter 3 gives some more guidance on the difference between these types of approach, but for now you should at least have some idea of the approach you want to adopt. In other words, do you want to write a documentary account, to find causes and explanations, to try to say something rather unusual about your subject, write something that is only distantly related to architecture, or speculate in a creative, propositional or hypothetical manner? All these may be possible.
- *Academic context.* Although no dissertation can be wholly original, your research should contain a significant element of research and interpretation that is unique to yourself. In order to do this, you first have to have an idea of what has already been studied in relation to your proposed dissertation subject and, therefore, of how your own line of enquiry will make an original contribution to the understanding of this topic. In short, who else has already explored this subject, and what do they say or propose about it? Is this a subject that has already been exhaustively covered, and/or can you add something relatively new?

If you apply each of these four criteria above to your proposed dissertation subject(s), and come up with some responses, you will very rapidly come to realise what is a runner and what is not.

There are also some very practical issues that you must consider if you are to get off on the right footing. Some of these may seem somewhat trite when viewed in the context of the intellectual parameters of an architectural dissertation, but they are in fact extremely important. Making a mistake here could seriously derail your project.

- *Size and scope of subject.* As already explained, you have to carefully match the objects of your study with the conceptual questions you wish to ask of it. This rapidly becomes a matter of the time available to you, and effort you can put into it (which has to be balanced with your other studies) and the words available to write it all out. Can you really cover in depth the decorative schema of all of the churches of Italy, or the way architecture is used in every single one of Franz Kafka's novels? Can you assess all of Merleau-Ponty's philosophy and relate it to the entire history of twentieth-century architecture? Conversely, is there really enough to say about a single Morphosis beach house, or about one film by Satyajit Ray?

  Bear in mind also that if you choose to do a comparative study – say, the historic marketplaces of Nottingham compared to their equivalents in the French *bastides* cities – then you will have to undertake double the amount of research and writing than if you studied just one of these places. Conversely, in a dissertation about, say, the idea of memory and architecture, comparing the work of, for example, architect Daniel Libeskind with that of artist Maya Lin, might help you to develop interpretations about monuments and memorialisation that otherwise would have escaped you.

- *Availability and access to sources.* To study something properly then at some point, no matter how many ideas you already have of your own, you are going to have to look at some other material: books, archives, buildings, films, individuals etc. are all possible sources. However, not all of these may be open to you, or even exist at all. For example, if you want to write a study of the Peter Jones department store in London, is there a company archive that has information on the building, and will they let you look at it? (Answer: yes and maybe.) Is there much written on Feng Shui? (Answer: not much, increasing all the time, but of patchy quality.) Where will you find information about graffiti art? Will Jean Nouvel/Toyo Ito/Zaha Hadid/Jacques Herzog talk to you? (Answer: you might be lucky.) Does the Barcelona Pavilion still exist? (Answer: depends on how you consider the authenticity of the recent re-creation.) Although you cannot foresee at the outset of your research exactly what sources you will be able to use, you need to have some idea that there is a reasonable variety of material to study.

- *Time.* Chapter 3 offers more advice about time-planning, but for the moment bear in mind that some projects take up more time than others: in particular, interviews may have to be planned many weeks or months in advance, cities in other parts of the country (or the world) take time to visit, and archives may require advance negotiations before access is granted or documents can be reproduced. As with sources, you need to have a general idea as to whether you have enough time for the kind of research which your dissertation research will entail.

- *Finance.* There are always cost implications in any research, if only for occasional photocopying. Some projects, however, are inherently more expensive than others. If you are planning to go to Chile or New Zealand, can you afford the travel expense? Would Brighton or New York be cheaper than Cairo?

Other projects which can prove expensive include those involving films (rare films, unavailable on video or DVD, may have to be viewed at national film archives with screening charges) or the study of rare photographs or drawings (you may not have to pay copyright charges for reproduction – see Chapter 4 – but you may well have to pay for staff to make copies or prints). Once again, make sure that you understand the cost implications of your research study before getting too deeply committed.

- *Personal strengths* and *weaknesses*. A dissertation should always be challenging, and you will no doubt be wanting to stretch yourself intellectually, but you should also be aware of your own limits. One of the mistakes that architecture students sometimes make is that they think they can be an expert in anything they care to turn their hand to. Sometimes this is true. Sometimes, unsurprisingly, it is not. Thus while you may want to study the depiction of architecture in the works of Thomas Hardy while using the techniques of the Russian formalist school of literary theory, or apply the technological speculations of Nicholas Negroponte to intelligent architecture, beware that you are not trained in literary criticism or advanced science and that you may, consequently, find such topics very difficult. Alternatively, if you happen, say, to speak Norwegian as well as English, and have a good knowledge of poetry, you may be able to undertake a study on the relation between the work of Olaf Bull and Alvar Aalto that would be quite beyond the reach of most other architecture students. In many ways this is simple common-sense. Try to devise a dissertation project which will best develop and exploit your own personal capabilities. This does not mean only intellectual strengths and weaknesses, there may be other more personal aspects that you may want to consider:

1   Interviewing. Do you enjoy meeting and talking to people? If so, an interview-based project would obviously be a good idea. Conversely if you are the kind of person who is happy digging around in archives, maybe a library-based project would be more appropriate.

2   Contacts. Who are the people you know? Is a family friend the building manager for Lloyd's of London? Did you once work for IBM or SOM?

3   Languages. What languages do you speak? Is your French good enough to read those Yona Friedman or Henri Lefebvre texts that are yet to be translated? Does your fluency in Japanese help with a study of Shogunal and Daimyo gateway buildings?

4   Travel. Which are the cities and buildings you have visited? How many people can honestly say that they have experienced Beijing at first hand? Does your first-hand knowledge of New Bedford or New Harmony offer any opportunities?

5   City of residence. Where do you live? If you are studying in Glasgow, or come from Stockholm, studying some aspect of Mackintosh or Asplund might be more feasible.

6   Technical equipment. Do you own, or have access to, the right technical resources? Such things as high-speed broadband internet access, a good-quality digital camera or voice-recording machine might be required for particular kinds of dissertation research.

In general, take a review of your life – where you are, where you have been, who you know – and make good use of what you have.

• *Risk*. It has to be said that some kinds of dissertation are inherently more 'risky' than others – by which is meant those dissertations which might fail, or which not be as good as they could be, because of factors which are often outside the control of the student. Four of the most high-risk dissertation projects are:

1   Historical research that tries to *prove* something. For example, if you want to show beyond all doubt that Piranesi was under the influence of opium when he prepared the Carceri drawings, that may be difficult to demonstrate convincingly. It would be better here to choose a dissertation question that seeks to show how the Carceri drawings *might* be interpreted as drug-inspired or otherwise fantastical invention.

2   Research that relies on other people or a particular set of data. If your whole dissertation requires Norman Foster to grant you two hours of his time for an extended interview, or on the existence of original photographs of the construction of Palau Guell, you may be disappointed. As the proverb says, don't put all your eggs in one basket. You will usually do better to choose a dissertation which draws upon a range of different sources. This way, not only are you more likely to get a substantial amount of information, but you will also get information of different types and shades of opinion, which will greatly enrich the interpretations you can offer.

3   Dissertations that make extremely unlikely connections. If you try to show that architect's spectacles are directly related to the design of their buildings, you may, or may not, make a highly original contribution to the history of fashion and architecture. If you want to undertake an unusual connection, make sure that you have something meaningful to say.

4   Dissertations that are purely speculative. If you write in a purely philosophical manner, you may end up saying little of great originality, or even of much sense. Again, make sure that you have something meaningful to say.

A balance of objects, interpretations and theorisation will always help protect against these kinds of risk. Your supervisor can always advise you as to which kind of topic is most likely to succeed.

Choosing and Working with a Supervisor

Not every school of architecture lets you choose your supervisor, often for reasons of staffing and/or other matters of practicality. Others, however, do let you make some kind of choice, and this can be an important advantage. To help you make your choice, you might like to consider the following.

Knowledge

Obviously it is a good idea if your tutor knows something about the kind of dissertation you want to write. However, just like you, even a large group of tutors cannot between them be an expert and authority on absolutely everything, and they consequently cannot be expected to be able to give you highly detailed advice about every subject that you might want to undertake.

This is particularly true with a dissertation, which at its best can be a highly original study and so, by definition, lies beyond the knowledge of most other people. You should therefore not be surprised if your supervisor sometimes seems to know less about your study than you do. Conversely, it sometimes can be a little daunting, even occasionally unhelpful, to have a supervisor who does know a great deal about your particular subject. In either case, your supervisor is not there to teach you, i.e. to tell you what to think and do, but to guide you through the project by discussing and testing your ideas and thus making sure that you explore different avenues of thought and structure your argument to the best possible advantage.

So when choosing your supervisor, in terms of their knowledge all you need to do is to try to make sure that there is a general match in interests: someone who has written about medieval architecture might be useful for a study of Scottish castles, or someone who knows about critical theory may be suitable if you are interested in the ideas of Michel Foucault. Beyond this, you should not have too many problems.

Personal Relations

It does help if you get on with your supervisor well enough to feel free to express your ideas. The way that a dissertation is 'taught' is, after all, usually through one-to-one tutorials at which you talk as much if not more than your supervisor. So the more relaxed you feel, often the better the conversations that ensue.

Experience and Reputation

Famous historians and theorists are always attractive options, and if you are lucky enough to have someone particularly renowned in their field by all means go ahead and capitalise on your good fortune. Beware, however, that such people are not always the best supervisors. Just because they themselves think profoundly and write beautifully does not mean that they will necessarily help you to do the same. They may also be less accessible, being constantly called to other conferences, teaching at another institution, or just plain busy.

On the other hand, less well-known or comparatively less experienced tutors may be much more keen to engage with you on your subject, and have the time and inclination to discuss your ideas with you at great length. They may also be more aware of new and interesting developments in architectural thinking. Then again, they might not!

The thing to remember when choosing a supervisor is not to prejudge anyone, particularly by their books or their appearance. Talk to them informally, go to one of their lectures, talk to other students about their experiences – all these things can help you find the right person to work with.

Working with a Supervisor

Remember that your supervisor is likely to be very busy, not only with other students on your programme but with other courses, projects and administration. In short, you will only have a limited amount of access to her or him. There are, however, a number of ways in which you can make sure you get the most out of their time:

- *Be punctual.* If you have a 30-minute tutorial, turning up 15 minutes late will mean that you immediately lose half of that time. If you cannot turn up to a pre-arranged tutorial, phone or e-mail in advance and ask to arrange another appointment. Conversely, if you always see your supervisor at the appointed time, you will get more and better advice.
- *Ask questions.* Probably you should not try to take control of the tutorial yourself, nor should you expect your supervisor to do all the running. Prepare some questions or issues which you would like to discuss, or at the very least think in advance about what you have done and what you can describe about your subject and research.
- *Allow time for feedback.* If you give your supervisor something to read, you should allow them at least a few days and often a week or more to do so. Otherwise you may well not get the quality of feedback which you would like.
- *Provide drafts in a suitable format.* Check with your supervisor if they would like to see draft work in sections or in larger components of the dissertation. And do they prefer to receive this digitally as e-mailed text documents or pdf files, or as hard copy print outs?
- *Use your supervisor.* Seeing your supervisor regularly is one of the best ways of making sure that your dissertation is of the very highest possible standard, yet you would be surprised how many students see their supervisor as little as possible, and sometimes only when they are summoned. Although your supervisor will probably ask to see if you have been invisible for a long period, in general it

is normally up to you to arrange tutorials. Find out what the system is for doing this, and do so as regularly as possible whenever you have something to discuss. Indeed, signing up for a tutorial is often a good way to make sure that you have done something more on your dissertation by that date. Some universities will now also require students to keep a "log book" or a similar record of when they met with their supervisor, what was discussed, and what was the agreed next course of action. For advanced research programmes, such as a PhD, keeping this record up to date may also be a requirement for progression for one stage of the programme to another.

Writing a Proposal

Once you have selected your dissertation topic, assessed that it is indeed a feasible project, and met with your supervisor, it is often a good idea to write a detailed outline of the proposed study. The purpose of this is to give yourself a clear and definite idea of what you are going to do, how you are going to do it, and when you are going to do it. It will also form the basis of a form of 'contract' that you make with your supervisor as to what you undertake to complete.

Dissertation proposals can take many forms, and often different universities have very specific instructions as to what a proposal should include. In general, however, your proposal should contain the following:

- *Title and subject matter*. Here you should give the title and sub-title of the dissertation. Try to be as specific as possible about what you are actually going to look at: for example, 'John Entenza and the *Arts & Architecture* magazine, 1945–1955' is more useful than 'Modern architecture in the United States.' You may be tempted at this stage to immediately give the dissertation a seductive title, and a more descriptive sub-title, such as 'Inference and Impossibility: the Influence of Roman architecture in Budapest'. This kind of title may be acceptable for the final submission, but may not be a good idea for a working title – after all, you have yet to complete the research, and your ideas may well change during this process.
- *Statement of research problem*. This is the most important part of the proposal and should include:
  1   Identification of the objects of study. What buildings, which architects, which cities and/or whose films do you intend to study?
  2   The significance of what you are investigating. What is interesting about it, and what ideas do you intend to pursue?
  3   The kind of approach adopted. How are you exploring and assessing the subject, and with what methodology?

4   Academic context. Who else has written about this subject already, and what kinds of things have they said? How does your proposed study differ from theirs?

Note: You do not normally need to produce a sample or extract of your dissertation text at this stage, but in fact the 'statement of research problem' can often go on to form the basis for the introduction to your final text.

- *Contents list*. You should list here the titles of each of the main 'chapters' of your dissertation. Bear in mind that although students and tutors alike often refer to these as chapters, it is in fact better to think of them as sections – remember that your whole dissertation may well be roughly equal in length to one chapter in a book, so each chapter of your dissertation therefore corresponds to one sub-section of a book chapter.
- *Sources*. You need to state here where you are getting your information from. List the main libraries, archives, key texts, people, buildings etc. that are of use to your project.
- *Timetable*. Give some indication of time. How far have you progressed with the work? When will the rest be done? If there are key events which need to take place – such as an interview, an art event, or a research field trip – make sure to identify these also.

The proposal is not, therefore, an actual part of your dissertation, but forms the main specification for what it is going to be and how you propose to do it. It should probably be no longer than 1 000 words or 2–3 pages of documentation, and can easily be shorter.

Once you have written your proposal, make two copies, keep one for yourself on file and give one to your supervisor. This can be a useful discussion document, and help make your tutorial as productive as possible, so ask your supervisor to respond with ideas and suggestions as to how your ideas and work plan might be improved.

References

1   Alice T. Friedman, 'Not a Muse: the Client's Role at the Rietveld Schröder House', Diane Agrest, Patricia Conway and Leslie Kanes Weisman (eds), *The Sex of Architecture* (New York: Harry N. Abrams, 1996) pp 217–32.
2   Mirjana Lozanovska, 'Abjection and Architecture: the Migrant House in Multicultural Australia', Gülsüm Baydar Nalbantoglu and Wong Chong Thai (eds), *Postcolonial Space(s)* (New York: Princeton Architectural Press, 1997) pp 101–29.

3 Researching

What is Research?

Exactly what research is can be a contentious issue – ask any two academics, and you will probably get two rather different descriptions. In particular, there is often some kind of narrow-mindedness about what constitutes 'proper' research – those with a scientific background may insist that research is only research when it proves or disproves the answer to a stated hypothesis, while, similarly, architectural historians of a certain ilk (now increasingly rare) may insist that research is only research when it uncovers new facts about a specific building or architect. In addition, there are differences in the definition of research in US institutions, where some doctoral programmes in architecture are located in schools of art history, architecture or even in programmes specialising in subjects such as gerontology or social factors and architecture. This can extend to the privileging of constructed aspects of architecture in one institution (studied through orthographic architectural drawings) or architecture as an artistic artefact (studied through photographs). Doctorates in design will emphasise still other issues, and vary between the USA, the UK and other countries. If you wish to read about this in more depth, see the extended discussion in Jane Rendell's article, "Architectural Research and Disciplinarity," in *ARQ (Architecture Research Quarterly)*, v. 8 n. 2 (2005).

As you might guess from all this, architectural research can adopt all manner of different forms and approaches, and to some extent you do not have to know exactly what research 'is'. However, there are a number of characteristics common to most if not all good architectural dissertations, which you would do well to bear in mind.

An architectural dissertation should rely on research that is:

- Original, in that it is undertaken by yourself, yet which also
- Acknowledges other people's ideas and work as appropriate.

'Originality' can thus mean examining material never before studied or providing new interpretations of well-known material. The process by which you do this should entail:

- The study of some specific architectural objects, e.g. persons, ideas, buildings or drawings, and/or
- The application of some interpretive or analytical framework, particularly one which
- Explores a particular theme or asks a specific question about architecture
- The writing or other exploration of these ideas in a way that conveys your investigation to yourself and to others.

The result is then a dissertation which:

- Provides new information and/or interpretations about architecture, and which, thus,
- Allows you to learn more about architecture yourself, and which also
- Makes a contribution to architectural knowledge in general.

Historical and Critical Methodology

One of the most difficult things for architecture students to get to grips with is a sense of the methodology they might adopt when writing about architecture. When producing an essay or shorter piece of writing this is less important, but for a larger research study the very best work is that which not only says something original about architecture, but which also understands exactly how those comments and that originality have been produced.

This problem is compounded by the fact that many architectural thinkers and writers have themselves adopted a wide variety of different approaches over the years. To give you some idea of this range, and of the kinds of challenge they would pose, one could identify (and this list is far from exhaustive) the following strains of exploration in the last 50 years or so (which are not necessarily mutually exclusive).

Empiricism

This is the idea that history can be constructed simply by setting out the facts, with the historian maintaining an 'objective' distance from their subject. Henry Russell Hitchcock's *Architecture: Nineteenth and Twentieth Centuries* is a good example of this kind of approach, which often does little more than describe the building and state the building's date and architect.[1] Challenges here include:

- Would you be content with this relatively limited approach?
- Can you be sure that the facts that you will uncover will be new and original pieces of information?
- Can you be objective about architecture?
- How do you know that the facts you select are the important ones?

Iconography and Iconology?

First developed in relation to art history by German art historians, the iconographic and iconological approach to architecture tries to identify particular ideas or themes as they recur in buildings over time. For example, Colin Rowe's famous essay *The Mathematics of the Ideal Villa* makes comparisons between the use of proportions by Palladio and Le Corbusier.[2] Studies with a similar methodology include Erwin Panofsky, *Gothic Architecture and Scholasticism*[3] and Robert Venturi, Denise Scott Brown and Stephen Izenour, *Learning from Las Vegas*.[4] Challenges here include:

- How familiar are you with this kind of technique?
- Are you willing to conduct highly focused research on one particular aspect of architecture?
- How will you show the connection between different kinds and periods of architecture?

Hegelian History and Theory

Influenced by the ideas of the German nineteenth-century philosopher G. W. F. Hegel, the Hegelian tradition pervades a large part of architectural history. Some of its most pertinent traits include ideas of progress (architecture is getting 'better'), that this progress is being achieved by specific individual architects (often men) in particular countries (often in the West), and that this architecture somehow represents a 'spirit of the age' or *zeitgeist* that pervades a particular historical period. For extreme versions of this kind of thinking, see Nikolaus Pevsner's *Pioneers of Modern Design,* any of Charles Jencks' innumerable attempts to capture the latest '-ism' in architecture[5] or Heinrich Wölfflin's idea of the *kunstwerk* in *Renaissance and Baroque.*[6] Challenges here include:

- Do you believe in the fundamental concepts behind this approach?
- If so, how will you justify your selection of architecture and your interpretation of it?
- How do you define the *zeitgeist* for your chosen subject?
- How is this *zeitgeist* manifested in a physical and visual medium?

Social History

Many architectural writers have paid attention to the social context of architecture. Historians like Marc Girouard or Spiro Kostof, for example, have both looked at the way people have commissioned, constructed and lived in buildings as well as how these buildings have been designed.[7] Other writers like Anthony Vidler have combined this with a Hegelian methodology, as in his study of the eighteenth-century French architect Claude-Nicolas Ledoux.[8] Challenges here include:

- What kind of context do you wish to look at? For example, party politics, gender issues, patronage, class relations, building occupancy? How will you justify this context over any other?
- Where will you gain your information from?
- How will you write about these kinds of events?
- Can architecture be entirely explained by its context, or are there criteria and goals particular to architecture that context does not explain?

Politicised History and Theory

Some architectural historians are concerned not only with relating architecture to wider conditions and circumstances outside of the architectural profession, but also with interpreting that context in relation to a particular political philosophy or position. Two of the most obvious instances of this have been the Marxist studies of Manfredo Tafuri and other Italian writers,[9] who have focused on notions of ideology and revolution, and feminist studies which seek to explore not only the role of gender relations in architecture but also the possibility for female and male emancipation from those roles.[10] Challenges here include:

- What particular political philosophy do you wish to refer to? For example, classical Marxism, structural Marxism, Anglo-American feminism, psychoanalytic feminism?
- How familiar are you with these concepts?
- How can you show the relevance of these ideas for architecture?
- Are you interested in using the analytical method of the writer you have chosen, or only in demonstrating the theory (these goals may not be the same)?

Operative History and Theory

Operative criticism or history is the term deployed by Tafuri for those architectural historians and critics who deliberately seek to use their writings in order to support the case for a particular kind of contemporary architecture today. Again, this kind of writing is particularly pervasive within architectural discourse, and can range from straightforward hagiographic biographies that simply praise a particular architect's work, such as Mary Lutyens's account of the work of her own father, Edwin Lutyens,[11] or those which construct a view of architectural history which by implication supports certain kinds of architecture today, such as Reyner Banham's advocacy of a technological modernism in *Theory and Design in the First Machine Age* and which has done much to support high-tech architecture,[12] or Sigfried Giedion's *Space, Time and Architecture* which performed the same task for much of the modern movement.[13] Challenges here include:

- Do you wish to write in support of a particular architect or kind of architecture? Do you wish to be an advocate of Bruce Goff and organicism, Kenzo Tange and metabolism, or Nigel Coates and narrative architecture?
- If so, why?
- How will you maintain a critical distance from the subject?

Theorised and Interdisciplinary Studies

Historians and critics today often make increasing reference to theories and disciplines from outside of architecture. For example, you will find elements of semiology in the work of Mark Gottdeiner,[14] Derridean post-structuralism and literary theory in that of Jennifer Bloomer,[15] psycho-analysis in Anthony Vidler,[16] phenomenology in Juhani Pallasmaa,[17] urban geography in Ross King,[18] post-colonial(ism) theory in Zeynep Çelik,[19] etc.[20] This is a growing area in architectural research which has emerged as architectural writers have begun to look to other disciplines to find interpretative frameworks, research methods, primary sources and secondary literature in order to explain architectural issues – see, for example, the wide range of theorised approaches adopted by the contributors to Iain Borden and Jane Rendell (eds), *InterSections: Architectural Histories and Critical Theories* (2000). It is unlikely that you will have time in one of the shorter kinds of architectural dissertation study to familiarise yourself extremely thoroughly with theoretical sources from another discipline. However, if you are undertaking a specialist architectural history or theory programme at masters, MPhil or PhD level, or if you have a first degree in another discipline, you may well find that you have much of the knowledge you need. Challenges here include:

- As with politicised writings, to which particular theory do you wish to refer?
- How familiar are you with these concepts?
- How can you show the relevance of these ideas for architecture and for the particular time and place you are studying?
- What role do these ideas play in your work? For example, do you wish to demonstrate Michel Foucault's ideas about power, use a conceptual category of Foucault's such as that of heterotopia, or use his analytical methods?

Social Science

Some architectural historians also make an attempt to use the various methods of social science to examine some point about architecture. For example, Alice Coleman made extensive use of social science survey techniques in her attack on social housing, *Utopia on Trial*,[21] as did Anthony King in his work on the bungalow,[22] while those like Kim Dovey and Thomas Markus have incorporated elements of space syntax methodology into their studies of building plans.[23] Challenges here include:

- What particular techniques do you want to adopt?
- Will you have the time and resources to carry them out?
- Will they show what you want them to show?
- What point of view about architecture does the use of these methods imply?

Personal Writing

Another kind of architectural writing is the highly personal one, where the author takes a highly subjective and often quite poetic approach to architecture. Examples here range from the journalistic invective of Michael Sorkin[24] to the thoughtful musings of Paul Shepheard[25] and the more philosophical writings of Jun'ichiro Tanizaki.[26] Challenges here include:

- How can you make this interesting and relevant for others to read?
- What style of writing will you adopt?
- How can you make this acceptable as a dissertation at your particular school of architecture?
- How precisely do you satisfy the 'original contribution to knowledge' criterion often employed to assess the validity of a dissertation? Personal is not necessarily the same as original.

Visually-based Studies

These range from studies which are largely design-based explorations, to those which use photographs, diagrams and other visual forms of analysis (such as Robert Venturi, Denise Scott-Brown and Stephen Izenour's *Learning From Las Vegas*) to intersections of multiple texts, images and graphic design (such as Rem Koolhaas and Bruce Mau's *SMLXL*).

Obviously there is an extraordinarily wide range of visual and creative strategy possible here. Challenges here are similar to those for 'Personal Writing' above, and also include:

- Which visual strategy will you adopt?
- How does this visual strategy relate to the textual strategy of the dissertation?

- How will the visual material contribute to the understanding or interpretation of the subject matter?
- How will you differentiate your dissertation from studio-based work?

All these different methods may seem a little daunting at first, but they are not meant to be overly problematic for you when thinking about your dissertation. You certainly do not have to understand all these methods before starting your own dissertation, but it is important that you know why you have chosen a particular theoretical framework.

Apart from the specialist and directed questions that the different methodologies identified above can help pose, there are also a number of very simple questions that you might ask of your subject. Some may not be relevant to your subject, but nonetheless often the most apparently straightforward inquiry can lead to the most intriguing of answers. Such questions, and again the list is far from exhaustive, might include:

Questions of production
- How was this architecture constructed?
- Who was involved?
- Where is it? Why is this?
- When was it built?
- How was it paid for? Who paid for it? Why?
- Has it been altered after its original construction? When? Why?
- What were the main intentions of the architects and other producers?
- Where did these ideas come from?
- What is the function of the architecture?
- Who benefited from this architecture? In what way?

Questions of interpretation
- What kinds of design ideas can be related to this architecture?
- What ideas from outside of architecture can be related to it?
- How are these ideas manifested in the architecture? Are they visible?
- How does this architecture compare with other examples of its type? How is it different?
- What is it trying to avoid? What is it trying to prove or show?
- What have people said about this architecture? Why was this?
- What is the significance of this architecture when it was built?
- Has this significance changed over the years?
- What is its significance today?

Questions of reception and experience
- What is the architecture like to look at?
- Can you experience the architecture other than by looking?
- Is it different on the inside?
- Is it different when you move around?

- Is it different in the flesh from its representation in books and articles?
- How do other media (e.g. films, novels, the internet) represent this architecture?
- Who are the different people who have experienced this architecture over time?
- How will you convey your own experience of the architecture?

Questions of use
- What was the intended use of the architecture?
- What was the actual use?
- Who used it? Were there different groups of users? How did they differ from one another?
- When was it used? Did use change over time? How and why? What is the use of the architecture today?

Research Techniques

Apart from the more cerebral questions of methodology, there are also a number of much more practical but nonetheless important research techniques which can be useful when researching your dissertation.

Note-taking

The biggest question when making notes is what to note down. The short answer to this is to note down only what is directly relevant to your dissertation subject. So if you were exploring the experience of verticality in modernist staircases, you would certainly want to note down anything that talked about movement up and down the staircase of, for example, the De La Warr Pavilion. You would probably want to note down details about the concrete and steel construction, but would ignore details about all the other buildings designed by the architects, Erich Mendelsohn and Serge Chermayeff. This is where your carefully prepared dissertation proposal comes into play – keep this with you at all times, mentally if not physically, and you can then assess everything that you come across in terms of where it fits into your proposal. If it doesn't fit, don't bother taking notes.

Other questions of note-taking include whether to take an exact transcription/quotation from the source, or whether to paraphrase it in your own words. Generally speaking, you should aim for the latter, and reserve quotations only for particularly pertinent phrases, sentences or statements. If you do take quotations, you should check them very carefully as it is almost impossible to transcribe a quotation without making at least one small error. You should also distinguish very clearly in your notes what is a quotation, what is a paraphrasing by you, and what are your own thoughts and observations (see below for an example of how to do this). Remember to write down all the relevant published information about the source. When taking notes, always include the page number (see below).

Recording Notes

Whenever you find a relevant piece of information, make an observation or have a new thought, there is one, absolutely essential thing that you simply must do: write it down. This may sound obvious, but it is very tempting to say to yourself that you will make a note later on, or just remember it. However, more often than not, you won't, or you will fret unnecessarily trying to remember whatever it is that you found earlier on!

In general, therefore, the main principle is to gather information and thoughts as you go along. Given the time restraints of a normal architectural dissertation programme, you will probably not have enough time to return to the same place twice, so treat each session as a one-off opportunity. Go somewhere (a book, a library, a person), get what you want, make good but concise notes, leave.

Remember that this applies to your own interpretive thoughts as well as to factual information. If you have a thought of your own about your subject, write this down too. You can do this either in your regular notes, in which case you need some kind of notation system (e.g. your initials) to signify to yourself that this is one of your own thoughts and not someone else's, or in a separate 'ideas book' (see below).

Many people find it easiest to keep their notes using a normal-sized pad of paper, and then to transfer pages into a ring-binder at the end of each day. This system has two main advantages:

- Pages can be rearranged in the ring-binder at a later date to suit the development of your ideas and the structure of your dissertation.
- Only the paper pad has to be carried with you when doing your research. This will be much lighter to carry and if you should be so unlucky as to lose the pad, then you will have only lost one day's work at the most, and not your whole set of notes.

Other systems involve using a kind of journal or diary, where you collect all your thoughts and notes in one place, or using a laptop or other kinds of portable computer. If you use either of these two methods, beware that you are running the risk of losing all your work if the journal or portable computer goes missing. With a computer, you should always make a back-up at the end of each day, which should solve this problem, but with a journal there is no simple safety procedure, other than regularly photocopying any new pages you make.

If you are using a laptop or other portable computer, one other thing to check, particularly if you are travelling a long distance, is that the archive or library in which you are going to research has suitable power sockets into which you can plug. Few portable computers have adequate batteries for a full day of research.

However you decide to keep your notes, another useful thing to do is to carry a smaller 'ideas book' with you at all times. (If you are particularly into gadgets, a small hand-held Palm-based or PocketPC computing device, or similar, can perform the same task). That way, if something suddenly occurs to you, you can always quickly jot it down.

Filing Materials

You will amass large quantities of information which you must be able to retrieve later. You can choose to file your notes by author or by broad subject categories relevant to your research topic. Whichever system you choose, keep all your research material together in one, easily accessible place, where they are logically stored and arranged.

Photocopying

It is often very tempting to make photocopies of things in libraries and archives. However, remember that photocopying texts is not the same as reading or thinking about them! Just because you have managed to collect a pile of photocopies 50 cm high on new museums in Sheffield and Minneapolis does not mean that you have done much real work on this subject. In general, try to keep photocopying at a minimum. This will help your bank balance as much as anything else.

Photocopies are, however, very useful in particular circumstances:

- Long quotations, of half a page or more, can be more quickly recorded using a photocopy, and also may help prevent transcription errors (see above).
- Tables, lists of figures and other lengthy pieces of factual information may also be best recorded by photocopy.
- Illustrations may also be usefully photocopied (see below). Line drawings and diagrams photocopy well, while for others you may need to use a colour or laser copier.
- Some archives are open only for short periods of time, offer limited access, or close for vacations etc. If you find yourself running out of time in this way, try photocopying as much as you can, to take away and read later – although note that not all libraries and archives will allow this, so check in advance if you think you are going to want to do this.

Illustrations

As with other kinds of information, you should try to gather as many of the illustrations that you think you will need as you go along. There are five ways in which you might do this:

- *Sketching.* If you are good at freehand or tracing, you may find it easiest to sketch illustrations. Beware, however, that they will lack a certain historical authenticity when you come to include them in your final dissertation, although this may not matter depending on the nature of your subject.
- *Photocopying.* Generally this is the easiest way to copy illustrations to a standard good enough for nearly all dissertations – this is particularly true if you can use a high-quality laser or colour copier. Beware, however, that although the first copy you make may look good enough, any second- or third-generation copies will rapidly deteriorate in quality. You may therefore need to make more than one first-generation reproduction, particularly if you want to keep one dissertation for yourself while the others are kept by the university.
- *Photography.* Some libraries or archives will let you take photographs of material in their collections, (although many will not). To do this well you will need a good-quality digital or 35 mm camera and probably also a macro lens, tripod or copy stand, and appropriate film, filters and lighting. Things to note here include:
  1 Digital images or normal prints will be easier and cheaper to scan or copy later on so that you can include them in your dissertation, but slide film will normally give a better quality. Digital cameras can produce good-quality results, but make sure you use a high enough resolution.
  2 Black and white film can be used regardless of the type of lighting, as it obviously is unaffected by colour-casting problems.
  3 Tungsten-rated film (slides only) can be used in combination with tungsten lights, as commonly found fitted to copy-stands.
  4 Ordinary slide or print film can both be used in daylight conditions.
  5 Ordinary slide or print film can be used in artificial light conditions, if used in combination with an appropriate filter. For example, the yellow cast given out by normal light bulbs can be largely corrected by using an 80B filter.
  6 Digital cameras are less directly affected by colour-casting, but be aware that colour accuracy is still very difficult under artificial light conditions.
  7 As you will often be using a macro lens, you will need a tripod or copy-stand and/or fast film in order to keep things steady.
  8 Shoot from above, and keep the image as flat as possible, parallel to the camera and in the centre of the shot. A piece of non-reflective glass or Perspex placed over the image in order to flatten it out can help here. Beware of using a wide angle setting in order to fit the image in, as this can distort the image considerably.
  9 If you are taking images from a video, DVD, television or computer screen, you should black out the room completely as annoying reflections in the monitor can very easily stray into the shot. You should use a shutter speed of 1/15 s or slower

(i.e. 1/8 and not 1/60), as this will eliminate the black banding that often occurs when taking images from television. Fast film, a tripod and a good four-head video player or DVD player with high-quality pause are all extremely useful.

10 Get permission for use of illustrations as you go along, as this can be very time consuming later (see also Chapter 5).

- *Scanning.* If you can take books or other materials out of the library or archive, you could scan images directly into a digital format. Most scanners produce results good enough for a dissertation.

- *Official reproductions.* Some archives and libraries will only allow illustrations to be reproduced by their own official reproduction service, either as photocopies, photographs or, occasionally, digital scans. Beware that ordering images in this way can be not only quite expensive but can also take up to several weeks or even months to arrive. Plan in advance. Note that some archives and libraries also charge a separate copyright fee for publishing the illustration con-cerned – but this should not apply to you as a university dissertation is not classified as a published work (see Chapter 5).

Interviews, Surveys and Questionnaires

Many students wish to conduct interviews or other forms of survey as part of their research. Although not an essential part of all architectural dissertations, in some circumstances and done properly, these can be an extremely good way of gaining primary data that are completely original to your own study. If you are conducting a large number of interviews such as a survey of opinion, it may be worth checking with your institu-tion whether it is necessary for your interview subjects to sign an agree-ment consenting to the interview. Some institutions nowadays also operate an ethics policy for any research involving human subjects, cov-ering matters of safety, consent, autonomy and privacy. Such issues are not normally relevant to most architecture dissertations, but if in doubt ask your supervisor.

Interviews can be difficult things to get right, but with a little foresight and advanced planning most problems can be avoided. If you are thinking of or intending to use interviews in your research you should consider:

- *Data targets.* What information do you wish to find out? Is there par-ticular data which you need (such as the percentages of architecture students who are female and male, broken down by architecture school and by year), or is it of a more general kind (such as different students' perception of whether being female or male makes a dif-ference to the kinds of designs they produce)?

- *Interview set.* Which people are you going to ask? How many? A lot, or are there just a few key people? Does it matter if some of them do not agree to participate?

- *Format.* What kind of format do you want to adopt? A statistical survey, a structured interview with exactly the same questions asked of all participants, or a much more general and open discussion format?
- Approach. How will you conduct the interviews? Depending on the format, you have a number of different ways in which you might conduct an interview or survey. Perhaps the easiest is to send a questionnaire to lots of different people by post, fax or e-mail. However, the response rate to this kind of questionnaire is typically very low, for recipients will often have neither the time nor the inclination to reply, or they will have every intention of doing so but somehow never quite get around to it. If you do send out a questionnaire, one trick is to say clearly and politely at the top how little time it should take to complete a response – asking a few, well-directed questions that take no more than 5–10 min to answer is usually about right. Do check with your institution whether it has guidelines on the conduct of interviews – this is likely to be the case if you are in the USA.

Other ways of conducting interview include speaking to people you meet in the street or at a building if this is appropriate to your study. If you want to explore ideas of what a building means to different people, say for the Neue Staatsgalerie in Stuttgart, you could interview visitors, guards, curators and anyone else that you can engage in conversation. Again, for large numbers of interviewees, you may need to check with your institution for procedures.

Telephone interviews are a good way of reaching some individuals, but make sure that they have time to talk to you before launching into your questions. If you are going to phone someone, writing to them in advance and letting them know what you are doing is often considered to be a polite course of action.

Of course, the main way of conducting an interview is to have a one-to-one and face-to-face meeting. If you wish to do this, you should:

1   Arrange the interview well in advance, and check a day or so before the interview itself that everything is okay. This is particularly important if you are going to be travelling any great distance.
2   Make sure you have done much of your other research in advance. An interviewee will probably not be very happy if you are clearly not well prepared, and if you have not bothered to read published material.
3   Take control of the interview yourself, and do not expect your interviewee to just perform (unless, of course, that is clearly how they prefer to operate!). Prepare some questions in advance and use these to run the interview – if you then move on to discuss other subjects, that is fine, but try to cover what you came to find out.
4   Ask your interviewee if you can record the conversation. He or she may need to sign an agreement – check with your institution

before you ask for the interview. Make sure that you have a good recorder, that you know how to use it, and that you have enough batteries, tapes, disks etc. If you cannot record the interview, keep good notes.

5   Keep the interview relatively short, and don't go on for too long: 30–60 min is normally more than enough.

6   Write and thank your interviewee for their time a day or so afterwards. You may also want to offer to send them a copy of your dissertation when it is completed.

7   Listen to the interview recording, or review your notes, as soon as possible. If you have a tape or disk, you can either transcribe the whole thing (although this can be very time consuming), or make a list of the issues covered and use the machine counter to identify where on the tape they occur.

8   You may find that as your research progresses you have additional questions for your interview subjects. Often, these supplementary questions can be broached by a follow-up phone call at a later date.

Visiting Architecture

Actually going to visit a building, city or other piece of architecture can often be an extremely good, not to say essential way of finding more out about a building. However many images, plans, descriptions, theories and DVDs you study, architecture is always different in the flesh. If you intend to visit architecture as part of your research, in order to make the best use of this experience you should consider the following issues.

- *Data targets.* What do you want to find out? Do you need to find out particular information, such as aspects of construction or sense of space, or is your visit more general in nature?
- *Interview set.* What people do you want to meet? The building manager or owner? Users?
- *Access.* When is the architecture open to the general public? Do you need to make another kind of arrangement? What will you be allowed to see? Can the architecture be easily viewed from the exterior? Where from? What can you see? When can you arrange a field trip? How much will it cost? From whom do you need permission to visit?
- *Records.* What records can you make of your visit? Will you be allowed to take photographs? Might video, sketches, or notes be better than photography? Can you obtain documentation while you are there (photographs, plans, visitor guides, other information)? Should you have information beforehand to help you understand the building and know what you want to record?
- *Experience.* What kind of experience have you gained from your visit? Was the architecture different in various parts, and/or when

you were moving? Were you allowed to see everything? How might your experience of the architecture differ from that of other people, particularly non-architects?

Recording Sources

Not only is it important to keep good notes of your subject material, it is also essential to maintain a meticulous record of where the information has come from. Thus for every single piece of information you need to note down the archive, book or article details, name of illustration etc. In general, you need to have all the information that you will have to include in your footnotes, references and bibliography (see Chapter 4). In particular, you need to note page numbers as well as publication details for all information, and especially for quotations, paraphrased notes, facts and other (and) precise data. Note that this applies to illustrations and diagrams as well as textual material. For example, part of a set of notes might look something like this:

Source
Georg Simmel, 'The Metropolis and Mental Life', P. K. Hatt and A. J. Reiss (eds), *Cities and Society: the Revised Reader in Urban Sociology* (New York: Free Press, 1951), pp. 635–46.
Notes
GS – Sees cities as a place of punctuality.   [637–8]

Quote –
If all clocks and watches in Berlin would suddenly go wrong in different ways, even if only by an hour, all economic life and communication of the city would be disrupted for a long time.
[end quote]   [638]

IB – does this apply to all cities, or just to Berlin??

GS – Quantitative nature of the metropolis leads to: [645]
• individual independence
• elaboration of individuality itself   [646]

IB – might this relate to Loos' interior designs for bourgeois houses in Vienna? See Ronstaid article for more on this.

Here, the source gives publication details, the numbers in square brackets on the right-hand side give the appropriate page numbers, while a notation system shows what is a paraphrasing of Simmel (GS), what is a quote (Quote) and what is the researcher's own thoughts or question (in this case, IB).

Deploying this kind of system methodically and consistently may seem like overkill at this stage, but rest assured it will save you an enormous amount of effort and potential trouble later on. This is particularly true when you are trying to avoid unintentional plagiarism (see below).

Reviewing Thoughts

One of the most important things you can do when researching your dissertation is to think about the subject as you go along – that is, do not just be content to collect facts and information, but actively consider what it is that you are finding out during the research process. To help with this process there are a number of things that you might try doing:

- *Write it down.* Write down any thoughts you might have. As stated above, jot down any particular ideas or questions among your notes (in which case take care to distinguish your own ideas from everything else), or in a separate place.
- *Reviewing notes.* Review your notes regularly by taking 30 minutes or so at the end of each research session to go over what you have noted and, once again, take care to write down any reflections you have on this. Some people even find it useful to keep a kind of diary, noting down where they have been and what they have thought.
- *Write as you go.* Although it is often, of course, very difficult to write major parts of your dissertation until you have done at least some of the research, as soon as you are in the position to write something, do so. These pieces of writing do not have to be very long – just enough for you to get some thoughts down on paper. Doing this will help to keep your thought processes active. You can also give some of this writing to your supervisor as something to discuss. And when you come to write the dissertation properly, you will often find that you have already done much of the thinking and writing.
- *Talk as you go.* Above all, talk to other people about your work, and not just to your supervisor (see below). Different people can often have very valuable things to contribute to your work, and often about matters which you may never have thought about on your own. Talking about your work, as with writing small excerpts, also helps you to keep your thought processes active and enquiring.
- *Reflection.* Refer back to your initial ideas and reasons for dealing with the subject. Every now and then, perhaps once a week or so, you should refer back to your proposal. This will help keep you focused on what you are doing, and also remind you of what stage you have reached in the overall project.

Timetable

Most diploma and masters dissertation programmes are run on fairly strict time schedules, at the end of which there is one, immovable date: the submission deadline. Doctoral dissertations have more flexibility, depending on the institution. Nevertheless, in general, you only have a limited amount of time to come up with your subject, begin researching, discuss things with your supervisor and other relevant people, complete the research, write a draft, make changes, produce the final document and hand in. All this has to be done in a limited period – for a diploma or masters dissertation this period of time may often be only 9–12 months, or even less. In the USA, a doctoral dissertation or thesis may take as much as 7–10 years after passing the examination stage, even though only 4 years of funding is typical in US programmes. In the UK, there are strong pressures on both institutions and students to complete dissertations within the specified time limits – usually a UK doctoral dissertation should be completed within 3–4 years for full-time study or 4–6 years for part-time study (in the UK, doctoral architectural studies are rarely funded by the institution itself).

In order to cope with these time demands, draw up a timetable showing the main periods of:

- Research
- Writing
- Draft submission
- Draft revisions
- Deadline for final submission

You should also include:

- Term/semester dates
- Important dates such as field trips, special archive trips, scheduled interviews etc.
- Dates when your supervisor or advisory faculty are and are not available
- Important personal dates such as birthdays, personal vacations, family events etc., with which you will not want to have a work clash.

Libraries and Archives

Where to find information is, of course, one of the single most important questions for any dissertation project. Exactly where you can find what you want will vary dramatically according to the architectural subject you have chosen, but there are nonetheless some simple rules and guidance that can help you.

In researching your dissertation, there is one thing to bear in mind: unlike most other essays and assignments, what you are doing is an original piece of research and it is therefore very unlikely that you are going to find everything you need in standard, published books. Instead, at the very least you are probably going to have a look at articles in the academic and professional architectural press, as well as conduct primary research yourself in archives, through interviews, surveys etc. Some of these have already been discussed above. What follows is particularly related to libraries and archives.

Bear in mind that you may also need to use a foreign language and foreign archives to access some primary sources of information. In the USA, for this reason, many doctoral programmes require the study of a second language beside English. In the UK, this may require taking special classes. You will also need to plan carefully with respect to time, transportation, accommodation and budget. You may need letters of recommendation or reference from your institution to obtain advance permission to use the archive as well as a general letter confirming who you are and what your research topic is. These documents can be particularly helpful if you need access to sources which you discover only after arriving at the research destination. It helps if these letters are in the language of the country you are visiting. It is also important that you remember to carry your student identity card with you, as this may allow you to enter other archives/buildings that you discover while in your foreign research location.

Books

Most architecture schools have reasonably well-stocked libraries containing a variety of older and more recent publications, some of which will undoubtedly be of good use to you. This is where you should start looking. In particular you should investigate:

- *Reference books.* There are a number of publications which give general introductions to architecture and architects, and in which you will find some initial references which you might want to follow up. These include:
  The Architects' Journal Information Guide (supplement to the *Architects' Journal,* published annually).
  Avery Obituary Index of Architects (Boston: G. K. Hall, second edition, 1980).
  Centre Canadien d'Architecture, *Guide des Archives d'Architecture du CCA* (Montreal: CCA, 1992).
  E. Beresford Chancellor, *The Lives of the British Architects from William of Wykeham to Sir William Chambers* (London: Duckworth, 1909).
  H. M. Colvin, *A Biographical Dictionary of British Architects, 1600–1840* (New Haven: Yale University Press, 1995).
  Nadine Covert (ed.), *Architecture on Screen: Films and Videos on Architecture, Landscape Architecture, Historic Preservation, City and Regional Planning* (New York: G. K. Hall, 1993).
  Alison Felstead, Jonathan Franklin and Leslie Pinfield, *Directory of British Architects, 1834–1900* (London: Mansell, 1993).

John Fleming, Hugh Honour and Nikolaus Pevsner, *The Penguin Dictionary of Architecture and Landscape Architecture* (London: Penguin, fifth edition, 1998).

A. Stuart Gray, *Edwardian Architecture: a Biographical Dictionary* (Ware: Wordsworth, 1988).

Pedro Guedes (ed.), *The Macmillan Encyclopaedia of Architecture and Technological Change* (London: Macmillan, 1979).

Joseph Gwilt, *The Encyclopedia of Architecture, Historical, Theoretical and Practical* (New York: Bonanza, revised edition, 1982).

John Harvey, *English Mediaeval Architects: a Biographical Dictionary down to 1550* (Hulverstone Manor: Pinhorns, revised edition, 1987).

Ruth Kamen, *British and Irish Architectural History: a Bibliography and Guide to Sources of Information* (London: Architectural Press, 1981).

James H. Maclean and John S. Scott, *The Penguin Dictionary of Building* (London: Penguin, fourth edition, 1993).

Ann Lee Morgan and Colin Naylor (eds), *Contemporary Architects* (Chicago: St James, second edition, 1987).

Adolf K. Placzek (ed.), *Macmillan Encyclopaedia of Architects* (New York: Free Press, 1982).

Royal Institute of British Architects, *RIBA Book List* (London: Royal Institute of British Architects, published annually).

Royal Institute of British Architects, *RIBA Directory of Practices* (London: Royal Institute of British Architects, 1997).

Royal Institute of British Architects, *RIBA International Directory of Practices* (London: Royal Institute of British Architects, 1997).

Dennis Sharp (ed.), *Sources of Modern Architecture: a Critical Bibliography* (London: Granada, second edition, 1981).

Jack Travis (ed.), *African-American Architects in Current Practice* (New York: Princeton Architectural Press, 1991).

Willem Van Vliet (ed.), *The Encyclopedia of Housing* (Thousand Oaks: Sage, 1998).

Randall Van Vynckt (ed.), *International Dictionary of Architects and Architecture* (Detroit: St. James Press, 1993).

Arnold Whittick (ed.), *The Encyclopedia of Planning* (Huntington: R. E. Krieger, 1980).

Joseph A. Wilkes (ed.), *Encyclopedia of Architecture: Design, Engineering & Construction* (London: Wiley, five volumes, 1988–90).

In addition, there are also now an increasing number of readers and other related books which deal with architecture-related articles or provide other overviews of the subject. These can be useful for finding 'classic' articles on architecture and city studies, and for gaining an insight into terminology. These include:

Architectural Theory: from Renaissance to the Present; 89 essays on 117 treatises (London: Taschen, 2003).

Eugenie Birch (ed.), *The Urban and Regional Planning Reader* (London: Routledge, 2004).

Gary Bridge and Sophie Watson (eds), *The Blackwell City Reader* (Oxford: Blackwell Publishers, 2002).

Michael Bull and Les Back (eds), *The Auditory Culture Reader* (Oxford: Berg, 2003).

Ulrich Conrads, *Programmes and Manifestos on 20th-Century Architecture* (London: Lund Humphries, 1970).

Keith L. Eggener (ed.), *American Architectural History: a Contemporary Reader* (London: Routledge, 2004).

Caroline van Eck and Christy Anderson (eds), *British Architectural Theory, 1540–1750: an Anthology of Texts* (Aldershot: Ashgate, 2003).

Adrian Forty, *Words and Buildings: a Vocabulary of Modern Architecture* (London: Thames & Hudson, 2000).

K. Michael Hays (ed.), *Oppositions Reader: Selected Readings from a Journal for Ideas and Criticism in Architecture, 1973–1984* (London: Academy Editions, 1992).

K. Michael Hays (ed.), *Architectural Theory Since 1968* (Cambridge, MA: MIT, 1998).

Charles Jencks and Karl Kropf (eds), *Theories and Manifestos of Contemporary Architecture* (London: Academy Editions, 1997).

Charles Jencks (ed.), *The Post-modern Reader* (London: Academy Editions, 1992).

Hanno-Walter Kruft, *A History of Architectural Theory: From Vitruvius to the Present* (London: Zwemmer, 1994).

Neil Leach (ed.), *Rethinking Architecture: a Reader in Cultural Theory* (London: Routledge, 1997).

Richard LeGates and Frederic Stout (eds), *The City Reader* (London: Routledge, third edition, 2003).

Setha M. Low, *Theorizing the City: the New Urban Anthropology Reader* (New Brunswick: Rutgers University Press, 1999).

Malcolm Miles and Tim Hall with Iain Borden (eds), *The City Cultures Reader* (London: Routledge, revised edition, 2003).

Kate Nesbitt (ed.), *Theorizing a New Agenda for Architecture: an Anthology of Architectural Theory 1965–1995* (New York: Princeton Architectural Press, 1996).

Joan Ockman (ed.), *Architecture Culture 1943–1968* (New York: Rizzoli, 1993).

Jane Rendell, Barbara Penner and Iain Borden (eds), *Gender Space Architecture: an Interdisciplinary Introduction* (London: Routledge, 1999).

Neil Spiller (ed.), *Cyber Reader: Critical Writings for the Digital Era* (London: Phaidon, 2002).

Simon Swaffield (ed.), *Theory in Landscape Architecture: a Reader* (Philadelphia: University of Pennsylvania Press, 2002).

You will also find a number of similar such readers in related or trans-disciplinary fields, such as cultural studies, postcolonialism, anthropology, art history etc.

- *General book catalogue.* Use your library computer to search by title, subject and keyword for books on your subject. Libraries often list books in only one of these formats, so check all three. This can be a laborious process, so be patient and take your time. In order to make your task more efficient, make a careful note of all the references which look like they might be interesting, and then go to the shelves and check them all in one go. *Note:* Many libraries have only their more recent acquisitions entered on the computer system. If you looking for older texts, you may need to look at a microfiche or even a card-indexed system to locate what you are looking for. You can also now interrogate on-line library catalogues semi-automatically, using purpose-designed reference manager software such as EndNote.

  When you have found a book on the shelf, take a few minutes to look at other things filed in the same part of the library that might also be of use to you.

  Make notes from the books you have found, and, in particular, look at their bibliographies and footnotes. This is often a good way to track down more obscure sources, such as chapters in edited books, articles in journals and so on.

Journals and Magazines

Much of the information you need is likely to be located in architecture journals, magazines and the trade press. Be warned that tracking down articles on a particular subject is a notoriously difficult and time-consuming operation. It is, however, a task that you simply must do if you are to research your dissertation properly. Fortunately, for architecture, there are two main indices that can help you.

- *Architectural Periodicals Index (API).* This is an index to all the periodicals held in the RIBA Library, so anything you find in here can be obtained at the RIBA in London if your own school does not have it. You can look up your subject in a number of different ways (author, architect, place, building type, etc.). The API can be consulted in a series of printed volumes, one per year going back to the early 1970s, and each volume contains references only to periodical issues published in that year – so you will have to look at each volume in turn to find out all the possible references.

Some schools now have an electronic version of the API, in which case multiple years can be searched in one go. However, as with the paper-based version, the index does not go back very far, so for publications from the more distant past you must consult the second option open to you. Alternatively, and perhaps easiest, consult the RIBA Architecture catalogue on-line via www.architecture.com. This on-line resource is fully searchable by keyword, author, title, subject, and series, and results can be printed, saved to disk or e-mailed. It contains:

– index to over 300 of the world's most respected architectural periodicals
– catalogue of books and audio-visual materials
– catalogue of RIBA Library Photographs Collection
– catalogue of drawings and other materials acquired by the RIBA Library Drawings Collection since 1986
– catalogue of the RIBA Library Manuscripts Collection
– biographical database of architects

- *The Avery Index.* This is an index to all the periodicals held by the Avery Library at the University of Columbia in New York, so not everything listed in here will be obtainable in your own school library. Its main advantage is that it goes a lot further back in history than does the API, indeed into the nineteenth century. As with the API, if you use the paper version you will need to look up keywords several times – for the Avery this means a set of volumes which go up to 1979, and then a series of supplementary series. Some schools now have an electronic version of the Avery, which should greatly aid you in your task – as with the paper version, subjects include the history and practice of architecture, landscape architecture, city planning, historic preservation and interior design. Coverage is from 1934 to the present with selective coverage back to 1741 and the database is updated on a weekly basis. In the UK and other parts of Europe, the Avery (and other architecture-related databases) can also be accessed off-campus via the 'Athens' access management system – ask your university librarian for details. Similar web-based access is also available in the US and other countries worldwide.

Between them, these two indices should give you everything you need for anything produced from within the discipline of architecture, and consulting them carefully is an important part of an architectural dissertation study. Keep careful note of article references you get from the API and the Avery – you don't want to have to repeat the task unnecessarily.

The API and Avery indices are not the only places to look for this kind of information: other useful sources include the Iconda, and the BIDS Arts & Humanities systems, and the Wilson Art Abstracts On Line. If you want to find the right index for articles written about architecture but published in journals associated with another discipline, i.e. articles that address a non-architectural subject, you may find that an appropriate one exists. For example, references in art history journals can be found in the Art Index.

Many journals and periodicals are now themselves on-line, often allowing you to not only search for but also download articles on your subject. For example, in 2005 the Environmental Studies library at UCL – covering architecture, planning and construction – offered the following journals with either full or partial on-line access:

> *ARQ: Architectural Research Quarterly; Assemblage; Bridge Engineering; The Builder; Building and Environment; Building Design; Building Research and Information; Building Services Engineering and Research; Cement and Concrete Research; Cities; City and Community; City: analysis of urban trends, culture, theory, policy, action; Construction and Building Materials; Construction Information Quarterly; Construction Management and Economics; CORDIS Focus; Design Studies; Development and Change; Ecotoxicology and Environmental Safety; Energy and Buildings; Engineering, Construction and Architectural Management; Environment and Planning A-D; Environment and Urbanization; Environment International; Environment, Development and Sustainability; Environmental Impact Assessment Review; Environmental Management; Environmental Modeling and Assessment; Environmental Pollution; Environmental Research; Environmental Science and Policy; Environmental Software; Ethics, Place and Environment; European Planning Studies; European Urban and Regional Studies; Facilities; Gesta; Grey Room; Habitat International; History and Theory; Housing Statistics; Housing Studies; Integrated Assessment; International Development Planning Review; International Journal of Project Management; International Journal of Urban and Regional Research; International Planning Studies; Journal of Architectural Education; Journal of Architectural Engineering; Journal of Architecture; Journal of Arid Environments; Journal of Ecology; Journal of Environmental Management; Journal of Environmental Psychology; Journal of Housing and the Built Environment; Journal of Housing Economics; Journal of Land and Public Utility Economics; Journal of Planning Literature; Journal of Property Research; Journal of Rural Studies; Journal of Services Marketing; Journal of Social Policy; Journal of the Society of Architectural Historian; Journal of Transport Geography; Journal of Urban Design; Journal of Urban Economics; Journal of Urban Planning; Land Economics; Land Use Policy; Landscape and Urban Planning; Landscape Research; Local Economy; Local Environment; Local Housing Statistics; Municipal Engineer; Online Planning*

Journal; Papers in Regional Science; PEB Exchange; Planning Perspectives; Planning Practice and Research; Planning Theory; Planning Theory and Practice; Policy and Politics; Progress in Planning; Regional Science and Urban Economics; Regional Studies; Space and Culture; Space and Polity; Spatial Vision; Structural Design of Tall and Special Buildings; Structures and Buildings; Technological Forecasting and Social Change; Town Planning Review; Transplantation Proceedings; Transport Policy; Transport Reviews; Transportation Research Parts A-F; Urban Design International; Urban Design Update; Urban Ecosystems; Urban Geography; Urban History; Urban Review; Urban Studies; Waste Management and Research; Work, Employment and Society.

Similarly, in 2005, the Columbia University Libraries list as e-journals the following titles within architecture:

Architectural Digest; Architectural Record; Architectural Review; Architecture; L' Architettura; ARQ; Assemblage; Baumeister; Better Homes and Gardens; Canadian Architect; Design Studies; Green Places; Home Cultures; Hospitality Design; House Beautiful; Inland Architect; Journal of Architectural Education; Journal of Environmental Planning and Management; Journal of the American Society of Architectural Historians; Journal of Urban Design; Journal of Urban Planning and Development; Nexus Network Journal; Places; Progressive Architecture; Residential Architect; Restaurant/Hotel Design International; and TD & T.

To access these journals, you will need to visit either your universities own on-line library resource, or the relevant internet portal (many of which are accessible via the 'Athens' access management system – ask your university librarian for details). For example, see the sites for BIDS (www.bids.ac.uk), Blackwell Synergy (www.blackwell-synergy.com), Cambridge University Press (www.cambridge.org/uk/journals), Cross Ref (www.crossref.org), Emerald (www.emeraldinsight.com), Extenza (www.extenza-eps.com), Highwire (http://highwire.stanford.edu), Ingenta Connect (www.ingentaconnect.com), JSTOR (www.jstor.org), Taylor and Francis/Metapress (http://taylorandfrancis.metapress.com), Oxford University Press (www3.oup.co.uk/jnls), Science Direct (www.sciencedirect.com), SwetsWise (www.swetswise.com) and the Web of Knowledge (http://wok.mimas.ac.uk).

Note, however, that it is the more 'academic' journals which tend to be on-line. The more design oriented architecture magazines, such as *A+U, Archis, Blueprint, Domus, GA* etc. are not yet available in this way.

Special Collections

Your university may well have one or more special collections, often related to the city you are in and the people who have lived there. If you are not sure about the existence of these, once again, ask the librarian and/or your supervisor.

On-line Resources

Many universities have invested greatly in CD-ROMs, on-line data streams and other forms of electronic information. These can range from the BIDS supply of data to indices of various kinds to major national newspapers and magazines. For example, you might consider on-line sources such as Art Abstracts, Arts & Humanities Citation Index, Art Index and Art Index Retrospective, Art Bibliographies Modern, BHA (Bibliography of the History of Art), Books in Print, Dictionary of National Biography, Dissertation Abstracts, Getty Information Institute, Historical Abstracts, Index to 19th Century American Art Periodicals (AAI), Oxford English Dictionary Online, Social Sciences Citation Index, Urbadisc and the Web of Knowledge (formerly Web of Science).

Most universities also carry CD-ROMs listing all PhD studies done on all kinds of subject, and not just architecture. You may want to consult these, and/or look at the on-line Dissertation Abstracts and consider the abstracts for relevant theses. You may also be able to order a copy of a particular PhD on an inter-library loan if necessary.

As you can tell from this, there is a vast range of information on-line, and you should ask your university librarian to advise you on what is available via your own institution.

Other Libraries and Archives

You will not, of course, find everything you need in your own architecture or university library. Although many books and articles may be ordered on inter-library loan, at some point you will want to move off-campus and get stuck into some serious digging around. This is where the real fun starts, and if at first it seems a little intimidating, then don't worry. Most people feel unsure of themselves when they first go to a new archive, or arrange an interview – but once you get into it, it soon becomes much easier than you might have thought.

There is an enormous variety of other libraries and archives which you might want to consult, and it is impossible to list all of them here. The best place to find the archives relevant to your research is often the footnotes and bibliography of the books related to your subject. Relevant libraries and archives can be relatively easily located using the Internet, and many resources also now allow you to search their catalogues on-line, so at least you can see what they have before setting off for a visit. Some of the most useful include:

- *National architectural libraries.* Many countries have one or more libraries with international standard collections of architectural material, where you can find journals, books and other publications on architecture from all around the world. If you need to make a very detailed inquiry into architectural theory or history, particularly for older subjects, you may well need to visit this kind of library. In the USA, one of the best architectural libraries is the *Avery Library,* located at Columbia University in New York (www.cc.columbia.edu/cu/libraries/indiv/avery). In the UK, the best architectural library is the *British Architectural Library* at the RIBA in London (www.architecture.com), which also has a very good drawings and photographs collection in its separate Drawings Collection.

- *National copyright libraries.* A 'copyright' library should, in theory, have a copy of absolutely every book or journal published in English and on all subjects, not just architecture (although in practice some of the more obscure architecture publications are easier to find at more specialist collections such as those at the RIBA or Avery). Copyright libraries include *The British Library* in London (www.portico.bl.uk), and with a separate newspaper and magazine collection also in London (tel 020 7323 7353). Others to consider are the *National Library of Scotland* in Edinburgh (www.nls.uk), the *Bodleian Library* in Oxford (www.bodley.ox.ac.uk), the *National Library of Wales* at Aberystwyth (www.llgc.org.uk) and the *National Library of Australia* in Canberra (www.nla.gov.au). In the USA, the *Library of Congress* is located in Washington (www.loc.gov). Most other national libraries can be located through the *Gabriel* Internet site (www.konbib.nl/ gabriel, mirrored in the UK at http://portico.bl.uk/ gabriel/en/welcome.html).

- *Research libraries, special collections and archives.* These can offer a bewildering range of specialist information, from architecture, films and design to agriculture, biographical archives and cult interests. The best way to find these is through the internet, and a search through some of the following sites should help you to locate what you need. A few of the collections that you can access through the Internet are also fully on-line, so you may not even have to leave your desk in order to access them.

  In the UK, look at web-listings offered by the very useful *National Register of Archives* (www.nra.nationalarchives.gov.uk/nra/), as well as *ARCHON/Archives On-Line* (www.history.ac.uk). For other library resources, *COPAC* provides unified access to the catalogues of some of the largest university research libraries in the UK and Ireland (www.copac.ac.uk), as does the *NISS* gateway (www.hero.ac.uk/uk/niss/niss_library4008.cfm).

The *Institute of Historical Research* of the University of London (www.history.ac.uk) lists linkages to history resources globally, as does the *American and British History Resources* at Rutgers (www.libraries.rutgers.edu). *Columbia University* is once again particularly useful, with a very impressive listing of linkages to university and other libraries (www.columbia.edu/ cu/lweb/eresources/catalogs/ index.html), and archives (www.columbia.edu/cu/libraries/subjects/ speccol.html). The enormous archives listing, for example, ranges from the NASA Historical Archive and the United States Holocaust Museum to the American Institute of Architects and the Smithsonian Institution Archives of American Art.

- *City, public and local libraries.* These are often particularly good for dissertation topics which are based on your local city. They can usually provide highly detailed information on such topics as city development and growth, topographical maps and photographs, street life, local industry and commerce, transport, population figures, archaeological data, etc. Local history groups can usually also be contracted through local libraries.

- *City government offices.* Like local libraries, the various offices of the city government can often provide data that would be completely irretrievable through any other source. The actual organisation of this material varies greatly from city to city and country to country, but of particular use are those offices which deal with planning in particular and with public works in general. Whatever the municipal system of your own city, you should be able to obtain information on such matters as planning applications, city plans, zoning and any civic building, as well as official statistics, local laws, city demographics etc.

- *Foreign archives.* Access to these is often difficult and, as noted above, will probably need prior verbal or written contact, with letters of recommendation. You will need to understand bureaucratic procedures, which may vary from country to country. In some archives, source material may not be made available if it is in use at the same time by another researcher. You should always check in advance so that you do not have a wasted journey.

- *Personal archives.* Personal papers and other documents may be in the possession of relatives and/or have access controlled by them. You may have to be very careful how you handle these, particularly if they are not in good condition, as you do not want to be held responsible for any deterioration in their condition. It is useful to check how they have been stored before you visit and inspect personal archives. You may also need to check whether you need to wear gloves to handle them or keep them out of bright light. Damage to personal papers leads not only to a loss of research knowledge but also of personal memory for the owner, so it is important to be very careful.

The Internet

As already noted above, an increasing amount of material is readily available on the internet. Apart from the archives and libraries identified above, a whole raft of other people are now putting material onto their internet sites. These include companies and other institutions, government bodies and special-interest groups.

Some architects also have their own internet sites. So if you want to go and interview an architect, or need more details about a particular project, before contacting them directly you should make sure that the information you need is not freely available on the internet.

The former Director of the RIBA British Architecture Library, Ruth Kamen, produced the following list of architecture-related sites. Although currently not being up-dated, it is still an incredibly valuable source of architecture internet links, and is available at http://members.riba.org/library/rlinks.htm. This site includes over 2 000 links, with some 29 000 words of descriptions and notes under the following headings: general (electronic lists and discussion groups, search engines, directories and news; architects, designers, engineers and critics (directories , contemporary, historical); architecture (associations, councils, institutes, internet sites, search engines and lists, databases, geographical, styles and periods, web sites); awards & competitions; building types; buildings; computers, cad & virtual reality; construction; design, interiors, art; education; environment; events; government; grants; heritage; landscape; law; libraries, archives & visual resources; maps; materials & products; museums, galleries & exhibitions; planning; property; publications; research; standards & testing organisations; subscription services; towns & cities; visual arts; web design & net services; and miscellaneous.

Another excellent set of architecture-related links is hosted by the University of Nevada, Las Vegas, and can be found at http://library.nevada.edu/arch/rsrce/webrsrce/contents.html. This set of links is organised under the following headings: reference tools; accessibility/universal design; bibliographies; biographical/directory information; dictionaries and thesauri; education-related; indexes to print material; information databases and image banks; internet sites: lists and architecture search engines; library catalogues; miscellaneous; product and manufacturer information; technical information; resources; accessibility/universal design; architects and designers; architectural anthropology; architectural archives; architectural firms; architectural services; architecture and music; associations; booksellers and publishers; building industry information; building types and styles; buildings; campus planning; competitions; computing; construction and computing; consultants; contractors and builders; cyberspace; databases; design: interior, industrial, graphic; discussion groups; education; electronic publications; facility and project management; GIS (geographic information systems); government; green design; historic preservation; history; houses and house plans; housing; HVAC; image collections; indexes to print material; internet sites: lists and architecture search engines; jobs; landscape architecture; Las Vegas & Clark County, Nevada; libraries; lighting; maps; news; places; planning; product and manufacturer information; real estate; research (centres and groups, databases, papers, tools); resources (booksellers and publishers, products and manufacturing information); safety; signs; standards and codes; themed architecture; tiles; urban environment; virtual galleries; women.

The Boston University Library offers a web-based guide to research in architecture, www.bu.edu/library/guides/architect.html. This covers general architecture sites, image sources, special topics such as film and architecture, bibliographic guides, indices for periodicals and dissertations, library catalogues and other useful information.

Although more planning than architecture-oriented, also worth looking at is Cyburbia, www.cyburbia.org, a portal site for urban planners and others interested in cities and the built environment. It contains a selective directory of internet resources relevant to planning and urbanism. Cyburbia also includes information about mailing lists and newsgroups, and hosts an active bulletin board and image-hosting gallery.

- *Searching*. When conducting searches on the internet, as with library catalogues, it is best to use a number of different key words and search engines as results can be extremely variable. Make sure you use the advanced search features of search engines such as A9, AltaVista, AllTheWeb, Google, Lycos and Yahoo. If you see any useful links, make an immediate note of the URL address or add a bookmark – it is very easy to move on and to forget what you have seen, even from just a few minutes before.

- *Information*. Exactly what information you will obtain obviously depends greatly on the subject you are investigating and the sources available to you. As with libraries, you may find a number of useful books, articles and statements. Unlike libraries, however, you may also find illustrations, document archives and other materials which can be directly downloaded for inspection at a later date. Contacts (names, e-mail addresses, postal addresses) and links to other sites are also often obtainable.

  Some internet sites, especially those on special-interest topics, also offer various forms of on-line discussion groups where you can pose specific questions which you may want to ask. Before doing so, however, make sure that you have checked out all the recent discussions. On the internet it is considered bad protocol to repeat oft-stated requests and questions when that information is already available.

- *Note-taking*. When you have found something useful, you can do the same kind of note-taking that you might do in a library or paper-based archive. On the internet you also have another choice, which is to simply download or cut-and-paste the whole of a page into another program on your computer. This can be very useful, but beware that the same kind of rules apply here as to photocopying – just because you have a copy of something does not mean that you have read it, still less thought about it. So try to be reasonably selective with your collecting procedures.

• *Recording sources.* As with all research, you have to be very careful on the internet to make sure that you carefully note down the source from which you gathered your information. This is particularly true of the internet, because the ability to download or copy over whole pages means that you will then have a complete, digital transcription of the source, ready to be used in your dissertation. Although this may seem to be a huge advantage (such as for extended quotations), it also means that unless you are extremely fastidious in your working methods it is very easy indeed to end up unintentionally plagiarizing a source. There are therefore two things that you need to note for any piece of information gained from the internet.

1   URL. First, you need to know the URL – web address – of the Internet site concerned. Ideally, this should be from the exact page rather than the general site address, i.e. www.hughpearman.com/articles5/pyramid.html and not just www.hughpearman.com. In order to do this, it is often easiest to copy and paste the URL, along with the information related to it, into a word-processing or similar program on your computer. (If you do this, ensure that you save the word-processing document at regular intervals as internet access can often cause computers to crash.)

2   Date. The other thing you need to know is the date at which you accessed the web site, e.g. www.hughpearman.com/articles5/pyramid.html (accessed 8 February 2005).

Besides the information and guidance given above, there are also several other things to bear in mind when researching on the internet. If you are going to do a great deal of internet-based research for an extended dissertation, you might consider consulting a specialist guide such as Niall O'Dochartaigh, *The Internet Research Handbook: a Practical Guide for Students and Researchers in the Social Sciences* (Sage, 2001), Carol Clark, *Working the Web: a Student's Research Guide* (Harcourt College, 2000), or Steve Jones (ed.), *Doing Internet Research: Critical Issues and Methods for Examining the Net* (Sage, 1998).

However, for most architecture students following a few simple rules will suffice. Kamen, who compiled the RIBA Architecture Links resources listed above, recommends the following:

• *Reliability.* With what authority has the website been written? Is the author/publisher/sponsor clearly identified? Was this resource found from another resource that is considered reliable? Do other reliable resources link to it?

What is the content and scope of the website? What is the point of view? Is it biased? Is it a spoof? Does the information appear to be accurate and/or complete? Can you verify it in other sources? Are there references to additional resources?

Is the website current? Is information up-to-date? Are there dates on the page to indicate when the page was written, when it was first published on the web, and/or when it was last revised? If not, can you discover this by, for example, viewing page information or page source?

- *Evaluation.* Be an internet detective, and consider whether the URL (Universal Resource Locator – the web address) contains a clue. For example, in www.sah.org 'sah' refers to the Society of Architectural Historians.

  Look at the domain suffix, which can you tell whether the website's producer is educational, non-profit, commercial, etc. For example, .ac=academic, .co=commercial, .com=commercial, .edu=educational, .gov=governmental, .net=Internet Service Provider, .org=non-profit making organisation.

Which country does the website come from? For example, .de=Germany, dk=Denmark, fr=France, nl=Netherlands, uk=United Kingdom, .com=USA or international.

Who published the page? In general, the publisher is the agency or person operating the server computer from which the document is issued. The server is usually named in first portion of the URL, between http:// and the first /, as with the RIBA for http://www.riba.org/library/ rlinks.htm.

Is the website someone's personal site? To discover this, read the URL carefully and look to see if the server is a commercial ISP or other provider of web page hosting (like aol.com or geocities.com). And look for a personal name (e.g. iborden or borden) following a tilde (~) or the word 'users' or 'people.'

Consider who is responsible for the website and who wrote it. For example, click on 'home' or 'homepage' or perhaps on a logo. Truncate back along the URL (also a good trick if you get a 'page not found' message). Look for 'about us' or 'biography.' Click on 'e-mail' or 'contact'. Or view the page source.

References

1   Henry Russell Hitchcock, *Architecture: Nineteenth and Twentieth Centuries* (Harmondsworth: Penguin, 1958).
2   Colin Rowe, *The Mathematics of the Ideal Villa and Other Essays* (Cambridge, MA: MIT, 1977).
3   Erwin Panofsky, *Gothic Architecture and Scholasticism* (London: Thames & Hudson, 1957).
4   Robert Venturi, Denise Scott Brown and Stephen Izenour, *Learning from Las Vegas* (Cambridge, MA: MIT, 1972).

5   Nikolaus Pevsner, *Pioneers of the Modern Movement: from William Morris to Walter Gropius* (London: Faber, 1936); and Charles Jencks, *The Architecture of the Jumping Universe: A polemic. How Complexity Science is Changing Architecture and Culture* (London: Academy, 1995).

6   Heinrich Wölfflin, *Renaissance and Baroque* (London: Fontana, 1964).

7   Mark Girouard, *Life in the English Country House: a Social and Architectural History* (New Haven: Yale University Press, 1978); and Spiro Kostof, *A History of Architecture: Settings and Rituals* (Oxford: Oxford University Press, 1985).

8   Anthony Vidler, *Claude-Nicolas Ledoux* (Cambridge, MA: MIT Press, 1990).

9   See, for example, Manfredo Tafuri, *Architecture and Utopia* (Cambridge, MA: MIT, 1976).

10   See, for example, Jane Rendell, Barbara Penner and Iain Borden (eds), *Gender, Space, Architecture: an Interdisciplinary Introduction* (London: Routledge, 2000); Diane Agrest, Patricia Conway and Leslie Kanes Weisman (eds), *The Sex of Architecture* (New York: Harry N. Abrams, 1996); and Deborah Coleman, Elizabeth Danze and Carol Henderson (eds), *Architecture and Feminism* (New York: Princeton Architectural Press, 1996).

11   Mary Lutyens, *Edwin Lutyens* (London: Murray, 1980).

12   Reyner Banham, *Theory and Design in the First Machine Age* (London: Architectural Press, 1960).

13   Sigfried Giedion, *Space, Time and Architecture: the Growth of a New Tradition* (Cambridge, MA: Harvard University Press, 1941).

14   Mark Gottdiener, *Postmodern Semiotics: Material Culture and the Forms of Postmodern Life* (Oxford: Blackwell, 1995).

15   Jennifer Bloomer, *Architecture and the Text: the (S)crypts of Joyce and Piranesi* (New Haven: Yale University Press, 1993).

16   Anthony Vidler, *The Architectural Uncanny: Essays in the Modern Unhomely* (Cambridge, MA: MIT Press, 1992).

17   Steven Holl, Juhani Pallasmaa and Alberto Pérez-Gómez, 'Questions of Perception: Phenomenology of Architecture', special issue, *A + U* (*Architecture and Urbanism*), (July 1994).

18   Ross King, *Emancipating Space: Geography, Architecture and Urban Design* (New York: Guilford, 1996).

19   Zeynep Çelek, *Urban Forms and Colonial Confrontations: Algiers Under French Rule* (Berkeley: University of California Press, 1997).

20   For an overview of the relation between critical theory and architecture, see Iain Borden and Jane Rendell (eds), *InterSections: Architectural Histories and Critical Theories* (London: Routledge, 2000).

21   Alice Coleman, *Utopia on Trial: Vision and Reality in Planned Housing* (London: Hilary Shipman, 1985).

22   Anthony King, *The Bungalow: the Production of a Global Culture* (Oxford: Oxford University Press, 1995).

23   Kim Dovey, *Framing Places: Mediating Power in Built Form* (London: Routledge, 1999); and Thomas A. Markus, *Buildings and Power: Freedom and Control in the Origin of Building Types* (London: Routledge, 1993).

24   Michael Sorkin, *Exquisite Corpse: Writing on Buildings* (London: Verson, 1991).

25   Paul Shepheard, *What is Architecture? An Essay on Landscapes, Buildings, and Machines* (Cambridge, MA: MIT, 1994).

26   Jun'ichiro Tanizaki, *In Praise of Shadows* (New Haven: Leete's, 1977).

4 Preparing

There are many ways to skin a rabbit. Writing is no different, and authors adopt a wide range of techniques, procedures and tricks in order to produce and structure their material. The advice in this chapter therefore should not be taken as a set of rules that you should follow exactly. That said, much of what is contained here summarises much of what might be considered to be the 'best practice' in dissertation writing. As with the other chapters in this book, if you follow the procedures outlined here then you should be able to produce work of a high standard.

A large number of books offer general advice on writing and referencing, which you might also like to consult. Some of the most popular include:

American Management Association, *The AMA Style Guide for Business Writing* (New York: AMACOM, 1996).

Judith Butcher, *Copy-editing: the Cambridge Handbook for Editors, Authors and Publishers* (Cambridge: Cambridge University Press, third edition, 1992).

The Chicago Manual of Style (Chicago: University of Chicago Press, fifteenth edition, 2003).

The Economist, *The Economist Style Guide: a Concise Guide for All Your Business Communications* (London: Wiley & Sons, eighth edition, 2003).

Joseph Gibaldi, *MLA Handbook for Writers of Research Papers* (New York: Modern Language Association of America, sixth edition, 2003).

Ernest Gowers, *The Complete Plain Words* (London: Penguin, 1962).

Modern Humanities Research Association, *MHRA Style Book:
Notes for Authors, Editors, and Writers of Theses* (London:
Modern Humanities Research Association, fourth edition,
1991).
Thomas S. Kane, *The New Oxford Guide to Writing* (Oxford:
Oxford University Press, 1994).
Thomas S. Kane, *The Oxford Essential Guide to Critical
Writing: Essential Resource Library* (Oxford: Oxford University
Press, 2000).
William Strunk and E. B. White, *The Elements of Style*
(London: Collier Macmillan, fourth edition, 2000).
Andrea Sutcliffe (ed.), *New York Public Library Writer's Guide
to Style and Usage,* (HarperResource, 1994).
Kate Turabian, *A Manual for Writers of Term Papers, Theses
and Dissertations* (Chicago: University Of Chicago Press, sixth
edition, 1996).

Structuring a Dissertation

The most basic rule in structuring any coursework – an essay as well as
a dissertation – is a triad:

> 1 SAY WHAT YOU ARE GOING TO SAY
> 2 SAY IT
> 3 SAY THAT YOU HAVE SAID IT

In other words, you should first introduce your subject in order to let the
reader know what it is you are trying to explore. Second, you need to
conduct your exposition. Third, you should retrace in summary form the
ground, which you have previously covered. In practice, this means
adopting the following structure:

- Introduction
- Main argument, divided into a number of sections or chapters
- Conclusion.

Each of these parts of a dissertation performs a specific role. It is important
that you understand what these roles are, and how they are carried out.

Introduction (Say What You Are Going To Say)

The introduction to your dissertation is exactly that: an introduction for
the reader that explains the main content, arguments and structure of
what they are about to read. As such, the introduction both orientates the

reader by letting them know what lies ahead and whets their appetite by providing a few clues as to what is going to be discussed.

Architectural students often get quite worried about the introduction to their dissertations, but in fact there is no reason for this as the introduction can be simply divided into five main components. The introduction should cover:

- *Objects of study*. Here you should briefly summarise the subject, indicating the main objects of study. This can be a simple statement identifying the main architects, buildings, texts, other cultural media etc. that the dissertation investigates.
- *Interpretive ideas*. Here you should introduce the main theoretical and other intellectual ideas you are bringing to bear on the subject. What are the main themes you investigate? Are there any particular sets of ideas that you use to do this?
- *Academic context*. In order that the reader has some idea of the originality of your own work, you should briefly identify other works already completed by other historians and theorists, and note how your own work is different. In short, what work has already been done on this subject, and what new ground are you covering?
- *Methodology*. Here you should briefly summarise the procedure you will be adopting. Is this a piece of history, theory or personal writing? Is it, for example, a piece of politicised history or a social science investigation?
- *Dissertation structure*. This is simply a description of each section in turn – as has been done for the introduction to this book under the heading 'The Handbook'.

You do not need to write a very lengthy introduction to your dissertation, and this should comprise no more than 20 per cent of the total wordage. For example, for a dissertation of 10 000 words in total, the introduction should be no more than 2 000 words of that total and often shorter. If you then also allow 300–400 words for each of the five sub-sections and write each one in turn, you will quickly find that the introduction is completed without too much pain or heartache.

Main Argument (Say It)

This is where the most important part of the dissertation is located – the investigation of architecture according to the questions and ideas that you pose. In order to achieve this target as clearly and successfully as possible, you should deploy the following five tactics.

- *Sub-division*. Divide the main body of the dissertation into approximately three to seven chapters or sections. Each of these sections should deal with a distinct aspect of the dissertation in turn.

Deciding exactly what these sections are, and the sequence in which they run, is one of the single most important acts when writing a dissertation.

- *Section focus.* Each section should be carefully focused on its selected topic. In other words, stick to the point. Try to keep various asides, discursions and any other extra information to a minimum. Your dissertation will be most successful if you select your particular theme for each section and doggedly pursue it.
- *Section size.* Keep each section to approximately the same size. Assuming once again that the dissertation is 10 000 words in total, and you have used approximately 2 500 words for the introduction and the conclusion, then clearly you have about 7 500 words for the main argument. You then sub-divide this again to produce, say, five sections of 1 500 words each. Alternatively, if you are dealing with a larger dissertation, the same process still holds – take the total number of words available to you, excluding introduction and conclusion, and divide that figure up into the appropriate number of sections on which you are working.
- *Section linking.* Link each section with the next. It is often helpful to the reader if they are guided through the dissertation. To do this, you can provide linking paragraphs at the end and/or beginning of each section, very quickly summarising where your investigation has got to, and where it is going next.
- *Section writing.* Work out exactly what you want to put in each section, and then write each in turn. Although working on a computer sometimes makes it tempting to adopt the scatter-gun approach to writing, doing a bit here and a bit there, most people find it easier to work section by section through their dissertation. This not only lets you keep your own mental health in order, as you have to cope with only one issue or question at a time, it also allows you to keep a careful eye on how well you are progressing. (For more advice on writing, see below.)

Conclusion (Say That You Have Said It)

As with the introduction, many students get somewhat worried about the conclusion to their dissertation. However, there are really only two things that you need to do here.

- *Summary statement.* You simply need to remind the reader of your argument and interpretations, drawing out the most salient points. Remember that although you will have written, redrafted and reread your dissertation many times, the reader will have been through it only once and will thus be much less familiar with your material. A simple recapitulation in the conclusion is of great help to a reader in recalling what they have just read.

- *Speculation.* The conclusion is also the place where you might speculate upon the value of your investigations for architecture in general, and perhaps outline any work that might be done in the future. Sometimes, particularly with dissertations that deal with contemporary topics, you can introduce a piece of 'late-breaking news' here, providing another twist or turn to the events that you have been covering (such as the developer has gone bankrupt, the architect has won a new competition, a new theory has recently emerged ...).

The conclusion is often slightly shorter than the introduction, and as a general rule should be approximately 5–10 per cent of the total dissertation length.

Working Methods

One of the most difficult things to do when working on a dissertation (and indeed to give advice about) is actually doing the writing. Nearly everyone you might speak to about this will have a slightly different way of going about it, and in the end you must do what suits you best. However, once again, there are a number of very useful tricks and techniques, which you may find helpful in smoothing your passage through the writing process.

Reviewing Notes

In order to write your dissertation, it is obviously extremely useful if you have an intimate knowledge of the material that you have gathered together during your research. This may sound obvious, but many people spend a lot of their writing time just going through their notes and files searching for something that they half-remember having written down. Conversely, knowing exactly what is in your notes and where to find the relevant information will immensely speed up your writing and also improve your argument.

You should therefore read your notes thoroughly before writing, and review them at frequent stages. Some people find it helpful to carefully arrange their notes: numbering pages, organising them into rough groups, and so on. Others even go as far as to prepare a rough index of their notes for all the main subjects that they wish to include in their dissertation – if you can bear to do this it may well save you a lot of time later on, particularly if you have collected a large quantity of research material.

Writing

If you followed the previous advice about researching a dissertation (see Chapter 3) then by this stage of your dissertation project you should already have a number of notes and interpretive thoughts written down, in which case it is now a case of arranging them and expanding them. If you have not done this, don't panic. Tackle each of your dissertation sections in turn, and think exactly what it is you want to say. Sometimes it can be of great help simply to get anything at all down on paper, and then to consider whether that really is what you wanted to say. Editing down your initial text can really help focus your thoughts. Talking to other people can also help, especially, of course, to your supervisor.

In general, most people write and think better without distractions. Turn the radio/iPod off, turn the answering machine on, resist the sudden temptation to do all your clothes washing, put the cat out … .

Arranging Thoughts

A successful dissertation is not just a collection of information and ideas but a series of these things arranged into a coherent whole. In order to produce this kind of dissertation, when writing you continually have to make decisions about what you want to say next. So in the same way that each of your dissertation sections addresses an issue and leads on to the next section, within each section you should again try to arrange your thoughts clearly and methodically. In practice, this means that each paragraph should contain a distinct thought, and should lead on to the next.

At the same time as writing each section and each paragraph (or even sentence) within it, you should at all times try to keep in mind the overall plan and structure of your dissertation. Ask yourself, what is the last thing I wrote, what do I need to say next, and where does this lead me in terms of my overall argument? The aim is, after all, not to write just anything but something that contributes to your dissertation as a whole.

Referring to the Subject

Make sure that you always refer to your subject. It is very easy in a dissertation, particularly when you have done a large amount of research, to try to include every architectural fact that you have uncovered and every idea that you have had about it. However, no matter how selective and accurate you have been in your research and note-taking, writing a dissertation is much like editing a film: a large percentage of it ends up on the cutting-room floor.

Above all, while you may, of course, want to make some parallel comparisons or contextual references, you should as much as possible try to refer directly to the subject you are investigating. Similarly, try to deploy only those ideas and arguments that are relevant to your interpretation. Adding in a load of other stuff will not impress the reader, and will only serve to cloud their understanding of what you are trying to say.

One trick to help you do this is to write about a specific illustration or quotation, which you have in front of you as you write and, which you include in the dissertation. That way, you can only write about something known to both you and the reader.

Assessing Work

It is a good idea to reread what you have written at regular intervals, especially after a day or so. Often you will find that something could be said more clearly, or that you have missed out an important thought. Ask yourself whether the text still makes sense to you. Could the ideas be presented more clearly? Could someone who knows little about the subject still understand it?

After rereading their work a number of times, authors often find that they cannot concentrate on their own words, which are beginning to look the same. If you find this happening, you can change the way that your text appears in much the same way that artists and designers often look at their work in a mirror in order to get a fresh perspective on it. For writers, if you have been working solely on a computer screen you can print out the text, or if you already have a print-out do so again but with a different font – both of these tactics will make the words seem very 'different' from how they read previously and will help you to get a new take on their sense.

Once again, your supervisor is the best person to provide a good assessment of how your work is progressing. Show her or him a sample of your work, even if only a small excerpt of the whole, as this will enable them to comprehend clearly how you are working and the kinds of things you are trying to say.

Dissertation Size

It is very easy when writing a dissertation to massively overshoot the total number of words allowed to you. In order to avoid the need for lengthy and time-consuming editing-down at a later date, you must keep a careful eye on the wordage you have written. Nearly all word processing and related computer programs now offer a 'word count' facility, so there is no reason why this should be difficult to do. You also need to know whether the number of words you are allowed includes footnotes, bibliography, appendices etc. For example, the 100, 000 word allowance for a text-based doctoral dissertation at University College London (UCL) *includes* main text, footnotes and references, but *excludes* the bibliography and appendices.

Grammar and Spelling

Although it is only the final dissertation and not the first draft that you will probably be assessed on, anything you can do to improve the standard of grammar and spelling in your manuscript will serve you well in the future. Try to correct grammar and spelling as you go along, or at the end of each day. Above all, try to resist the temptation to leave all this to the end – a badly constructed draft text will only serve to hinder your thought-processes, make it very difficult for anyone else to respond to your work in progress, hide the real word count and in the end will just store up additional work for later on down the line. If grammar is not your strong point, and the suggestions that the grammar check on your computer brings up do not all make sense to you, find a friend or relative who is willing to go through a section of your text. He or she can annotate the errors, and also explain why these are grammatically wrong.

Illustrations

Illustrations usually form a very important and frequently essential part of an architectural dissertation. Architecture is, after all, very much a visual entity and consequently some form of illustrative material often plays an integral role in any discussion of it.

However, just as you take great care to choose your words and arguments, so you should pay equal attention to the illustrations, which contribute to your dissertation. Things to consider include the following:

- *Type of illustration.* What is the best kind of illustration to use at any particular moment in your dissertation? A plan, section or elevation? An interior or exterior view? A conceptual sketch or diagram? A map or site-plan? A photograph with people, giving a sense of social use and the time at which the photograph was taken? Each of these conveys a different kind of information, and you should therefore match the right illustration with the appropriate text and argument.
- *Atmosphere.* Illustrations have an atmospheric 'mood' as well as a technical quality. Thus a dramatic black and white photograph with heavy contrasts and red-filtered sky, showing, for example, a public square with civic buildings and lots of people, will have a very different effect from a hard-lined architect's plan of the same urban space. Your choice of what kind of illustration to include may depend on, apart from your argument, the kind of study you are undertaking: if you are writing a more interpretive account, the black and white photograph may be more appropriate, but if you are doing a social science study then the architect's plan may be better.
- *Usefulness.* Although many illustrations are, of course, very useful indeed, architecture students can sometimes put too many illustrations into their text. This is doubly ineffective, as not only do the extra illustrations draw attention away from those which really are adding something to the argument, but the reader of your dissertation may be cynical enough to think that you are trying to cover up for a lack of work and thought in your text. Each time you place an illustration into your dissertation, ask yourself whether it is really needed. What information does it show? Would it matter if I left it out?
- *Textual comment.* One test of whether an illustration is really useful to your dissertation is whether you refer to it in the main text. In

general, you should try to refer to all illustrations, and use them to drive the main argument.

Referencing

An important part of any architectural dissertation is the referencing system – footnotes, references and bibliography – adopted in order to inform the reader as to where your information and main ideas have been derived from.

*   *Footnotes.* Footnotes are extra pieces of information that provide additional clarification or comment to that which is contained in the main body of the text. In general, footnotes should be kept to a minimum.
*   *References.* References are shorter pieces of information that state the source for the facts or ideas concerned. In particular, references should be given for all quotations, specific pieces of information and for ideas that you have found in other texts.

There are two main systems for dealing with footnotes and references.

Harvard

In the Harvard system, as it is often called, you simply place any reference in the main body of the text. For example,

> Spiller argues that the influence of new biological and mechanical systems on architecture means that we must now re-assess architectural space (Spiller, 1998).

Here, a quick cross-referencing with the bibliography would provide the full details for the Spiller publication listed for the year 1998. If there are more than one publication by that author, these can be listed as 1998a, 1998b and so on.

A slightly more detailed version of the Harvard system is to include the exact page number(s) for the publication concerned. For example,

> Spiller is particularly concerned to address the surface qualities of architecture and how these might be represented in drawings (Spiller, 1998, 85–94).

The advantage of the Harvard system is that it makes references to particular authors very clear within the main body of the text. Its disadvantage, however, is that these same references can easily disrupt the flow of the main text, particularly when used in a historical or critical dissertation where a great deal of different sources are used (thus requiring many references) and/or where the writing style otherwise tends to be quite fluid. Furthermore, the reader, of course, has to look at bibliography to find the full reference, while any footnote material still has to be dealt with in the usual manner, using superscript footnote markers (see below).

For these reasons, the Harvard system tends to be favoured predominantly in science and social science disciplines. The kind of architectural discourse which focuses on critical, cultural, historical or theoretical interpretations of the built environment, however, tends to avoid it.

Humanities

The more common way of including footnotes and references in architecture is therefore the humanities system. Here a superscript marker in the main body of the text refers the reader to extratextual material containing either footnotes or references. For example, both footnote and reference are dealt with in the following sentences:

> Spiller argues that the influence of new biological and mechanical systems on architecture means that we must now re-assess architectural space.[1] His argument ranges from alchemy and secrecy to cyborgian mutation and genocide.[2]

> 1 Neil Spiller, *Digital Dreams: Architecture and the New Alchemic Technologies* (London: Ellipsis, 1998) pp 1–13.

> 2 Spiller is thus more concerned with the possible impact of these technologies on the architectural imagination than with their objective, technical effects.

These footnotes and references would, of course, usually be placed elsewhere in the dissertation, at the foot of the page, at the end of the current section, or at the end of whole dissertation – any one of these is usually acceptable.

When giving the reference information for a source, note that along with the usual publication details you should also cite the exact pages to which you are referring (in the case above, pp 1–13 inclusive). Note also that the use of the prefix 'pp' denotes multiple pages, while 'p' is used to refer to one page only. Another convention is to abbreviate page numbers so that 42–44 becomes 42–4 (similarly, 101–192 would become 101–92 and 241–249 would become 241–9, while 59–61 or 98–104 would stay in this form).

The first use of a work in the footnotes/references should always be given in full, such as

> 1 Philip Tabor, 'Striking Home: the Telematic Assault on Identity,' Jonathan Hill (ed.), *Occupying Architecture: Between the Architect and the User* (London: Routledge, 1998) pp 217–28.

> 2 Adrian Forty, *Words and Buildings: a Vocabulary of Modern Architecture* (London: Thames & Hudson, 2000) pp 23–5.

This, as with all other forms of full reference, should follow the system you have adopted in your bibliography (see below). Subsequent references can then be given in abbreviated form, such as:

3   Tabor, 'Striking Home', p 223.
4   Forty, *Words and Buildings*, p 38.

You can also use two other forms of abbreviation. The first of these is *ibid.*, short for *ibidem*, or Latin for 'the same place'. Here you could have a series of references, all for the same source, which ran:

1   Jane Rendell, 'Gendered Space: Encountering Anthropology, Architecture and Feminism in the Burlington Arcade', *Architectural Design*, special issue on 'Architecture and Anthropology' (October 1996) pp 61–2.
2   *Ibid.*, p 60.
3   *Ibid.*, p 62.

Alternatively, you may use *op. cit.*, short for *opere citato*, which is Latin for 'in the work cited'. Here you can refer back to previous references, such as:

1   Iain Borden, *Skateboarding, Space and the City: Architecture and the Body* (Oxford: Berg, 2001) pp 42–3.
2   Allen Cunningham (ed.), *Modern Movement Heritage* (London: Spon, 1997) pp 22–3.
3   Borden, *op. cit.*, p 95.

However, while *ibid.* and *op. cit.* are much loved by academic publishers, you would do well to avoid these abbreviations. This is for the simple reason that both *ibid.* and *op. cit.* depend greatly on there being a full, prior reference to which they can accurately refer. It is all too easy when writing a dissertation to remove the full reference in the draft or final production stages, thus leaving any subsequent *ibid.* and *op. cit.* references floating without substance. At least with the abbreviated form of reference (i.e. of the form, Borden, *Skateboarding, Space and the City*, p 95) you and the reader still have some clue as to what the full reference might be.

Bibliographies

Bibliographies are an important element of any dissertation, itemising all the sources and major influences for the work in hand. Your supervisor and examiner will normally pay close attention to the bibliography, checking it both to see what it contains and for its formatting and attention to detail. If your bibliography is full of mistakes or otherwise incorrectly produced, this can drastically undermine the confidence that the reader will have in the rest of the dissertation.

Content

The bibliography to a dissertation should contain two kinds of information:

- *References from main text.* This includes all books, journal articles etc. that are included in your footnotes and references, and any other sources mentioned in the main body of the dissertation.
- *Other sources.* This includes other books, articles, archives etc. that you have consulted, but which otherwise do not appear in your footnotes and references. This does not mean that you should include every book or article you have ever read or heard about (and your dissertation assessor will probably be very cynical of bibliographies padded out with irrelevant or unlikely sources), just those which have been of use to you in this dissertation.

Arrangement

It is sometimes a good idea to sub-divide your bibliography into different sections. For example, if your dissertation was an investigation into the Situationist idea of psychogeography as expressed in the work of architect Constant Niewenhuys and the painter Asger Jorn, you might want to have distinct sub-sections on Situationists in general, Constant and Jorn.

Format

There are many different ways to format a bibliography, and it would be possible to fill up this whole book with all the various systems, rules, conventions etc. However, in general, you need to provide all the information that you can possibly think of:

- *Books.* For whole books, you should include author(s) and editor(s), title of book, place of publication, publisher, revised edition (if appropriate), and date. The names of translators, where appropriate, are also often included.
- *Book essays and chapters.* For essays and chapters in books, you should include author, title of essay, together with the place of publication, i.e. editor(s), title of book, place of publication, publisher, revised edition (if appropriate), date and page range.
- *Journal articles.* For articles in journals, you should include author, title of article, together with the place of publication, i.e. title of journal, volume and issue number, date and page range.

Exactly how you provide this information is largely up to you. The most important thing is that you are absolutely consistent in your methods. This means not only making sure that you include all the necessary information in each bibliographic entry, but that you also pay very close attention to your use of commas, brackets, periods etc. as well as to the use of italics and quotation marks.

Note that chapters, articles, dissertations and unpublished material etc. are all put in quotation marks. This is because they are not published in themselves, but are only parts of published works, or are unpublished at all. Conversely, all book titles, journal titles, films, government reports and similar materials are set in italics, as these are published documents.

You may see older dissertations and government reports with book titles set not as italics but as underlined text. This is because nearly all typewriters had no facility for italic font faces, so underlining was used instead. Similarly, typed manuscripts used underlining to clearly indicate to the typesetter what needed to be placed in italic. These old, historic reasons for using underlining rather than italics are, however, by now more or less redundant – italic font faces can easily be selected on any computer program, and a file version can be given to the typesetter if required at a later date. So use italics, not underlining.

An example of a typical humanities bibliographic system is as follows:

- *Authored book*. Nigel Coates, *Ecstacity: Guide to* Ecstacity (London: Laurence King, 2003).
- *Multi-authored book*. Bill Hillier and Julienne Hanson, *The Social Logic of Space* (Cambridge: Cambridge University Press, 1984).
- *Edited book*. Andrea Kahn, (ed.), *Drawing/Building/Text: Essays in Architectural Theory* (New York: Princeton Architectural Press, 1991).
- *Multi-edited book*. Duncan McCorquodale, Katerina Rüedi and Sarah Wigglesworth (eds), *Desiring Practices: Architecture, Gender and the Interdisciplinary* (London: Black Dog, 1996).
- *Chapter in an edited book*. Carol Burns, 'On Site: Architectural Preoccupations', Andrea Kahn (ed.), *Drawing/Building/Text: Essays in Architectural Theory* (New York: Princeton Architectural Press, 1991) pp 147–67.
- *Chapter in a multi-edited book*. Henry Urbach, 'Closets, Clothes, disClosure', Duncan McCorquodale, Katerina Rüedi and Sarah Wigglesworth (eds), *Desiring Practices: Architecture, Gender and the Interdisciplinary* (London: Black Dog, 1996) pp 246–63.
- *Journal/magazine article*. Anthony Vidler, 'Bodies in Space/Subjects in the City: Psychopathologies of Modern Urbanism', *Differences*, v. 5 n. 3 (Fall 1993) pp 31–51.
- *Published interview*. You should treat this as if it were a book chapter or journal article as appropriate, e.g.:
  'Space, Knowledge and Power', interview with Michel Foucault, Paul Rabinow, (ed.), *The Foucault Reader* (New York: Pantheon Books, 1984) pp 239–56.
  'An Interview with Fredric Jameson', *Diacritics*, v. 3 n. 12 (1982) pp 72–91.

- *Self-conducted interview.* Here you just need to give the participants, place and date of the interview:
  Interview between author and Zaha Hadid (London, 9 November 2005).
- *Dissertations/Theses.* These should be treated like a conventional book, but as the work is not published the title is not set in italics but is placed in quotation marks:
  Edward Dimendberg, 'Film Noir and the Spaces of Modernity' (New York: New York University, unpublished PhD thesis, 1992).
- *Archives.* Each archive has its own reference system, so you must provide not only the archive name but also enough information for someone else to locate the material you have found, e.g.:
  Ebenezer Howard, speech at the opening of Homesgarth, *Papers of Sir Ebenezer Howard*, Hertfordshire County Record Office, Hertford, folio 3.
- *Internet.* Give title and web address of the site, and date accessed, e.g.:
  'Burford's Hall of Fame', http://www.vvcom/~gilmore/head/ (accessed 11 April 1995).
- *Broadcasts.* Give programme title, channel/station and date.
  Heaven, Hell and Suburbia (BBC2, 17 April 2005).
- *Film/video.* Give film title, studio, director and year:
  Playtime (Specta-Films, dir. Jacques Tati, 1967).

Plagiarism

Plagiarism is becoming an increasingly important issue for architecture schools and universities, who are clamping down hard on anyone found plagiarising work. Several internet sites have sections devoted to this practice – see for example http://webster.commnet.edu/mla/plagiarism.shtml, or the *MLA Handbook for Writers of Research Papers* on which this website is partly based. As deliberate plagiarism is a form of cheating and fraud, penalties for proven cases are, rightly, quite severe, and often include fines and/or retaking of an academic year, substantial downgrading of the degree award, and even expulsion from the institution concerned.

The problem for anyone undertaking a dissertation is that it is actually quite easy to unintentionally plagiarise someone else's work. To prevent this, you need to know what plagiarism is, and take steps to avoid it.

What is Plagiarism?

If you include distinctive phrases, sentences or paragraphs from other authors, you must put this text into quotation marks, and acknowledge the source with a reference. If you do not follow this procedure, it is very likely that your work will be viewed by the examiners as an act of *plagiarism* – using someone else's ideas and words directly, while presenting them as if they were your own.

Dissertations are usually read by at least your own supervisor, and are often second-marked by another member of the faculty staff. Most dissertations in the UK are also read by an external examiner, regardless of the level of study. In the USA, masters dissertations may have an external reviewer. In addition, many academics now use bespoke plagiarism-detection software such as EVE2, Glatt Plagiarism Screening, iThenticate, Turnitin and WCopyfind – see www.plagiarism.com and www.plagiarism.org for details. It is therefore extremely likely that any plagiarism contained in your dissertation will be spotted by at least one of these assessors.

Prevention

To prevent your work from containing plagiarised elements, there are a number of easy steps that you can take.

- *Research*. As described in Chapter 3, you should at all times keep a careful note of the sources from which you have made your notes, collected information etc.
- *Quotations*. Enclose in quotation marks every extract that you have reproduced as a quotation from a book, periodical or other source.
- *Other data*. Provide a reference for all other specific pieces of data or key ideas that you have derived from other sources.
- General writing. All other information should be rewritten in your own words. However, in general, it is not enough to (a) simply change the wording of an extract and to claim it as your own, or (b) simply mention the author or title in a bibliography or elsewhere. If you rewrite someone else's ideas in your own words you should still provide a reference to this source next to the sentence or paragraph concerned.

    You are, of course, expected to read books and articles and to quote them with appropriate acknowledgements. But you are also expected to ensure that your dissertation is not just a collage of other people's words and ideas – you need to have digested your sources sufficiently to be able, in your own words, to summarise their contents and to draw conclusions from them. See http://webster.commnet.edu/mla/plagiarism.shtml, which provides several useful worked examples of this in practise.

    One way to help avoiding deliberate or accidental plagiarism is to write with all books, articles (and even your notes from them) out of sight. So refer to your research files, think about what you want to say about the specific issue you are concerned with, and then remove the research file from sight before writing a paragraph, page or section of your dissertation.

Submitting a Draft

Apart from the final dissertation, the draft of your dissertation is the single most important document that you will produce in your dissertation studies. This is the moment at which you and your supervisor can see for the first time the totality of the research and the argument that you are putting forward, and can assess it accordingly. It is also the moment at which advice from your supervisor can make a radical difference to the success of the final dissertation, by suggesting changes of emphasis, detail, argument and so forth. If you prepare a good draft and give it to your supervisor with plenty of time in which they can respond, you can make a massive improvement to the final result.

- *Contents.* Generally, your draft should contain all the textual parts of the dissertation – the introduction, main sections and conclusion. All essential illustrations, appendices and bibliographic information should also be provided. Footnotes and references in drafts are often not fully polished, but bear in mind that your supervisor will need to be able to see the sources from where you have obtained your information and ideas.
- *Quantity.* As stated above, the draft should normally be presented as a complete document. Some supervisors, especially in the case of longer dissertations, will also ask to see drafts of each section or chapter of the thesis as you write them.
- *Format.* Some supervisors prefer to be given drafts as hard-copy. Others will accept e-mail and disk version, or even faxes. Check with your supervisor in advance which format they require.
- *Questions.* Along with the draft itself, it is often a good idea to provide your supervisor with a list of questions that you yourself are not sure about. Is the second chapter correct in emphasis? Does the argument in the third section make sense? Does the conclusion say appropriate things? Are there too many illustrations?
- *Timing.* Bear in mind that your supervisor will need adequate time in which to read your draft and give feedback. Discuss this with your supervisor carefully. When is a good time to submit? When can you expect feedback? Remember that the more time your supervisor has, the better the feedback you can expect and the better your final dissertation can become.

Word-processing

Many if not all architectural students use a computer to word-process their dissertation draft. This book is not the place to discuss hardware and software capabilities in detail, but make sure that you follow the usual basic rules:

- *Spelling and grammar.* You should use the spell checker and grammar functions on your software, but it is also important to proof-read the hard copy carefully. It is amazing the number of errors that are either missed by the software (such as, for example, typing 'from' rather than 'form', or 'tot he' rather than 'to the') or by the eye (repeated words, such as 'the the', are particularly difficult to spot on the screen).
- *Word counts.* Use the word count regularly in order to keep a check on length. You should do this for both the total length of the dissertation and for the size of each section or chapter.
- *Fonts.* When you come to print out your draft, make sure you use a decent, readable font – not fonts designed for use on the screen, like Monaco, Geneva or Chicago. Serif fonts like Bookman, Palatino or Times are generally easier to read in longish documents like dissertations than are sanserif fonts like Avant Garde, Ariel, Helvetica, News Gothic or Verdana. Personally, I now use Courier, a typewriter-like serif font for my own article drafts, as it is one of the easiest to read – although it is not very space-efficient and therefore is less suitable for longer documents. The print-out should be in 10- or 12-point text, double- or even triple-spaced for easy reading.
- *Saving.* Save your work regularly, and at least once an hour. Many word-processing programs can be set to do this automatically or to prompt you to do at, say, 15-min intervals. In fact, it is very easy to get into the habit of saving more or less constantly, and this will help minimise the incredible sense of frustration and annoyance when the computer crashes and work is lost.

  It is also a good idea to do a 'save as' at regular intervals, such as once a week. This is useful for two reasons. First, if you make a wrong turn in your dissertation at some point, it is then relatively easy to go back to a previous version of your work. Second, files sometimes get corrupted, and if you copy that corrupted file onto your back-up (see below), then you will have no usable version. If you have done a recent 'save as', however, there is a good chance that you will still have a relatively up-to-date version available. You will almost certainly have lost some work, but at least not everything.
- *Back-ups.* MAKE REGULAR BACK-UPS OF YOUR WORK. Every year, every dissertation programme in every single architecture school has at least one person who loses their entire dissertation because they kept it all on a disk (hard-disk, Zip, USB-drive or whatever) without making a copy, and at the last, crucial moment the disk did what all disks eventually do, which is either to get lost or stolen, or to crash horribly without any chance of repair. Even more frequently, one or more of the files on the disk can easily become corrupted through a virus, weird computer gremlins or just plain old bad luck. Either way, if this happens to you then you will have lost all of your work. You have been warned. Do not let this person be you.

> **If you are reading this and have not already made a back-up of your work, stop immediately, put the book down, go to the computer and do a back-up – do this now, and repeat the process at least once a day.**

To be really safe, it is also a good idea to have an off-site back-up, which will help reduce the risk of damage if you should be so unlucky as to suffer a burglary or a fire. For example, you can keep one back-up at home and another copy at your studio in the architecture school.

Alternative Dissertations

So far, in this guide we have discussed dissertations mostly as textual documents, which have been written in an academic writing style with footnotes etc., which may be augmented with images, and which are produced as artefacts printed on paper. For most architectural students, this will no doubt be the case. Indeed, many architecture schools also require that dissertations take this kind of format.

However, in some architecture schools, for some students undertaking particular kinds of research project, it may also be both possible and desirable to deviate from this model of what a dissertation might be. So instead of a text plus images, the dissertation might be produced as a video, multimedia disk, performance event etc. The potential here is enormous, for there are, of course, a near-infinite number of ways of producing an expressive and theoretical document. That said, there are a number of things that you might consider.

- *Format and design.* Architectural documents, of course, have very often had considerable attention paid to the way in which they are formatted and designed. However, in recent years the relation between form and content has become even more intense, with documents like *S, M, L, XL* designed in conjunction with Bruce Mau or *Strangely Familiar* designed in conjunction with Studio Myerscough.[1] If you take a look at these and other similar publications you will see that the way in which the design works is not just as an aesthetic gloss but as an integral part of the content of the book – something which helps communicate as well as make more attractive. For example, in the *Strangely Familiar* publication images are used as identifiers, concepts and diagrams, and in series, singly, temporally and dialectically. In *S, M, L, XL*, information is presented as body text, list, table, graph, banner text, layers and numerous other devices. In the case of *Strangely Familiar,* the graphics relate to the manifold experience of architecture, while in *S, M, L, XL* they are related to the interdisciplinary way in which Rem Koolhaas and the OMA office undertake the design process. So such devices can be far more than just another 'style' of presentation, and instead represent a different way of thinking about what architecture is and might be.

- *Writing.* The way in which people write is often described as their writing 'style', suggesting that writing about architecture is just a matter of choice of language and tone. In fact writing is much more complex and fundamental in nature, such that *how* people write can largely determine what it is that they wish to say. For example, the kinds of analytical writing about Le Corbusier's villas by, say, Stanislaus von Moos, and which concentrate on notions of design method, are very different in character from, say, John Berger's prose musing on one of Le Corbusier's villas and which, although much shorter, conveys a great deal about personal memories and meanings for its occupant.[2]

  Similarly, employing different structuring devices and varying the manner of writing within a dissertation can also convey different effects. Long passages can be interspersed with shorter ones, or with quotations, graphic elements and poems. The dissertation can be circular in structure, with no obvious beginning or end, or it may be bound in an unusual manner.

- *Other formats.* The most radical form of alternative dissertation is often one that changes the format of the dissertation altogether. Possibilities here are, of course, legion, but some of the most common in architectural schools include those produced as CD-ROMS, video presentations, television or radio-style documentaries, or films. Others have included poetry, performance events, installation artworks, sculptures and animation. Such formats often allow something very different to be said about architecture from what is possible with a textual document: for example, sound, body movement, change over time and personal emotion are all often much more easily conveyed than they can be in a non-textual way.

If you wish to undertake an alternative form of dissertation, there are a number of things that you simply must consider even before starting work.

- *Regulations.* Will your architecture school allow this kind of submission? If so, are there any precedents (who has actually completed an alternative dissertation)?
- *Supervision.* Who is willing to supervise you in this project? Do they have the necessary skills and experience?
- *Hardware.* Do you have intensive access to the kind of equipment you are going to need? This is particularly true for dissertation projects involving computers, film and video hardwares.
- *Risk.* Experience shows that many alternative dissertations fall into the 'high-risk' category discussed in Chapter 2. This is because they

frequently require a high degree of technical as well as intellectual capability, as well as the fact that the architecture school itself may not be used to dealing with this kind of project.

If you have considered all the above, and understand what you are getting into, then by all means go ahead. This kind of dissertation can be extremely rewarding. In doing so you should bear in mind the following issues.

- *Form/content relation.* A dissertation, no matter what format it adopts, is not usually assessed primarily for the technical skill used in putting it together. As with architectural design, where a beautiful drawing of a poor building does not usually attract good marks, so in the dissertation it is the ideas, argument and coherence with which you articulate these thoughts that matters – not the graphic design or film-editing skills. What this means is that, for an alternative format of dissertation, you must avoid one of the biggest kind of trap: namely of concentrating on the medium or form of the project at the expense of the content or ideas expressed within it. Instead, you should work simultaneously with form and content, and continually ask yourself the questions as to how the ideas you are working with are being articulated through your chosen medium. What are these ideas? How are they manifested? How precisely can they be understood? Do you need more than one kind of medium (e.g. a CD-ROM animation and a textual document) to complete the task? It is usually better to choose a format whose rules you already understand well so that you can concentrate on forming the content and not on inventing new rules for the format. If you combine more than one format, this advice is even more important. Do not spend most of the time you have available to you by inventing new formats.
- *Relation to design work.* One of the problems that students sometimes face with an alternative format dissertation is how to distinguish it from their design work. Bear in mind that the dissertation is normally considered to be a different arena in which to explore architecture that is separate from the design studio. When undertaking this kind of work you should constantly ask yourself whether you are in fact learning and communicating anything different from your portfolio and studio-based projects.
- *Examinability.* Although you may become technically very adept, bear in mind that your supervisor and examiners may not have the same kind of skill capability as yourself. If you have prepared, for example, a virtual reality or computer-based presentation, how will they view it? What hardware requirements must be satisfied? Will they know how to operate the equipment? Bear in mind also that many architecture schools send away dissertations for review by an external examiner, so you may need to consider how transportable

and readable your dissertation must be in order for it to be properly examined. Finally, you should make it clear (in whatever format is most appropriate) exactly how your assessor is to understand and 'read' the medium you have used, and why its use is important: what issues it allows you to highlight that a conventional dissertation cannot, how it changes the audience for your dissertation, and why it is appropriate for a piece of work in an academic setting. A clear understanding of the methodology of your alternative dissertation is even more important than that of a conventional one, because your reader will be encountering it for the first time.

* *Archiving.* Some architecture schools require students to place a copy of their dissertation in the school's library or other permanent archive. If you have undertaken, for example, an installation or performance-based dissertation, how will this requirement be satisfied? One possible solution may be, for example, to submit a paper-based record of your dissertation project (rather than the dissertation itself) for archiving purposes.

References

1   Rem Koolhaas and Bruce Mau, *S, M, L, XL: Office for Metropolitan Architecture,* Jennifer Sigler (ed.) (New York: Monacelli, 1995); and Iain Borden, Joe Kerr, Alicia Pivaro and Jane Rendell (eds), with Studio Myerscough (designers), *Strangely Familiar: Narratives of Architecture in the City* (London: Routledge, 1996).
2   Stanislaus von Moos, *Le Corbusier: Elements of a Synthesis* (Cambridge, MA: MIT, 1979); and John Berger, *Photocopies* (London: Bloomsbury, 1997) pp 52–8.

5 Presenting

The presentation of the final dissertation is obviously an integral part of the assignment. After all the hard work selecting, researching, developing and writing your dissertation, this is the final stage necessary to ensure that you present your efforts in the best possible manner.

It is surprising, however, how many dissertations are let down at this stage by relatively small errors which detract from what would otherwise be a much better product. Architecture students can occasionally be somewhat slap-dash with their dissertation in a way that they would never countenance for their design work as drawings, models or renderings.

General Presentation

In most cases, dissertations are not intended as exercises in graphic or typographic design, so considerable efforts in this direction will not usually gain extra marks from the examiners (although a different set of criteria may apply to the kinds of alternative dissertation discussed in Chapter 4). Nonetheless, all dissertations, of whatever format, should meet certain standards. You should consider the following:

- *Multiple copies*. You probably will have to submit more than one copy of your dissertation, so if your architecture school asks for three copies of your dissertation, give them that number. Many schools return one copy to you. In many institutions, one of the submitted copies can be a 'best version' or 'top copy' containing, for example, full-colour or laser-copied illustrations, while the others can be of a slightly lower reproduction standard. If this is the case, you may want to check in advance that the superior version is the one which will be returned to you. No matter how many copies your architecture school asks for, and whether one is going to be returned to you or not, it is always a good idea to make an additional best version for yourself. Although your school should look very carefully after dissertations submitted to it, there is always a chance that your dissertation may be mislaid during the examination process.

- *Print output*. A clear text will enable the reader to work more easily through the text, and so better comprehend what you have said. To achieve a high print standard, use word-processed or typed text, ideally printed on a high-standard laser or letter-quality device. Inkjet printers are usually acceptable, but old dot-matrix printers should be avoided. Print on one side of the paper only.
- *Paper*. Print on a good quality paper, at least 105 gsm rather than 90 gsm, which will prevent too much 'show through' from one page to another. Do not use very thick paper, however, as this will unnecessarily bulk out the dissertation.
- *Size and shape*. In general, most dissertations use an A4 portrait or US letter layout. Some institutions may insist on only one size. You are well advised to adopt this format unless you have a particular reason to do otherwise. If you do use a different paper size and shape, particularly anything larger than A4, bear in mind that this must be transportable and legible.
- *Binding*. Many architecture schools require submitted dissertations to be properly bound at a professional binders, with specific conventions as to colour, lettering, dating etc. Other schools simply ask for spiral or another suitable binding system. Whichever system your school requests, make sure that you follow the rules precisely – most PhD theses, for example, will simply not be accepted unless they exactly follow university requirements.

  You should also allow plenty of time for binding to be done – it can easily take a whole day to take your final manuscript to the copy shop, make copies, and bind the result. If you are using a professional binder, choose one well in advance, and preferably one who is based locally. Professional binders often need 2–3 days in which to turn a job around, and possibly even more during busy examination periods.
- *Title and title page*. Many architectural students give their dissertations a graphic front cover, often with one large illustration relating to the dissertation subject. If you do this, make sure your name and the year of submission is also included on the front cover and/or on the spine. Immediately inside, the first page should then include the same information, together with the title and sub-title of your dissertation. As with your original proposal, this title should be meaningful, indicating the subject matter as well as the kind of interpretation you have undertaken.

- *Contents page.* Include a contents page with a listing of all chapter or section headings, together with page numbers.
- *Acknowledgements.* You may wish to include an acknowledgements page, where you can thank teachers, friends, family, archive staff etc. who have helped you in your work. If you have completed a PhD, then this list will probably be quite extensive, less so for a shorter undergraduate dissertation. Whatever the kind of dissertation, try to keep the acknowledgements relatively short, as lengthy and overly effusive acknowledgements are often seen by examiners as being somewhat indulgent.
- *List of illustrations.* It is good practice to include a list of all the illustrations used in the dissertation, together with their figure number (see below) and the source from which they have been obtained.
- *Font.* As for the draft, use a 10- or 12-point serif font for the main text of your dissertation, such as Bookman, Palatino or Times for the main body of the text. Sanserif fonts like Avant Garde, Ariel, Helvetica or News Gothic can also often be used. Do not use screen fonts like Monaco, Geneva or Chicago.
- *Paragraph formatting.* Arrange the main body of the text with lines that are double-spaced, and with no more than 20 words per line (although 13–15 words is more usual). These conventions help the reader to locate the beginning of the next line more easily without getting 'lost' on the page.

  Dissertations should normally be set with the text left-justified and right-ragged (meaning that the left-hand edges are all flush together, while the lines vary in length creating an uneven right-hand side). You can set your software to produce fully justified text (flush on both left and right sides) but be aware that convention dictates that this is usually done only for published documents such as books and journal articles.

  Resist the temptation to use right-justified and left-ragged text, or, worse still, centred text. These formats, if used at all, should be deployed extremely sparingly for header quotations, chapter or section titles etc.
- *Section and chapter headings.* These are usually set in bold, sometimes also with capitals and in a larger font size than that used for the main text (e.g. 14- or 18-point). Double-check that the headings correspond to the numbering and titling given on your contents page.
- *Sub-headings.* Clearly distinguish sub-sections in your main text with sub-headings. These can be set in bold or italic, and in the same font size as that used for the main text.
- *Quotations.* Separate quotations (i.e. those which are not run into the main body of the text) are usually inset slightly in from the left edge by about 1 cm, and are also often single-spaced. You do not need quotation marks for quotations formatted in this manner.

Resist the temptation to set quotations in italics, as this style can get rather tiring after a few pages.

- *Amendments to quotations*. Often you will need to slightly modify a quotation in order that it suits the grammar of your own prose, or for other purposes. For example, you may wish to start a quotation at a point which is mid-sentence in the original. This is usually dealt with by adding a capital letter within square brackets. Thus the sentence 'It is possible to say without equivocation that today in Australia a new form of ecological architecture, dependent on both natural resources and political commitment, is emerging' may be quoted as:

> [T]oday in Australia a new form of ecological architecture, dependent on both natural resources and political commit-ment, is emerging.

Conversely, but using the same rule of putting amendments in square brackets, the original sentence of, for example, 'No-one is more focused on bodily architecture than Kas Oosterhuis' could be inserted directly into your main text (i.e. not used as a stand-alone quotation, but embedded in the main flow of your own writing) as '[n]o-one is more focused on bodily architecture than Kas Oosterhuis'.

The same rule of using square brackets to identify your own actions also applies to omissions within quotations. For example, if you wish to miss out part of a quotation, you can add an 'ellipsis' – a series of periods and spaces – to indicate this omission. There are various ways of doing this, but one of the most accurate is to use an ellipsis in square brackets, thus indicating that this is your own act, and not that of the original author. Thus, the quotation about Australia above could be further edited as:

> [T]oday in Australia a new form of ecological architecture [...] is emerging.

Finally, you may wish to emphasise some word in the quotation that the original author had not emphasised. The way to do this is to note your act in square brackets. Thus, the original sentence 'Architecture is a purely imaginative activity' may be reproduced as:

> Architecture is a purely *imaginative* activity. [emphasis added]

Note that because this is a frequent practice on the part of academic writers, when the emphasis has not been added but is indeed in the original, the dissertation writer may acknowledge this fact. For example,

> Nothing is more central to *pleasurable architecture* than gender, sexuality and bodily matters. [emphasis in original]

- *Footnotes and references.* This material can be placed at the bottom of the page, at the end of the relevant section or chapter, or collected together at the end of the dissertation. The font is usually the same type and size as the main text, but can be smaller (say 9-point) and use a different font face (if a serif font is used for the main text, a sanserif one might be used for footnotes). Footnotes and referencing can be either continuous and run in one range from beginning to end of the dissertation, or can be reset at 1 for each new chapter or section. Formatting should otherwise follow the instructions given in Chapter 4.
- *Page numbers.* Page numbers (sometimes referred to as 'folios') should be included on every text page, and are normally placed centrally at the base of the page, or in the top right-hand corner. It is often not essential to number pages with only illustrations on them, although different schools may have different rules about this.
- *Bibliography.* The font type and size for the bibliography is normally the same as that used for the main text of the dissertation. As for footnotes and references, formatting should otherwise follow the instructions given in Chapter 4.
- *Appendices.* An appendix is a useful place to put any extra data, tables, interview transcripts or other material which is original to your dissertation but which is too detailed or too obtrusive to include within the main body of the text. An appendix is not the place to put any extra thoughts, interpretations or any other information which is essential for the reader to understand your investigation. For example, an architectural dissertation might use an appendix as a place in which to put a complete list of buildings by an architect and which are otherwise unrecorded, a set of illustrations that have not previously been published, or such things as additional statistical analysis of, for example, different construction methods used in a large house-building programme. The font type and size for an appendix is normally the same as that used for the main text of the dissertation.
- *Index.* An index is not usually required for a dissertation.

Illustrations

Which illustrations to include in your dissertation is considered in Chapter 4. When it comes to presenting your final submission, however, there are several other factors to consider.

- *Quality.* Make sure that the illustrations you include are of a good quality. For an architectural dissertation, you will frequently need to depict a high degree of detail, so a laser copy, print or high-definition scan will frequently be required. Note also that quality degradation will also set in rapidly if you make copies of another copy. The higher quality the original, the better you can prevent this image quality from falling with subsequent copies.

- *Colour.* Colour copies may look good, but they are expensive and may not add anything to your argument. Indeed, many people prefer the look of black and white illustrations. However, in order to get a high-quality black and white reproduction you have to use a colour copier or printer in order to get a good definition grey-scale reproduction. If you are not sure about this, the trick here is to experiment with some differing processes for one or two different kinds of image. You can then pick the process which gives you the best quality/cost compromise.
- *Size.* You may need to include images which are larger than your dissertation, in which case will need to fold these into the binding, or into a pocket at the back, or other such technique. Or you may wish to request to be allowed to submit a landscape-format or oversize dissertation that can more easily cope with your illustrative material.
- *Positioning.* In general, it is a good idea to position illustrations next to or near to the text to which they refer. Usually, it is considered adequate to place illustrations on separate pages, inserted between text pages at appropriate intervals. Alternatively, you can place them on the same page as your text, in which case be sure that your paste-up and/or computer skills are good enough to do this effectively and neatly. You should normally avoid placing all illustrations together in one part of the dissertation, although in some cases there may be a particular reason why you might want to do this, for example when comparing the evolution of a particular building type or detail over time. If you need to refer to an illustration on several occasions, you do not have to reproduce it more than once – just refer back to the previous usage.
- *Figure numbering.* You should give all your illustrations a unique figure number. As with footnotes, this numbering can either run in one continuous range from beginning to end, or can be divided up into sections. In the latter case, it is conventional to use 1.1, 1.2 etc. for illustrations in Section 1, then 2.1, 2.2 for illustrations in Section 2, and so forth. These figures can then be referred to at the appropriate juncture in the main body of the text.
- *Captions.* Illustrations are usually given a caption, identifying the subject and sometimes making an interpretive comment. The source of each illustration can also be given next to the caption, or this information can be given for all illustrations on the 'List of Illustrations' page (see above).
- *Copyright.* One issue that many architecture students are becoming increasingly concerned about with regards to illustrations is the thorny issue of copyright. Although this is indeed quite a complex area for commercial publications, the good news here is that unless you are copying a large part of someone else's book (say, a chapter or more of an image-based publication), or you are going to actually

publish your research, you do not normally have to worry about copyright. In short, unless you have been expressly forbidden from doing so by a particular archive or source, you should not have to worry about copyright for use in an unpublished dissertation that has been undertaken for education purposes. If you are in any doubt, however, you should check with the source concerned.

Computer Software

Some of the basic rules of word-processing are explained in Chapter 4. For your final dissertation submission, you may well find that the same word-processing software, particularly an advanced one such as Apple Mac Pages, Microsoft Word/Office or Corel WordPerfect, will be more than adequate.

You may, however, wish to investigate the potential of desk-top publishing programs such as Quark XPress or Adobe InDesign, which give much greater control over text and image manipulation. Although often quite difficult to learn, once mastered, these pieces of software can be particularly useful for doing things like integrating images closely with text, rotating or resizing images, deploying graphic elements, or other such advanced techniques. Beware, however, that these kinds of program may also have considerable drawbacks, such as their capacity to include footnotes. In general, you should probably use these programs only for the very final version of your dissertation, when you are quite sure that any changes you make will be minor in the extreme, and/or if you are already skilled at using them.

Assessment Criteria

As with all work submitted as part of a university degree, it is a good idea if you know the grounds on which that work is going to be assessed. Indeed, many universities now require departments to make these assessment criteria (as they are often called) known to students. Assessment criteria, of course, vary greatly from one architecture school to another, and are frequently quite general in character in order to allow the broadest possible range of work to be included within the architectural education process.

An architectural dissertation is no different, and you should always check your own school's assessment criteria for dissertations. To give you some indication of what might apply, the following is a typical set of assessment criteria for an architectural dissertation programme.

- *High Pass*, i.e. an A grade, or first-class degree in the UK, or commendation standard piece of work. Dissertations assessed at this standard would generally be expected to show very good critical understanding of the topic – very good knowledge of the objects of study, and of the various intellectual, theoretical and interpretative ideas used to understand, analyse and assess them. An originality of research evidence – using primary and other student-discovered materials – would almost certainly be required.

- *Pass*, i.e. a B grade, or second-class degree in the UK, or other good, average standard piece of work. Dissertations assessed at this standard would generally be expected to show an understanding of the subject matter, to use a range of different evidence and materials, and to demonstrate some ability to question the issues involved.
- *Low Pass*, i.e. a C grade, or third-class degree in the UK, or other low standard piece of work. Dissertations assessed at this standard would generally be expected to show a basic understanding of the subject matter, and have no fundamental errors, but probably would lack any evidence of awareness of the problems of interpretation or questioning of the subject. In many US institutions a C grade may well be a failing grade, and the advice above will refer to a low B pass.
- *Fail*, i.e. a D grade, or non-honours degree in the UK, or a C grade in some US institutions, or other sub-standard piece of work. Dissertations assessed at this standard would generally offer only a little or a confused understanding of the subject matter. Such dissertations might also contain basic errors of fact or argument. Dissertations which plagiarise or otherwise simply reproduce information from other sources, without the student making any sense of it to herself/himself, would also normally be assessed as being at fail standard. Clear and intentional plagiarism may also have far more serious implications, as already stated above.

Oral Examinations

Apart from submitting the dissertation itself, some dissertation programmes may also require you to undertake an oral examination in the subject – sometimes referred to as a defence, or a viva. This is common for PhD and MPhil dissertations, but less so for masters, diploma or first degree programmes.

If you are required to undertake an oral examination, you should bear the following points in mind.

- *Purpose*. In general, the purpose of any oral examination is not to test your powers of recall down to the last detail of your dissertation, but to see if you are in command of the material through your powers of spoken expression as well as through the written word.
- *Examiners*. You should find out in advance who the people are who are going to conduct the examination. Other information you might

seek out is the interests and expertise of these people, and whether you have any say in their selection.

- *Examination process.* Finding out a few practical details in advance can also help you relax. Where will the examination take place? Will anyone other than yourself and the examiners be present? How long is it likely to last? How and when will you be informed of the result?
- *Questions and answers.* In preparing for an oral examination, you should carefully consider the kinds of questions that you might be asked. These are likely to range from the strategic (why, for example, did you choose the work of Marc Augé in order to interpret both airports and art galleries?), the methodological (how, for example, did you select the interviewees from within SOM's offices?) to the particular (was there, for example, any possibility that the American planner-architect Clarence Stein would have read the influential book *Der Städtebau* by the Austrian Camillo Sitte?).

  Try to prepare your answers to these questions not as readymade, off-the-pat responses but as the kinds of things that you would want to talk about. The more discursive and thoughtful you can be in answering, the better.

  Remember also that you are not expected to know absolutely everything about your subject, just to be aware of what it is that you have done, and what it is that you have not done. So if necessary do not be afraid to show that you understand the limitations of your dissertation, or of your own knowledge. Realising what work needs to be done next, and communicating as much, can be a very effective way of convincing your examiners that you really do understand the research process.

- *Attitude.* The examiners are not there to catch you out, but to engage you in an intellectual debate. So try to be as relaxed and positive as possible in what you say. Take your time, and speak as slowly or quickly as you would in any conversation with your peers. If you get the chance, you can turn the examination into a kind of general discussion, and even put propositions to your examiners.

6 Afterwards

Once you have completed your dissertation, and undertaken your oral examination if appropriate, there is little more you can do other than to wait for the result. If you have followed this handbook carefully, and you have put in some hard work and diligent thinking, then you should have done very well, and may be now thinking of ways of pursuing this kind of research further. If not, then you may be thinking of how you can redress the situation. Either way, some advice on what to do after the dissertation follows. Also included here is some advice about what to do if something has gone badly wrong during the research process, or if you have been faced with other, unavoidable difficulties.

Further Research and Study

Depending on the kind of degree you have just undertaken, there are a number of different courses, which you might consider taking in order to further your studies and development in the area of architectural history, theory and writing. To find out about these, you can consult the various listings of courses, which will be available in your campus careers office. Many universities also give details of their courses on the Internet.

In general, however, there are a number of distinct different kinds of programme, which you might consider.

- *Specialist first degrees*. Many art history courses offer a substantial architectural component, although you should always double-check exactly what is on offer, as this can vary greatly from year to year. These types of courses will complement your existing degree with greater insight into the history of art and architecture in general, and will often raise questions of methodology and interpretation. They normally take 3–4 years of full-time study to complete.

* *Diploma/masters conversions.* Many architecture courses at diploma level, such as those in the UK, often offer an extra period of study by which to obtain a master's degree. This typically involves a 3-month full-time or 9 months part-time study, usually in the form of a short dissertation. These types of courses are very useful for pursuing a particular interest in some more detail, and will give you an MA or equivalent qualification after your name, but will not provide the kind of specialist training offered by most dedicated masters or even some first-degree programmes.

* *Masters degrees (MA, MArch, MSc etc.)* Typically, these types of courses offer a period of seminar or lecture-based instruction, followed by an in-depth dissertation of substantial intellectual rigour. They are ideal for those wishing to pursue a higher research degree (see below), to enter academia, to pursue architectural journalism of arts and architectural policy, or for those who simply wish to have an extensive grounding in the possibilities of historical, critical and theoretical discussions of architecture. Most masters degrees take between 1 or 2 years (usually 12 months in the UK, often longer in the USA) for full-time study, or a part-time equivalent.

  Although there are a number of history and theory masters degree courses on offer, they can be hard to locate. For the USA and Canada, where the choice is wider, see the list under Student Resources on The Society of Architectural Historians' web site (www.sah.org). In the UK, there are various specialist architectural history and theory masters on offer, including the Masters in Architectural History at The Bartlett School of Architecture, University College of London (UCL) (www.bartlett.ucl.ac.uk/history_theory/programmes/msc_ah.htm). For these and other countries, you can also consult the guides to graduate course, which should be available in your university careers office.

* *Higher research degrees (MPhil/PhD).* Although sometimes including a period of seminar- or lecture-based instruction, these degrees focus in particular on the completion of a substantial 40 000–100 000-word thesis, consisting of largely original research and interpretation. In the UK, good PhD programmes should include an element of taught seminars on methodology and research skill, such as, for example, the modules on "Critical Methodologies of Architectural History" and "Research and Dissemination of Architectural History" at the Bartlett School of Architecture, UCL. Thereafter, the focus is on the individual student's research, typically allowing them to complete their PhD in 3–4 years. In the US universities, the period of seminar or lecture-based instruction varies – if you hold a UK degree recognised as equivalent to a US masters degree it is generally 2 years or, if you do

not, then it is often 3–4 years. In the USA, this period usually concludes with an examination in your major and minor fields. On successful completion of these exams you move into the candidacy phase, and write and defend your dissertation proposal. The total period of study is therefore usually much longer than in a European university, and often reaches 6 years or more in total.

If you are thinking of starting this kind of dissertation study, check carefully with the institutions that interest you, as the institution, the discipline and the dissertation topic may all play a role in this process. In particular, as well as identifying a suitable supervisor, find out what the overall research environment is like. How many other PhD students are there? What methodology and training pro-grammes are available? When can PhD students present work in progress to their peers? What funding is available for you to attend conferences? How many other academics, besides your supervisor, are working in the same general area? When checking where you might wish to apply, it may also help to know that many doctoral programmes dealing with architecture are in schools of art history. Again, for north America, see the list on The Society of Architectural Historians' web site (www.sah.org).

Higher research degrees are particularly suitable for those wanting to enter academia, and/or those wishing to focus in great depth on a particular research topic. Such degrees often take from 2 to 3 years to complete for an MPhil, or anywhere from 3 to 10 years for a PhD. Part-time study is also often possible. Many US institutions offer fee remis-sion or scholarships to attract research students with an already strong academic record, which in the case of overseas applicants can significantly reduce the cost of study. The UK institutions attract awards from the Arts and Humanities Research Board, British Council and other funding bodies. Do not forget to enquire about these as you are researching which institution is most suitable for you.

- *Non-degree courses and study.* It is, of course, not essential to take a degree at a university in order to continue studying architectural his-tory and theory. Many universities, colleges and other educational institutions offer less formal courses in the subject, while you can also pursue your own course of study by simply reading whatever you want, and discussing it with like-minded friends and colleagues.

Publications

If your dissertation has been particularly well received, and/or you feel that you have been able to make an original contribution to architectural thinking, then you may want to see if you can publish your work and make it available to a wider audience. There are a number of possible ways of doing this, but beware that in all cases you will often have to make some considerable changes to your dissertation in order to suit the requirements of your intended place of publication and its readership.

- *Competitions.* Perhaps the easiest way to further publicise your work is to enter your dissertation into one of the many competitions available to student dissertations. For example, most of the examples included in this handbook have been submitted to the competition for student dissertations held annually by the RIBA (Royal Institute of British Architects) in London. Many other countries and institutions have similar competitions, some with significant funding attached, and you should ask your supervisor and other teachers for their advice on this matter.
- *Publishers.* Publishers are generally only interested in publishing doctoral dissertations, but in some instances a masters dissertation may be sufficiently original to develop into a publication. If you think this might be the case, discuss it with your tutor and any other teacher at your institution who have publication experience. If they agree with your view, they may be able to suggest the best publishers for you to contact. Alternately, you may wish to contact a publisher whose books come closest to your subject area – your bibliography should be a good source. If the initial informal contact with the publisher is encouraging, you will probably need to write a book proposal. If so, you should ask for the guidelines from the publisher. It may take a long time – as much as 2 years – for a book to develop from proposal to full manuscript, often with no guarantee of publication at the end of the process. You should be prepared for a lot of revisions and additional research for little or no financial remuneration.
- *Academic journals.* Many architectural journals will consider publishing articles based on dissertations. The best way to do this is to look in your institution's architecture library, and select, say, three or four journals, which seem most likely to be of interest in your work. Again, your supervisor and other teachers can also give you advice here. You can then follow the chosen journals' instructions as to length, formatting etc. (and make sure you follow these closely) and send it off for consideration. Many journals operate a referee system, where each submission is considered by one or more independent academic advisors, so you may have to wait a while before receiving a response.

  However, before going to all the trouble and effort of turning your dissertation into an article form, which can take much longer than you might think, you may want first of all to approach the journal's editor on a more informal basis, just to see if they would be willing, in principle, to consider your work. You can then avoid wasting your time by making an inappropriate submission.
- *Professional magazines.* The various monthly or weekly architectural magazines may also be interested in running a feature on your

dissertation, particularly if it deals with an architect or architectural issue in current debate. Again, an informal approach to the features editor is always a good first step in this direction.

- *Student publications*. Publications and other events, such as conferences and symposia, organised by students (usually graduates) are another way of furthering your work, and can often involve very useful intense discussions. They are also often much quicker in turnaround times than other academic journals, and much less beholden to market forces than professional magazines, so your chances of seeing your work published and discussed in the near future is much more likely.
- *Internet*. Depending on your dissertation subject, a relevant interest group or site-leader may be interested in including your work on their internet site. Alternatively, you can, of course, easily set up your own personal web page, and post up the dissertation yourself. Either way, you can reach potentially enormous numbers of people very quickly, and at minimal cost.

If you are intending to use your dissertation for publication purposes, you should also be aware that there may be copyright and privacy issues that were not important when doing the original dissertations, but which are very important indeed when publishing in the public domain. These are likely to fall into one or more of the three areas.

- *Illustrations*. If you have used any illustrations other than those taken by yourself, then you must seek permission from the owner of the original source before you can reproduce it in the public realm. So for any painting or artwork in a gallery, any map or diagram in an archive, any photograph taken by another photographer, any illustration taken out of another book or other publication, their source must be consulted and their permission sought in writing. This may apply even if you have taken the photograph yourself, particularly if you have taken it out of a book, of an artwork or film or in the interior of a building. (Note, however, that if you have taken a photograph of a building, and particularly of the exterior of a building, you will not usually need to seek permission.)

  In the USA, most images belong in the public domain if they are more than 50 years old – otherwise you must get permission to publish them, or you will have to publish without illustrations. In the USA it is also customary to publish your PhD dissertation with UMI (University Microfilms Inc.), in which case you must get permission to use all other illustrations, or alternatively publish the dissertation without illustrations.

  Furthermore, many sources or copyright owners may charge you a fee to reproduce an illustration. Charges vary, but can be anything from a few pounds or dollars, to two, three or even four-figure numbers.

The other problem is the quality of the images that you have. Photocopies or scans of images, while good enough for a dissertation, are not normally of an acceptable standard for publication, and you may need to obtain higher-quality images for inclusion in any published version of your dissertation.

- *Privacy.* If you have interviewed or obtained other private information from an individual in the course of your dissertation research, you must seek their permission before you can publish it elsewhere. Just because someone was willing to speak to you as part of your educational research does not mean that the same person will be as keen to see their private views or details placed into the public realm. Many will be happy to oblige, but check first – this is very important, particularly in the USA, where you might be barred from publication or sued if prior permission is not obtained.
- *Commercial sensitivity.* In a similar manner, if you have obtained information of a commercial nature directly from an organisation, such as the economic turnover of an architectural practice or construction company, then you need to check first that you can reproduce this information in the public realm.

One final point about publishing your work. Most academic texts – journals, magazines and books alike – are printed in very small production runs, and do not generate substantial income for the publisher. As a result, authors often receive only a very small fee, or a small percentage of the royalties. If you are intending to publish your work, you should therefore bear in mind that you are very unlikely to make much profit, if at all, from your efforts.

Troubleshooting

As in any educational programme, sometimes something can go wrong during an architectural dissertation project, often for a reason beyond anyone's control. This section identifies some of the most common problems and some of the possible responses that may be open to you. But be aware that this part of the handbook, perhaps more than any other, requires you to check with the specific regulations and options of your own institution. In any case, the general rule with all the circumstances listed below is to talk to your supervisor and/or other tutors as soon as you think that something might be wrong. Keeping the issue bottled up inside of you will not help matters, so the earlier you discuss the problem, often the easier it will be to sort something out.

- *Wrong subject.* Sometimes students realise, and often at a stage when they are quite well advanced with their project, that they have chosen the wrong subject. This can be for a number of reasons, from the intellectual, to the personal, to the pragmatic. Either way, the best thing to do here is to discuss the matter with your supervisor at the earliest possible opportunity. It may well be that you do not need to completely alter the topic of your dissertation, and that a relatively simple reorientation of the project may be all that is necessary. Alternatively, you and your supervisor may be able to come up with a new but related topic that will be comparatively easy to develop.
- *Dyslexia and personal problems.* A comparatively large number of architecture students – many more than in most other disciplines – suffer from dyslexia. The exact nature of dyslexia and its cause are a matter of some debate and dispute, and it is enough to say here simply that it produces in sufferers a difficulty in reading, writing and general information processing. Many architecture students suffer from this condition because their dyslexia means that they tend to move away from text-based disciplines and towards visually based ones. So architecture does not make you dyslexic, but dyslexia may encourage you to become an architect.

  Furthermore, there are strong suggestions that the particular spatial and visual skills, which architects use, and the part of the brain, which deals with these processes, may somehow correlate with other information processes within the brain, including the ones that lead to dyslexia (and, incidentally, left-handedness). Here, one could argue that dyslexia and architectural invention are correlated conditions or activities.

  If you know that you suffer from dyslexia, or even if you just think that this might be the case, you should talk to your tutors – most architecture schools have one member of the faculty who has been specifically nominated to deal with this problem. He or she can then take you through your institution's procedures for dyslexia, and explain to you the possible responses. These may include giving extra allowance or marks for coursework, time extensions to submissions and examinations etc. Some universities also have schemes whereby dyslexia sufferers are provided with special computers and/or software to help them in their writing assignments.

  The same applies to any other personal problems that you may be faced with over the course of your architectural studies. If, for example, you have particular difficulties concerning your health, family, personal relationships, finances, accommodation and so forth you should discuss this in confidence with your tutors. They can direct you to possible sources of help, as well as making sure that any serious problems are accounted for during the examination process.

- *Lost dissertation.* Sometimes students lose their entire dissertation, or all the work done so far, before the final submission. Normally this is because they have suffered a computer crash and not made a back-up, although sometimes it is because they lost the only hard copy and had no computer version. If this happens to you, and it is a computer problem, try to speak to an advanced computer expert, who can often recover files that a normal person could not. If this does not work, and your dissertation really has been lost, you have no option than to repeat the work. Your supervisor can advise you as to the procedures for doing this, and any time extensions, resubmission procedures etc. that may be open to you.
- *Missed deadline.* If you accidentally miss the deadline for the final submission, you should inform your supervisor and/or programme leader immediately, and often something can be worked out. Do not just stay silent and hope that things will be sorted out later.
- *Retakes.* An architectural dissertation is rather like a driving test: not everyone passes the first time. This can happen for a number of reasons, not all of which are necessarily the students' own fault. As an independently researched and written document, there are many things that might go astray with your dissertation (although following this handbook should help to prevent the vast majority of these).

  If you do happen to fail your dissertation, you should talk to your supervisor at the earliest possible date and discuss what was wrong with your submission. In many cases, you may only have to make relatively minor alterations in order to raise the dissertation to a pass standard for resubmitted work. Alternatively, you may be better advised to start afresh on a wholly new topic.

  It is also worth checking with your supervisor exactly what opportunities for resubmission are allowed under your institution's regulations. If you are allowed only one resubmission, then it is obviously important in the extreme that you pass the next time around, particularly if you also need this pass standard in order to satisfy the requirements for professional architectural accreditation. In such circumstances you would want to make the dissertation resubmission the very top priority of your current list of tasks to complete.
- *Appealing against results.* If you have failed your dissertation, or you feel that you have received an unjustly low mark, you may wish to appeal against the result. Here you should check first of all with your institution's regulations for allowing such an appeal. Many, for example, have quite complex marking systems involving two internal markers and an external examiner for all assessed material, and will therefore not allow any appeal simply on the grounds that these people might have somehow got it wrong.

  However, if you believe, and have some evidence to support your belief, that, for example, your tutors were prejudiced against you, that marking and examination procedures were not followed correctly, that you received wholly inadequate supervision, or that extenuating circumstances should have been taken into account when assessing your work, you may indeed want to launch an appeal. Although emotion can obviously run high in these kinds of cases, try to put forward your case as rationally and as briefly as possible, while including all relevant detail and supporting evidence. An appeal explained in this manner, rather than one full of vitriol and heated opinion, is much more likely to be considered and to be accepted.

7 Dissertation Excerpts

The dissertations contained here are all prize-winning submissions from architectural students around the world. Extremely varied in subject matter, approach and tone, they are nonetheless all exemplary examples of how good a dissertation can be, when pursued with verve, creativity and rigour.

In most cases we have selected just one part of the dissertation – usually one particular chapter – along with appropriate introductions, conclusion and so forth which delineate the overall scope of the research project. Please note that for reasons of copyright, as explained previously, it has not been possible to reproduce in this book all of the illustrations used in the original dissertations.

Susannah Bach

ORIGINALITY *of IDEA*

The Barber-Surgeons' Anatomy Theatre

Combining extraordinarily thorough research in primary archives with exemplary scholarly presentation, Bach's dissertation is original for its excavation of a now-lost piece of seventeenth-century architecture. More than that, it offers a reinterpretation of this architecture in the light of more modern critical interests of the context of the architecture (such as the body and architecture) as well as the stated concerns of client and architect. The text reproduced here is part of a reworked and shortened version of the original dissertation, produced for an essay competition and publication.

THE BARBER-SURGEONS' ANATOMY THEATRE:

> *'This frame coagmented for the service of the Soule we have compared to the whole world or universe.'*
>
> Susannah Bach

PART I

The Barber-Surgeons' Anatomy Theatre in an Historical and Intellectual Context

'The Theater shalbe ... built according to the plotts drawn by His Majestie's Surveigher'

On 6th April 1638, the 'Lords of ye privye Counsell & other persons of state' attended the inaugural dissection at the newly built anatomy theatre of the Worshipful Company of Barber-Surgeons.[1] The event was marked by a lavish banquet that cost over £100 and Liverymen of the company were required 'to give their attendance in the Hall upper parlours & Theater at the enterteynment of the lords'.[2]

The Barber-Surgeons' Company was one of London's oldest City trade guilds. Its premises, initially its Hall, were in Monkwell Square, just inside the Roman wall. Within was Holbein's famous painting commemorating the union of the Barbers' Company with the Guild of Surgeons in 1540. From then until 1745, as the Barber-Surgeons' Company, it was responsible for the training and licensing of surgeons in which anatomical demonstrations played an important

---

[1] Sidney Young, *The Annals of the Barber-Surgeons of London, compiled from their records, and other sources*, p 452.

[2] The total cost of building was £722 7s 6d. £1 in 1636 is equivalent to about £100 today. See *Bank of England Quarterly Bulletin, May 1994*.

role. In the Act of Incorporation of 1540 the Barber-Surgeons was given the right to

> *take without contradiction foure persons condemned, adjudged and put to death for knowlage instruction in sight learnying & experience in the sayd seyence or facultie of Surgery.*[3]

By 1635, the existing facilities for anatomies had become inadequate and it was ordered by the Court of Assistants that 'a Theater to the largenes of the upper ground betwixt the goldsmithes' tenemt & the clothmakers tenemt on the one side & London Wall on the other side shalbe ovally built for the worship and comiditie of this Companie at the Charge of this house'.[4] England's foremost architect and Surveyor to the King, Inigo Jones, was chosen to be the designer. The accounts for 1635–6 record money spent when 'Mr Inigo Jones the Kinges Surveyor came to view the back ground' and that 'spent by water tymes when wee went to Mr Surveigher about the theatre'.[5] In 1636 the building began, and was 'built according to the plotts drawn by His Majestie's Surveigher'.

Jones's initial sketch of the design is kept at Worcester College, Oxford, together with John Webb's more finished drawings, two plans and an elevation.[6] It has been suggested that Webb intended them to form part of a compilation of Jones's designs to be produced after his death.[7] There is also a section through the theatre drawn by Isaac Ware for his compilation of *Designs by Inigo Jones and others*. It is likely that this work was initiated by Lord Burlington, who greatly admired the theatre, and offered to pay for its restoration in 1730.[8] A final drawing, by William Newton (1768) is annotated 'idea of ye Theatre in old/Surgeons Theatre in Barbers Hall' and differs from Webb's and Ware's drawings by including niches and Corinthian columns. This suggests that it was part of a proposal for a refurbishment, which was never undertaken. Just seven years later the building was demolished.

The anatomy theatre was on two floors. On the lower ground floor there were two 'private dissecting rooms'. Above was the tall auditorium linked to the main Hall by a balustraded arcade. The brick and

[3]*Annals*, p 588.
[4]*Court Minutes*, 11 February 1635, *Annals*, p 132.
[5]*Annals*, p 402.
[6]J. Harris and A. A. Tait, *Catalogue of Drawings by Inigo Jones, John Webb and Isaac de Caus*. Worcester College Collection, drawing numbers 1–2.
[7]Webb made similar presentation plans of Jones's designs of Temple Bar, York Water Gate, Star Chamber and the Cockpit Theatre. See *RIBA Catalogue*, notes for drawing number 170.
[8]*Annals*, pp 153–4.

tile building, punctuated by large windows, was austere from the outside, 'solid proportionable according to the rules, masculine and unaffected', but inside it was painted and ornamented, and contained numerous artefacts relating to the ritual anatomy.[9] The Barber-Surgeons' anatomy theatre was Europe's third after those at Padua and Leiden, and emphasised England's place as a contemporary leader in medicine.[10]

Inigo Jones's theatres designed for plays and his masque and stage scenery have been well documented.[11] Little has been written, however, about his links with the London medical profession. The picture in this essay of the architecture and functioning of the theatre has been derived principally from contemporary sources: drawings, records of the Company and also descriptions by visitors to the building in the seventeenth and early eighteenth centuries. It is the purpose of this essay to consider its form, internal arrangement and ornamentation in relation to contemporary intellectual and anatomical thought.

The 'Anatomical Renaissance' and the First Anatomy Theatres
The development of anatomy as a science from the fifteenth century arose in part from a renewed interest in Greek, especially Galenic, texts. It was, however, Vesalius, Professor of Surgery and Anatomy at the University of Padua, who made the most important impact on the discipline. He helped to restore Galenic anatomy only in order to correct it and go beyond it relying on close observation of the body as the key to understanding. His major work, *De Humani Corporis Fabrica* (1543) was based on first-hand experience.

That 'fabrica' means building reflects the analogy between anatomy and architecture. The development of anatomy was concerned with an understanding of three-dimensional space – the interior of the body – and was inter-related with the work of Renaissance artists and architects in painting, perspective drawing and sculpture. As Sebastiano Serlio wrote:

> *And as those paynters are much perfecter that have seene and perfectly beheld, right Anatomies, then others that only content themselves with the outward bare show of superficiecies, so it is with perspective workers.*[12]

---

[9] J. Alfred Gotch, *Inigo Jones* (London 1928) pp 81–2.
[10] See W. Brockbank 'Old Anatomical theatres and what took place therein', *Medical History* Vol. XII (1968) pp 374–6.
[11] See John Harris and Gordon Higgott, *Inigo Jones Complete Architectural Drawings*, and John Orrell, *The Theatres of Inigo Jones and John Webb*.
[12] Sebastiano Serlio, *Regole Generali de Architettura de sopra le cinque maniere degli edifici* (Venice 1537). English translation by Robert Peake, *The Booke of Architecture* (London 1611).

The frontispiece of Vesalius's book gives prominence to the setting in which the anatomy takes place. It shows a circular structure with classical columns. The development of specific structures, theatres for the performance of dissections, marked the growth and rise in status of anatomical science. Initially, these were temporary structures. At the Universities of Padua and Bologna, the principal centres of medical study in the fifteenth and early sixteenth centuries, anatomical dissections took place in temporary seating erected outside or in a convenient room, sometimes a church.[13] Benedetti, a hellenic scholar and teacher at the Padua Medical School was the first writer to discuss such structures:

> *For this a very cold winter is required, so that the cadavers do not immediately putrefy. Moreover, in a spacious ventilated place a temporary theatre is to be set up with seats around a hollow, like may be seen at Rome or Verona, of such a size that the number of spectators may be accommodated, and so that the surgeons should not be inconvenienced by the crowd.*[14]

Similarly, the sixteenth-century demonstrations at the Barber-Surgeons' took place in the main hall. Initially there was no seating. Presumably, surgeons and students stood around the large dining table, as shown in Nicholas Hilliard's painting of a visceral lecture. In 1568, the Court of Assistants of the Barber-Surgeons' Company ordered the temporary construction of wooden raised seating in the hall during each anatomy.[15]

In 1594, the first permanent anatomy theatre was constructed within the university buildings at Padua; it was followed by the anatomy theatre at Leiden, converted from an existing church (1597). Anatomy was increasingly understood to be an important part of knowledge and learning. It became fashionable for the educated élite, courtiers and wealthy merchants to attend anatomies to expand their knowledge and satisfy curiosity, and to provide entertainment. The anatomy theatres of Italy and the Low Countries became part of the experience of the English traveller. The diarist John Evelyn recorded visits to Padua in February and Leiden in August 1646.[16] George Hakewill in 1627 complained on his return about the lack of anatomical demonstrations.[17] The new anatomy

---

[13]In Venice, a law of 1386 ordered a month of dissection. Locations included the Church of S Paterniano, the Carmelite monastery, S Stefano and the Frari.

[14]Alessandro Benedetti (Alexander Benedictus) d. 1512, *Anatomice, sive historia corporis humani* (1502), trans. Andrew Cunningham, *The Anatomical Renaissance* (Scolar Press 1997) p 67.

[15]*Court Minutes* 1 Feb 1568. *Annals*, p 315.

[16]Ernest Rhys (ed) *The Diary of John Evelyn*, p 475ff.

[17]*Ibid.*

theatres were a register of civic pride, an 'index of intellectual advancement for the City's flourishing cultural and artistic life'.[18] London needed a permanent anatomical theatre to rival those at Padua and Leiden. It was to be 'soe necessarie and comendable a worke tendinge to the generall good of the whole kingdome'.[19]

The London Medical Profession and the Public Anatomies

On the Continent the new anatomy theatres were university based, but in England it was the professional institutions which were to embark on similar elaborate building programmes. By the late sixteenth century the medical profession in London had separated into three bodies: physicians, surgeons and apothecaries. The latter two had guilds which assured independence and freedom of operation. The physicians formed their own college and rapidly grew in power over the following century.

Despite the assignment of monopoly rights by Charter, there remained intense rivalries between the branches of the profession. Complaints and arguments over infringement of the rights were frequent occurrences. The Barber-Surgeons jealously guarded their right to the teaching of anatomy. This was particularly important since in 1564 Elizabeth I had granted to the College of Physicians rights similar to those granted by Henry VIII to the Barber-Surgeons a quarter of a century earlier. The building by the Barber-Surgeons' of their anatomy theatre enabled them to assert authority and maintain their privileges. Subsequently, the Physicians commissioned the ageing Inigo Jones to design an anatomy theatre. The project was entrusted to John Webb on Jones' death. The building, completed in 1653, was destroyed in the Great Fire of 1666.

Anatomical demonstrations were termed 'public anatomies' because the malefactor was termed a public body. They took place four times a year, one for each of the four 'condemned'. Of necessity they coincided with public executions, although generally they took place during the colder months of the year when the body could be preserved more easily and there was less risk of plague.

Each public anatomy consisted of three lectures over three days. Despite intense rivalry between surgeons and physicians, the lecturer, 'the Reader of Anatomy', was either a Barber-Surgeon or a physician. Attendance was compulsory for all 'free' surgeons including the Master and Wardens as well as the apprenticed surgeons. Guests were often invited by the Company to the lectures and sometimes to

---

[18]J. Sawday, *The Body Emblazoned*, p 42.
[19]Indenture of Lease between the Mayor & Co of London and the Masters & Co of the Barber Surgeons, 5 May 1636, *Annals*, p 132.

a dinner following. Samuel Pepys, one such guest, describes his visit on 27th February 1663:

> *About I o'clock Commissioner Pet and I walk to Chyrurgeon's Hall, we being all invited thither, and promised to dine there, where we were led into the theatre; and by and by comes the reader, Dr Tearne, with the Master and company, in a very handsome manner: and all being settled, he began his lecture; and his discourse being ended, we had a fine dinner and good learned company, many doctors of Phisique and we used with Extraordinary great respect.*[20]

Inigo Jones and Anatomy in the context of contemporary cosmology and theology

Inigo Jones's skill in numerous fields including architecture, masque making and military engineering led John Harris to describe him as 'a true uomo universale in the Renaissance mould and perhaps the only man in England who could so be described'.[21] Through his patrons and travels abroad he was attuned to current intellectual thought in Europe and England including scientific and anatomical knowledge. He was acquainted with members of the London medical profession including William Harvey and Robert Fludd. It is these connections which most probably led to his involvement in the design of anatomy theatres for the two most influential medical establishments.

Today the study of the human body is seen purely within a scientific context. By the end of the seventeenth century, the advances of Newton, Locke and other rationalists signalled a transition to scientific methodology. There was, however, no abrupt change or break with the past, and at the time of the building of the theatre anatomy was linked to other disciplines: cosmology, theology and penology. To Inigo Jones anatomy encompassed much more than simply dismembering the human body. It brought into question the place of the body within, and its relation to, the universe as a whole and aroused concerns over the after-life and Christian beliefs in death and judgement. It was connected to the penal system and the maintenance of order and hierarchy in society.

The work of two English physicians, Helkiah Crooke and Robert Fludd, is important in understanding this period of transition from traditional to modern thought and in demonstrating the interconnection of different areas of intellectual thought within the development of medical science. Their work is of particular interest

---

[20]*The Diary of Samuel Pepys*, 27 February 1663.
[21]John Harris and Gordon Higgott, *Inigo Jones Complete Architectural Drawings*, p 13.

due to their connection with the Barber-Surgeons and with Inigo Jones.

Helkiah Crooke had studied at Leiden under the well respected Professor Peter Pauw, who had been responsible for the building of the anatomy theatre there. The first edition of Crooke's *Mikrokosmographia* (1615) was the first comprehensive textbook to be compiled and illustrated in the Vesalian manner by an English author. It provided a synthesis of both ancient and modern accounts of the structure of the human body, accepting the prevailing contradictions in anatomical understanding. The first edition was dedicated to the Barber-Surgeons:

> To the Worshipfull Company of Barber-Chyrurgeons, the
> Master, Wardens, Assistants, and Communality of the same;
> Helkiah Crooke, Doctor in Physicke, wisheth Happie and
> prosperous successe in your Profession. From my house in
> S. Annes Lane, this last of May 1615.

It has also been suggested that the Frontispiece to the Second Edition (1631) to 'The Younger Sort of the Barber Chyrurgeons' shows an anatomical demonstration taking place at the hall where Crooke himself lectured on several occasions.[22]

Robert Fludd is best known as a Renaissance philosopher and mystical scientist. His ideas, although emanating from Ancient and Renaissance sources, were elaborated, co-ordinated and synthesised into an immensely detailed concept of the universe, placing great emphasis on magical and mystical concepts. Yet he was a respected practitioner and not just a philosopher in an ivory tower. It was through Michael Andrewes, Physician to the King and Reader of Anatomy at the Barber-Surgeons' between 1628 and 1632, that Fludd joined the Company in 1634, just as the initial plans for the new theatre were being discussed.[23]

The historian, Frances Yates, put forward circumstantial evidence supporting the conjecture that Jones was acquainted with Robert Fludd.[24] Research for this essay has confirmed this. Jones's notes in the flyleaf of his copy of Palladio's *I quattro libri dell'architettura* reveal that, not only was he a friend of the King's physician, William Harvey, but that he also knew Fludd and had consulted them both concerning his ailments. In notes dated October 4, 1638 in the flyleaf he wrote:

---

[22]J.M. Ball, *The Body Snatchers*. The clothing suggests it is probably in Leiden.
[23]Huffman, *Robert Fludd and the End of the Renaissance*, fn 31, p 186. *Court Minutes* 1621–1651, pp 123 and 171. See R.S. Roberts, 'The personnel and Practice of Medicine in Tudor and Stuart England, Part II London', *Medical History* 8 (1964) pp 233–4, n. 93.
[24]*Theatre of the World*, Chapter 5, 'Inigo Jones in a New Perspective' pp 80–91.

> *Doc: Haruy tould mee that barbares beaten and as much of it*
> *putt in to ye glister as all ye other seeds will doe the effecte*
> *Doc Flud discommendes glisters for weakning the guttes.*[25]

Both Fludd and Crooke demonstrate a view of the universe which owes much to Neoplatonism, which had considerable impact in Elizabethan England through men such as John Dee, the mathematician, poet John Chapman and playwright Christopher Marlowe.[26] The Neoplatonic tradition considered the material world changeable and corrupt and consequently the lowest realm of existence. Perfection lay in the spiritual world. Neoplatonism was influenced by hermetic ideas.[27] Science and medicine could not be separated from magical/mystical traditions.

An important aspect of Neoplatonism was that a system of correspondences existed. Man, for example, formed a microcosm of the macrocosm of the spiritual world. As the title *Mikrokosmographia* suggests, Crooke's anatomical text was deeply rooted in this relationship:

> *Man's Body the temperature thereof and the proportion of the*
> *parts;..it may worthily be called a Little World, and the paterne*
> *and epitome of the whole universe.*[28]

He describes the universe as consisting of three worlds: the 'sublunary', the 'coelestiall' and the 'highest heaven'. Within this framework Crooke considered that each part of the human body had its equivalent in each of these worlds:

> *For as the world there are three parts, the sublunary which is*
> *the basest, the coelestiall wherein there are many glorious*
> *bodies and the highest heaven which is the proper feste of the*
> *deity. So in the body of man there are three regions. The*
> *lower belly which was framed for the nourishment of the indi-*
> *vidual ... The Middle Region of the Chest, wherein the Heart*
> *of man the sunne of this Microcosm perpetually moveth ...,*
> *and the Upper Region is the Head wherein the soule hath her*
> *Residence of estate.*[29]

---

[25]J. Bold, *John Webb: Architectural Theory and Practice in the Seventeenth Century* on the friendship between Jones and Harvey p 165. Inigo Jones on Palladio. Facsimile edited by B. Allsopp, p 72 on Flyleaf three verso.

[26]On John Dee (1527–1593) see Yates, *Theatre of the World, p xi*. Cornelius Agrippa's *De Occult philosophia*, in English libraries from 1550s, was an important Neoplatonic work with particular mystical and occult content.

[27]Hermetic ideas derive from the ancient Egyptian Hermes Trismegistus. See Yates, *Giordano Bruno and the Hermetic Tradition*.

[28]*Mikrokosmographia*, p 6.

[29]Ibid. pp 428ff.

Similarly Fludd in his extensive work *Utriusque cosmi historia*, published in two volumes *On the Microcosm* and *On the Macrocosm*, structured man and universe into three parts. It is interesting that Harvey's revolutionary *De Motu Cordis* on the circulation of the blood makes similar analogies.

A concept implicit in the microcosm–macrocosm relationship was that of theatrum mundi. This considered the world as God's own theatre. The idea was widely understood in Renaissance Elizabethan theatre.

> *All the world's a stage*
> *And all the men and women merely players.*[30]

Thus, the theatre could reveal truths to man and teach him about human nature. If the theatre could be a representation of the universe, to Fludd it also provided a suitable mnemonic as part of the 'ars memoriae', the art of memory which he described in his *Technical History of the Microcosm.*[31] The concept of teatrum mundi and memory systems reflected Vesalius's analogy between the building and the body in his use of the word 'fabrica'. For his exploration of the human body Crooke used the analogy of the rooms within a house:

> *The glory and beauty of this stately mansion of the Soule*
> *we declared in the first Booke. The outward walles we*
> *dismantled in the second. The cooke-roomes & sculleries*
> *with all the houses of office and roomes of repast we*
> *survayed in the thirde ...*[32]

In the early seventeenth century religious beliefs affected the practice of anatomy as well as almost every other aspect of daily life. Dismantling a human corpse was believed to violate Christian eschatology. The body, 'the stately mansion of the Soule', was seen in Christian terms as the house of the immortal soul. Thus, as well as the unnatural disfigurement and dismemberment of the physical elements of the body, it was feared that anatomisation tampered with the soul of man and would prevent passage to heaven. This doctrine led to extreme opposition to and fear of dissection:

> *I had rather be a sot than an Anatomy; I will not have my flesh*
> *scrap'd from my Bones. I will not have my skeleton in Barber*
> *Surgeons' Hall.*[33]

---

[30]William Shakespeare, *As You Like It.*
[31]See Frances Yates, *The Art of Memory* (Routledge 1966).
[32]*Mikrokosmographia*, p 907.
[33]Crispin in *The Anatomist* by Edward Ravenscroft (1674).

Furthermore, it was a strongly held belief that a good Christian burial would assist the passage of the soul to the after-life. Clare Gittings
writes of people's 'intense preoccupation with decent interment'.[34]
The Barber-Surgeons were obliged to give the body a ritual burial. It
was written in Article 60 of the 1606 By-Laws: 'Anatomies to be
decently buried'. The Court Minutes and Accounts demonstrate the
Company's concern for 'Proper Burial' and give details of the close
connection with the nearby Church of St. Gyles at Cripplegate.

The use of criminal bodies for dissection linked dissection with the
ritual execution which preceded it. Furthermore, since it was feared
that anatomisation affected a man's soul, it was available as a pun-
ishment additional to execution, and therefore could be used by the
State to widen the spectrum of punishments available to it. Only trai-
tors and heinous offenders were subjected to posthumous tamper-
ing. The Murder Act of 1752 codified the established practice of the
use of a criminal's corpse after execution for the purpose of dissection. Anatomy thus played its part in the system of judicial punish-
ment. This demonstrated the power and status of the Crown, part of
the whole structure of earthly and divine authority. Maintaining this
structure was important for the prevalence of order over disorder in
society. Every living thing had its own God-given place within the
universe, but in a strictly ordered way. Contemporary writers and
moralists often presented their view of order and hierarchy in society as an analogy between the nature and composition of the body.
Shute's *Chief Groundes* reads:

> *as the members of the body doing without impediments their
> naturall dueties, their whole body is an healthful harmonye*[35]

Against the backdrop of contemporary views of the universe, the
afterlife and authority, the building and its ornamentation is now
considered.

'In form all round': an Amphitheatre for Anatomy
The form of the Barber-Surgeons' anatomy theatre is derived from
Greek and Roman structures. Jones had studied the theatres and
amphitheatres of antiquity during his Italian visits, and was familiar
with Vitruvius.

He is well known for his extravagant masques and stage sets for
the Stuart courts. He was also a master of theatre design. Drawings
remain of structures for court theatres, such as, for example, the
Paved Court Theatre at Somerset House. Of particular interest are

---

[34]Clare Gittings, *Death Burial and the Individual in Early Modern England* (Routledge 1988).
[35]John Shute, *Chief Groundes of Architecture*.

those showing a public playhouse.[36] These designs derived mainly from the classical theatre, interpreted by Jones to suit his audience. The uni-directional hall theatre, with elaborate sets and machinery was most appropriate for the popular Italian-style productions. The anatomy theatre, although similar in detail to these projects, is derived not from a classical theatre but from the amphitheatre, defined as 'in form all round', a 'double theater'.[37] Here the auditorium circumvented the central arena and spectators looked down on to the performance. Conversely, in the classical theatre the audience was separated by a proscenium arch through which to view the stage. As Benedetti wrote an anatomy theatre should be 'set up round a hollow, like may be seen at Rome or Verona'.[38]

The separation between actors and audience in the court theatres was understood by Jones as the separation between representation on stage and the actuality of the corporeal world, and was intended to foster wonderment and imagination. By contrast, the drama in the anatomy theatre was based on scientific truths discovered through investigating the human corpse, not on fiction. The oval auditorium wrapped itself around the corpse allowing observers proximity to the body and an intimacy in which the mind would be inspired to focus on the lecture. Here, audience and 'actors' were part of the same physical realm.

If Jones's anatomy theatre was to be an emblem of the 'teatrum mundi' then according to Heywood the 'all round' form, emblematic of the universe was most appropriate:

> If then the world a theater present
> As by the roundness it appeared most fit.[39]

Similarly Donne wrote:

> An amphitheater consists of two theaters. Our text hath two parts in which all men may sit and see themselves acted.[40]

Further, the amphitheatre form was appropriate in its association with the brutality and civic glory of Rome. Here, the ancients had viewed savage spectacles, violent fights between man and animals. In London, rings for bear-baiting and circular wooden cockpits were to be found in such places as Bankside. Yet, amphitheatres were also representative of the golden age of Imperial Rome. Inigo Jones used the image of a Roman amphitheatre in the masque *Albion's Triumph*.[41]

---

[36]See also John Orrell in *The Human Stage* (1985) and *The Theatres of Inigo Jones and John Webb* (1988).

[37]Puttenham, *English Poesie* 1589. Donne 1631, OED.

[38]*Anatomice, sive historia corporis humani* (1502).

[39]Preface poem to Thomas Heywood, *Apology for Actors* (1612).

[40]Donne, 1628, *OED*.

[41]See *The King's Arcadia*, pp 71–2.

Jones was designing for a London audience, and his classical ideas had to engage with an established set of theatrical expectations. London was unusual in its large number of public theatres, and their distinctive all-round forms stand out in contemporary views of the City. Jones developed his design using antiquity as an idea which could respond to local tradition, rather than exact imitation.

Jones exploits the antique as a paradigm in his choice of the amphitheatre form for the anatomy theatre. The dissections undertaken within were associated with violence. Yet the Company and anatomists wanted to demonstrate that their art was constructive in its teaching about man and God and that the amphitheatre 'all round' form was appropriate as a representation of 'teatrum mundi'. This paradox creates a tension which is resolved in the proportioning of the amphitheatre and the vertical structuring of the theatre.

PART II

The Oval Form and the Body

'Ovally built for the Worship & Comiditie of this Companie'

Square, Circle and the Human Figure: The Body as Focus of the Anatomy Theatre

Contemporary belief in the resemblance between the corporeal, ethereal and spiritual realms of the God-created universe has been discussed. Consequently, architects strove to echo the structuring of the universe in their designs in order to awaken man to the spiritual. This could be undertaken by designing with numbering systems and harmonic ratios, representing the mathematical structure of the universe. Furthermore, since Man's form represented a microcosm of the universe, it was desirable to echo the proportions of the human body. Crooke wrote:

> Now the due proportion, composition or correspondences of the parts of man's body, with respect each to other and of them all to the whole, is admirable. This alone (for a patterne) doe all work men ..., doe the surveighers, master carpenters and masons, referre all their plots and projects they build temples, houses, Engines, shipping, Forts.[42]

Interestingly, Inigo Jones annotated his copy of Barbaro's commentary of Vitruvius with these words: 'the boddi of man well proportioned is the patern for proportion in building.'[43]

---

[42] *Mikrokosmographia*, Book One, p 6.
[43] *The King's Arcadia*, p 63.

One method of proportioning based on the human form was that of 'homo ad circulum' and 'ad quadratum' which arose from the idea that an outstretched man could be inscribed within a circle and a square. Vitruvius's famous description of this relationship was the inspiration for numerous pictorial representations.[44] The square and the circle emulating cosmic and human structuring in basic geometric terms was an important system of proportions encompassed by Renaissance architectural theorists, including Leon Alberti and Sebastiano Serlio. It was also practicable for use with compasses on paper and for laying out a building site.

Serlio and the Development of the Oval for Building
Early Renaissance churches mainly followed the pattern of the longitudinal or the perfectly round form because, according to Lotz, the oval was considered

> *a heresy in the eyes of those theoreticians of the cinquecento who, as disciples of Alberti, acknowledged only the circle or the regular polygon as ideal forms.[45]*

Interest in the use of the oval arose in the early sixteenth century. Michelangelo's proposal for the tomb of Julius II in the new St. Peter's would have been the first oval space in Europe and Peruzzi proposed an oval plan for S. Giacomo degli Incurabili, the syphilis hospital in Rome. Neither project was realised.[46]

It was not until the second half of the sixteenth century that the oval became an acceptable form. Sebastiano Serlio, a pupil of Peruzzi, wrote in Book V of *De Architettura* (1547): 'Following the circle in perfection, oval shapes are the next closest. Therefore I thought it good to form a temple from this shape.'[47] The first oval buildings began to materialise: in Rome Vignola was responsible for two projects and Francesco da Volterra's S. Giacomo degli Incurabili (1592) followed Peruzzi's earlier proposal. In Venice, Sansovino designed the oval Church of the Incurabili Hospital (c. 1565).[48] It is particularly interesting to note that the latter two were churches built in connection with medical establishments.

---

[44] *The Ten Books of Architecture*, Book 3, Chapter 1.
[45] Lotz (ed. D. Howard) *Architecture in Italy 1500–1600*, p 49.
[46] Howard Colvin, *Architecture and the Afterlife* pp 232–9. On Peruzzi's design see W. Lotz, 'Die Ovalen Kirchenraume des Cinquecento,' *Romisches Jahrbuch fur Kunstgeschichte* VII(1955), 26ff.
[47] S. Serlio, *Regole Generali di Architettura di sopra le cinque maniere degli edifici* (Venice 1537 and 1551). Book V, 'On temples', 7r Hart and Hicks English translation, p 402.
[48] See Deborah Howard, *Jacopo Sansovino: Architecture and Patronage in Renaissance Venice* (New Haven and London 1987) pp 88–94.

The oval was associated with several memorials associated with the after-life, such as the chapel attached to the mausoleum of Emperor Ferdinand II at Graz (1614–38). Since the anatomy theatre was to provide a reverent setting for the dissection of the corpse, associated with death and judgement, its chosen form was appropriate.

Within intellectual circles, moreover, the oval form was of topical interest, because the Copernican theory that the earth and planets revolved around the sun was being discussed, as well as Kepler's discovery that the orbits of the planets were elliptical rather than circular. The mathematics was not then available to create a physical theory involving ellipses, and the term ellipse only acquired its present precise definition much later.[49] Even in 1636 there were few oval buildings in Europe. Borromini's oval design for San Carlino in Rome (1634) was innovative in design. That Jones' design is contemporary emphasises its uniqueness in the history of English architecture.

Constructing the Oval Anatomy Theatre

The *Annals* suggest that considerable effort was spent in laying out and measuring Jones's oval plan on site. The shape was more complex to set out than a simple rectilinear or circular building and payments for 'measuring' were made on several occasions:

> Paid to Mr Wilson a mason to Measure Stanleys worke in the Theater & spent then xiijs – ixd Given to Robert Butler and John Pullen for their measuring the Theater xls[50]

Close study of the drawings at Worcester College, Oxford, reveal small compass points in a diamond shape, almost identical on both the initial sketch by Jones and John Webb's later drawing, demonstrating how the oval was constructed on the plan and subsequently transferred to site. In Book I of *De Architettura*, 'On Geometry', after a consideration of regular polygons, Sebastiano Serlio illustrated the oval: 'Oval forms can be drawn in many ways but I shall only give the rule for four.' The construction of the anatomy theatre corresponds to the first of these diagrams.

The theatre's oval shape was derived from the triangle and the circle. Two equilateral triangles formed the focal points of the arcs which inscribed the outline. Borromini's design for San Carlino was also based on these shapes although the oval was constructed in a slightly different manner.[51]

Although perhaps not apparent at first, the square and circle relationship can also be identified in the plan of the Barber-Surgeons'

---

[49]M.S. Longair, *Theoretical Concepts in Physics* (new edition in preparation).
[50]*Annals*, p 403.
[51]Anthony Blunt, *Borromini*, pp 47–84.

theatre. If the stairtowers were to form the bottom corners of a square, then the top edge delineates the upper limit of the central dissecting stage. When a circle is inscribed within that square the newel post of each staircase is located on its circumference.

In the Preface to Book Two of *Mikrokosmographia*, Crooke's admiration of geometrical proportioning of the circle, the square and of the triangle, is described through the poetry of Edmund Spenser:

> *The frame thereof seem'd partly circulare,*
> *And Partly Triangulare. O worke Divine!*
> *Those two, the first and the last proportions are*
> *The one, imperfect, mortall, feminine:*
> *The other immortall, perfect, masculine*
> *And twixt them two, a Quadrate was the Base*
> *Proportioned equally by seaven and nine;*
> *Nine, was the circle set in Heavens place,*
> *All which compacted, made a goodly Diapose.*[52]

Jones within the Neoplatonic tradition desired to create architecture which he believed would reflect the structuring of the universe and the microcosm–macrocosm relationship. The plan of the anatomy theatre was based on geometrical shapes and proportioning which were understood to imitate the proportions of man and the universe, essential in a building whose focus was the human frame. Jones was also aware of the need to choose a form with sacred overtones. He knew of Serlio's work and of the new oval churches, and wanted this new 'laboratory' to be in line with the most innovative architecture so as to reflect the cutting edge of contemporary thought.

PART IV

'This frame coagmented for the service of the Soule we have compared to the whole world or universe.'

H. Crooke, *Mikrokosmographia*
Preface to Book Seven

The title page of *Mikrokosmographia* shows a remarkably similar dispositioning and vertical proportioning of elements to those in the anatomy theatre. The lower part of the image represents the sublunary realm where an anatomy demonstration of the brain can be seen. As on the concave ceiling of the anatomy theatre, the celestial zone shows stars, planets and the sun. The illustrator has used visual conventions

---

[52] *Mikrokosmographia*, p 61.

from celebrated Renaissance paintings, such as Raphael's so-called 'Disputa'. In the central portion two statues, probably derived from Vesalian figures, together with Father Time and a figure of death pointing to the book offer the art of anatomy as a means to unveil human truths and are a reminder of human mortality.

The anatomy theatre, an emblematic theatre of the world in a cosmic sense, is also compatible with Christian eschatological teaching. As it was feared that dissection of the body would deny its redemption and eternal life, it was important that the form and interior of the theatre should provide a setting which would sanction anatomy by metaphorically aiding the passage of the soul to the after-life – the (building) frame 'coagmented for the service of the soul'. Jones was aware of the use of the oval form associated with the after-life, but acknowledged the sacred role of the anatomy theatre in its vertical structuring. The strata within the building are reminiscent of a Renaissance painting, such as Michelangelo's *Last Judgement*, which illustrates the eschatological journey, the final destiny of man.

The lower ground floor of the building, where the dissection and preparation of the body took place, is associated with blood and gore, a representation of subterranean Hell – the final destination of the sinner in Christian belief. In the main theatre, the auditorium area below the cornice represented the world of the living, with the heavens painted on the ceiling symbolising the resting place of those men who were redeemed. Crooke's Frontispiece exhibits eucharistic symbolism. The anatomy lecture depicted in the lowest part of the engraving is reminiscent of the Last Supper, and the sacraments and shedding of blood are images of redemption.

The anatomy theatre also represents hierarchy and stability within the universe and within society. This careful structuring of the elements and the decorum in which dissections were undertaken, compared with the turmoil of the preceding execution, reasserts the prevalence of order over disorder and the solemnity of justice. Although the amphitheatre form is a reminder of brutality, it is also representative of civic glory and the authority of the ruler.

Architectural historians, writing about Inigo Jones, have placed little emphasis on the Barber-Surgeons' anatomy theatre. It was, however, a remarkable building which encompassed numerous facets of early modern thought and identified a fusion between them. Its study gives an exciting insight into the lives and beliefs of Londoners in the mid-seventeenth century. The theatre brought science and classical humanism into a Christian framework.

Megha Chand

Interrogating the Indian Condition: Some Problems with the Frameworks of Architect Charles Correa

Chand's dissertation combines three distinct components all concerned with issues of colonialism and postcolonialism: a personal interest in postcolonial construction, critical and cultural theory, and architecture. In this dissertation all three are interwoven into a beautifully written text which oscillates from academic analysis to poetic and personal discourse. It has an air of commitment and passion that keeps the reader glued to the development of the argument.

Megha Chand

INTERROGATING THE INDIAN CONDITION

Some problems with the frameworks of architect Charles Correa

I would like to thank Andrew Higgott for all his help in the writing of this essay.

ORIGINAL CONTENTS

An informal introduction to frameworks for thinking in postcolonial India
Acknowledging the Other
The space of the 'Difference'
Framework
Case Studies
Words spoken in a dream
Of Suppressions
Rethinking Frameworks
Summing Up
Bibliography

Excerpts

AN INFORMAL INTRODUCTION TO FRAMEWORKS FOR THINKING IN POSTCOLONIAL INDIA

Several years back, in 1992, I wrote a test to gain admission to a school of Architecture in New Delhi. The test comprised of two stages and in the second stage, one of the tasks given was to draw the image of an iron from memory. The iron, a common household object. I drew one, just like everybody else, meticulously, careful that it fulfilled all the specifications of the one lying in the corner of my room, disused, but nevertheless there. The proportions had to be right – it was a drawing test – the steel base shone against the dark plastic body and the handle and the regulator had to be in the right place and the tip of the iron was sharp in contrast with the curvy upper body. I drew it the way I remembered my personal one, standing upright as if somebody had left it there on purpose. Just when I had nearly finished the drawing, I wound an electric coil around it so that now the whole body was hidden behind the coil and one had to guess that what it hid was the body of an iron. The coil just trailed off on an imaginary table and instead of a plug at the end of it, I drew three wires hanging loose.

I made it to the third and final stage, the interview, where amidst other fairly straightforward questioning, I was asked one, which has troubled me persistently ever since. "Megha, tell us *why* you haven't drawn a plug at the end of this coil?". . . . I didn't have an answer. I had drawn it because I had drawn it. Before I could fumble some understandable form of explanation one of the members on the panel said, "What you are saying truly speaks of the Indian condition."

The Indian condition

Maybe I am trying to read too much into what could have been a casual remark, a kind of a warning to a novice that there are better answers than 'I don't know' because every action of ours is inexorably tied to a context. Certainly to me his comment could have meant at least two things: that the drawing spoke about the status that technology (represented by the iron) has in Indian households – the status of the 'Other', a certain foreignness in its existence which persists because Indians are averse to using industrialised 'hi tech' products. This sounds like a gross generalisation for a country where a certain section of the population are the driving engines behind Bill Gates' feverish imaginations, where multinational brands of Coke and Nike are more than just household names which manifest their presence at every street corner in miniscule quiet hamlets as well as busy metros through billboards, screaming their manifesto – 'Just do it'. Yet it is true that despite owning three irons (two Indian made and one British), freshly washed clothes from our household are ironed *every day* by Hari, the dhobhi, who lives under the staircase soffit of our block of 28 flats in New Delhi. Hari was born into this profession – he is the 19-year-old son of Ram Prasad, who after having passed on the profession to his son has retired to his village in Bihar to pursue a livelihood in agriculture.

Hari uses an iron which runs on coal (not electricity) – an object double the size of our light weight models, made of cast iron and when full of burning coal, which needs to be stoked by a hand fan, Hari needs to use both his hands and the force of his body in order to iron out the creases in the clothes. Clothes sensitive to high temperatures are just dealt with at the end of the day when the heat of the coal has simmered down.

Or perhaps in order to understand my critic I must distance myself from the immediate effect of his words and locate him in that web of life which has given him the right/confidence to use the term 'Indian condition'. A mind which has observed the nuances of other cultures varied in habits (including ironing habits), a mind which has had the fortune (or misfortune) to dislocate itself from a highly contextualised and focussed world constitutive of its own history to give it the power to *compare*, can see things 'in perspective' and is capable of such a comment. For I cannot imagine Hari the dhobhi carrying out the daily business that he was born into under the self conscious framework that constitutes what the 'Indian condition' might be. For him it is a way of life and I won't be wrong in saying – the only way of life.

Such is the story of this common household object – the iron – which rests peacefully in the corner of rooms of millions of households in India – the story of purchases of maybe a foreign returned family coexisting with the dhobhi industry in New Delhi, the story of the latest washing machine wrapped in muslin in my grandmother's kitchen, used only occasionally for 'special' washes, the story of the Mercedes on its virgin trip to the temple where it is blessed with God's watchful eye, the story of the inexorable movement of signification that both constitutes the exorbitant image of power and deprives it of the certainty and stability of centre or closure.[1]

To transgress a little further, into the realm of what primarily concerns this essay, one could begin to see the story at work in the guise of collisions between processes that make contemporary architecture in India today. Collisions between the 'contemporary and the ancient', to put it very crudely, but more importantly collisions between processes of thinking of an archaic worldview that still has a steady grip and is a result of a historic cultural conditioning and the world that constitutes a more recent phenomena of the 'hybrid'. Between the two there emerges an ominous silence that utters an archaic colonial 'Otherness' that speaks in riddles, obliterating proper names and proper places that turns imperial triumphalism into the testimony of colonial confusion and those who

---

[1]Bhabha, Homi, *the location of culture*, p 147.

hear its echo lose their historic memories. This is the Voice of the early modernist colonial literature, the complex cultural memory of which is made-in a *fine tension between the melancholic homelessness of the modern novelist, and the wisdom of the sage like story teller whose craft takes him no further afield than his own people.*[2] (my emphasis)

A. K. Ramanujan, noted poet, muses over this condition in his wonderful essay 'Is there an Indian way of thinking?' and gives us insights into the janus faced nature of thinking that prevails in India. I quote:

> "*Stanislavsky had an exercise for his actors. He would give them an everyday sentence like, 'Bring me a cup of tea', and ask them to say it forty different ways, using it to beg, question, mock, wheedle, be imperious etc. My question, 'Is there an Indian way of thinking?' is a good one for such an exercise. Depending on where the stress is placed it contains many questions – all of which are real questions – asked again and again when people talk about India.*
>
> *Is there an Indian way of thinking?*
> *Is there an Indian way of thinking?*
> *Is there an Indian way of thinking?*
> *Is there an Indian way of thinking?*
>
> *The answers are just as various. Here are a few. There was an Indian way of thinking; there isn't anymore. If you want to learn about the Indian way of thinking, do not ask the modern day citified Indians, go to the pundits, the vaidyas, the old texts. On the contrary India never changes: under the veneer of the modern, Indians still think like the Vedas.*
> *The second question might elicit answers like these: There is no single Indian way of thinking; there are Great and Little traditions, ancient and modern, rural and urban, classical and folk. Each language caste and religion has its special worldview. So, under the apparent diversity, there is really a unity of viewpoint, a single supersystem. Vedists see a vedic model in all vedic thought. Nehru made the phrase 'unity in diversity' an Indian slogan. The Sahitya Academy's line has been, 'Indian literature is one though written in many languages.'*
> *The third question might be answered: What we see in India is nothing special to India; it is nothing but pre-industrial, pre printing press, face to face, agricultural, feudal,*

---

[2]Benjamin, Walter, *Illuminations*, pp 98–101.

Marxists, Freudians, McLuhanites, all have their labels for the stage India is in, according to their schemes of social evolution; India is only an example. Others of course would argue the uniqueness of the Indian Way and how it turns all things, especially, rivals and enemies, into itself. Look at what happened to Indo Europeans in India, they would say: their language gets shot with retroflexes, their syntax with nominal compounds, they lose their nerve – the British are only the most recent example (according to Nirad Chowdhri). Look at what happens to Buddhism, Islam, the Parsis. There is an Indian *way, and it imprints and patterns all things that enter the continent; it is inescapable, and it is Bigger Than All of Us.*

The fourth question may question whether Indians think at all: It is the West that is materialistic, rational; Indians have no philosophy, only religion, no positive sciences, not even a psychology: in India matter is subordinated to spirit, rational thought to feeling, intuition. And even when people agree that this is the case, we can have arguments for and against it. Some lament, others celebrate India's unthinking ways. One can go on forever."[3]

These questions, posed informally by Ramanujan, are focussing on an idea of the 'Indian condition' in constructing a notion that represents a post-colonial democratic nation. These ruminations have an echo in my critic's comment, in that both are in relation to an 'Other' an anterior system of codes which give it definition, without which the uttering of these observations and questions would have been impossible. In other words, the message of Ramanujan's lucid answers has a meaning only in relation to all those things which are not Indian. (Like the materialistic west, the industrial society, depending on the question being answered.) So that throughout the passage one is being made aware of the traits of the Indian mind in relation to *something else*.

The presence of the Other problematises matters tremendously when it comes to interrogating what constitutes the identity of the post-colonial hybrid psyche. Once it is acknowledged, a *'difference'* comes into focus, the space of which is marked by an ambivalent temporality, one which makes it extremely difficult to rely on the stability or the fullness of the past in defining the contemporaneity of the nation. Also, apart from being a generalised condition of post-modernity into which all contemporary cultures are now irretrievably ushered, it is specific to the post-colonial, more pointedly the

---

[3]Ramannujan, A. K., *Is there an Indian way of thinking? An informal essay.* Contributions to Indian sociology, pp 1–2.

post-colonial intellectual living and working in the Indian metropolis.[4]

The course of contemporary Architecture in India is, by and large, determined by individuals who are part of a metropolitan culture – some of whom have a nationalist agenda which comes from a sense of 'losing identity' in the wake of colonisation and then the adoption of modernist frameworks for the conception and production of projects. The frameworks which helped them regain a sense of the Indian identity are heavily dependent on the revival of tradition and its representation, which may suppress other ambivalent signs of the present – and are therefore in danger of producing oriental stereotypes by romanticising the past.

To my mind it is extremely critical to restructure this way of thinking so that the 'Indian' in the 'modern Indian' is not simply represented by stereotype exotica but by something much more urgent and less stable. To recognise this is the purpose of the dissertation.

The following two chapters lay down the rules of this restructuring and come out of some observations during the course of my shift from living in the Indian metropolis of New Delhi, to a recent one of living in the western metropolis of London.

FRAMEWORK

The notion of nationhood and therefore identity is important to a postcolonial autonomous nation. But how does one construct one when the only structures available are inventions of western ideology? For instance the very idea of 'nation' (from which comes nationalism) is an eighteenth-century European concept.

How does one negotiate between the archaic and the contemporary without suppressing truths which are very real and happening – like the suppression of the skilled craftsperson who still exists as a migrant in the city in search for jobs – or at a larger scale, the fact that technological advancements in the Indian context is a misnomer as 70% of the population is engaged in the production of agriculture in an effort to feed 5 billion people annually?

How does one account for the space of the 'difference' which comes about from the act of mimicking a prototype ?

What is the process through which the idea of the signifier is constructed when it comes to producing a building with an 'Indian Identity'?

These are some of the questions that inform the reading of the following two projects by Charles Correa. The intention of the reading,

---

[4]Ahmed, Aijaz, *Post Colonial Theory and the 'Post-' condition. Lecture delivered at York University, Toronto on 27.11.96*, p 25.

using the above frameworks, is to expose the inconsistencies in conceiving the ideas by the architect, thereby putting the conception in danger of its own myth and assumptions.

CHARLES CORREA'S STRATEGY

Correa's nationalist strategy is dependent on a formal representation of the archaic on the skin of the building. There is a definite preoccupation with 'traditional architecture', a search for one's roots in an authentic past, and on finding it in places such as ancient temples, ancient water tanks and palaces and forts the images are grafted to not only the skin of the building but also into the narratives that accompany the imagined experience of the spaces.

One encounters 'sudden' confrontations with astoundingly specific symbols which refer, directly, to another time and another place.

THE JAWAHAR KALA KENDRA (JKK)

Jaipur 1992

An Arts Centre devoted to the memory of Nehru, it was designed by Correa for the government of Rajasthan.

In Correa's words, "The JKK is double coded like the city of Jaipur: a *contemporary* building based on an *archaic* notion of the cosmos."[5]

The reference selected by Correa to model the building on is archaic indeed. It is based on the *Vastupurush mandala* of the *Vedic* shastras where Architecture is conceived as a model of the cosmos; the specific *mandala* invoked here is the *Navagraha* consisting of nine squares. Each square corresponds to a different planet.[6]

The original city plan for Jaipur drawn by Maharaja Jai Singh is also based on a spatial matrix – with one of the nine squares removed to the east due to the presence of a hill. The JKK directly invokes this original Navagraha with one of the squares displaced to create an entrance, thereby recalling the gesture that created the original city plan of Jaipur.

It is interesting to note that the personality of Raja Jai Singh who commissioned the building of the city of Jaipur has a resonance with Nehru's to whom the building is dedicated. Both were profound believers in the newest myths of science and progress. Jai Singh constructed the Jantar Mantar; astronomical instruments that could measure with greatest possible accuracy the movement of sun and stars and Nehru laid the foundations of the modern Indian nation in

---

[5]Correa, Charles, *Charles Correa*, p 218.
[6]A+D, Sept–Oct 1991.

theory and practice. Yet it is extremely ironical that in choosing the symbols that signify/remember Nehru, Correa doesn't go beyond the realm of *recalling the archaic*. Almost as if he *doesn't know* that there exists a significant lump of the present marked by signs of split identities, a presence of otherness and a sense of the ambivalent all of which have evolved from colonial suppressions and later the efforts of the modern movement. But ... then how does one represent these 'senses' or rather can one represent them formally in images?

By literally mimicking the plan of the city of Jaipur to create the plan of the JKK one senses a divorce and a 'difference' between it and the prototype which is marked by the emptiness of the symbolic gesture. There is no sign of transcending the image of the model which is grounded in its own myth and economy of means. The questioning space of the difference becomes apparent in the knowledge that the grid of the city of Jaipur was displaced because of real topographical constraints. Perhaps the idea of 'displacement' could have been the mark of *its own* identity in the way *it* reflected the nuances of *its* site to create *its* own order in plan ... but the preoccupation seems to be otherwise.

One notices in the 'setting out' of frameworks (and also in the detailed description later) that the conception is based on the *creation of binaries*. By creating the binary of 'archaic' and 'contemporary' ("a *contemporary* building based on an *archaic* notion") Correa creates two neat categories into which must fit all ideas – 'either here or there'. The danger with this classification to my mind is that it doesn't problematise the 'in-between', the intrinsic and invisible manner in which signs of the archaic disrupt signs of contemporaneity and vice versa, an unstable relationship where it's difficult to say which is which, perhaps because the two are so absorbed in feeding each other. As a result the binaries 'miss out' on their internal and invisible relationship because all the effort has been spent in defining them, through formal symbols, *against* one another. Which leads to the observation that they the (binaries), in their earnestness, also suppress other possible truths which, for instance, could be about accommodations in the production of the project (between the contractor and those very 'carriers' of archaic knowledges who ultimately build it) or any other kind of accommodation that is borne out of real and eccentric conditions of the site located in its specific region. In a simplistic way, yes, the building is contemporary, but only because it happens to be built in the last century. Its potential contemporary-*ness* marked by the interstitial processes and passages of shifts during colonial governance and now the efforts of globalisation (and therefore hybridisation) remains conveniently overlooked due to the easy categorisation of the binaries.

But the binary is established and there's no going back!

Now the functional programme of the building is fixed neatly onto the nine square plan that mimics the plan of the city of Jaipur. Each of the nine 'Mahals' (palaces) has been named after a particular planet – *Mangal, Chandra, Budh, Ketu, Shani, Rahu, Guru, Shukra* and *Surya* and is designed to express its special quality.

For instance the 'Mangal Mahal' is based on the planet 'Mangal'. "Since this planet represents power, it was decided to house the Director and his administrative offices here. (Such esoteric connections are made for each of the squares.) This planet becomes the entry point to the whole complex – so along the walls of the 'Mangal Mahal' is an explanation of the *Navagraha*, and on the ceiling under the dome is painted a Jain cosmograph depicting all the rivers, mountains, animals and vegetation of the manifest world around us."[7]

"On the external surfaces (of each Mahal) the presence of each of the planets is expressed by its traditional symbol inlaid in white marble, embellished in polished black granite and mica slate, recalling again the precisely calibrated surfaces of the Jantar Mantar Observatory."[8]

'Since this planet represents power . . . .' In the since-*ness* of the 'since' there is a sense of blindness that speaks about the menace of logical connections in the same way that the binaries are rationalised and executed. This too is a symbolic gesture forced on the nine square plan which immediately leads one to ask why the 'quality' of 'power' was considered appropriate for the Director instead of 'Education' or 'Knowledge' or 'Devourer/Restorer' or even 'Heart'. In other words, what is the *critical relationship* that has given these functions their place in the scheme of things? If the logic of the association, Power = Director has a ground, then why is it that the association of Anger = Textiles seems like one borne out of default, almost like a farce of the former? It's a small point but it brings into focus the danger of nurturing a bias for pedantic social hierarchies which give rise to such esoteric connections and also the carelessness with which the myth is constructed. Is there anything in the sense of the physical articulation of the rooms that alludes to these qualities?

The fact that things are a 'given', right from the symbolic significance of the interiors to the symbolic treatment of the façade dressed in red sandstone – "the same materials used for the Jantar Mantar Observatory, in the Red Fort at Agra and in Fatehpur Sikri"[9] and adhered to dogmatically, makes the question of their relationship to the building itself and the site on which it stands come into

---

[7]Correa, Charles, *Charles Correa*, p 223.
[8]Correa, Charles, *Charles Correa*, p 220.
[9]Correa, Charles, *Charles Correa*, p 220.

focus. Is there a critical relationship that informs the placing of all? And then is it not absolutely critical to acknowledge the fact that the sandstone in Fatehpur Sikri is primarily used as a structural material, before any embellishments are carved on its surface? So that when the structure of the JKK is *clad* in the same sandstone only to serve the purpose of *recalling* it, a difference appears that speaks, in its silence, of the devastating consequences of glossing over the truth of the prototype, in other words, fetishising it – to produce the *oriental stereotype*.

Similarly, the precious inlays on the Jantar Mantar, recalled on the external surface of each of the mahal, have come out of a judgement related to the working of the instrument – they have a place, in that it is through them and their instrumental quality that the movement of the celestial bodies is gauged. Therefore they establish a real relationship with the earth and the sky and in doing so they also establish their *critical* position in the whole conception. This act of judging the 'location' of the inlay (so precise dimensionally that mms. would make a world of a difference) is amiss on the façade of the JKK where, by referring to the precise design, it begins to focus on the lack of judgement in its own presence.

To explain this idea further, one has looked at the 'Surya Kund' in detail.

THE SURYA KUND

The Surya Kund ('water tank dedicated to the Sun God') occupies the central square in the plan of the JKK. In Correa's words, "It is a void as specified in the vedic shastras, representing nothing – which is the true source of all energy."[10]

Its purpose is loosely defined, unlike the other eight squares, and lies in making space, in an open-to-the-sky courtyard, for visitors to rest before moving on to the next 'Mahal'.

The physical articulation of the 'Surya Kund' and its name is derived, directly, from the Surya Kund in Modhera, Gujrat, which was built in 1026 BC.

Here lies the problem – in its precision in choosing the reference and in its inability to transcend itself in doing so.

Firstly, Correa embraces the questionable strategy of *thematising the text* of 'tradition' as opposed to sensing it in its specific context. Whereas thematising involves glossing over the text of history and seeing it in themes, of 'Kunds' in this case, sensing it in its *location*, inverts the emphasis on the gaze of the onlooker, on the lens through which it perceives the object of desire, to ask for the specific

---

[10]Correa, Charles, *Charles Correa*, p 225.

context in which it would like to see. In doing so it challenges the former's universal appeal by saying, "*there is no such thing as a universal kund.*"

It is interesting to note that the theme of the 'kund' appears in the following projects in the oeuvre of Charles Correa:

- Jawaharlal Nehru Centre for Advanced Scientific Research (Bangalore, 1994)
- Inter University Centre for Astronomy and Astro Physics (Pune, 1992)
- Jawaharlal Nehru Institute of Development Banking (Hyderabad, 1991)
- New Bagalkot Township (Karnataka, 1985–)
- Surya Kund (New Delhi, 1986)
- Vidhan Bhawan, State Assembly (Bhopal, 1980–)

The superficiality of Correa's universal order becomes quite stark when one looks at the myth and the economy of means that gave rise to its model in Gujrat: The prototype, Surya Kund in Modhera, Gujrat is extremely specific in the myth that gave rise to it and also its relationship with the topography of the region. The Surya Kund was constructed for sun worship which goes back to Vedic times when the Aryans first established themselves in India. Originally intended for use by those who came to worship at the temple of Surya on its banks, the tank is still used for sacred baths by Hindus.

Located strategically as a water collector in an area of Gujrat which remains hot and dry through most of the year, the structure is essentially subterranean with a depth of 15 m. The 'real' constraints of erosion and subsidence of earth has informed its form – of a complex sequence of steps pitched on an inclined surface of earth and this protects the earth from eroding ... but also makes a processional way to reach the water ...[11]

But when universalised into a theme and grafted literally by Correa, the kund becomes an object fetishised and divorced from its model, but more devastatingly, from itself. In its mimicry, it produces a difference, a returning gaze, a dissembling eye, that looks at the kund of the JKK AND at Correa's synoptic gaze, to ask for that nuance that marks its own reason.

If the central square represents a void in Correa's imagination, then one wonders if the void is a void because of a lack of functional specificity or whether there is a spatial sense to this 'nothingness'. I only bring up this point because I am reminded of the sense of disruption and negation I felt while peering into, walking into and

---

[11] Jain, Kulbhushan, *The Architecture of India*, p 53.

around the uncanny installations of Anish Kapoor, whose specific preoccupation is also to do with representation of the void.

The *depth* of the *physicality* of the objects is the frame through which the void engulfs the viewer's space.

The *presence* of the object renders a space more empty than mere vacancy could ever envisage[12] ... so that the expansion of available space – the making of emptiness – never fails to register a lateral movement, a transitional tremor, that disorders the boundedness of the void. The void slips sideways from the grasp of frame and figure: its visual apprehension as contained absence, made whole and present in the eye of the viewer, is attenuated. The enigma of the void ... supplements it with a disruptive, disjunctive time through which the spectator must pass – 'reverse, affirm, negate'.[13]

Consider, for instance, the figure of *Adam*. A cavity set so deeply in stone that its pigmented pitch *defies* the depth of the rock, and floats weightless to the surface. Suddenly the stone has shifted mass, leaving only its shadow, making more ground than it stands on . . . .

Or consider the material possibility, in the meditative recess of *My Body Your Body*. As the viewer enters the oblique membrane of pigmented blue, the void speaks of the elusive object of the body: the father's absent body, the mother's missing body, the lover's longed for body, my empty body. Then, the work shifts, and from the darkness of loss there emerges a fold of light and longing: a fluctuating form of a rim, a lip, a lid, a limb, a line of life . . . a fragile meeting of space and emptiness, and in that ambiguous adoration, the discovery of your body, my body . . .[14]

And in their own way, through their displacement, they allow us to decipher emptiness as a 'sign'.

And in their own way, also, in the interventions of the material, they describe the obliquity of the present, not a primal past, but not as yet the future either. In transition between the material and the non-material.[15]

In relation to Correa's void, Kapoor's void is about the tangential touch of the *material* and non-material. "Only when things are truly made, in the sense of possessing themselves, are they beautiful. If they are not truly made, the eye is a very quick and very good instrument . . . . The idea of the truly made does not only have to do with truth. It has to do with the meeting of material and non material."[16]

[12]Bhabha, Homi, *'Making Emptiness'*, from Anish Kapoor, p 12.
[13]Bhabha, Homi, *ibid.*
[14]Bhabha, Homi, *'Making Emptiness'*, from *Anish Kapoor*, p 28.
[15]Bhabha, Homi, *ibid.*
[16]Kapoor, Anish, *Anish Kapoor*, p 18.

The sense of *fragility* with which Kapoor conceives of his 'void' in terms of idea and construction is amiss in Correa's conception. Apart from the fact the space has a name 'void', one doesn't sense it in any way that engages the notion, in terms of being engulfed by it. The name remains a name, a bland symbolic gesture.

From the plan of the building to the interior of rooms, Correa is excessively concerned with 'tradition' and its revival – and the focus is on the image of the building rather than its location and its construction.

It is ironical to see this project in relation to Buckminster Fuller's, Correa's tutor at the MIT, where the preoccupation is wholly with the technology of construction and its relation to usefulness, exemplified by projects like the Dymaxion House and the geodesic dome.

In the effort of recalling the past Correa also overlooks truths that may surround the project – like the craftsperson who is the carrier of archaic knowledge systems of construction now becomes a mere tool that actually builds this archaic/contemporary building. In the process he creates stereotypical images of traditional Indian architecture with great emphasis on the look of things.

The thinking of the JKK exemplifies the inevitable dangers of the 'difference' produced in the act of mimicry – being almost the same but not quite; as the symbol of identity and its content have between them a disturbing disruptive gap.

I can only sum up the magnanimity of the crisis of this kind of thinking by pointing out the ease with which it fits into the critic's preoccupation. Here is Kenneth Frampton's view who most definitely (I assume) sees this project as the enshrinement of critical regionalist values:

> *"The most surprising and* **refreshing aspect** *of this entire complex is the way in which a* **radiant, popular** *architecture,* **replete** *with icons is* **combined** *with* **antique lore**, *while at the same time retaining the* **vitality** *of contemporary* **craft** *activity. The* **implicitly regional** *character of this institution* **finds** *expression in the red Rajasthan sandstone with which it is faced, topped by copings in beige Dholpur stone. These are the same materials that were used at the Jantar Mantar observatory, at Fatehpur Sikri and the Red Fort in Agra. In each mahal, this* **revetment** *is* **enlivened** *by appropriate icons inlayed in white marble, black granite and grey mica stone."*[17]
> *(my emphases)*
> *The architect and the critic.*
> *The orient and the occident.*

[17]Frampton, Kenneth, *Charles Correa*, p 14.

One created by the inquisitive energies of the other.
Never mind the truth.

WORDS SPOKEN IN A DREAM

... ... *Why are you so selfconscious. ... you seem to say,
"Look at me! I am Indian because ..."*
.... *things are so neatly classified in your words ... in your universal 'kunds' and 'bindus' and 'mandalas' and 'darwaazas' and
all that ... But you always forget the other things, things about
the ambivalent nature of the present ... .where it's impossible to make distinctions ....like 'archaic' and 'contemporary'.
Look at Hari the dhobi ... .his use of his cast iron iron when
there is no dearth of irons around him speaks of the contemporary condition .... in the way his past disrupts the present
.... so that he becomes the present .... more cunningly than
the self-concious binaries and categories you resort to. ...
You prefer to step out and* then *signify some 'meanings'
through some visual signs.
Can you not think of a way in which the scene and agent are
one? Can you not just be? ... without having to mention the
word 'Indian'? .... where your building is it.... explanations
cancelled.
Listen to this ancient poem called 'What his concubine said
about him (within earshot of his wife's friends, when she
heard that the wife had said disparaging things about her)'....*

> You know he comes from
> where the fresh-water shark in the pools
> catch with their mouths
> the mangoes as they fall, ripe
> from the trees on the edge of the field.
> At our place
> he talked big
> Now back in his own
> when others raise their hands
> and feet,
> he will raise his too:
> like a doll
> in a mirror
> he will shadow
> every last wish
> of his son's dear mother

*... ... to describe the exterior landscape is to inscribe the
interior landscape: the landscape that man owns in which he
lives, represents him: it is his property in more senses than*

one. ... (the place where sharks do not have to work for the
mango, it falls into its open mouth.)[18]
Here the scene and agent are one; they are metonyms for
each other[19].... ...

RETHINKING FRAMEWORKS

The rethinking of frameworks must begin to accommodate signs
that do not dogmatically look at culture as a homogeneous pool of
meaning but as something that is living and in flux – brought about
by a process of assimilation and accommodation of the new.

The frameworks of Charles Correa, in operation at the moment, do
not recognise this as a result of which contemporary Indian
Architecture sees its 'Indian' in the purity of the realm of tradition.
However, the demand of contemporaneity is to dwell in the present
which is made up of incommensurable demands and practices –
brought about by the presence of the Other which can be discerned
in shifts, adjustments, assimilations and suppressions – processes
which are inscribing the identity of the nation and indeed architecture now.

To my mind it is extremely critical to acknowledge these processes
and use *them* as frames to construct an architectural strategy for
identity. Needless to say that deploying visual representations only
succeeds in divorcing the building from its ambition.

SUMMING UP

In this essay I have attempted to bring to focus some of the problems confronted by architects in India who have a nationalist agenda
in that they are trying to formulate strategies of representation to
project notions of selfhood or identity through their work. Their
work is critical to my mind, because they bring to focus some dominant themes concerning the framework of representation, the
framework being the 'lens' through which one's gaze is directed.

The ambition of Correa's architecture is to redefine the course of
contemporary Indian architecture by recalling the past, the preroga-
tive being that the richness of it needs to be accounted for in the
reconsidering of architecture in the aftermath of the modern movement, which didn't recognise it.

---

[18]Ramanujan, A. K., *Is there an Indian way of thinking? An informal essay. Contributions
to Indian Society*, pp 9–10.
[19]*Ibid.*

In the two projects discussed, this is achieved by a visual representation that refers to tradition as a wholesome and static product rather than a body of meaning that is in a mode of *constant flux* brought about by collisions of an archaic worldview that still has a steady grip in the scheme of things and the more recent phenomena of the modern movement, seen in the conception of the stone masons and their suppression in the architectural profession.

Today, however seductive the past might be, it is impossible to look at it with a loving gaze that ignores the hybridity of the Indian psyche from the point of view of the individual and the collective – the identifying mark of which is a splitting of identities, but one which is more subtle and ambivalent than the creation of binaries. For this reason I found it necessary to highlight the experience of my simultaneously double coded childhood in New Delhi, and later, the literary work of Bombay poet Adil Jussawalla whose preoccupation is to define identity by dwelling in the space of the difference that emerges in the invocation of the Other. Jussawalla's poem emphasises that identity emerges in the invocation of the two AT THE SAME TIME.

It is difficult to transfer the same sort of literary sense directly to architecture, but in a sense one can feel it in the production of the Corinthian column whose antecedents lie in ancient Europe while simultaneously being grounded in the Indian archaic.

In this sense, the richness of tradition lies in its powers to assimilate and accommodate the alien through the building process, not in its image, which is all Correa can see. If acknowledged, it is inevitable that the building will be Indian, without trying to be it, although it may not be immediately recognisable as something 'traditional'. A nationalist agenda that overlooks this crucial 'sign of the present' is in inevitable danger of suppressing it and in doing so is in danger of being divorced from its ambition of producing a 'contemporary' 'Indian' building. In the process, stereotype images are evoked which mimic the look of tradition but can never satisfy its truth as the crisis of its present are not included in the framework.

Keeping this in mind, I would like to urge Charles Correa to shift his attention from the image of the past to its urgent living present.

Nic Coetzer

The Production of the City as a White Space: Representing and Restructuring Identity and Architecture, Cape Town, 1892–1936 (PhD)

Coetzer's doctoral dissertation explores how English values, architects and architectural ideas played a major role in shaping identities, architecture and power relations in Cape Town between 1892 and 1936. Driven by an uncompromising belief in the universal desirability of Englishness and Western architecture and culture, they manifested a tension between a romanticised, historical, rural ideal, and an urban dystopia, the compromised resolution of which lay in suburban housing schemes. Ranging across discourse, images, public events, built space and buildings, the dissertation investigates notions of preservation, national identity, land possession, civilisation, the city, socio-cultural conditions, race and colonialism, and architectural materiality and aesthetics. The depth and detail of empirical research is thus matched by an intensity and breadth of interpretation, as befits a comprehensive historical PhD study.

ORIGINAL CONTENTS

Table of Figures
Acknowledgements
Preface
Abbreviations
Introduction

The Issue
The Existing Field
Areas of Focus, Methodology, Archival Sources0
Introduction and Overview of Part One
Introduction and Overview of Part Two
Introduction and Overview of Part Three
Conclusion and Beginning

PART ONE: THE HISTORICISED COUNTRYSIDE AND THE VALORISED SELF

1 A Common Heritage/An Appropriated History: Cape Dutch Preservation and Revival Movements and the Restructuring and Representation of a Common English/Afrikaner Identity

Introduction
Background
Cecil Rhodes, Herbert Baker and Groote Schuur
The Closer Union Society: Cape Dutch Architecture as a 'Common Heritage'
Conflated Histories: Writing Commonalities between Afrikaner and English
The South African National Society: Representing A National History in Monuments
Groot Constantia and Other Wilful and Spurious Restorations
Promotion and Dissemination of Cape Dutch as a National Style
Slavish Copyists: Mapping the Cape Dutch Gables
Official Buildings and the Cape Dutch Style
Waning Enthusiasm
Conclusion

2 Markers of Western Civilisation: Cape Dutch Homesteads and the Absence of "Others"

Introduction
Graham Botha and the Popularising of Settler History
Markers of Civilisation and "Great" Men
"Civilised European Races," and their "Superlative" Architects and Architecture
The Mud and Earth of the Vernacular
Here: the Future in the Past/Cape Dutch as Integral to the Landscape
'Barbarians' & the Absence of Others
Architectural Fetishism, Disembodied Images, and 'Beauty'
Conclusion

3 Possessing the Land/Possessing the History: Cape Dutch Country Houses and the Empire's New Landed Gentry

Introduction
Romantic Portrayals: Cape Dutch as Manor House, Country House and Home
The Past in the Present: Rhodes and the English Possession of Dutch History
Cecil Rhodes, Herbert Baker and Groote Schuur
Literal Possessions: Stewards of the City as Landed Gentry
Invented Possessions: Stewards of the City as Landed Gentry
Conclusion

PART TWO: THE CITY AND THE ALLOCATION OF OTHERNESS

4 The City as a Visual Problematic: Town Planning, Tourism, "Unsightliness" and Slums

5 Ascribing Otherness and the Threat to the Self: Representations of Slums and the Social Space of Others

PART THREE: THE SUBURBS AND THE NEUTERED SAME

6 Models of the Self: Englishness, Environmental Determinism, The Garden City Movement, and "Model" Cottages

Environmental Determinism and Instrumentality
The Garden City Movement in Cape Town
Competitions, Exhibitions, Models and the "Supra-Real"
Conclusion

7 Boundaries to the Self and Other: Legal Restrictions, The Development of Restructuring Institutions, and Non-Project-specific Restructuring

Introduction
Early Statutes and Regulations, City Council Committees, & Restructuring
'Temporary' Buildings, Corrugated Iron Areas and Rural Ideals
Compromises to the Building Regulations and Rural Ideals
Density: Municipal Structuring of Class and the Villa and Cottage as ideal
State Structuring: The Public Health Act and the Slums Act
Housing legislation and the Assisted Housing Schemes
Conclusion

8 The Specific Restructuring of Other as Same: Inner-City & Suburban Projects, The Location as a White Space

Introduction
The Anti-urban projects: Wells Square Clearance, MGV, Roeland Street Scheme
Municipal Control and the Structuring of the Self
Early 'Native' Statutes and Legislation and the Design for Ndabeni
The Native (Urban Areas) Act
Langa and Pinelands: An Appraisal of Garden City Ideas
Conclusion

Conclusion
Bibliography
Primary Archival Sources
Primary Printed Sources
Primary Published Sources
Secondary Unpublished Sources – Academic Texts
Secondary Published Sources – Books
Secondary Published Sources – Journals
Appendix A: Who's Who
Appendix B: South African National Society, 1923
Appendix C: Koopmans-de-Wet, Special Committee, 1913
Appendix D: List of Photographs, Empire Exhibition, 1924

INTRODUCTION

The Issue

This thesis initially arose out of a seemingly simple question: 'How does architecture (or things architectural), come to be used to promote specific political agendas and ideological values?' The 'how' of the question obviously refers to the techniques involved, which include written and graphic representations as well as the material reality of buildings, places and spaces – what I have identified elsewhere as discourse, space and image.[1] For its part 'things architectural' hints that the concern is a broad one, and not just a focus on architect-designed buildings, but includes many aspects of the built environment and issues related to it. The final part of the question continues this broadening not only to include the kind of politics-as-culture of Albert Speer's architectural visions for Hitler,[2] but also the idea of culture-as-politics bubbling under in Gramsci's "hegemony"[3] and Foucault's "productive" power.[4]

A study of Cape Town in these terms, from 1892 to 1936, is fair game, as would be just about any time and place in the world touched by human intervention. Obviously though, Cape Town during this period brings with it a set of peculiar conditions. Firstly, it should be noted that the city (and its architects), was particularly English and English leaning during this phase.[5] English architects, clients, officials and bureaucrats (the stewards of the city),[6] controlled most of the means of representation and economic production, and were thus at the centre of this activity of making politics-as-culture and culture-as-politics. Furthermore, these stewards of the city simply looked to England for most of their architectural ideas. At its most simple then, this thesis *narrates* the ways in which architecture, or things architectural, came to be used to promote the specific political agendas and ideological values of the English at the Cape at the time.

A study of the unofficial journal of the Cape Institute of Architects, the *Architect, Builder & Engineer*, brings to light four issues of the day, namely, the promotion of the preservation and use of the

---

[1]Coetzer, N., 'Building Power. Frank Lloyd Wright and the Structuring of Power Through the Built Environment,' (University of Colorado: Unpublished M.Arch Dissertation, 1996).
[2]Speer, A., *Inside the Third Reich*, (London: Weidenfeld and Nicolson, 1970).
[3]Gramsci, A., *Selections from the Prison Notebooks*, (London: Lawrence & Wishart, 1971).
[4]Rabinow, P., *The Foucault Reader* (New York: Pantheon Books, 1984) p 61.
[5]Bickford-Smith comments that 'To be acceptably English all one had to do was to be White, English speaking, in favour of the Empire and, that ubiquitous Victorian virtue, respectable,' Bickford-Smith, V., *Ethnic Pride and Racial Prejudice in Cape Town* (Johannesburg: Witwatersrand University Press, 1995) p 39.
[6]See Appendix A.

Cape's early colonial architecture – now commonly known as Cape Dutch – as a national style; the use of town planning and other citywide interventions in the appearance and fabric of Cape Town; the presence of "slums" in Old Cape Town; and finally, the need for the "proper" housing of the urban poor, especially "natives" in what were then called "locations". The question that should be asked then, is, why are these issues necessarily to be considered political? Surely, they simply were indicative of the values that the English possessed rather than being motivated by some political agenda. Or, surely they were simply the politically neutral interests of the emerging modernist agenda: better housing, efficient traffic, in short, a well-managed city?

Given that this study concerns Cape Town from 1892 to 1936, it seems that postcolonial theory may provide some answers. The basic concept common to most of the exponents of this complex theory[7] is that the cultural activity of the coloniser is not neutral but an essential part of the process of political domination and continued exploitation. Central to this culture-as-politics are processes aimed at representing and restructuring the identity of the coloniser and the colonised such that the "self" (in this case the English stewards of the city) finds confirmation of "his" supremacy through representing the colonised as not being similar in culture and society or in any other way, to "himself". In short, the "English gentleman" sees himself as an "English gentleman" by not being a "barbarian". This conveniently hierarchical opposition between the "self" and "his" constructed Other has the effect of justifying the often-brutal subjugation and exploitation of the indigenous population. Yet the coloniser's unshakeable self-belief, or rather, belief in the Self (White, English and *cultured*), sets up a series of moves that attempts to render "the other" as "same". It is precisely at the point when the colonised begins to take on the traits and foibles of the coloniser, only, in a half-complete manner, that the convenient hierarchies central to colonisation start to unravel – not only is the destabilising hybridity that emerges impossible to manage and define, but the coloniser also sees the tenuous nature of his being in the disfigured representation of himself that "the other" as "same" presents. Here the coloniser sees, at last, the truth of the destructive rapacity of colonisation and attempts to resolve the contradictions of

---

[7]For the pioneers and main exponents of postcolonial theory see, Fanon, F., *Black Skin, White Masks* (London: Pluto Press, 1986); Said, E. W., *Culture and Imperialism* (London: Chatto & Windus, 1993); Said, E. W., *Orientalism. Western Conceptions of the Orient* (London: Penguin Books, 1995); Spivak, G., *In Other Worlds. Essays in Cultural Politics* (New York: Methuen, 1987); Bhabha, H., *The Location of Culture* (London: Routledge, 1994). For a summary see, Young, R., *White Mythologies. Writing History and the West* (London: Routledge, 1990).

colonisation be removing the presence of hybrid-Otherness. In short, the visible disorder of hybridity must be made to disappear and the hierarchical order of Self and Other be maintained.

Yet the issues of identity in South Africa were far more complex than a simple polarity between the English as "self" and "Native" as "other" would allow. There was a hierarchy of Otherness that ranged from Afrikaans to Greek, Portuguese, Jewish, and other "dark" Europeans being closest to the idea of Englishness, followed by the predominantly Muslim "Malays", the creole "Coloureds", and Indians, whilst "Natives" were considered so distant as to instigate a debate as to whether or not "civilising" "them" was a plausible undertaking. Natives were further categorised as Christian "married Natives", or the "better class of Natives" as compared to the "migrant worker" or "raw kafir". Thus, the capitalised word "Other", as used in this thesis, mostly refers to all those who would have been considered non-English or "different" to the middle-class English who were so dominant in Cape Town during the period of study. In a similar manner the use of the words "Otherness" or "Other-spaces", refer to a generalised condition that was contrary to an English ideal. Those familiar with South Africa's racist history will be aware of how problematic some of the names of the groups listed above are. I have chosen to retain these names in this thesis, obviously not because I condone their use, but because they indicate the racial and ethnic identities that were being constructed, and largely given, by the English to these Others during the period of study. Furthermore, direct quotations contain original terms, some of which are offensive and illegal under recent South African legislation.[8]

Taking postcolonial theory into account suggests that this thesis cannot simply *narrate* the ways in which architecture, or things architectural, came to be used to promote the specific political agendas and ideological values of the English at the Cape at the time. It necessarily needs to interpret these events as largely the culture-as-politics of the British Empire and Englishness that, through the representing and restructuring of identity, had the continued dominance and exploitation of South Africa as its goal or effect. Put in its most simple form, the Cape Dutch preservation and revival movement was used to represent and restructure a valorised Self and legitimise the possession of the land whilst simultaneously dispossessing Others of History; the slums and town planning considerations were part of the representation of Otherness and allowed their dispossession from the fluid opportunities of the city; and finally the rehousing programmes can be seen as an attempt to restructure the Other as Same whilst removing the signs of hybridity.

---

[8]Act 4, 2000 (Promotion of Equality and Prevention of Unfair Discrimination Act).

This thesis thus has two aims, namely to find "evidence" of the values of Englishness at work in the issues of the day, and to interpret the architectural representations and restructuring arising from these as part of the culture-as-politics motives of the coloniser (as defined through postcolonial theory).

But what were the ideological values of the English at the Cape at the time? Or rather, what defined Englishness? Obviously, the following eight chapters will find "evidence" of these characteristics, but I would like to briefly introduce, in the broadest terms, the cultural context that dominated much of the discourse at the Cape. For the middle class, Western civilisation was the apotheosis of human achievement, and England, its Empire and its middle class was the natural conclusion to this Hegelian sense of history that had begun with the Greeks. In short, the middle class believed in the supremacy of the cultural artefacts and ideas of Western civilisation and became the promoters and warders of these at an almost religious level. Indeed, John Ruskin's conflation of art and religion in his writing perhaps reflected the loss of Christianity's omnipotence. For William Morris art, or Culture with a capital "C", *was* the new missionary work to be undertaken; whilst class "upliftment" did have a concern with material conditions it was also largely driven by the naïve belief that if the working classes could just see the beauty in art, the troubles of the world would disappear. Or, as a corollary, if material ugliness could be removed from the world a "fuller" life – the only life worth living – would be had. Of course Morris can be noted for his anarchist and socialist leanings, but the Romantic undercurrent in his ideas also located this "fuller" life as only plausibly flourishing in a rural ideal. Even town planning, a practice so seemingly technicist and modernist to us today, had its partial roots in visions of an aesthetic and bucolic Medieval past as promoted by Raymond Unwin and the Garden City Movement. Englishness was thus a peculiar mix that valued the "high" art of Western civilisation, and the Romantic imagery of picturesque English villages. This then, is the White supremacy that I would like to suggest was the context of the Cape; not just the theories of racial superiority given via blood, but a belief in Englishness (having as it did the Culture of Western civilisation as its dominant legitimising force) as the only "proper" way to be in the world.

CHAPTER THREE: POSSESSING THE LAND/POSSESSING THE HISTORY: CAPE DUTCH COUNTRY HOUSES AND THE EMPIRE'S NEW LANDED GENTRY

> *As I sit and sip 'Schoongezicht,' the thought comes – is it not possible that the released component elements of long dead and gone occupants, duly absorbed by the soil and*

reabsorbed by the vines, may pass into the wine of the country, such is this excellent Heritage, and assume within ourselves fresh life and shape? Why should not the personalities of the departed live again in our wine, as their intellects may be said to in the architecture bequeathed to us, such as we have been enjoying to-day.[9]

F. Masey, 'The Beginnings of our Nation.'

Introduction

In the first part of the twentieth century, a number of politicians playing a dominant role in South Africa's wealth and future, either bought existing Cape Dutch homesteads, or had versions thereof built. Chapter One laid out how the need for a common English/Afrikaner identity gave a nationalist focus to the building preservation movement, which may partly explain the sudden interest in Cape Dutch homesteads by these politically active individuals. Furthermore, events in England may also shed some light on the phenomenon: the *nouveau riche*, for reasons of status, had begun to purchase, build and occupy country houses in a grand manner.[10] Certainly this forms part of the analysis undertaken here, and, one could argue that Cecil Rhodes started a *nouveau riche* Cape Dutch buying craze when he bought a few homesteads in the 1890s, ostensibly to start his fruit farming enterprise.[11] However, there are another two distinct considerations, related in some way to the issues raised in the previous two chapters that need their own further differentiation. This chapter first investigates the discourse supporting the notion that Cape Dutch homesteads were manor houses whose social relations and social space were considered a reflection and model for South Africa's emerging racial order. This idea of the justification of the present through the past is the basis of my interpretation of the design in 1892 for Rhodes's new house Groote Schuur that symbolically legitimised the project of Empire as the continuation of South Africa's early history. The second part of this chapter uses the findings of this discourse analysis and Rhodes's motives as the basis for an interpretation of the literal and symbolic possession of Cape Dutch homesteads by some of the country's elite and politicians.

---

[9][Mag]*The State*, v.1, n.6 (June 1909) p 657.
[10]Stamp, G., *Edwin Lutyens. Country Houses from the Archives of Country Life* (London: Arum Press, 2001) pp 14–18.
[11]Baker, H., *Cecil Rhodes*, p 64.

Romantic Portrayals: Cape Dutch as Manor House, Country House and Home

Central to the production of the discourse around Cape Dutch architecture was the romanticising of the period, particularly through the imagining of the homesteads as manor houses inhabited by settler versions of the English landed gentry. As we saw in the previous chapter, the early settler period was often portrayed as a dangerous time during which "civilisation" triumphed over "barbarism". However, there was also a tendency to imagine that time as a period of idyll. Both these stances were used to valorise the "miraculous" production of the Cape Dutch homestead as manor house. Consider Prime Minister J.C. Smuts' preface to Dorothea Fairbridge's *Historic Houses of South Africa*:

> *It is evident that this noble architecture could only have arisen in times of comparative quiet and leisure. And of this there must have been plenty in the secluded sun-filled valleys of the Cape in those far-off times.*[12]

The leisured class that constituted the English landed-gentry seems to be lurking in the background of Smuts' understanding of the social conditions at the time of the production of the Cape Dutch homesteads. Alys Trotter's *Old Cape Colony* echoed Smuts' sense of the period being one of idyll. She depicts the arrival of Willem Adriaan van der Stel in 1699 to, as she imagines it, the Cape as a paradise:

> *White walled farms gleamed with their enclosures on the distant mountains, young oak trees were everywhere planted; vineyards and gardens, vital with the wonderful vitality of virgin soil made the peninsula a paradise in the eyes of the tired seafarers.*[13]

The 'paradise' being depicted was characterised as being distinctly European in appearance and highly romanticised. The Van der Stels – Simon as Governor of the Cape from 1679 until his son Willem Adriaan assumed control in 1699 until 1708 – were the two individuals who received the greatest overlay of romanticism by the early historians, in a process verging on adulation. Certainly, Willem Adriaan was not everyone's firm favourite, thanks to his somewhat heavy-handed exploitation of the settlers during his office and his dubious accumulation of wealth represented by his large homestead of Vergelegen. His twentieth-century apologists argued his case around the thesis that he was a highly civilised and cultured individual who

---

[12]Fairbridge, D., *The Historic Houses of South Africa*, p ix.
[13]Trotter, A. F., *Old Cape Colony*, p 96.

should be venerated whatever his supposed ill-doing to those under his control. Alys Trotter understood the paradox that Willem Adriaan's case presented to the twentieth-century production of discourse around Cape Dutch architecture: Vergelegen, so it seemed at the time, was the very building that, along with Groot Constantia, was the template by which all other homesteads were developed, and yet was the physical object that galvanised a mini-revolution at the Cape leading to the departure of the "great man". She writes the following of Vergelegen: 'It is sad and curious to reflect that had this house never been built, the clever Van der Stel family might still be represented in South Africa.'[14] The extension of this scenario was (had this been the case) that Cape Dutch homesteads would not have existed. Even after it was discovered that the gabled Groot Constantia was not the original form of the homestead of Simon Van der Stel, it did not preclude the continued romanticising of the man through the place and *vice versa*. An example of this can be found in a 1931 edition of *The Cape*:

> *[Groot Constantia] is not as originally built by Van der Stel [...]*
> *Yet, whether you visit Groot Constantia when big purple and*
> *red clusters are still hanging, or perhaps in late autumn, when*
> *the leaves of the grape vines are yellow and crimson, or when*
> *the pale, fresh green of spring weaves a fairylike enchant-*
> *ment, there is always an appearance of ancient grandeur*
> *about the place.*[15]

Along with the implicit romantic images such as these of the Cape Dutch homesteads and their occupants, there is evidence of their literal representation as manor houses. Consider, for example the speech of the Administrator of the Cape at the Opening ceremony of the restored Groot Constantia:

> *What is it that makes Groot Constantia a precious heritage to*
> *us to-day? It is the association of the homestead with the*
> *name of Simon van der Stel, one of the greatest names of all*
> *times in South African history [...] I have now very much*
> *pleasure in declaring the restored manor house of Groot*
> *Constantia open.*[16] *[emphasis added].*

Trotter's Christmas article in the *Cape Times* suggested that 'the populous and busy modern South Africa of the future will make pilgrimage to the Old Homesteads of the Western Province as Americans make pilgrimage to-day to the old Manor Houses of England'.[17] This

---

[14][News]*CT* 1898.12.25: 'Old Cape Homesteads'.
[15][News]*The Cape*, 1931.04.10: 'The Constantia Valley.'
[16][News]*CT* 1927.09.22: 'Groot Constantia.'
[17][News]*CT* 1898.12.25: 'Old Cape Homesteads.'

vision of the Cape Dutch homestead as a manor house was suggested through the use of other words. Consider, for example the following excerpt from the editorial of the *AB&E* describing the adaptation of European society to local conditions by the settlers: 'The free worker of the Lowlands of Europe was replaced by the coloured *serf* of the Cape'[18] [Emphasis added]. These verbal references then, have the effect of establishing Cape Dutch homesteads within the traditions of a European landed gentry.

Not only were Cape Dutch homesteads imagined as manor houses, but were also imagined as places where the values of a "home-life" had been a priority. The nuclear family was pictured as part of the general romantic assembly of the settlers' manor houses. It is worth quoting an excerpt from the following article which appeared in the *Cape Times* in 1931 under the pseudonym 'Progress,' concerning the reconstruction of the homestead Bien Donne following the damage done to it by a fire. The full title of the article is 'Old Cape Homestead Restored. A Genuine Echo of the 17th Century. "Bien Donne" reconstructed on original plans':

> *Here, far from the country of their birth, they raised as enduring monuments to their industry, courage, faith and culture, those glowing jewels of architectural beauty that remind us, in the hectic rush of twentieth century life, of the days when the home was the centre of human endeavour, and reflected the thoughts, aspirations and culture of an age of gracious courtliness [...] But of Bien Donne, the well given, it may be written that, lacking the place in history that Van der Stel's homestead occupies, it is yet nearer to the heart of the people, because it idealised the people's home of that period [...] None who pass that way can fail to visualise those stirring adventurous days – when the labour and joy of creation was centred in the Home Beautiful, and the years passed lightly in the pleasant valley of the Huguenots.[19]*

Bien Donne and other homesteads similar to it are thus presented as potential templates for the middle class of the increasingly conflict-ridden twentieth century. It is 'nearer to the heart of the people' because it is less ostentatious than Simon van der Stel's Groot Constantia but still provides a model for 'the Home Beautiful'. House museums such as Koopmans-de-Wet, which had been instituted to preserve 'the fast-disappearing emblems of the home-life of the people, for future generations',[20] were part of this valorising of the past

---

[18][Mag]*AB&E*, v.17, n.6 (January, 1934) p 7.
[19][News]*CT* 1931.06.09: 'Old Cape Homestead Restored.'
[20]Finch, J. R., *The Cape of Good Hope. Being the Official Handbook of the City of Capetown* (Cape Town: City of Capetown, 1926) p 28.

life of the early settlers. An article titled 'Our Old Houses' contains this idea of domestic tradition, and thence didactic importance of the preservation of Cape Dutch homesteads:

> *The nation that despises its traditions must lose its soul. If we are not called upon to sacrifice our lives in defence of the ashes of our fathers and the temples of our gods it would appear to be at least reasonable that we expend thought and care and cash upon the preservation of the worthy hearths and homes of our forebears.*[21]

[*Masthead of Die Huisgenoot (The Home-Enjoyment), illustrates a Cape Dutch homestead as exemplifying the Home Beautiful: 'Pa' returning home from work being greeted by two children, 'Ma' at the threshold to the "Home," and perhaps 'Grandpa' on a bench on the front stoep. Source: [Mag] Die Huisgenoot, v.7, n.81 (January, 1923).*]

This idea, that Cape Dutch homesteads, and the idealised lifestyle associated therewith, were being imagined as templates for the twentieth century, brings us to the following section.

The Past in the Present: Rhodes and the English Possession of Dutch History

The stewards of the city saw the past in the present, or rather, the idealised and hierarchical social structures of the Cape Dutch period as models for the twentieth century. Consider the following extract from the December 1920 edition of the *AB&E* article on 'The Need for a South African Architecture' in which the Cape Dutch homestead has provided a model by which South Africans (meaning White South Africans), could live:

> *The high dark room and tree-shaded grounds have become the agreeable retreats of all from the glare of the sun and the aridity of the plains. The 'stoep' has become the outward and visible sign of a love for the open air. The separated outbuildings have afforded appropriate housing for the black and coloured servants. A love of green and white has been engendered by experience gained in sun-swept spaces [...] Out of these and similar expressions of the emotions of memory or the clamant needs of our present life a concrete expression in domestic architecture may most certainly be predicted. It will derive much from the Cape Dutch style.*[22]

---

[21][Mag]*AB&E*, v.15, n.1 (August, 1931) p 7.
[22][Mag]*AB&E*, v.4, n.5 (December, 1920) pp 10–11.

That the separated outbuildings of slave lodges 'afforded appropriate housing for the black and coloured servants' is a statement of fairly astounding hierarchical sentiments. This then is the model for the twentieth century: White masters living a refined and cultured home-loving life whilst the slaves are separated into a one dimensional existence, housed in quarters sustaining their health and maintaining their status, always present but never near, White, but not quite. Indeed, it is exactly this model of housing for Cape Town's "non-White" population that is the focus of Chapters Six and Seven.

Trotter's early article on Cape Dutch homesteads in the *Cape Times* also offers a glimpse at the way stewards of the city saw the past in the present:

> It was here that [Simon Van der Stel] built the well-known country house of Constantia [...] The vines still grow there in the sunshine, for Constantia is a successful wine farm whose labour is carried on by convicts; and the men calling to each other in the quiet of the great heat are picking the purple and golden bunches, much as the old Governor's slaves would have done [...] Constantia is a wonderful place for dreaming.[23]

Solomon's article on the 'The Architecture of South Africa' in 1914 suggests that he saw the 'labourers' (as he called them) as having helped develop the country under the guidance of the settlers and carries on to consider that:

> Here in South Africa it seems to be a legitimate use of our vast native population for the purpose of building roads to traverse our country, and dams and barrages wherewith we might develop schemes of irrigation.[24]

The excerpts from Solomon and Trotter above also point to another aspect of representations of Cape Dutch homesteads that need to be explored. This is the sense of continuity, represented in Trotter's case by the vines (believed to have been planted by Van der Stel), and by the labourers in Solomon's case, in which the past is ready to be possessed and re-enacted by the present. The finding of legitimacy of the present social structure in the valorised past also extended to the idea of individuals and their right to possess artefacts of the past, or simply, to establish a lineage of possession from then till now. Returning to Solomon's article we find the following example of this:

> It required a great personality like Simon van der Stel, who, in the face of tremendous opposition and continual fault-finding

---

[23][News]*CT* 1898.12.25: 'Old Cape Homesteads.'
[24][News]*Transvaal Leader* 1914.02.23: 'Architecture in South Africa.'

on the part of 'The Seventeen' – the name by which the
Company was known in Holland – centred his ideal of life, just
as Cecil Rhodes did in later years, in homes of quiet dignity
and beauty amidst orderly plantations of avenues and
groves.[25]

Solomon's connecting of the venerated Van der Stel to the slightly
more dubious Rhodes would have been a conscious move to give
credence to Rhodes's imperialist vision. There was, however, a far
more literal connection between Rhodes and the "grand" past of the
original Governors at the Cape, and one which he himself enacted.
It is to the design and building of Rhodes's Groote Schuur that we
now turn.

Cecil Rhodes, Herbert Baker and Groote Schuur

I have already noted in the first chapter the symbolic act of concilia-
tion between English and Afrikaner that Rhodes made in his building
of Groote Schuur. But Rhodes' Groote Schuur could also be read in
another way in which Rhodes' gestures towards Cape Dutch architecture were perhaps more founded on visions of Empire rather than
nation. Rhodes, who had attended Balliol College in Oxford, had also
listened attentively to John Ruskin's lectures. Baker identifies this as
the source of Rhodes' imperialist drive and that he was following
Ruskin's suggestion to found colonies for the Empire and teach
England's colonists to 'make England a centre of peace, mistress of
learning and of the arts'.[26] By literally building his new house on the
foundations of one of the first Governor at the Cape's buildings,
Rhodes can be understood to possess that past for himself.
[*Groote Schuur, bronze relief depicting the arrival of Jan van
Riebeeck, and indigenous inhabitants. Source: [UCTimage] BC206.*]
[*Alabaster frieze at South Africa House, London, showing Groote
Schuur at the time of the first settlement of the Cape. Source:
McNab The Story of South Africa House.*]
There were also symbolic acts, one of which was the implementa-
tion of a bronze relief sculpture above the main door of Groote
Schuur showing the arrival of Van Riebeeck at the Cape receiving
supplication from the indigenous population: Rhodes simply *is* Van
Riebeeck, or else, is simply continuing the process of colonisation
that van Riebeeck helped implement. Another symbolic act is illustrated by the fact that he changed the name of what was called The

---

[25][News]*Transvaal Leader* 1914.02.23: 'Architecture in South Africa.'
[26]Baker, H., *Cecil Rhodes*, p 11.

Grange to Groote Schuur, thereby reconnecting the building to its past by using the Dutch words for "Big Barn." In addition, its first use as a grain store is perhaps indicative of his intent to possess the present and the future *development* of South Africa through the past. In a more subtle way, and perhaps through the efforts of Baker and Trotter rather than Rhodes himself, Rhodes's parity with Cape Dutch historical figures is reinforced in *Old Colonial Houses of the Cape of Good Hope*[27] where a photograph of Groote Schuur makes an appearance amongst original Cape Dutch homesteads. Even after his death he was still possessing South Africa through representations in South Africa House in London: Groote Schuur's relief sculpture of Jan van Riebeeck being met by the indigenous inhabitants was recreated for the foyer, whilst an alabaster frieze depicts Rhodes's Groote Schuur being approached anachronistically by original settler ships [*Groote Schuur, bronze relief depicting the arrival of Jan van Riebeeck, and indigenous inhabitants. Source: [UCTimage] BC206.*]

These acts amount to a literal and symbolic possession of history to which Dorothea Fairbridge was well aware. In her *The Historic Houses of South Africa*, she points to Groote Schuur as the re-manifestation of the original Dutch barn, and Rhodes as the descendant of Van Riebeeck:

> But when we stand on the stoep behind Groote Schuur and look out across the blur of colour under the stone pines in the garden – cannas, bougainvillea, and plumbago – across the soft turquoise of the hydrangeas on the hillside and up the silver-clad slopes of the grey mountain, we are only conscious of the two great spirits of the past – the two pioneers – Jan van Riebeeck and Cecil Rhodes. As long as this South Africa of ours endures their names will be linked together in this lovely spot – the corn lands of the one, the home of the other. Even the house reflects the work of both, for underneath the building – the fourth erected on this site – are the foundations of the great barn in which van Riebeeck stored his grain, found by Mr. Herbert Baker in making the necessary excavations.[28]

Through the possession of the past, then, authors such as Fairbridge were aware that individuals such as Rhodes could lay a legitimate claim to the land that had been settled by Europeans more than two centuries before. That this land was not simply South Africa but in fact the whole of Africa to be kept and contained by the Empire, is suggested in this following quote taken from the City of Cape Town's official guide to the Cape from 1909:

---

[27]Trotter, A. F. and Baker, H., *Old Colonial Houses of the Cape of Good Hope*, plate xxxiv.
[28]Fairbridge, D., *The Historic Houses of South Africa*, p 66.

> *Van der Stel was the great pioneer of his day and an enthusi-*
> *astic farmer. His first Colony was named after himself. Two*
> *hundred years later the Pioneer of the North bequeaths his*
> *name to his first settlement – Rhodesia! To-day, in a part of*
> *the former's original colony of Stellenbosch we are to revive*
> *many memories of both, – to renew our acquaintance with the*
> *past and see the developments effected by the industry of*
> *people of English, Dutch and French descent.*[29]

This is not to suggest that Rhodes did not also consider Groote Schuur, in its lavishness and its pretences, as a status symbol, or as a signifier of "nobility". That Rhodes's Groote Schuur had been designed along the lines of a country house was not missed by the author of an article in the *Rand Daily Mail* in 1931, who, in writing on the home of the Prime Minister, reported that it 'has been described as one of the most beautiful country seats to be found anywhere out of England'.[30] Rhodes had started a trend whereby Cape Dutch came to signify status and gentility. In fact, by 1935,[31] C.P. Walgate had taken to describing the existing Cape Dutch homesteads as 'country houses' which indicates the extent to which these once dilapidated working farmhouses had been reinterpreted and purchased by the elite in the 40-odd years since Rhodes's initial endeavours. It hardly seems surprising to read that Edwin Lutyens, long in the service of providing country houses for English clients, offered this advice to architects at the Cape on his visit in 1919:

> *Finally, look to your old homesteads; reverence them and use*
> *them as models intelligently, not copying them without the*
> *understanding that those old Dutchmen were gentlemen.*[32]

This, then, forms the basis for the next two sections: Cape Dutch homesteads, and Cape Dutch revival country houses, as literal and symbolic possession of status and the rightful possession of the land of South Africa in the service of the project of Empire.

Literal Possessions: Stewards of the City as Landed Gentry

Along with Simon van der Stel's Groot Constantia, Willem Adriaan van der Stel's Vergelegen emerged as one of the most highly venerated Cape Dutch homesteads. It is not surprising then, that Vergelegen became the object of possession when it was purchased

---

[29]Finch, J. R., *The Cape of Good Hope*, p 55.
[30][News]*Rand Daily Mail* 1931.05.30: 'Permanent Home of the Premiers.'
[31][Mag]*AB&E*, v.19, n.2 (September, 1935) p 7.
[32][Mag]*AB&E*, v.2, n.10 (May, 1919) p 15.

from Samuel Kerr in 1917 by the Johannesburg mining-magnate Lionel Phillips, thanks to the efforts of his wife Florence.[33] This following section considers the event of the purchase and "restoration" of Vergelegen southwest of Stellenbosch, as well as the Cape Dutch homestead of Lanzerac, east of Stellenbosch. Also under consideration is the extent to which a number of highly influential people – mostly politicians – were involved in possessing Cape Dutch homesteads during the period of study.

With thoughts of retirement, the erstwhile President of the Chamber of Mines, Lionel Phillips, under pressure from his wife Florence, chose to purchase the Cape Dutch homestead of Vergelegen near Somerset West in 1917. Although it is plausible to consider that, perhaps like some people nearing retirement, a place in the country was an obvious choice, and whilst it is important to acknowledge that Vergelegen was subsequently turned into a productive and profitable farm which may have been part of the initial plan, there is enough evidence to suggest that the Phillips had other very specific reasons for purchasing Vergelegen. These, I would like to argue, were fundamentally linked to notions of Englishness, the general ending of the uprightness of the project of Empire in the period after WWI, and the emerging threat of urbanity, democracy and modernism to the existing class- and race-based social order.

Vergelegen, as has already been mentioned above, was the original but partly modified homestead of Willem Adriaan van der Stel, son of Simon van der Stel and governor of the Cape from 1699 to 1708. That the homestead, along with Groot Constantia, had been represented during the first few decades of the twentieth century as an almost mythical exemplar of a country or manor house has also been considered. It was none other than Florence Phillips' good friend, Dorothea Fairbridge, who was at the forefront of this adoration, defending the name of Adriaan and rewriting the history of his exile. At the time, England's country estates were being represented, through institutions such as the National Trust, as part of an idyllic and ideal rural past. In fact, Lionel Phillips had purchased Tylney estate outside of Reading in 1898. That Phillips was willing to sell Arcadia, the elaborate house Herbert Baker had designed for him, and move from an increasingly urban Johannesburg to rural Vergelegen should also not go unmentioned. Vergelegen required extensive and expensive alterations and additions to make it "habitable" which suggests that its purchase was motivated more by ideological reasons rather than utilitarian or economic ones. It seems very likely, then, that the Phillips' purchased the estate for the

---

[33]Gutsche, T., *No Ordinary Woman. The Life and Times of Florence Phillips* (Cape Town: Howard Timmins, 1966) p 342.

ready-made identity that its originator, and the building itself, represented to them. Exactly what this identity was is fairly complex and needs to be mapped out below.

During the late nineteenth and early twentieth centuries, the rural past of England was beginning to be revered by proponents of the Arts & Crafts movement as an idyllic and ideal condition to be returned to. Not only did the rural unpolluted landscape offer the promise of relief from industrial cities such as Manchester, but others have suggested that the hierarchical world of the past that it represented offered a sense of order to those whose class-values were being confronted in the urban chaos of cities such as London.[34] The revering of the "landed gentry", although not in keeping with William Morris's egalitarian and socialist visions, emerged at the end of the nineteenth century as a particularly English undertaking, through which much emphasis was placed on the landed gentry representing the value of culture, learning, refinement and history.[35] Thanks to the efforts of Florence Phillips' friend Dorothea Fairbridge and others, Adriaan Van der Stel would easily have fitted the concept at the time of a country gentleman and Vergelegen itself would have matched the representation as a country house with its fine gables, symmetry and large garden, whilst simultaneously fitting in with the less ostentatious emerging aesthetic of the Arts & Crafts movement. Possessing Vergelegen would have been an opportunity for the Phillips' to assert their desired class-values and literally remove themselves from the democratic messiness of the city.

Vergelegen and Van der Stel may, however, have had a stronger and more personal resonance with the Phillips's. There are a series of parallels between the lives of the Phillips and Van der Stel that need to be exposed. Firstly, if Van Riebeeck was acclaimed as the symbol of the first permanent White settlers in South Africa, and Simon van der Stel as the bringer of colonists, then Adriaan was represented by authors such as Dorothea Fairbridge as the first entrepreneur and agriculturalist. In essence Adriaan was a developer who "opened up" the country with his agricultural almanac and colonisation of the interior for development.[36] Lionel Phillips, a man who had been at the forefront of the development of the mining industry in South Africa, would quite possibly have seen himself as some kind of spiritual descendent of Van der Stel. Florence Phillips, as an avid farmer, modelled herself on Adriaan's achievements in

---

[34]Hawkins, A., 'The Discovery of Rural England,' in Colls, R. and Dodd, P. (eds), *Englishness. Politics and Culture, 1880–1920* (London: Croom Helm, 1986).

[35]Meacham, S., *Regaining Paradise. Englishness and the Early Garden City Movement* (New Haven: Yale University Press, 1999) p 9.

[36]Fairbridge, D., *Historic Farms of South Africa. The Wool, the Wheat, the Wine of the 17th and 18th Centuries* (London: Oxford University Press, 1931).

Current front façade of Vergelegen, Somerset West. Source: Author.

this sphere. Much was made in discourse around Adriaan and Simon van der Stel of their hospitality and the focus of the political world around both Vergelegen and Groot Constantia. The potential for the Phillips to re-enact those early "grand" days of the Van der Stel period may have suggested itself to the Phillips when considering Vergelegen as a retirement home. Florence Phillips' biographer, Thelma Gutsche notes of the Sunday lunches held at Vergelegen:

> The Prime Minister, the Admiral, the Archbishop, members of Parliament, distinguished overseas visitors (it was said of the Phillips that "they knew everyone" and were correspondingly influential), professors, artists, editors, scientists, writers, would find themselves at the same table and exposed to her uninhibited outbursts.[37]

Even the Governor-General and Princess Alice (the Athlones) were often visitors to Vergelegen.[38]

This is not to suggest that the Phillips' identified with Van der Stel as a Dutchman. The possession of Vergelegen was not in any way part of the general English/Afrikaner reconciliation others such as J.C. Smuts had attempted to engineer through Cape Dutch architecture. In fact, Florence Phillips had no qualms about discrediting Afrikaans and Dutch history in the development of South Africa, preferring to locate its importance with the English.[39] As a true believer in bolstering the supporters of the Empire in South Africa, Florence Phillips even campaigned for new immigration from England upon the centenary celebration of the 1820 English settlers through the

---

[37]Gutsche, T., *No Ordinary Woman*, p 365.
[38]*Ibid.*, p 376.
[39]*Ibid.*, p 376 and 390.

1820 Association.[40] Rather than simulating any reconciliation between the English and Afrikaner, the Phillips' were occupying the space of the image created of Van der Stel as being a fine and civilised gentleman living in a fine manor house – a particularly Romantic and English image of the life of the landed gentry of the eighteenth century. In fact, I would go so far as to suggest that Van der Stel was never particularly Dutch, and Somerset West and the Cape Peninsula was more part of the English landscape than South African – to those purchasing the homesteads at any rate.

Purchasing Vergelegen and "restoring" it must be understood as part of the general stewardship that the English at the Cape felt was a necessary protection of History itself – here I mean the concept of Western civilisation, which the English understood to be the sole constituent of History. For individuals such as the Phillips, the English were, in South Africa, the natural heirs and conclusion to a story of Western civilisation begun in the time of Van der Stel and left incomplete by the "boorish Boers" who had had him exiled; the Afrikaners in their part could not carry the task as the general impression at the time was that they had lost their "civilisation" when they went off into the wilderness that was the Great Trek in the late 1830s. This gives credence to the suggestion that the English – even one born in South Africa as Florence Phillips was – were claiming the early settler past as their own through a moral necessity. The purchase, "restoration" and living in of Vergelegen was more than an act of possession of grandeur and status; it was the restitution and securing of "European civilisation" as tautology, the very definition of civilisation itself. The self-assured cultural chauvinism that saw Western civilisation as essential to all humankind was a fundamental part of the narrative of legitimacy of the project of Empire in a period of increasing threats to the seemingly indubitable veracity of the project itself.

Another example of Vergelegen's symbolic power in the services of Empire is to be found in the City of Cape Town's reaction to the arrival of the Prince of Wales on an official visit in 1925. As has been mentioned in the previous chapter, the Prince was taken on a motorcar tour of Cape Dutch homesteads in and around the Peninsula. As part of the gifts given to him on his departure, the Prince was to receive a photograph album of amongst other things, Cape Dutch homesteads.[41] This photograph album was to bear the coat of arms of the Van der Stels, as well as have its cover made from wood from the Camphor trees Willem Adriaan Van der Stel had planted at Vergelegen some 225 years previously. The future

---

[40]*Ibid.*, p 354.
[41][News]*CT* 1925.02.20: 'The Prince's Visit.'

C.P. Walgate's side addition to Vergelegen showing front façade of main house to the right. Source: Author.

C.P. Walgate's side addition to Vergelegen, showing pond. Source: Author.

king of England not only possessed images of the grand past of part of the Empire, but literally possessed that past as future through his proxy possession of Vergelegen as symbolised through the camphor-tree photo-album.

But what of the restoration itself? The task of the restoration fell to J.M. Solomon, a protégé of Bakers, who was being extended beyond his capacity in the design of the new campus for the University of Cape Town. At Solomon's request, Baker sent Percy Walgate, who he had in Delhi, to work on Vergelegen. When Solomon committed suicide, Walgate had full responsibility for the design and restoration even though his knowledge of Cape Dutch architecture was limited. Florence Phillips had sponsored Fairbridge's *Historic Houses* and she was a source of instruction for Walgate. Despite this, the work Walgate achieved was, like so much of the "restoration" of the time, a rather less than sensitive intervention. The back gable was torn down and replaced by one copied from the old church at Paarl.[42] Contrary to Gutsche's findings that Walgate used 'authentic joinery' and metalwork 'to conform to early Dutch patterns',[43] the whole design was clearly driven by Arts & Crafts sentiments. The two courtyards and the hipped-roof side-wings with their fountains and reflecting ponds beyond, the planting of cypress trees, and the inserts and detailing on the shutters,[44] all point to the workings of an Arts & Crafts architect not thoroughly familiar with Cape Dutch nuances and operating through current European considerations.

Contemporary to the Phillips' restoration and a fairly short distance away, Elizabeth Katherina English, the wife of a mining pioneer,[45] bought the Cape Dutch homestead, Schoongezicht (Lanzerac) from J.H. Wicht in 1914.[46] In 1920, Kendall and Morris were commissioned to provide a series of options for extension of the old Cape Dutch homestead with the work being undertaken in 1921. Minor work included the addition of chimneys, new doors and *stoep* to the southwest, and the replacement of the screen between the hall and what became the dining room. The majority of the work eventually involved adding two new rooms at each end of the front façade, adding a new kitchen and bedroom/bathroom placed symmetrically about a new courtyard at the back, and the addition of servants' rooms and guests' rooms in the attic. The somewhat extensive changes in space, form and function that resulted may suggest that Kendall and Morris were less than committed in their historical sensitivity and in their work with the SANS. Kendall and Morris would later insist that old Cape Dutch dwellings could and should be altered to include the conveniences and comfort expected of a modern home[47] thereby making them even more desirable possessions.

[*Kendall & Morris's alteration to Schoongezicht (Lanzerac), Stellenbosch, including the symmetrical addition of a study and bedroom bay to the front and a bedroom and kitchen at the back, and attic bedrooms for guests and servants. Source: Lanzerac Auction Catalogue, 1934.*]

[*Kendall & Morris's 1921 addition to Schoongezicht (Lanzerac) changed the proportion of the front façade through the addition of a bay at each end. Source: Author.*]

---

[42]Gutsche, T., *No Ordinary Woman*, p 362.

[43]*Ibid.*, p 368.

[44]I am grateful to John Rennie, the architect of a recent restoration of Vergelegen, for pointing this out.

[45]Gutsche, T., *No Ordinary Woman*, p 374.

[46]Unauthored Fact Sheet from Lanzerac Hotel.

[47][News]*CA* 1925.03.28: 'Part of Old Wynberg: An Experiment in Restoration.'

An article was written in the *Natal Mercury* by L. Cumming-George concerning the recent alterations and additions to the Cape Dutch homestead of Parel Vallei originally owned by exiled Frans van der Stel, son of Simon van der Stel. In commenting on the project designed by C.P. Walgate for James Head, the article adds an almost teleological necessity to the idea of bettering the building by insisting that the modern kitchen brings the building 'no doubt nearer to-day [to] that which Van der Stel dreamed when he planned and which he regretfully and reluctantly had to abandon'.[48] The sense of completing the project of the past is a theme that was noted above as an interpretation of the Phillips' purchase of Vergelegen.

It was quite clear that extensive alterations done sensitively for a worthy client – a steward such as Elizabeth English and her house at Lanzerac – was far more desirable than having the buildings grow derelict through abandonment or, worse, having them disfigured through the boorish, corrugated-iron additions made by farmers themselves. Furthermore, what seems to be a rather excessive and irreverent alteration and addition was in all likelihood not viewed that way by Morris and Kendall and their contemporaries. The Cape Dutch homestead was represented as part of an Arts & Crafts genre, and in that sense the additions were simply an extension of a pre-existing fabric that resonated with the dominant stylistic and ideological architectural movement in the Cape and Britain at the time. The new elements such as the "leg-of mutton" dormer window to the maids' rooms literally creeps into the very fabric of the old building. Possessing the original through additions such as this was an important part of the possession of the land through the object.
[*Kendall & Morris addition to Schoongezicht (Lanzerac) showing servant's window at eaves. Source: [UCTimage] BC206.*]

48[News]*Natal Mercury* 1930.05.16: 'Fine Old Architecture of the Cape.'

It is, however, important to note that Lanzerac was not in any way seen as a simple Arts & Crafts cottage; it was more correctly imagined as a modest country house with seven bedrooms, three maids' rooms, a study, a drawing room, large hall and living room, a morning room and kitchen area. It is interesting to note the extent to which typical Edwardian concerns for separating servants (and those they served) through space had on the design. Thanks to the late addition of attic guest-rooms to the programme towards the end of construction, Morris insisted on adding another staircase to avoid 'young men having to go from the Bed Rooms to the Bath Room' past the maids' rooms.[49] This decision effectively led to the addition of a two new bays to each end of the front façade instead of the low minor additions originally planned, and thereby bringing a radical change in the front proportions of the building. Whilst some may argue – despite the general ideological climate at the time – that Elizabeth English quite simply wanted to "farm grapes and make wine" there is a simple detail designed presumably by Morris that suggests that her intentions, or her architects intentions for her, were more grandiose. An eight-sided star inlayed into the panel above the new fireplace in the dining room suggests she was marking herself with the Van der Stels' emblem.

[*Kendall & Morris alteration to Schoongezicht (Luncarty) showing design for fireplace with star perhaps symbolic of Van der Stel. Source: [UCTbox] BC206, 90.*]

As has been mentioned above, Rhodes, through his purchase and rebuilding of what became Groote Schuur, lay possession to a settler past. Rhodes also set about purchasing a number of Cape Dutch homesteads including Nooitgedacht, Good Hope, Boschendal, Rhone, Lekkerwyn, Weltevreden, Vredenburg, and Bien Donne, in and around the Simonsberg and Drakenstein Mountains in order to establish his envisioned fruit-farm empire.[50] Apart from the few politicians who had ancestral claims to the Cape Dutch homesteads they occupied during the period of study – such as "Onze Jan" Hofmeyr at Welgemeend – Rhodes seemed to have sparked a purchasing craze of Cape Dutch homesteads in and around Cape Town by the city's elite. John X. Merriman, Prime Minister of the Cape from 1908 until Union, was the owner of the Cape Dutch Homestead Schoongezicht in Stellenbosch at least during the period 1900 – 1910.[51] J.W. Sauer, who held the cabinet post of Native Affairs and

[49][UCT]BC206, 90: 1921.10.21, Letter from Morris to Devenish.
[50]Baker, H., *Cecil Rhodes*, pp 243–4.
[51]Merriman was also the first Chairman of the Van Riebeeck Society, which published out of print historical documents, see Fouche, L., *The Diary of Adam Tas, 1705–1706* (Cape Town: Van Riebeeck Society, 1970).

introduced the Land Bill leading to the racially segregationist and disempowering Land Act of 1913,[52] was the owner of Uitkyk, north of Stellenbosch. Richard Stuttaford, who, as a member of parliament in 1919, motivated for and partly financed Pinelands Garden City – "South Africa's first Garden City" as the saying goes – following a visit to Letchworth in England with Raymond Unwin in 1917, also commissioned Baker in the Cape Dutch inspired design of his house Lidcote in Kenilworth in 1904.[53] Some 20 years later Stuttaford went on to purchase the old Cape Dutch homestead of Rustenburg east of Stellenbosch whereupon Morris was involved with some restoration work.[54] The man from whom Stuttaford purchased Rustenburg, was Lord Percy De Villiers, the first president of the SANS.

[*Baker & Kendall, addition to Lidcote, Cape Town, for R. Stuttaford. Source: [UCTbox] BC206.*]

Whilst the same suggestions made at the beginning of the section on Vergelegen could be made on these individuals and their possession of Cape Dutch homesteads – that they were retired, wanted to farm, or perhaps were investing in economically lucrative property – it is quite clear that some of them were committed to the Cape Dutch restoration and preservation movement for ideological reasons. This can be inferred from their membership to either the CUS or the SANS, and the general ideological motivations of those movements. Meiring Beck was president of the SANS and it seems likely that his purchase of the Tulbagh Drostdy was motivated by a sincere desire to preserve the settler past. That Stuttaford was a committed possessor of the Cape Dutch homestead of Rustenberg is supported by his membership to the SANS and the CUS as well as in a letter sent by Kendall to him in 1926.[55] Although Sauer was more of a Republican than an Imperialist,[56] his wife was a member of the SANS at least in 1923 suggesting that protecting identity and preserving Cape Dutch homesteads was an active consideration. Other minor players in the future of South Africa such as Julia Solly of Knorhoek, James Rawbone of Broadlands, were also possessors of Cape Dutch homesteads in and around Stellenbosch and were both members of the SANS.

---

[52]Davenport, T. R. H., *South Africa: A Modern History*, p 336.
[53][UCT]BC206,67.
[54][Mag]*AB&E*, v.11, n.11 (June, 1928) p 7.
[55][UCT]BC206, 155: 1926.01.23, Letter from Kendall to Stuttaford.
[56][Mag]*The State*, v.3, n.4 (April, 1910) p 526.

Invented Possessions: Stewards of the City as Landed Gentry

In the first decade of the twentieth century, Herbert Baker was able to develop a fairly distinctive Cape Dutch revival style, perhaps more simply called Baker Cape Dutch, that became somewhat popular with wealthy suburban house-owners at the Cape and in Johannesburg. Predominantly double-storied and characterised by twirled chimneys and Baroque gables such as those at Lidcote and Groote Schuur, Baker's Cape Dutch perhaps spoke more about his desire for originality in design and the progressive development of style in architecture than about a literal or accurate historical investigation and replication. It also seems fairly plausible to discount Baker Cape Dutch as having originated from any real desire to lay claim to a settler past, and to consider it more the work of an individual opportunist intent on using generous commissions to explore building as an artistic and creative medium; Baker was more of an aesthete than an ideologue.

[*Kendall & Morris's design for R. Stuttaford, Lourensford, Somerset West. Source: [UCTimage]BC206, Portfolio of Images.*]

When Kendall and Morris took over the reins of Baker's firm after Masey and Baker left Cape Town, the Cape Dutch revival became distinctly more political in its proliferation. A large number of Kendall and Morris' clients were members of the SANS and CUS and were actively involved in Union ideology. This gives support to the proposal that the use of Cape Dutch elements such as gables in their houses was more than simply part of a contemporary stylistic trend. In fact, as Radford has noted, the Cape Dutch revival had a very limited impact on domestic architecture in Cape Town in general.[57]

Aside from the initial enthusiasm generated by Rhodes' example of Groote Schuur, its occurrence seems to have been based on two ideological premises: either as symbols of Union and the possession of a settler past, or as symbols of the life of a landed gentry. The two were not exclusive and in fact complemented each other. Cape Dutch gables became totemistic additions to buildings otherwise clearly Arts & Crafts country houses in their design and detailing. In fact, what was only later classified as the Peninsula type gable,[58] became almost exclusively used, perhaps as a way of recapturing the "pure" gable form supposedly represented by Groot Constantia. That the proponents of the Groot Constantia or Peninsula gable as "prototype" were using it as a political symbol, and were in fact

[57]Radford, D., 'The Architecture of the Western Cape, 1838 to 1901', p 2.
[58]Walton, J., *Homesteads and Villages of South Africa*, p 14.

unaware of its future classification to a geographic region, is indicated in its widespread usage in areas beyond the Peninsula.

[*Kendall & Morris's design for R. Stuttaford, Lourensford, Somerset West – ground floor plan. Source: [UCTimage] BC206, 481.*]

Lourensford estate (later known as Fleur-du-Cap) was purchased from Sir James Sivewright in 1916 by J.W. Jagger, the leader of the Union Party at the Cape and President of the Cape Town branch of the pro English-immigration lobby, the Overseas League.[59] Jagger commissioned Kendall and Morris in 1924 to design a new house on the Lourensford estate. Although the design may have been a collaboration between Kendall and Morris, the project seems to have been a point of dispute between the two, leading to Morris leaving the partnership. Kendall was later involved in some alteration work to the drawing room fireplace in 1932, but the construction administration of the house-proper was left to Morris who maintained the contract through arbitration.[60] Consequently, the contract files are not to be found with the Baker and Kendall archives at the University of Cape Town, leaving only a few copies of the design drawings and contemporary photographs as the basis for analysis.

Given the extent of the project and its broken symmetry, hipped-roofs, expressed chimneys and windows set at the eaves level, the house carries all the characteristics of an Arts & Crafts house designed for a country gentleman. The maintenance of social hierarchy in the project and the house is fairly obvious to read in the plan as is similarly found in Rhodes' Groote Schuur. At Lourensford it is hardly remarkable that the design provides spatial and visual separation of served and servants' areas through the restriction of the latter to the right of the main, symmetrical, double-storied house, although three of the nine servant bedrooms did creep their way into the upper floor of the main house. It is also fairly telling to note that the servants' rooms in the service wing all have windows that face onto internal courtyards and are located away from the extensive and elaborately designed back garden. Presumably this was to prevent any "intrusion" of the servants into the backspace with its Palladian follie, which no doubt would have been greatly used.

[*Kendall & Morris's design for R. Stuttaford, Lourensford, Somerset West – first floor plan. Source: [UCTimage] BC206, 481.*]

These design elements and concerns were very typical of an Arts & Crafts country estate in England. A minor element on the sketch plan illustrates the general conflation of race and class that had occurred in the colonies at the time: three small rooms in the servant's wing are

---

[59]Gutsche, T., *No Ordinary Woman*, p 342.
[60][UCT]BC206, 172: 1925.08.18, Letter from C.H. Smith to Morris.

tellingly labelled 'Boy', indicating the status of a black, male servant, and thereby locating the project in the nexus of South Africa's paternalistic and hierarchical race relations. The clearest indication of the house as clear political status is indicated by the inclusion of the Groot Constantia or Peninsula type gable at the front entrance. Whilst it may be argued that Jagger was simply following the stylistic trend of Cape Town's elite, his commitment to the SANS and the CUS suggest that the Cape Dutch gable was used as a symbol of rootedness and possession of the geography and history of a settler past. Two slave bell-towers can also be noted at the northeast corner of the house.

[*Baker's Groote Schuur, design for Rhodes. Source: Le Roux, W.J., Groote Schuur.*]

Many of the observations made regarding Lourensford could be made with regard to Kendall's design of Luncarty, which, in some way, can be seen as a predecessor to Lourensford. Although not on such a grand scale as Lourensford, it carries similar aspirations of presenting itself as the house of a country gentleman. In this instance the separation of servant and served spaces is not carried through as clearly as in Lourensford, however, there is a room for a 'boy' with its entrance off a kitchen-yard, whilst the servant's rooms and storage rooms were the only rooms to be located in the attic. The house, originally commissioned by Commander Sereld Hay, was in all probability designed by Kendall. Even though the drawings credit Baker as well as Kendall, Baker, who at that stage was in India, would most likely have acted simply as a design consultant on the project. Again, what is striking about the project is the inclusion of the Groot Constantia or Cape Peninsula gable at the entrance and back façade looking out over the garden. Hay was not active in either SANS or CUS circles which suggests that his motivations for including the gable in the house may have not been political and may have come from Kendall.

In 1927, Kendall was involved in designing an additional artist's studio space for Edith Struben, Luncarty's new owner, whose father had been a member of the CUS and a treasurer of the SANS, and who herself was a member of the SANS. Kendall spent considerable time and effort tracking down some 200 Delft tiles to be set around the fireplace adding to the "authenticity" of the home as a Cape Dutch homestead.[61] It was, however, a specific instruction on the part of Ms Struben that confirmed her purchase of Luncarty as part of the possession of original settler history. At the beginning of the design process she wrote to Kendall stating that 'if feasible and possible [I] should like to use my copy of Constantia Cellar Frieze over the fireplace and the rest to accord in treatment with it'.[62] Although the

---

[61][UCT]BC206, 95: 1927.04.12, Letter from Kendall to Struben.
[62]*Ibid.*, 1927.01.14, Letter from Struben to Kendall.

overall feel of the room was not particularly Cape Dutch, the minia-turised moulding of the frieze was indeed inserted, affording Struben the possession of both the history of Groot Constantia and the settler past of its "great men", such as Anton Anreith, the sculptor.

[*Kendall's design for Luncarty, Cape Town. Source: [Mag]AB&E September, 1927.*]

[*Plan of Kendall's design for Luncarty, Cape Town. Source: [UCTbox]BC206, 95.*]

[*Kendall's design for H.E. Hockly. Source: [UCTbox] BC206.*]

There are many more examples of the Groot Constantia or Cape Peninsula type gable being "attached" to the front façade of new fairly ostentatious and not so ostentatious houses developed in the suburbs of Cape Town and its surrounds. A double storey house on Greenfield Road in Kirstenbosch, designed by Kendall for H.E. Hockly, illustrates this quite clearly as well as making use of fairly typically proportioned, paned and shuttered Cape Dutch style windows on the ground floor, and more Arts & Crafts inspired windows up against the eaves on the first floor. The Greenfield house retains the gabled ends characteristic of Cape Dutch homesteads, making a fairly convincing double-storey adaptation of a typical Cape Dutch homestead front façade.

The same cannot be said of a house designed by Walgate in Somerset West. Although its plan roughly resembles the 'H' typical of many old Cape Dutch homesteads and its sash windows seem to have been carefully proportioned and positioned along Cape Dutch lines, its hipped roofs present the Groot Constantia or Peninsula type gable as an unconvincing and somewhat arbitrary addition to the house. Contemporary photographs and descriptions of the inte-rior – its black-stained ceiling beams and picture rails, and its many fireplace alcoves – suggest that the hipped roofs were part of the general Arts & Crafts aesthetic that was being pursued. Although its large planks of yellowwood floorboards suggest more attempts at greater authenticity in the design, the pretences and attempt at pos-session is to be found in the name given to the house and in a detail on the front façade. Called Stellandal in honour of the Van der Stels, the front gable also bore their coat of arms.[63]

[*C.P. Walgate, House in Somerset West, [Mag] AB&E, April, 1926.*]

Chapter Conclusion

Spurred by the building preservation movement and nationalist sen-timent, the nouveau riche at the Cape, as mirrored in England, set

---

[63][News]*Daily Dispatch* 1929.02.19: 'The Home Beautiful.'

about purchasing, at the turn of the nineteenth century, existing Cape Dutch homesteads or building simulations thereof as signified through Groot Constantia's gable. Possessing Cape Dutch homesteads became a way of possessing the "noble" past that these homesteads were represented as having. Alternatively, Cape Dutch homesteads were also considered to be iconic of the "Home Beautiful" and thus were considered models to be emulated in terms of "proper" housing for middle-class families, whilst simultaneously suggesting a lineage for the middle-class extending back to the original settlement of the Cape. The hierarchical space of these homesteads were also considered as appropriate models for the contemporary society at the Cape, and gave further legitimacy to the exploitative interests of Europeans in South Africa. Furthermore, as a new "landed gentry" (as signified through the Cape Dutch homesteads), the politicians and upper middle-class in the Cape and South Africa were able to literally lay claim to the history and geography of the land of South Africa, and thereby legitimise the project of Empire in South Africa and Africa beyond. Precisely whilst pretences of high society and civilisation were being made, an extensive and consuming discourse was emerging that began to represent the racially heterogeneous dwellers in the old parts of Cape Town as uncivilised and bestial, making them vulnerable to being dispossessed of the land they occupied. In a similar manner, the old parts of Cape Town were represented as squalid slums, without any aesthetic merit, making them vulnerable to eradication. It is these two considerations that form the next part of this thesis.

Conclusion

> On the steps of an old Dutch house the Guide broke the silence. 'Here in this place you see the Divine plan; order out of chaos, light from darkness, reversed. The new order is corruption after decency, foulness where once cleanliness and beauty reigned. Once this dwelling was a home – one family dwelt here – the name____ You remember it in the old Cape books. The old man – I see him now – found pride in the spotless white steps, the well-oiled doors and the shining brass. Not far away stands the old Theatre, and down this road the nobility of the day walked in the cool of the evening. Lady Anne Barnard was no stranger here; it seems as yesterday. But come, let us enter.'
> Archdeacon Lavis, 'The Pity of It... and Bethlehem.'[64]

---

[64][Mag]*The Cape*, v.19, n.492 (December, 1924).

A few days before Christmas 1924, Archdeacon Lavis (later Bishop), a crusader of Cape Town's slum clearances and housing reformer, provided the readers of *The Cape* with a Grinch-like horror-story. In the article Lavis presents a protagonist called Tomkins who is visited on Christmas Eve by 'The Spirit of Cape Town as God Meant It To Be' and taken on a journey – and the specific spatiality involved should be noted – from the suburbs into 'Old Capetown'. Under the direction of his 'Guide' he enters his 'pet aversion – a slum dwelling' where 'foulness reigns'. After their tour where 'devils lurk', the Guide petitions Tomkins that a '"Home" and not a "hovel", is the right of the poorest men and women and of each little child', and this right extends to having 'an environment which will develop and not retard the upward, onward, physical and spiritual movement in each human life!' An environment that the Guide suggests is not obtainable in the city itself, the place of which 'entails the loss of happiness, beauty, power and love.'

There are a number of reasons why I have chosen to conclude this thesis with Lavis' article. Firstly it is the perfect example of how different identities can become represented and structured through representations of domestic space. The second reason is that it is offers a convenient summary of the chapters of this thesis. The phrases 'old Dutch house' and 'Lady Anne Barnard was no stranger here; it seems as yesterday,' not only place an English presence side-by-side with Cape Dutch architecture, but also telegraphs both into the present: it is obvious that the building requires preservation to protect this "common" past. This is the central idea dealt with in Chapter One. There is also the expectation that the "heroes" of the past are to be known and are to be remembered 'in the old Cape books'.

The phrase 'Divine plan; order out of chaos, light from darkness' suggests an almost religious conviction in the cultural artefacts of Western civilisation. As shown in Chapter Two, a Cape Dutch building is not simply a relic from the past, but is evidence of Western civilisation's, or rather, the British Empire's, unquestionable mission to the world.

The ideas of Chapter Three are also present in the phrase 'the nobility of the day,' and suggests the Romantic undertone with which politicians and main players of South Africa and the Cape invented themselves as a landed gentry through the Cape Dutch homestead.

The idea of the aesthetics of the visual, as investigated in Chapter Four, is also present in the valuing of 'cleanliness and beauty' and the 'spotless steps' and 'shining brass'.

Chapter Five examined the way in which slums were represented as places where 'devils lurk,' and where an ascription of Otherness was made through the dwelling and the use of its space. The phrase 'let us enter' also indicates the way in which these Other-spaces came to be mapped.

The last three chapters of this thesis are hinted at in a number of ways. The idea of the "home" as being a single-family detached dwelling located in the suburbs is suggested in the fact that Tomkins himself is from the suburbs, and that the old Dutch dwelling was 'a home – one family dwelt here'. The other idea of Chapter Six, that of environmental determinism, is also suggested in the words 'develop' the 'upward, onward, physical and spiritual movement in each human life'. Finally, the Garden City Movement is hinted at in the idea that an urban environment entails the 'loss of happiness, beauty, power and love'.

Lastly, Lavis's article also offers a description of the key ideas that have led to the structuring of this thesis into three parts. The Self is manifested through a cultural life based on the History of Western civilisation, typically located outside of the city (although located in the city in Lavis's article for greater effect) and symbolised through the "beautiful" artefacts of "high" architecture. These buildings are also symbolic markers of the legitimate and necessary possession of the land by the coloniser. In contrast, the threatening Other is located within the city with its lack of boundaries, order and aesthetic appeal. Here the Other works away at the Self, posing his very undoing by putting in danger that which represents his very Self, namely the "high" architecture of Western civilisation. The "solution" is the removal of these Others from the dangerous fluidity of the ugly city into the Whiteness of the suburbs where boundaries are maintained and where the Other can be made into the Same and where hybridity is eradicated. The Other's absence from the city and ordering and restructuring in the garden suburbs (even only if as a simulacra of the Self), then, is taken as an effective resolution of the contradictions of colonisation.

Yet Cape Town, or South Africa, was not alone in this kind of representation and restructuring of the Self and "his" Others. Consider, for example, Octavia Hill's simultaneous efforts aimed at valorising and protecting England's bucolic heritage through the National Trust and her slum clearance and rehousing activities. Her work was born out of the same concerns for "culture" and the "proper" way of living that we have seen evidence of at the Cape. Thus, it is easy to hear the words of her friend and mentor, John Ruskin, or see his influence, permeating through in the representations and restructuring of the spaces of Cape Town that we have looked at. As J.R. Finch, Town Clerk and author of the official guidebook to Cape Town, says: 'Bring your trout rod and your books on nature, your gun, your volumes of Ruskin, when starting Southward Ho!'[65] It is in this sense, that the pre-Apartheid restructuring of the spaces of Cape

---

[65]Finch, J. R., *The Cape of Good Hope*, p 12.

Town was not simply the result of an early desire for racial segregation, but also the effects of a set of particularly English values that saw the stewards of the city set about restructuring Cape Town into a set of spaces after their own image. Nor was this simply the "neutral" effect of cultural activity. It was this representing and restructuring that set up a series of inclusions and exclusions, of legitimate and illegitimate ways of being, that in turn legitimised the possession of the land and its history, and effectively dispossessed Others from the land and made them History-less.

The writing of a cultural history framed through postcolonial theory obviously has the potential to deliver some new insights into South Africa's pre-Apartheid cities. This thesis has shown, that to consider, for example, the design of Groote Schuur in 1892 and the design of Ndabeni in 1900, or the design of the Cape Dutch South Africa pavilion in Wembley in 1924 and the beginnings of the design of Langa location in 1923, or the declaration of Groot Constantia as a national monument in 1936 and the Slums Act in 1934, is not to simply study events in the built environment held together by time and place, but is to get to the heart of how culture and identity are integral parts of the processes of colonial possession and dispossession. What this study perhaps lacks is a more explicit investigation into two issues, namely, the relationship between gender identities and architecture, and what Henri Lefebvre[66] identifies as "the space of representation", which have become marginalized as this thesis has focussed on the values and concerns of the "producers" of architecture. Although the issues of gender have been touched on in this thesis, a more thorough analysis of the period in these terms is in order. For its part, concerns for "the space of representation", tends to be focussed on the "users" of space and how identity is constructed *on their own terms*. Whilst this more anthropological concern is obviously an important issue to be dealt with, my interests as an educator and an architect have tended to problematise the role architects played in imagining or creating "ideal" spaces. The issue of how those "ideal" spaces were or were not used "correctly" and were perhaps adapted to "other" uses has not been tackled in this thesis.

What, then, is 'The Production of the City as a White Space'? Obviously it can be literally read as the racial segregation that was undertaken in South Africa's cities in the pre-Apartheid era. It can, however, also be understood as the result of the failed attempts at the production of the city as an English space. At the heart of the humanist project of the Garden City Movement, with its visions of a universal Englishness, was a desire to bring to the world that which

---

[66]Lefebvre, H., The Production of Space.

was "proper" and "ideal", namely, the English village and its cottages. The City, with its messy vitality, fluidity of identities and uterine spaces, needed to be eradicated, or made uninhabited, or turned inside-out to be bleached in the bright light of Whiteness, or, at the very least, just made to look correct and ordered. As such, other, or new forms of being in the world, were necessarily excluded, and hybridity was hastily removed. Yet the models of the Self prevailed in forms far removed from the ideal. Garden City representations of the cottage and its wisps of chimney-smoke became, in reality, the neutered, isolationist space of the homogenous suburb of modernism. Looking on, to the gridded and arid landscape of suburban Apartheid townships that followed these initial housing schemes, there is a sense that they were somehow construed as a punitive measure, a sort-of intentionally dehumanising project that only the monster of Apartheid could construct. Perhaps, though, this dehumanised landscape was simply born out of the "humanist" and anti-urban project that the English and their Empire brought with them to the Cape.

But the production of the city as a White space is not just about housing models and slum clearances. It is about how Whiteness legitimised its dominance in the world, how it produced and managed its identity through the control and representation of cultural products such as the socially and spatially decontextualised "high" architecture of Western civilisation, whilst simultaneously delegitimising the activities and spaces of otherness. It is about the protection and production of the city as the space in which only Whiteness appears – and in the abstracted space of the White city, things appear, before they *are*. Everything has its place and its boundaries; the Self there in the museum and the Home, and the Native there in his "hut". On the other hand, the condition of hybridity, like urbanity itself, is demanding and even dangerous in the muddled vitality and disorder it creates. It cuts through the boundaries of the White city, requiring inventiveness and work, denying the easy polarities of Self and Other.

Kathryn Ewing

Investigation of a Traders' Route: Analysis of the Street Edge which Informs Public Space, with Reference to the Indian City of Jaipur, Isfahan in Iran and Harare, Zimbabwe.

Like Chand, Ewing combines the poetic with the analytic and the historical, but here the emphasis is also very much on the first-hand experience and analysis of cities. As a result, the dissertation is conducted not only by text but also through images – both photographic and personal sketches. The wide geographic range (although only the study of Jaipur is reproduced here) of the study is likewise extremely impressive.

Kathryn Ewing

INVESTIGATION OF A TRADERS' ROUTE

The analysis of the Street Edge that informs Public Space, with reference to the Indian city of Jaipur, Isfahan in Iran and Harare, Zimbabwe

You live in time; we live in space.
You're always on the move; we're always at rest.
Religion is our first love; we revel in metaphysics.
Science is our passion; you delight in physics.
You believe in freedom of speech; you strive for articulation.
We believe in freedom of silence; we lapse into meditation.
Self-assertiveness is the key to your success;
Self-abnegation is the secret of our survival.
You're urged every day to want more and more;
We're taught from the cradle to want less and less.
Joie de vivre is your ideal; conquest of desires is our goal.
In the sunset of life, you retire to enjoy the fruits of your labour;
We renounce the world and prepare ourselves for the hereafter.
                                                  Hari N. Dam
                                       'Reflections on Life East and West'
                  (Extract from 'Travels through Sacred India', Roger Housden)

ORIGINAL CONTENTS

Preface
Introduction
Introduction to Case Studies
The Street
The Street Edge

The Senses, Poetry and Illustrations

My reasons for using poetry:

> *The taste of the apple ... lies in contact of the fruit with the palate, not in the fruit itself; in a similar way ... poetry lies in the meeting of a poem and reader, not in the lines and symbols printed in a book. What is essential is the aesthetic act, the thrill, the almost physical emotion that comes with each reading.*
>
> (Jorge Luis Borges)

My reasons for using illustrations:

> *Draw me your words and I'll understand your meaning*
>
> (Igor Stravinsky)

Introduction

Collage of Trading Street

> *I watched the crowds of people pour into the marketplace.*
> *I watched the chaotic movement and wild exchanges*
> *And the load carriers staggering under sacks.*
> *It seemed as if the whole world was there.*

I saw people of all shapes and sizes.....
They buy and sell, browse and investigate [1] (Okri, 1992)

This essay intends to explore the meaning and significance of trading routes, the market being of major importance, as a positive integrator in the continuity of the urban fabric. By understanding the immediate interaction of the street edge, the debate will revolve around the idea of the 'positive utilisation of public space', which form complex systems within the trading route. This can be seen in the traditional city of Isfahan, Iran, where the bazaar forms the intricate network of public space, to the convivial street life along the linear markets in Jaipur, India and informal market streets in Harare, Zimbabwe. The case studies will be the main focus of the paper. Why is the street edge of importance? Does it provide a vital source within the urban environment in terms of positive, open, public space? Is the street still considered to be public space?

This paper will constitute the notion of montage text as a medium which 'introduces and reproduces the complex multivariate and fragmentary experience' of the street and sensuous trading routes. The diagrams have been placed in an ordered, yet fragmented arrangement, as to emphasise the complexity of the informal sector, integrating colour and composition.

> *Besides this symbolic discontinuity, a new perceptual continuity can be set up through the intrinsic qualities of the fragments, colour, texture, opacity etc.... a new whole is developed via these very tangible elements.* (Oeschlin)[2]

Introduction to Case Studies

- Isfahan, Iran – a defined bazaar route connected by public squares.
- Jaipur, India – positive open spaces where trading exists on the street.
- Harare, Zimbabwe – a spontaneous, temporary, informal trading route.

This paper will deal with case studies in developing countries, namely Iran, India and Zimbabwe. The reasons for choosing these particular case studies is that they deal with various aspects of convivial street life and constructive occupation of space, which many

---

[1]Okri B. – Extract from *'The Famished Road'* (1992). Okri talks of the street and marketplace as the central hub of the town, the heart of the urban environment, as seen through the eyes of a young spirit boy. A place where people meet, buy, sell, sit, listen, gossip, interact, participate.
[2]Oeschlin W. – Working with fragments: The Limitations of Collage.

Western cities have disregarded in the recent years with the introduction of the motor car.

The examples, although similar in nature in the idea of trading routes, display differences of formality and informality, temporary and permanent, regular and irregular. **Isfahan** displays traditional concepts of the trading route from the sixteenth century, which are still relevant today, although they have been disrupted by the introduction of the vehicular roads. The formal bazaar of Isfahan forms the major structural arrangement of movement systems from the Friday Mosque to the Maidan.

Indian streets present a "rich diversity of social activity. . . . which interpret their experience through social, sensual and symbolic processes"[3] (Edensor, 1998). **Jaipur** is a combination of informality within the formal framework. A linear bazaar of continuous public space, expanding and contracting at various points along the street, allows trading to happen informally around the basic formal framework.

Harare, as a developing country, has a rapid rate of urban expansion, where informal employment forms the main source of income for many people living in the city. Due to a lack of space, spontaneous informal trading develops along streets on the periphery of the CBD. A high proportion of hawkers live and work on the pavements and around markets, which are found often near to the main public meeting place.

The Street

Imagine a trading route.

> *A vigorous street,*
> *Along which people inhabit, travel, and occupy.*
> *An activity corridor, forming the 'back bone' for development.*
> *A bazaar hosting a variety of exchanges,*
> *Selling, buying, trading, and operating.*
> *People moving, walking, wondering,*
> *Pondering the thoughts for the day.*
> *Stopping at points to breathe, gather, wait, talk.*
> *The street expands into public spaces – markets.*
> *Alive and vibrant, the heart of the city.*
> *Creating a network of intricate spaces and niches,*

---

[3]Edensor T. – Culture of the Indian Street, Chapter 14 from Fyfe N., *Images of the Street* (1998).

Kashmiri Bazaar
Lahore
Activity along the street
Canopied Walkway

Paharganj Bazaar
Delhi
Trading, living in the city
Streets become 'alive'

> *The street edge; public, private, opening, closing, up, down,*
> *Inhabited by the trader – people existing together, convivial life.*
> *Conviviality and the sensual experience of the market street*
> *Seeing, smelling, hearing, touching, tasting – living.*
> *Night and day, every day.*
> *A trading route.*[4]

The Notion of Trading Routes in Developing Countries

> *Think of a city and what comes to mind? Its streets.* [5]
> (Jacobs)

Many developing countries such as India and Zimbabwe, although rife with many social and economic problems, have managed to maintain the social life of small urban spaces, creating liveable habitats and allowing informal activities to happen impulsively in the street.[5]

---

[4]Author's own.
[5]Jacobs J. – Reading the street, Introduction by Fyfe N. – *Images of the Street* (1998) p 1.

Main Street
Lahore
Linear element of street
Freedom of boundaries

Main Street
Amritsar
Complex spaces
along street edge

The notion of the 'Traders' Route' as a major collector and integrator[6] of spontaneous activities is one of fundamental importance in any developing country. The informal sector in developing countries forms a means of survival for the majority of the urban poor. This informal lifestyle normally depends upon trading routes along important streets, which inform the city fabric. The idea of 'street', a linear element, needs to be understood as the 'lifeline to the city', as part of a 'social complexity'.[7] Streets capture the vitality, tension and excitement of the city, acting as social and spatial integrators, not separators. The streets are public space and should be open to all.

> *Streets are by far the most commonly recurring elements in the fabric of a city; yet all of them are different – no two streets in the world are alike...... Their inherent complexity is*

[6]Uytenbogaardt R. – Notes from a lecture with Uytenbogaardt, Urban Planning Issues, Housing Lecture Series (1995).
[7]Edensor T. – Culture of the Indian Street, Chapter 14 from *Images of the Street*, Fyfe N. (1998).

thus immense and they are decisive for the quality of the city.[8]
(De Carlo, 1988)

Edensor explains that streets have various activities, where

> *The street is located within a cellular structure that suggests a labyrinth, with numerous openings and passages. The flow of bodies and vehicles criss-cross the street in multi-directional patterns, veering into courtyards, alleys and cul-de-sacs. The busiest streets are the main arteries of this spatial network, are never merely 'machines for shopping' but the site for numerous activities.*[9]

Boddy claims that "streets are as old as civilisation, which have come to symbolise public life, with all its human contact, conflict and tolerance". However, over the years, this idea of the public street in the West has been turned into a vehicle moving device, where the "pace and rhythm of the real urban street seems to matter less and less". Boddy further states that the West is changing the functional active use of the street and the "other, older streets, with their troubling smells and winds and unpredictability, swirl into a distant and wispy memory, as vaporous as the smoke and rain outside".[10] Davis continues to argue that the public spaces of the new mega structures and shopping malls of the West (predominantly America) have removed the traditional streets and destroyed their spontaneity, where public activities are turned inwards and divided into strict compartments.[11]

Durbar Square, Kathmandu Celebration of public space

[8]De Carlo G. – Do City Squares still matter? Space and Society Journal, Vol. 42, April–June (1988) p 5.
[9]Edensor T. – Culture of the Indian Street, Chapter 14 from Fyfe N., *Images of the Street* (1998) p 206.
[10]Boddy T. – Underground and Overhead (1992) p 123.
[11]Davis M. – The Militarization of Urban Space (1992) p 155.

In a sense, this converts the public space into a private sphere, with the destruction of a lively, spontaneous 'street-life'.

> *It simply never occurs to us to make streets into oases rather than deserts. In countries where their function has not yet deteriorated into highways and parking lots, a number of arrangements make streets fit for humans; pergolas and awnings (spread across the street), tent-like structures, or permanent roofs. All are characteristic of the Orient. The most redefined street coverings, a tangible expression of civic solidarity ... are arcades ... . Apart from lending unity to the streetscape, they often take place of ancient forums ... incorporated into 'formal' architecture.[12]*
> (Boddy, 1992)

Collective public open spaces occur at the junction of one or more streets, forming a break in the route, "a meeting point of several communities".[13] These positive, public spaces celebrate every-day living and promote and enhance shared urban life. Uyentbogaardt describes public spaces as "containers for urban activities.....which should be made as positive multi-functional urban spaces".[14]

> *The street is an elongated line pulsating at various points.[15]*
> (Alexander, 1979)

Open spaces form a complex hierarchy in the make-up of the fabric, where the quality of the space depends on the degree of correspondence between solids and voids and on the amount of energy flows of human activities passing through or in them. Public space has an ability to draw energy from the street flowing into them or radiate energy back to the street flowing off them.

> *The perfect street is harmonious space... where the street is not an area, but a volume....it cannot exist in a vacuum; it is inseparable from its environment... The street is a matrix: urban chamber, fertile soil and breeding ground.[16]*
> (Rudosky, 1969)

How do the street edge and public space inform the market or trading routes?

---

[12]Rudofsky B. – Architecture without Architects, extract from *Streets for People* (1965). Quote at the beginning.
[13]Edensor T. – Culture of the Indian Street (1998) p 206.
[14]Dewar D. & Uytenbogaardt R. – *Creating Vibrant Urban Places to Live* (1995) p 29.
[15]Alexander C. – *A Pattern Language* (1979).
[16]Rudofsky B. – *Streets for People*, Introduction (1969).

The notion of trading along a street

Living and working in the street – the idea of a Tapestry of Space.

Energy flows (people, goods, investment, traffic) are channelled along defined routes, activity spines (streets), which generate a variety of intense activities (economic enterprises, commercial facilities, social and cultural activities, habitation) at dominant points along the line.[17] Doshi argues that

> *People have their most profound spatial experience on the route from one place to another or at the boundary between places* [18]

The traditional trading routes or bazaars maintained a quality of conviviality[19] and spatial order, where people congregated to enjoy the aspects of everyday living.

> *Streets should be for staying in and not just for moving through, the way they are today*[20] (Alexander, 1977)

Present day society seems to have moved away from this idea of human thriving in the street, where the "thrills of the bazaar are traded in for the conveniences of the sterile supermarket,"[21] which

Harare – Informal trading in the urban environment. The idea of social interaction in the street and informal activities are present in many developing countries, compared to modern Western Streets, which have been disrupted by globalisation and modern movements, such as the introduction of the motor car.

[17]Dewar D. & Uytenbogaardt R. – Continuity of the Urban Fabric, *A Manifesto for Change* (1990) p 48.
[18]Doshi B. V. – Quote from 'Doshi, the Architect', A&U, July–August (1997) p 137.
[19]Convivial living is one where 'people live together' with a unique set of social arrangements, which encourage a lifestyle of diversity and identity. References to conviviality: Illich, Peattie, Fyfe, Friedman, Boddy, Sorkin.
[20]Alexander C. – *A Pattern Language*, Oxford University Press, New York, America (1977) p 590.
[21]Chakrabarty (1991) – Extract from *Images of the Street* (1998) Introduction.

erases the sensuous feeling and rhythmic diversity of 'being' in the street. Crawford argues that the bazaars and marketplaces have been exchanged for the 'window shopping' idea in a shopping mall, where the shopper has been converted into the passive spectator, an isolated individual, silently contemplating merchandise.[22]

Sorkin regards this as the emergence of a new kind of city, a "city without a place attached to it",[23] where a disaggregated patchwork of fabric forms a bland, senseless urban environment. People enclose themselves indoors, along corridors or passageways, thus removing themselves from the activity of the street. This is partly due to the fact of the motorcar and globalisation. The vehicle has taken possession over the street converting the idea of 'street' to a passage of movement along a 'road'. Le Corbusier envisaged the street as a "machine for traffic, used exclusively by fast-moving mechanical vehicles, and free from pedestrians and building fronts".[24] This paper will challenge this idea of the street acting as a 'machine', where 'street' is rather viewed as both

> *'Representations of space' and discursively constructed spaces of the planner and architects and the 'spaces of representation', the space of everyday life of the 'inhabitants' and 'users'.*[25] (Lefebvre, 1991)

De Carlo emphasises the "crushing presence of the car",[26] which disrupts the balance between the built-up and open spaces in an urban environment. This in turn segregates the rich complexity of human activities and eventually eradicates them, as the positive open voids become filled with the solid mass of freeways. This is a sad loss of the pedestrian world and living on the street.

The Street Edge

Imagine a street edge.

> *The street edge defined by building fronts –*
> *A variation of terraces, porches, balconies, stairways, and arcades,*

---

[22]Crawford M. – Chapter 1, The World in a Shopping Mall, in Sorkin M. – *Variation of a Theme Park* (1994) pp 17–18.

[23]Sorkin M. – *Variations on a Theme Park,* Introduction, Hill & Wang, The Noonday Press, NY (1992) p xi.

[24]Fyfe N. – Le Corbusier's idea of the 'Machine City', extract from Fyfe N., *Images of the Street* (1998) p 3.

[25]Lefebvre H. – The Production of Space, (1991) extract from *Images of the Street,* Fyfe N. (1998) p 4.

[26]De Carlo G. – Do City Squares still matter? Space and Society Journal, Vol. 42, April–June (1988) p 5.

*Openings
Patankot*

*Developing a continuously discontinuous pattern of spaces.
Textures exposed, materiality uncovered.
The corner shops opening onto the street,
Day and night, supplying the pedestrian,
With an array of goods and daily supplies.
This open becomes closed,
As solid becomes void,
The tissue becomes object.
Moving through arched entrances,
Where public becomes private,
Commercial integrates with residential.
Reacting together to form a flexible, mixed-use environment.
One experiences the street by understanding
Free boundaries divided by people and their make-up
Living, working, playing.*[27]

The street edge forms an important part of the trading route. The edge forms a boundary between public and private, open and closed, solid and void. It is the integration of these aspects in forming the public spaces in the street that needs to be explored. Various architectural boundaries help to form these undulating, irregular spaces of the street edge. Staircases rising up off the street floor, balconies overhanging the shop below, corner shops celebrating the junction of many streets, thresholds changing the surface texture, openings with workshops spilling onto the pavement – a constantly changing edge filled with identity and swirling confusion.

*The more public a place – the more the fronts of the buildings
need to play a role of defining and articulating. People who opt*

---

[27]Author's own.

to live in this sort of location do so because they enjoy the sort of lifestyle associated with the public spaces. The fronts and the buildings themselves must be able to adjust and accommodate this preference as well as to the changing commercial and cultural activities associated with the central places – flats above, shops below – commercial and residential purposes.[28]

(Andrew P. & Japha D.)

The case studies are specifically chosen examples of trading routes, which incorporate a high degree of pedestrian movement combined with a small proportion of cars using the same streets. These examples reveal a sensuous nature of trading along a street edge, creating diverse and flexible complexities within the urban environment, managing to capture and stimulate different aspects of sight, sound, hearing and touching.

---

[28]Andrew P. & Japha D. – *Low Income Housing Alternatives for the Western Cape* (1978).

This paper will not be dealing with the underlying history of the case studies concerned, but will give a brief understanding of how the city originated in terms of movement routes, public spaces and street paths, the bazaar (market-street) being of main significance.

> *One moves through the entrance gate,*
> *Into the unknown world of **Isfahan Bazaar**,*
> *The winding cavern of the pedestrian world.*
> *A thriving tunnel of market life,*
> *Narrow channels flowing to other destinations,*
> *Spilling into introverted courtyards*
> *The private life for the inhabitants.*
> *The breathing point at a fountain,*
> *Cool water emphasising*
> *Stop.*
> *The public square terminating the route,*
> *The relifious spiritual world of congregating*

Isfahan, Iran

> *Life can only be understood backwards, but it must be lived*
> *forwards* [29] (Kierkegaard, 1983)

Isfahan became the capital of Iran in 1587.[30] (See footnote 30 for further references that will supply a basic outline to the history of Isfahan.) It is a city where a pedestrian trading route in the old town acts as the 'activity spine', (a collection of spaces and public facilities creating a diverse and unique trading route). The quality of the structure and importance of the bazaar of the city is clearly revealed. Structural clarity in the areas of generated activity implies an intensive ordered public conviviality.

Market Streets as urban Generators

'Convivial Living' in the Urban Environment

The urban markets of Isfahan exist in the public street, growing at certain points to form larger areas for public life. This forms an

---

[29]Kierkegaard S. – Quote from *Community and Unity*, Al-Bayati, Academy Editions, London (1983).

[30]Herdeg K. – *Isfahan – Formal structure in Islamic Architecture of Iran and Turkistan* (1990) p 13.

Further references: Ardalan N. & Bakhtar L. – Sense and Unity; Cantacuzino S. & Browne K. – Isfahan, Why Isfahan? Architectural Review, May (1976).

Further account on History of Isfahan see Golombek's 'Urban Patterns in Pre-Safavid Isfahan', Journal of the Society of Iranian Studies, Vol. VIII, Nos. 1–2.

Sketches of the Bazaar Route showing convivial living in the city of Isfahan

interesting concept of the market along the street – the trading route connected by gathering points, a life of conviviality.

Peattie describes a new way of understanding human living.[31]

> *A central goal is thought to be 'building a community' or 'preserving a sense of community' that exists. I would propose an alternative cultural concept: '***conviviality***'*

Ivan Illich describes conviviality as "autonomous and creative intercourse among persons; and the intercourse of persons with their environment". [32] In recognising this concept of convivial living, one can understand the idea of the Market Street as a generator in an urban environment.

Friedman describes conviviality in terms of architecture, as being the "spaces belonging to the outside of a building" which are "components of the city", where a "building is convivial if those spaces can be appropriately directed by people in the street.....The approach of convivial buildings is linked...to the 'interwoven design' of functional spaces."[33]

The market place forms a place of convivial living, where people are attracted to in any urban environment. A trading street has the same effect. A market may grow from a street to form the public space and convivial institution, where "convivial space is not separate from public space; it is part of it, freely accessible".[34] Dewar and Uytenbogaardt define urban markets as "the physical agglomeration of a large number of traders in (usually public open) space".[35]

[31]Peattie L. – Convivial Cities, Chapter from *Cities for Citizens*, Friedman J. (Also *Thinking about Development*, Plenum Press, New York, 1981).

[32]Illich I. – *Tools for Conviviality*, Harper and Row (1973) p 11.

[33]Friedman Y. – Architectures for the People, S&S, Vol. 50 (1990) p 60.

[34]Friedman Y. – Architectures for the People (1990) p 59.

[35]Dewar D. & Uytenbogaardt R. – *Creating Vibrant Urban Places to Live* (1995) p 53.

Friedman argues that the 'conviviality' of a "stopping place" (piazza, stairs, tribune) is evidently more intense than that of "transit places" (streets, corridors, passages). This is apparent in Isfahan, where the bazaar forms the movement route to the main public spaces, or the smaller spaces around entrances, or fountains, the convivial institutions, which are part of the urban tissue, with people coming and going at all times of the day. The creation of usable "gaps" between the buildings has formed convivial space, a positive volume and not negative leftover space.

Movement Systems and Harmonic Order

Traditional sixteenth century Isfahan consisted of diverse, simultaneous systems, interwoven and connected in a meaningful way to create a complex "harmonic order".[36] Primary (the bazaar route), secondary (residential pathways) and tertiary movement (water channels) systems form this intricate network of spaces. 'Street wandering' is an important aspect of life in Isfahan. As Ardalan and Bakihtar describe it, it is "man moving through unobstructed space rather than solid mass" which is dependent on "positive space continuity",[37] so as not to interrupt the flow of man and energy channels.

> *Man moves continuously in an undulating and expanding space that is forever united.*[38]

Primary Movement Systems

The bazaar route is the "commercial back-bone of the city"[39] and the "main street" of Isfahan. This is the primary movement within the city. It is a street where people meet their colleagues, gather for events, play with friends, shop for food, a very sensual and exciting place to enter in to and move through. The main ***Bazaar*** route begins at the North Gate and moves south towards the *Seljuq Maydan-I-Qadim* (Old Square) growing towards the *Zayandah River* (the eternal river).[40] It forms a shaded pedestrian walkway supplying the primary commercial, religious and government activities of the city.

---

[36]Ardalan N. & Bakhtar L. – Isfahan and Harmonic Order, *Sense and Unity* (1973) p 97.
[37]Ardalan N. & Bakhtar L. – *Space, Sense and Unity* (1973) p 17.
[38]Ardalan N. & Bakhtar L. – *Space, Sense and Unity* (1973) p 17.
[39]Herdeg K. – *Formal structure in Islamic Architecture of Iran and Turkistan* (1990) p 34.
[40]Ardalan N. & Bakhtar L.– Isfahan, Primary Movement Systems, *Sense and Unity* (1973) p 97.

Secondary Movement Systems

Residential quarters are accessible through the secondary movement systems of narrow pathways, which are enclosed on both sides by built form. These paths are considered to be the 'veins' along which the pedestrians flow, supplying the city to work as a 'whole'. Small bazaars, local mosques, shrines and bath-houses are found along this route. The *Chahar Bagh of Shah Abbas* (running north from the *Allah Wardi Bridge* in the south) is considered to be the "super pathway"[41] of Isfahan celebrating a 'ceremonial way'. It contains a row of trees and water channels interspersed with fountains.

Tertiary Movement Systems

The *Zayandah River* supplies the tertiary movement system with water for the channels, which run along the pathways, supplying the bathhouses, gardens and residential components of the city.

Superimposed Transport Network

A transportation network of the twentieth century has been super-imposed over the city plan, to act as the 'motor city'. This introduction of the road system has disrupted the original trading route and there are several aspects which have ruined the flow of people and energy along the street. This paper will not deal primarily with this aspect, but it is however worth noting the change in the outlook on the use of the street.

The Lifeline of Isfahan

The Bazaar Route

> *The bazaar presents the story line – the continuity – which is enriched throughout its length by the events which occur along the way – some big and important, some small and delicate: all close knit to the main thread..... The bazaar is an organism with a life of its own fed by supply routes extending far into the surrounding countryside.*[42] (Browne, 1976)

---

[41]Ardalan N. & Bakhtar L. – Isfahan, *Sense and Unity* (1973) p 100.
[42]Browne K. – Life Line, Bazaar Route, AR, Vol. 159 (1976) p 265.

The bazaar route shows clear definition of **public space** along the **street edge**. The plan of the bazaar is a network of streets covered with vaults and domes, often with higher domed or open areas at the crossing points. It is a miniature city consisting of dozens of streets (the bazaar being the main street), linking the urban fabric of mosques, caravanserais, hammams[43] and houses. The route carves its way through the city structure from the Friday Mosque to the Maidan. It is a pedestrian route where each space becomes a new adventure and experience. The bazaar route displays a simple concept, but of highly complex order.

Browne describes the bazaar as

> *A cavernous world...where no space is wasted and everything has a purpose, yet the structural system never dictates.*
> *Instead it produces an essentially human environment with a sculptural plasticity and unity far removed from the fractured environments which result from modern town planning.*[44]

The bazaar forms the lifeline of continuity in the city, enriched with activity, forming a tapestry of spaces linked together. Moving within the solid mass of the built form, positive spaces interact with passive negative shapes to create a spatial link, which provides an ordered system of geometric volumes that allows for constant change.[45] The linkage of these spaces depends upon the basic framework of "connections, transition and culmination".[46] Isfahan is....,

> *... ...a covered market which links up all parts of the community*[47] (Al-Bayati)

The central spine contains a series of independent spaces of the shops, each with their own unique character. It is these spaces of the street edge that is of particular interest in understanding the nature of the trading route. The bazaar route is ordered in a formal manner, yet gives one the feeling of informality and mystery. What happens beneath the domed roof of the street, or behind the closed doors of the shops, are both questions that the observer will ask. In discovering the city, one walks through the bazaar as if on a winding trail as the ambiguity is revealed and presents itself as a maze of human life, living on and above the street.

> *It is a kaleidoscope of sights, sounds, smells*[48] (Browne, 1976)

---

[43]Hammam – Bathhouse, which was an institution inherited by the Muslims from the classical world.

[44]Browne K. – Isfahan, Why Isfahan? Architectural Review, May (1976) p 265.

[45]Ardalan N. and Bakhtar L. – Space, *Sense and Unity* (1973) pp 11–19.

[46]Ardalan N. and Bakhtar L. – Space, Positive Space Systems, *Sense and Unity* (1973) p 17.

[47]Al-Bayati B. – Quote from *Community and Unity* (1983), Chapter on Courtyards and Markets of Islamic Architecture.

[48]Browne K. – Life Line, AR, Vol. 159 (1976) p 265.

Positive Space Systems

The concept of public space has a specific meaning in Islamic society. The normal idea of public space in the western world is generally considered to be any empty open space which is bounded by public or civic buildings, the town hall and cathedral. In the Islamic culture, public space is the central space where all social, commercial, political and religious activities take place. This leads to the creation of architectural complexities within Islamic cities, due to the concentration of important functions happening in certain areas. Eslami states that "**public life is broken up into many different places and distributed throughout the whole urban space**: from the market to the neighbourhood of the city gates, from the shapeless squares to partially covered pathways, cafes or corners of alleyways".[49]

Within these public spaces the boundary between public and private is blurred, they become free to integrate various functions at one particular time in numerous spaces. Eslami describes open space as "open to everybody".[50] This is an incredibly different concept to the West, where distinctive boundaries demarcate different properties or private land that is governed by municipal principles or rules. Life in the public space of Isfahan is open to all, a gregarious, changing space occupied by many people, moving through or remaining in the space. Dewar and Uytenbogaardt state that public space should be seen as the "social outdoor room of urban settlements", where these spaces are containers for urban activities, a celebration of life, and should be viewed as positive multi-functional urban spaces.

> *Positive urban spaces are clearly defined and have a sense of enclosure.... The nature and feel of a space is significantly affected by the way in which the edges are made. Edges can be made in many ways – planting, walls, buildings, colonnades, mixture.*[51]

Positive 'blossoms' or expanding areas develop at the intersections of the movement routes, allowing people to stop and breathe along the route. Isfahan is made up of a complex hierarchical system of spatial arrangements. Browne describes the orderly system of Isfahan as

> *Instead of exclamation marks you have sentences, sentences containing exclamation, emphasis, punctuation, but all in the context of a whole rather than in isolation.*[52]

---

[49]Eslami Naser A. – Public space in Islamic Cities, S&S, Vol. 58 (1992) p 115.
[50]Eslami Naser A. – Public space in Islamic Cities, S&S, Vol. 58 (1992) p 111.
[51]Dewar D. & Uytenbogaardt R. – Urban Markets, *Creating Vibrant Urban Places to Live* (1995) p 19.
[52]Browne K. – Life Line, AR, Vol. 159 (1976) p 260.

The primary system relates to the bazaar route, the main channel of flow. This begins at the main gates and frequently continues through the city to the culmination in the public square space of the Maidan. Ardalan states that there is a "hierarchy of spatial linkages that provide an orderly system that allows for both constancy and change".[53] The regular, public spaces like the Royal Square create a large area in which to break out and breathe, unlike the irregular, bustling, public, trading streets surrounding the complex where the crowds are shoulder to shoulder, but all are positive public space for the people to inhabit. Ardalan manages to capture the idea of positive public space in the quote;

> .....Man creates spaces within which man's essential soul can breathe.[54]

Freedom of Boundaries

> Symmetry and rhythm are combined in motion, as in a wave. The rhythm is time, its place is space and its motions the soul moving between the two, making the city into a total fabric. The boundaries of the system which delimits space may be distributed regularly or irregularly, they may fill space in rapid succession or leave it empty for long periods of time, they may be crowded together or spread thin, they may follow the pattern of space with certain variations or run contrary to it, creating secondary movement systems... ..... Results in the architecture of harmonious order. It allows the breath to penetrate and the soul to flow.[55]
>
> (Ardalan & Bakhtar, 1973)

By understanding the basic principle of public open space which occupies the space between the buildings (not necessarily the main city squares), it is easier to recognise the freedom of boundaries that exists in the streets of Isfahan. These boundaries are 'usable' spaces (shops, workshops, caravanserais, hammams, madarais), living environments, which are dependent upon the primary movement system (the bazaar) for their existence and shape the architectural expression that is formed. Solid spaces are seen as voids, negative space is not the leftover area between buildings, but the positive, active space, the functional 'gaps in-between'.

---

[53]Ardalan and Bakhitar – Isfahan, *Sense of Unity* (1973) p 100.
[54]Ardalan and Bakhitar – Isfahan, *Sense of Unity* (1973) p 17.
[55]Ardalan and Bakhitar – Freedom of Boundaries, *Sense of Unity* (1973) p 96.

Conclusion

> The city should be seen as a stimulating and exciting mael-
> strom of cultural conflict and change and should not be some-
> thing that should be deconstructed into a whole, rather we
> should celebrate and dissect the fragments and empathise
> with the multiplicity and contradiction which exists in such
> public spaces.[92]

By understanding the importance of convivial life in the street as
seen in Isfahan, Jaipur and Harare, one can understand the concept
that public street life must be maintained as a positive attribute
informing the integration of the street edge so that it becomes a
boundary unmarked by set parameters. Harare, being an African
city, has many different social systems, compared to the Asian
examples, but yet all the case studies have numerous ideas, which
are combined, to display the fundamental idea that the street
becomes a 'living environment, alive with humanity'.

The market places and bazaars of the case studies supply a large
range of social and economic activities, where the visitor and inhabitant are immersed in a complex network of spaces, on an interrupted
journey through the streets, only to stop at specific encounters or
public spaces along the way. There is a daily gathering of festivity and
mingling in a chaotic dynamism of city life. People passing through
the bazaars of Africa or Asia are continually exposed to the sensation
and sights, stimulated to a diverse world of excitement, compared to
the Western streets, where urban living has rendered street life as
being predictable, monotonous and lacking in sensuous nature.

This confirms that trading routes are positive integrators into the
urban fabric and should not be viewed as dirty, dusty places with
many problems and negative activities where only the urban poor
exist. Thus, the streets are public spaces, which contain a host of
many cultures, traditions and economies, packed full of energy.
These streets develop informal, irregular trading routes, creating a
versatile street edge, which is vibrant, multifarious and exhilarating.
The African and Asian trading street offers an environment where
there are numerous smells to be smelt, sights to see, people to meet
and memories to take away.

---

[92]Morgan S. – Notes from discussion about 'living in the city' (1999).

Alvin Foo Tze Yang

A Society in Transition: the Social and Spatial Production of the Aged Identity in the Changing Landscapes of Care Environments

Foo Tze Yang's dissertation is somewhat different from most of the others printed here, in that it offers a more social-science approach to architecture. This is a particularly timely study, as it investigates an aspect of architectural design and provision – for more aged members of society – that is becoming increasingly important in the context of demographic shifts in urban populations world-wide.

Alvin Foo Tze Yang

A SOCIETY IN TRANSITION

The Social and Spatial Production of the Aged Identity in the Changing Landscapes of Care Environments

ACKNOWLEDGEMENTS

I would like to express my gratitude and thanks to all those who have encouraged and supported me in the course of preparing this dissertation. Particularly to my supervisor, Associate Professor James D. Harrison and his colleague, Mr Kenneth Parker for their direction and encouragement and also to my family for their support.

I would also like to express my gratitude and appreciation to Ms. Vijaya Sreenidhi, Manager of Elderly Service Department, NCSS, for her hospitality and also for her generous insights into the current development of elderly care services in Singapore. Thanks.

ORIGINAL CONTENTS

ACKNOWLEDGEMENTS
ABSTRACT
INTRODUCTION: BACKGROUND

Chapter 1: The Spatial and Social Production of the Aged Identity

Chapter 2: Blurring the Boundaries: In Sharing of Power

Chapter 3: Changing Landscapes of Care Practice and Environment

APPENDICES

1.1 INTERACTIONISM
The reflexive aged identity

Interactionism is a useful concept in understanding the variables operative in elderly participation within the community, peer groups and family. According to Wallace and Facio, it provides a concept of an individual, "as creatively acting to define and shape the world around them, in contrast to the functionalist theory that tends to portray individuals as reacting to structurally defined roles and sanctions." To Wallace and Facio, it replaces a more deterministic view posited by 'disengagement theory' with a more volitional theory of human action. This concept is akin to Kaufman's definition of an 'ageless self' which contends that the aging and the aged cannot be viewed as passive actors who assume 'socially constructed roles' at every stage of their life cycle. They are active participants who maintain a notion of self and identity through continuous 'reconstruction' of their 'selves' to adapt to the changing contexts.

> *"The notion of agelessness provides a framework for understanding the problems and needs that accompany aging. For old people do not think of themselves in a linear way – a succession of roles, or a trajectory of gains and losses. Nor do people think themselves as purely "socialized" beings, learning, and then performing a set of socially appropriate behaviors. Instead people dynamically integrate a wide range of experience including values, family and educational backgrounds, work experience, and cultural ideals to construct a current identity. Decisions about what services to demand and what services to accept will depend on how perceptions of those services fit into their scheme of priorities – their ideas of what is important to them at that moment in time."*
>
> Sharon Kaufman

The implication to the care and service providers is that, in order to provide for interventions that are congruent to the client's needs and priorities, they must take into careful consideration the dimension of the 'ageless self' or the social self of the elderly person, which is most reflective of historical and social context from which the client makes his/her decisions. The elderly individual will most often "hold on to a sense of self and a sense of purpose that they generally refuse to have violated."

From an Interactionist's point of view, any social interaction between individuals or individual and community is seen as a process of exchange. Dowd contends that this exchange process explains that any "disengagement of the elderly from society is not due to role loss, but due to the deterioration of their ability to profit from exchanges made in such interactions. Because they can no longer profit, they withdraw from exchange networks." Dowd conceptualises the 'resources' that the elderly person brings into their interactions and social exchanges into three main categories, such as material (wealth), symbolic (physical appearance) and relational (friendship) resources. However, the use and control of such resources of the elderly individual can be limited by certain situations or environments that they are placed in. How successful the elderly person is able to control and make gainful use of such resources is noticed to raise the level of activity amongst their communities. In such instances, as observed by Hoschild, they have been observed to develop active communities with distinctive subculture and mutual aid patterns. What is significant in this observation is how the elderly individual can and will actively manipulate his or her 'resources' in reconstructing their social worlds especially in 'new' environments, where they are seen and made to feel valued and useful as social beings. Hence, it is important to recognise the 'motivational forces' behind their interactions and the role of care environments in facilitating and encouraging the elderly in the gainful use and control of such resources, to raise the level of activity. The Report of the Committee on The Problems of the Aged in Singapore noted that the mental and physical well-being of Elderly Persons depends greatly on how well they spend their time: maintaining interest in work, keeping up existing social contacts, and pursuing new interest and activities.

Pia Kontos observes that the emerging focus of the aged as a subject constitutive of individual experiences and not as an object of social practices is a reaction against conventional positivism and empiricism which until now has continued to characterise care practices and services. She feels that in conventional practice, old age is "treated as part of the natural order to the exclusion of the cultural order." In short, old age is treated as a biological phenomenon and the role of culture (the subjectivity of the aged) in such a framework is relegated to explaining surface variations of statistics, while the depths of individuals are presumed to involve the same physiological and organic processes and changes." As critical gerontological theory has become more sophisticated in terms of its dynamism and comprehensiveness, this has begun to pave the way for the inclusion of personal narratives to serve as a basis for alternative interpretations of the experience of ageing. She feels that this is necessary in providing a critical subjective dimension as a basis of critique against the scientific claims of social sciences.

Susan Pickard also observes that the self-image of the elderly individual is very much bound to the way the elderly see themselves as part of the wider community. Many elderly people considered that being sociable was a positive personality attribute as important as being part of the community or a neighbourhood. Keeping active and possessing a healthy social network resulted in promoting a 'youthful outlook' among the elderly compared to those who have withdrawn themselves from social circles. Susan Pickard observed that when people see themselves as not 'old' regardless of chronological age, it is a positive indication of high morale and general well-being.

What is also significant in Pickard's observation is that the perception of 'old age' even amongst the elderly is very negative and they wished to distance themselves from this condition. She also noted how some likened being old to the 'unreal quality' of being in a bad dream. The ageing body betrays the identity within as it does with the rest of society who gaze upon it. We must appreciate the significant amount of entrenched negative stereotypes that are attributed to the ageing body both by the elderly individual as well as society and this belies an often ignored 'ageless identity'. When we respond to stereotype, we respond not to this ageless identity but subsume it under a popularly constructed image, which results in the estrangement of the body from its identity; this will continue to heighten this sense of the 'unreal'.

1.2   EVOLVING LANDSCAPES
Embodied spaces and spatialised identities

Glenda Laws offers an interesting perspective on how the spatial environment and the body that inhabits it are mutually constitutive components, constantly reshaping each other over time. What is significant here is the understanding of the dynamics (of discursive and non-discursive powers) at work here in the constitution of the aged identity as well as how evolving forms of spatiality effects changes in social practices and age relations.

> *Identities are spatialised, in that where we are says a lot about who we are. There are pervasive links between social and spatial positions; we hold 'geographically specific' stereotypes of people because there are equally powerful stereotypes of places.*
>
> Glenda Laws

1.2.1 CHANGING AGED IDENTITY AND SPATIALITY

The public identity and status of the elderly within the past 5 decades of Singapore has been through a tremendous transformation. From images of elderly people residing in 'death-houses' in the 1930s, to images of the elderly people residing in old-age homes or one room HDB flats, to recent granny flats and sheltered housing initiatives, and to retirement villages or communities in the near future. The term 'retirement' also signifies connection with the work force, hence this attributes a measure of worthiness to the image of the old as having served society. It is important to note how the changing aged identities over the years were reciprocated by changing spatial types.

1.2.2 IDENTITY MARKERS:

Spatial influence in the production of new identities and social attitudes

Just as aged bodies are attributed symbolic capital in places or spaces that imbue them with positive meanings it follows that dis-empowerment is the consequence of the reduction of symbolic cap-ital of the body as in when a body declines and can no longer fulfil the 'role' that is required of that space or place. This can become problematic especially if one has bought into a developer's lifestyle or a care scheme, which does not factor in a degree of decline from the user or is adaptable to differentiated needs. This could affect the self-image of the user and as we can see, the experience of being old varies accordingly to one's environment.

Using Sun City retirement communities in the United States as an example, Laws observes how developers are mindful that in order to be successful they must market for a certain identity and actively construct such an identity. The marketing of images of residents engaged in various activities around the community is representa-tional of both the place and the 'identities' the developers seek as residents. This is illustrated through images of well-heeled elderly people, presented in the brochures, who are seen to be making the most of the country club-like facilities and actively taking part in sports activity. In this instance, we see how identities are being spa-tialised and spaces embodied.

> Real estate developers have been particularly cognizant of the need to spatialise these identities in order to make their own projects profitable. As these identities are constructed and adopted by an increasing number of people, demand for lifestyle retirement communities also increases.
>
> Glenda Laws

Soja's *socio-spatial* dialectic describes how spaces also alter social practices. The introduction of retirement communities and nursing homes are a result of changing social practices and values, and since their introduction, attitudes toward care for certain cate-gories of the elderly have changed. What is important to recognise is that certain types of physical environment limit the way or ways in which a community can develop in terms of potential social interactions and networks. Environments can be seen as age-graded or user-graded in that we only expect to see a certain cate-gory of people there. However, Massey argues that spatial boundaries are permeable in that "within any one location, local and extra-local forces can combine to produce the place and the character". Appreciation of this can suggest how complementary environments can be creatively combined so as to promote new attitudes of social engagement within the community as well as positive perceptions of the environment.

> *The material spaces and places in which we live, work and engage in leisure activities are age-graded and in turn, age is associated with particular spaces and places.*
>
> Glenda Laws

1.2.3 RENEGOTIATING SOCIAL RELATIONS:

Evolving new identities

Each cohort of the elderly is now expected to have a longer life expectancy and are generally healthier than past generations. The ageing and the aged now participate in activities that once fell within the domain of younger people. Senior citizens now take on roles as volunteers, educators, mentors, students and staff workers in fast-food restaurants. Undertaking these 'roles' and making their presence felt within respective setting challenges perceptions of whom we expect to see in certain types of spaces or places and in so doing, redefines age relations between all members of society. Laws contends that the aged identity remains fluid and is constantly being renegotiated over time. Moody concurs by acknowledging that changing social policies and institutions are factors that determine life-cycle transitions and roles hence identities. The educational system determines the transition from youth to adulthood; similarly retirement marks the transition from middle age to old age. What is significant now is that mid-life transitions are no longer clearly regulated. The disappearance of mandatory retirement, the 'culture' of retraining and life-long learning being expounded by ageing societies out of economic necessity are blurring and merging the boundaries that describe the role of the student, part-time worker and the retiree. The aged identity of today is perhaps more multi-dimensional than in the past. More importantly, Moody shares Neugarten's view that with the increasing ambivalence in the meaning of old age; one must redefine the bases for understanding 'old age' other than just the 'last stage of life'.

> *On the other hand, as the stages of life have evolved and become blurred, the entire image of 'old age' is giving way to more of an 'age-irrelevant' image of the life course. As an empirical matter, chronological age, by itself, loses predictive value and importance for many purposes.*
>
> Moody

The meaning of retirement has changed significantly over time; the growing visibility of the active and affluent retired people of the present has replaced the images of retirees suffering from social exclusion upon retirement. This is a significant turning point in what

Jamieson and Victor observe as a shift in focus from the productive versus the non-productive aspects of life stages to that of patterns of consumption. In Laws' case example of the American Sun City retirement communities, they commented that it is a "spatial representation of a particular retirement culture, a particular construction of retired life as happy, communal activity, protected from, yet in touch with, the surrounding community". They felt that this "focus on the consumption of different forms of living space would certainly seem to provide further understanding of the diversity of old age". Consumerism can be seen as liberating, and has undeniably enabled diversity and choice, and as a result, broke down certain ageist assumptions of how a retiree should live in society or be confined to certain locations. We must also recognise that such patterns of consumption are also shaped by economic interests, the question that must be continually asked is, "how well does it reflect contemporary 'realities' in responding to the real needs of the elderly person?"

1.3   THE 'OLD' IN THE IMAGE OF THE 'YOUNG':

In denial of the declining body

Sarah Harper contends that the negative image of the frail body is a construction of a male-dominated knowledge system, which is fundamentally premised on certain ageist assumptions. These assumptions fail to recognise bodily decline as a natural process of ageing hence tend to 'legitimise' certain care needs that are established through a biased criteria, which in turn dictates what the experience of 'successful ageing' should be.

This concept of 'embodied and disembodied' knowledge has implications on our understanding of the ageing body in relation to concepts of control. Harper notes, "Control under the dominant system of knowledge can be directly related to gendered experience of the body." This implies that in wanting to achieve 'disembodied' control, one favours absolute control over the body and suppresses the 'other' which is the ageing body with regard to physical decline. This inevitably leads to the denial of the 'lived' or 'embodied' body, which is categorised as 'unnatural'; hence something to be feared or at worst, treated with contempt or denial. Under patriarchal knowledge, premised on 'disembodied control'; men are enabled by this system of knowledge to deny the body for much of their lives. In the same line of argument, men become 'embodied' as they age because they begin to lose essential control over their body. "It is only later in life that men like women, through the experience of the experiential and constructed body, are forced to recognise the 'other' as a defining force in their own construction and experience".

However, this is not to say that women are more adaptable to changes in late life. As Susan Pickard comments, women and men are no less different in wanting physical independence. She disclaims the belief that women can cope with dependency better than men because they have been socialised to be more dependent to certain extent. She contends that both men and women do have certain domains in their lives in which they find it acceptable to be dependent but also other domains where they feel it is unacceptable. Thus it is important to investigate such domains that define and sustain notions of independence and self.

Cole observed in that the 'scientific management of ageing' in nineteenth century America, scientists sought after the ideal of a 'normal old age' premised on the image of the functional capacity of a youthful body as a key criterion of successful ageing. They sought solutions against senility, sexual impotence, decline in productivity etc. of the ageing body, which revealed a relentless hostility to physical decline in its fervent search for the 'elixir of youth'.

What is noteworthy is that such a notion of 'successful ageing' might be biased towards social perceptions of the natural processes of ageing. The advancement of medical technologies has offered 'ageing' bodies a temporary reprieve from the onset of physical decline. However, we have to be very careful that such innovations do not overstep its moral imperative as Cole forewarns:

> *By transforming health from a means of living well into an end in itself, 'successful aging' reveals its bankruptcy as an ideal that cannot accommodate the realities of decline and death. To create genuinely satisfying ideals of aging, we will have to transcend our exclusive emphasis on individual health and find renewed sources of social and cosmic connection.*
>
> Cole

Moody points us to the wider implications of the 'bio-medicalisation' of old age in relation to opposing forces of social, economic and technological developments:

> *Optimists believe that medicine will soon permit us to displace ageing-related diseases and declines until later and later in life, a pattern known as 'compression of morbidity'. Yet economic forces seem to move in opposite direction from biology. Changes in the job market and in technology can make previously useful skills irrelevant. Biology promises to postpone ageing, but social forces, such as age discrimination, make the impact of ageing more important than ever.*
>
> Moody

Featherstone and Hepworth identify the continuous tension that exists between the external appearance (the face and the body), the functional capacities and the construction of the personal identity of an elderly person. This tension is further exacerbated by stigmatisation and exclusion of the elderly from society through denial of inadvertent mental, physiological and sexual decline as a natural process in chronological old age. Thus, Frank (1991) and Kleiman (1988) argue for this need of acceptance on the part of society and self, in relation to the elderly community, which desires to be recognised in their condition and to be acknowledged that their conditions are both natural and human.

> *Old age is bio-medicalised, its symptoms treated by physicians and nursing home attendants. The old person's identity is fixed upon the body by its changes and by the experts on longevity who surround the process of ageing in Western society.*
>
> Warren

> *We learn to define ourselves by the roles and diagnoses given to us by psychiatrists, take them into ourselves and feel helpless to influence our own lives.*
>
> Lindow

Both Warren and Lindow capture the sense of 'helplessness' experienced by aged people in such circumstances, which underscores the importance for the voice of the aged to be heard and represented. Susan Harper elaborated on the concept of 'sexed' knowledge and its relationships to explain the dominant notions of control and management of the body. She believes that by recognising and challenging the fundamental assumptions entrenched within our beliefs this will "help in the forming of a new concept of later life which fully accepts the loss of bodily control, rejects the stigmatization of the declining body, and acknowledges the possibility of peace between meaning and control, symbol and experience, thus allowing the frailty of extreme later life to be fully integrated into mainstream social experience".

1.3.1 IN SEARTH OF A MYTH:

Identity and social place of the aged in pre-modern and modern times

Pre-modern elders were regarded as wise and accorded high social places until the onset of the industrial revolution which changed the face of societies and unwittingly eliminated the social sources and places of the elderly person for their wisdom, their know-how and their experiences, etc. This was seen to have eroded their status. Warren regards this as myth of modern ageing. What she proposes for both premodern and modern western culture is that the ageing body "forms the link between the ageing process and the social place of the elderly – and thus their social and personal identity".

The postmodern condition in Western culture describes a social phenomenon of the identity as constituted through political, social, gender, even sexual orientation; identity is constituted in the collective. Postmodern social movements in the light of evolving political and gender roles have given a social place and a voice to minority groups, women's rights groups, gays and lesbian groups, paramilitary groups etc. which were once 'faceless' (also without place) in premodern times. Warren observes that the body in the postmodern condition is no longer the *locus of self;* identity goes beyond "the body and its physical markers; it can be constituted in terms of political claims and powers devoid of physical components". Hence in this line of reasoning, some feel that once again in this era, the aged identity will find new sources of alternative social place and role just as other minority groups have done so just as in the myth of the pre-industrial past. However, Warren argues otherwise, she states that "bodily decay is the fulcrum of the ageing process in Western culture (and any other culture we might know), the *sameness of identity* is always challenged by the ageing body. And furthermore, this same process of bodily decay makes it unlikely that the aged will find personal identity within postmodern social movements". In other words, "the body is where ageing takes place and the body is where the social order takes note of ageing". (Karner) Unlike other social movements that distinguish its identity from one another in terms of cause, gender and sexual orientation the ageing body does not discriminate. The 'biomedicalisation' of ageing was never a new concept as it had its roots in antiquity even though its remedies then were much less refined but more fantastic. Nevertheless the principle remains the same, it is still a dominant aspect in the discourse of ageing. Warren laments:

> Social policies of old age in modern society risk absurdity to the precise extent that they become or remain ahistorical or anti-developmental. To ignore the long history of ageing as change and decay, the betrayal of the body, and the ambivalence of the young and old toward ageing and the elderly is to fly in the face of the wisdom of generations past and those to come.

Warren

Warren is critical about the fundamental approach to understanding the experience of ageing which has not moved beyond the preservation of the physical body. In our efforts to prevent its decline we ignored the reflexive identity or 'interactionist self' within the body. This 'blind-spot' has contributed to the continued ambivalence experienced by both young and old in the process and experience of ageing.

1.4   CONTESTED SPACE:

The arena of 'power and resistance'

'Space is a social construct' was an aphorism used in the seventies. It reflected the belief that space is constituted through social relations and material social practices. However, Massey felt that while it is correct to say that space is socially constructed, it is the one-sided formulation which implies that geographical forms and distributions were simply outcomes which merely described the spatial form of the social and were explained in other disciplines like sociology or economics. (41) This belief did not serve any function nor saw the need for furthering understanding in the relationship between the social and the spatial.

In the States during the 1980s, it became apparent that social and economic changes were also integral to the major spatial restructuring experienced both intranationally and internationally. Hence, the inclusion of the phrase, 'the *social is also spatially constructed'* was added to the aphorism of the 1970s. This implied that "in its broadest formulation, society is necessarily constructed spatially, and the fact that spatial organization of society makes a difference to how it works" is the fundamental difference in the conception of space as seen in the past. This has brought into focus the *centrality of space* in social sciences today.

1.4.1 POLITICS OF SPACE

There is a difference between an activity taking place in an informal setting such as a leisure centre or public space compared to the same activity taking place within an institutionalised setting, a home, hospice, day care centre etc. Within institutionalised settings, to perform an activity sometimes is tantamount to an imposed obligation. Refusal to take part is likely to be seen as being difficult or anti-social. Insensitivity to the feelings and perceptions of the elderly in the way activities are conducted may result in embarrassment and discomfort to the elderly person performing it. That is to say, programs or activities that become ends in themselves to keep the elderly occupied without taking into account how the elderly understood or were engaged with the activity will lead to rapid disengagement. The experiences of users are frequently constructed through the range of existing services; hence the recipients of such services – the aging and the aged – may well have absorbed ideas about their 'marginal role and limited capacities'. Thus it is necessary to ensure that 'practices' or 'initiatives' remain progressive in that they are capable of being self-reflective – being conscious of its assumptions and relevance. Fundamentally to challenge stereotypes rather than reinforce them.

*Confronting an image of the old tilted to the dimensions of
incapacity and death can initiate drastic changes in the attitudes and behavior toward those so labeled.*

Sokolovsky

Rather than having practices or initiatives that are designed purely
from functional attitudes and concerns that cater to perceived needs,
we need to look at practices or initiatives that work to promote
notions of 'empowerment' and 'self-development'. These concepts
should not relate just to the users themselves but also to how they
impact the rest of the community in terms of challenging mindsets
and encouraging participation and acceptance. Creating a less for-
malised environment and management will ensure less obligatory
'role-playing' or expectations to 'live-up' to. 'Power and resistance'
operate differently in different settings. We should be aware of such
'unspoken politics'. In short, activities will be 'framed' differently
under different circumstances and this will determine the extent to
which the elderly will participate or disengage or at worst be forced
into 'role-play'.

1.4.2 A FAMILIAR VIEW FROM HOME

Place beyond its physicality is also a symbolic construct. It serves as
a psychological construct of locating oneself in the scheme of
things. It is invested with immense social capital and also an intimate extension of the body. Such conceptual mapping is a powerful
medium that defines how an individual negotiates daily processes
with ease and success and what Kontos describes as a "vital facet of
self-identity".

Home is a familiar conceptual construct intertwined very much
with the concept of self in late life. A senior's strategies in coping with
the environment is to transpose the multi-faceted 'concept of home'
into settings like congregate or sheltered housing in which they
inhabit.

*The tenants adopt strategies, which allow them to retain con-
trol over many aspects of their lives and maintain the fabric of
home at standards they recognize as being appropriate for
themselves. Strategies for coping with declining health
involve the construction of home as a meaningful context,
one that affords independence, and shapes and maintains
seniors' self-identities. Declining health does not lead
inevitably to the disintegration of self-identity.*

Kontos

Even with the overall built environment, in this case, a nursing
home, Kontos observed that certain spaces are particularly invested
with more significance than others are. In this instance, the Tea

Room is seen as a symbolic 'territorial stake' between the residents and the administration. For the residents it is an expression of culture, embodying collective interests, activities and identity of the users whereas to the staff its symbolic value represented part of their work in maintaining the place, which transcended the activities that took place within it. Due to ideological differences, the Tea Room becomes a 'contested space' – a psychological hinge point that serves to sustain the overall perception of the support environment as a 'home' or as 'an institution'. Any attempt by the staff which is read by the residents as upsetting the status quo or an invasion into their 'home domain' will have a significant impact on the residents' experience of the place as a home.

> *Tenants justify their existence and assert their self-identity through the processes of resistance to the staff. In terms of identity, the ability to control intrusions into 'home territory' is a salient issue. Home plays an important part in framing the experience of independence, since independence is so closely linked to control.*
>
> Kontos

This study highlights the fact that beyond the considerations of designing physical environments for support and socialisation etc. one must be aware that a space can have totally different symbolic values to the parties involved. Encountered resistance from the residents cannot be resolved within administrative confines or logic. Meaningful intervention can only come from an appreciation of the existence of such value systems and requires a willingness to redefine working relations which also include the sharing of power.

The significance in observing how elderly people cope in supportive environments, even under conditions of physical decline and loss of mobility, underscores the importance of examining the role of personal construction of meaning of place by the elderly resident. As Kontos identifies, "Home space provides the material resources necessary for the senior tenants to maintain their independence, sustain a meaningful existence and resist institutionalisation." And just as importantly, "Place construed as home plays a critical role in maintaining a sense of personal identity."

3.3 CONCLUSION

From this discussion, we realise that the quality of care provision cannot be measured quantitatively by the provision of an extensive range of care services and environments. Firstly, it needs to be appreciated from a wider spectrum of issues that occur beyond the boundaries of care provision for the elderly community. Secondly, there is a need to relook at the boundaries and even to problematise them from which the discourse of ageing is structured upon.

Professor William Liu best sums up Singapore's multi-pronged approach to community care as:

> *The philosophy of individual responsibility and self-reliance, the family as the primary pillar of support, the community as the provider of support services and the government as facilitator, helper and catalyst.*

However, these initiatives only set out the parameters from which community care initiatives in Singapore are prioritised. One must be reminded that understanding the *Aged Identity* is the key to maintaining the relevance of these initiatives. The *Aged Identity* is a multidimensional one and is constantly renegotiated. Its richness can only be fully appreciated through multi-disciplinary efforts.

The medicalisation of health care services in its obsession with preserving the full range of control over the body has unwittingly transmitted the notion of a perfect body as the primary condition for successful ageing. This has recalibrated the expectations of the individual and society at large. Societal changes in terms of familial structures, care-management and government policies will also continue to redefine engagement between the various parties involved.

The 'role of place' in modern life course has been altered and will continue to change; the impacts of such changes are just beginning to be felt in terms of 'global' communities and evolving landscapes.

As the '*centrality of space*' acquires greater prominence in social sciences, this will further inform us on the workings of spatial organisation in how it better facilitates processes. Massey best captures the centrality of space, observing that "space is conceptualised as created out of social relations, space is by its nature full of power and symbolism, a complex web of relations of domination and subordination, of solidarity and co-operation".

Complexity and diversity characterise the various innovative and critical approaches adopted in gerontological discourse. However, in our continued endeavour to formulate better approaches and models of care we must not cease to question the ideological bases from which they spring. The concept of empowerment remains an elusive one, filled with contradictions and needs be answered differently under different contexts.

We are also reminded that things can only work if societal values are in concert with current developments and ideals expressed in community care models. Hence, to begin our daunting task of removing the stain of ageism still entrenched within our collective psyche – a necessary challenge – we must all engage. The 'push and pull' forces generated by social, political and environmental changes will continue to create undercurrents and the effects ripple through the whole of society's processes. In this continuous 'flux' of events, we (young and old) cannot afford to be ambivalent towards the processes and experience of ageing. These developments represent a simultaneity of positions, locations and meanings and has opened up 'traditional space' to dislocations and hence to 'politics' or power play. As the graying horizon dawns on us within the next three decades we will find ourselves in the *world* we now talk about. Until then, how well we are able to come to terms with it will depend on how well we understand it in the here and now.

Alexander Franklin

The Architecture of Omniscience: Codes, Grafts and the Representation of the Work of Michael Sorkin

Very often architectural dissertations make the mistake of tackling a subject that is far too large for the time and space available. Franklin's research dissertation shows the merits of tackling large issues concerning the way in which architecture may hover between text, representation and idea, but investigating them through the work of a single figure, in this case the American writer, critic and designer, Michael Sorkin.

Alexander Franklin

THE ARCHITECTURE OF OMNISCIENCE:

Codes, Grafts and the Representation of the Work of Michael Sorkin

ORIGINAL CONTENTS

Acknowledgements
Preface
0] Prelude
1] Writing as the [Clarifying] Architectural Act.

[PAIR ONE]
Criticism and the Political Act
2] Texted Architectures

[PAIR TWO]
The Code and Point of View
3] The [Written] Gap

[PAIR THREE]
The City and Propinquity
4] Exeunt:

PREFACE

I'm interested in a frankly visionary discourse of urbanism, and it's very little seen. And when I say that I'm interested in a visionary discourse I'm not simply interested in a formal discourse but a social discourse as well. In a way that

*conversation is somewhat more advanced than the formal
component, which we desperately need to reintroduce."*
*"I would say that from my own experiments in teaching, one
of the methods that I'm interested in investigating is a way of
thinking about the city, or the design of cities, that's more
inductive. This I understand not only as a design strategy but
as also a strategy for participation.*

Michael Sorkin, interviewed by Peter Hennessey[1]

My interest in studying the work of the critic, writer, architect and
professor of urbanism, Michael Sorkin, stemmed from a curiosity at
what seemed to me to be two independent discourses: the abstract
legality of the Local Code, and the fantasy of his colourful
Urbanagrams. Sorkin has two, or more, faces: the gravity of a critic,
and an inter-disciplinary method of seduction that draws one into
his visionary thought. Seduction through beautifully drawn plans
and evocative perspectives: sometimes these are funny, sometimes
ironic. But his underlying polemic is verging on the humorous, to
make cities fun to live in again, to find the qualities that help us get
the most out of where and how we live.

My questioning has always arisen from an interest in the multiplic-
ity of reading: situations, places, texts – and what lessons are there to
be learnt from the shifts that Sorkin makes from one field of architectural production to another. In an age where the validity of architectural writing has never been so prominent, I was interested in
analysing why more architects are finding their ways back into texts
as a way to help establish their aims, to convey their architectonic
expression. It seemed a natural synthesis of these two interests could
be found, first through studying the methods of texts, and then applying these literary techniques to an analysis of Sorkin's drawn work.

0] Prelude

*A scene is never viewed 'at a glance' – rather, it is recon-
structed via a scanning sequence in which the eye flits continuously from point to point to complete an almost
instantaneous visual reconnaisance of the situation. This
visual scanning process is an issue-oriented operation, and so
people with quite different motives and interests will view the
same scene in quite different ways.*

Tom Porter, *The Architect's Eye*[2]

---

[1] *Transition* No. 39, pp 19–20.
[2] Tom Porter, *The Architect's Eye* (London: E&F Spon, 1997) pp 28–9.

Michael Sorkin, who both writes and designs, speaks of "empty style", as a negative description of the status quo of architecture and urbanism in the United States during the last 20 years. In the pre- amble to *"Local Code"*, he states that, "the code and the plan are the armatures for the expression and extension of such preferences and the protocol for experiment. Their fulfilment acts as stimulus to art, in its friendship with the private and the collective imagination".[3] This study, is concerned with mapping the work of an architect who adopts different viewpoints within the range of architectural media that he uses, illustrating the liberating effect that independent, dia- logic projects might afford the work of other individual architects. Hence the text is loosely based on the work of Michael Sorkin, with other specific parallels drawn as appropriate.

Before I started studying architecture, the thought had never occurred to me that there might exist more than one way to do archi- tecture. Into the summer-break between my First and Second years, I sought to study the failings and strengths of my design work to date, and I ended up with finding and studying a book to which I owe a great deal, for it opened to me the reality of architecture as a mul- tifaceted process, of which there co-exist many means of represen- tation. In truth I picked out the book because it seemed to portray convincing tips on graphic techniques that the accomplished archi- tect as draughtsman and creative designer must have at his dis- posal, and I was desperate to improve my presentational skills. The effect however, has been subtler than a quick-fix, brassy suping up of weak First Year design work. It taught me that there was more to architectural representation than I had bargained for. The book was entitled *"Drawing As a Means To Architecture"*.[4]

The fact that drawing is only one means to architecture is a fun- damental, but neglected issue: as architects in their training become more comfortable in their ability to convey an expression of their architectonic image, the result is often the dependency on the draw- ing to get the message across. The process of architecture, if docu- mented fully, would have to incur thousands of references which lie beyond drawing. How many ways are there then to do architecture? What does the drawing do for the architect? Obviously, the fact that an architect must be able to draw, and draw convincingly, means that the profession will for the interim remain somewhat exclusive. And yet there is the contention that this is wrong, that architecture could and should be created by a far greater field of professionals other than those who are able to draw plans, sections and elevations.[5]

---

[3]Michael Sorkin, *Local Code,* (New York: Princeton Architectural Press, 1993) p 11.
[4]William Kirby Lockard, *Drawing As a Means to Architecture* (New York: Van Nostrand Reinhold, 1978).
[5]Jonathan Hill, *The Illegal Architect,* (London: Black Dog Publishing, 1998) pp 32–36.

Through reducing architecture to merely the construction and assembly of buildings from the architect's set of instructions, the scope of the architect's work is reduced to the pseudo-technical artist acting as the hidden foreman of a building project. Drawings can describe a building, but do they convey architecture proper?

> *It would appear that the drawing as a tool in some cases impedes the architect.*

It is not a new concept to question the convention of drawing as a means to architecture, indeed architectural drawing was born out of a necessity to add to the art of building a sense of precision. But the affect of precision that drawing has on architectural production can be limiting, and proponents such as Jonathan Hill, Bernard Tschumi and Michael Sorkin through their work suggest that there is another way to construct an image, an impression of space, which the drawing inherently cannot access. These architects, with differing results, have turned to the written text as a means to develop their architectural discourses.

Roland Barthes states that the reader is the space "on which all quotations that make up a writing are inscribed without any of them being lost; a text's unity lies not in its origin but in its destination". [6] For Barthes, the limitations of a text are not those of the translation of the text in the reader's mind, but that to give a text an author in itself imposes its own limits. It furnishes the mental construct with a final signified, which he contends results in heightening the reader's interest in the author and his setting, interests and impulses.

> *Experimental video, computer graphics, and virtual images have radically transformed the late twentieth-century understanding of reality and continue to challenge the complex discourse surrounding visual representation. The fragmentation and temporalization of space initiated by film montage and modernist collage have opened up a truly infinite realm of poetic places for the human imagination, which await their transformation into architecture.*
>
> Alberto Perez-Gomez, Louise Pelletier *Architectural Representation and the Perspective Hinge*[7]

This study of point of view is ultimately concerned with the influence that writing has on architectonic space. Itself a text, I have used a series of interwoven suggestions to question the issues of writing and drawing architecture, as an attempt to map the notion of point

---

[6]Roland Barthes, "The Death of the Author," in *Image, Text, Music* (London: Fontana, 1977) p 148.
[7]Alberto Perez-Gomez, Louise Pelletier, *Architectural Representation and the Perspective Hinge* (Cambridge, MA: MIT, 1997) p 3.

of view primarily in written architectonic space, and subsequently to look at how written (texted) conventions might benefit the conventions of space delineated through drawing. The marriage of the study of viewpoint and written architectural production stems from the influence that photography, and later cinematography, has had on the way we have come to think, to work, to live. Both still and moving images have opened our eyes to many new worlds, both through the act of instantaneous representation and reproduction; but equally through the actual development of photographic techniques, and the effects that they have had as they are crossed over into fields such as architecture. Thus the way many architects write, and the reasons for which they turn to writing, is to explore the possibilities of the blank sheet in evoking spaces through the frame of the imaginary camera, pushing the boundaries of written space and consequently they way we come to accept architecture, what it is, and what it could be.

3] The [Written] Gap

Misconstruing the omitted

> *Karen Franck: "...you, Nancy, get to choose the forms in a way that architects don't have an opportunity to do because they are restricted so much by the programme (brief) or by the site or by the budget. So you have a chance to pick and choose."*
> *Nancy Wolf: "But that's the role of the artist."*
> *Karen Franck: "Yes, and that's what some architects miss."*[30]

When we write architecture, we are constructing spaces which we will experience through the ways that we have been taught to read. We read differently; intonation allows the reader to read into the text issues which subconsciously are the most important and relevant to this cause; but are we given this same latitude with architectonic drawings? Roger Connah poses the central question to this train of thought: what would happen to (written) architecture if we had not been tempted to misconstrue language?[31] He concedes that some architects such as Reima Pietilä "consciously ask words to perform too much; unlike the film-director or the critic he asks them to over-achieve. In relation to his architecture, he often wants words to do more than they possibly can". [32]

---

[30]Karen A. Franck, *Nancy Wolf – Hidden Cities, Hidden Longings,* p 41.
[31]Roger Connah, *Writing Architecture* (Cambridge, MA: MIT, 1989) p 233.
[32]*Ibid.* p 230.

All narratives are different, but it is when the designer realises that it is not only the media that he chooses to utilise but the stance within the media which determines the product's formation and its success, that he will be in a position to impart the narrative correctly. The gap between his mind's image and that which she/he (re)presents shortens. Increasingly, architects are turning to media other than drawing and models through which they can shape their architectural forms. Writing has received a renaissance within the profession, precisely because, as Wiel Arets states, we think in words which are easier to grasp with little deviation in meaning occurring (when written in a language understood by all parties involved.) It is not a new concept, but the film-maker's frame has taught architects the value of the temporal gap, and through montage, the spatial gap. The film director Wim Wenders calls the gaps in Berlin wounds that have remained left over, untouched. For him, this city is defined through where it is empty.[33] It is through these gaps that we come into contact with the true city, for these gaps ask for our engagement with their story. "Some films are like closed walls: there is not a single gap between its images that would allow you to see anything else than what this movie shows you. Your eyes and your mind are not allowed to wander. You cannot add anything from yourself to that particular film, no feelings, no experience. You stumble out empty afterwards, like you have been abused. Only those films with gaps in between their imagery are telling stories, that is my conviction."

Omniscience

> The objective idea of a building – sets of conventional projections. These projective representations rely on reductive syntactic connections; each projection constitutes part of a dissected whole. They are expected to be absolutely unambiguous to avoid possible (mis)interpretations, as well as functioning as efficient mental instruments devoid of inherent value other than their capacity for accurate transcription. Professional architects generally see architectural drawing from this light.
>
> Alberto Perez-Gomez and Louise Pelletier, *Architectural Representation and the Perspective Hinge*[34]

Essentially all architects love drawings, but even the act of drawing has become such a tested issue in recent debate that it would appear that it is almost no longer appropriate for the student to draw

---

[33]Wim Wenders, *The Act of Seeing* (London: Faber, 1997) p 98.
[34]Perez-Gomez and Pelletier, *Architectural Representation and the Perspective Hinge,* p 3.

architecture. In opting to study new media, the limits and the conviction in the architecture become entirely different. We move on from the image if it doesn't impress, thus the view point of many students and practitioners is to strike the viewer with the image which sums up a project. Such an omniscient viewpoint, the assumption that there will exist one drawing for each project which can fully describe the intricacies of spatial sequences and the thought invested in generating them, is unattainable.

Important to note here is the influence of visual media on architectural production, to the extent that it gets in the way of the focus of work, blurring the architect's understanding of the parameters of the stance. Questioning might start with the type of drawing allowing me to best express the feel of the enclosure, and yet does the typology of the actual medium restrict the endeavours of the architectural proposal in any sense? Can one try to establish a condition where one is not dismissive of the work, simply on the grounds of the medium through which it is portrayed?

Journeying

Many architectures place great emphasis on the journey, the directional. One is constantly aiming at somewhere, blurring the notion of placedness. In many respects, the actual architectural event becomes this journey, and thus the paradox is that although this enhances the interest in the object, its detachment from the centre has shifted many cities' centres of gravity. Confusion at the periphery has not been helped by policies of decentralisation employed by both the authorities and business corporations. City centres are emptied, and whilst the romantic view shared by many planners is that the centres are being given back to the citizen, this is not the case when the vacated offices are left empty, untouched, dead, doing nothing. Sadly the hidden stimuli of the city are eroded through such missed opportunities; the dérive as a "technique of transient passage through varied ambiences...entails playful-constructive behaviour and awareness of psychogeographical effects, which completely distinguishes it from the classical notions of the journey and the stroll"[35] is something that is not commonplace today.

A closer look at a series of urban projects by Michael Sorkin Studio, such as the monumental project at Weed, Arizona, or the Acupunctures of East New York, lead one to notice the idea of the insertions creating new senses of localities. The focus lies in how

---

[35]Michael Sorkin, quoting a section from "Theory of the Dérive," in the Internationale Situationiste #2, December 1958. Quoted in *A City Nearby* (Vienna: Böhlau, 1996) p 18.

these relationships span between parts of existing city grids, or between entirely new, free-formed neighbourhoods. Again there might be a sense of movement of the journey, but this is coupled with the search for equipping the city once again with the potential for dérive. This city shifts the journey/destination relationship away from a transient idea of that which lies between place of origin and the destination. The destination is the possibility (ability?) to lose oneself, to find new destinations devoid of premeditation.

Extruding Movement

> *Maps are all present at once, physical as bibliographies which could be spoken are not, but...contain more information than we need or can absorb, a plenitude which lends conviction, because there is no way of exhausting these little worlds.*
> Robert Harbison, *Eccentric Spaces*[36]

Where are narratives constructed? To locate a physical or even a mental site of origin is no doubt a subjective issue, but a more objective view might not try to determine exactly where, but how? How is the narrative constructed, and specifically, how does one move through it? The movement that the reader has to adopt signifies the process of the narrative's evolution, but equally the scope. Discovering how to use it tells us where it comes from. To place the origins of the narrative is not always easily achieved, which Mark Rakatnsky finds virtuous. "It is within this struggle, between the inability to narrate in a seamless and definitive manner and the inability not to narrate, that narrative is constituted."[37] Rhythm is important to many narratives, such as Tschumi's *"Manhatten Transcripts"*, which depend, in their reproduced format, on the flip of the pages to tell the story at a speed slow enough to grasp the traces of the last distortion. Some texts are very slow, such as Sverre Fehn's numerous essays in *"The Thought of Construction"*, where each sentence asks the reader to pause, digest and reflect. Others however are very quickly grasped, such as Roger Connah's *"Welcome to the Hotel Architecture"*, in some cases possibly even quicker than a drawing or photograph. The temporal layers of a narrative however can allow the architect to influence the way you consume the work. You might want to speed through it, but it demands you to slow, to adopt the still silence of the words. Sorkin's *"Local Code"* differs in that a rhythmic notion exists through repetitive legislation, to the point of confusion.

---

[36]Robert Harbison, *Eccentric Spaces* (London: Secker & Warburg, 1989) p 125.
[37]Rakatnsky, op. cit., p 104.

One of the difficulties in grasping an understanding of Sorkin's drawn architectural work is for the very reason that it is all presented from a global point of view, that is to say, the plan is the prominent form of projection. Although the drawings of the New York Shrooms (1994) all appear to be exhaustively worked out, through using the plan predominantly, an interchangeability of layers is afforded through allowing oneself the freedom to not fix the delineated spaces at a given level in the viewer's mind. This freedom from determining the imaginal sectional qualities allows the focus to remain fixed on the possible relationships between distinct spaces within the plan. Because the focus of Sorkin's work is at the level of the city, the plan avoids the confusion of the specificity of an aesthetic, three-dimensional appearance of the proposal. So unlike the work of another experimental urbanist, Lebbeus Woods, whose work in the Saint'Elia visionary tradition focuses on perspectively conceived spaces, Sorkin often omits representing the extruded form that he plans. Woods' work, which is more politically cutting, is viewed from the safety of not knowing where these worlds are – bar his work for Sarajevo and Havana. Sorkin's drawn view is however always firmly fixed in cities that exist, whether or not they are actually known to him and us. In many ways this is why it is difficult to understand his drawings, because more often than not, as architects, we are interested in how something looks. Yet with the plan, we can understand the limits of spaces, and even vertical relationships. One is simply asked to change how one, as a viewer, moves through the drawing. Much is still left to the imagination, but the imagination is still an omniscient one; so when Sorkin does reveal a section, or a perspective, one is met with surprise. Perhaps this is the fault of the viewer, for reading what you want into a drawing, as you attempt to inhabit the parts of the spaces which evoke the most interest.

Reading Space

The interest in the question of choosing a medium of representation lies not in the spectra of media which the architect has at his disposal, but rather in the point of view which he chooses to describe his architecture from. Equally, filters which the spectator utilise veil and delude the narrative of the architectonic event. How different can differing narratives as descriptions of the same architectural event actually be?

Two novels by Italo Calvino illustrate how alternate descriptions of a city in *"Invisible Cities"*, or even of one and the same story, in *"If on a winter's night a traveller"*, can be constructed. *"Invisible Cities"* allows the protagonist to portray Venice as descriptions, grouped around 11 themes, of displaced hidden aspects of the same city. The fact that the story is based on Venice is almost irrelevant. The enigma of the story-telling lies in suddenly discovering that you can recognise these traits in cities which you have inhabited. In the way that Helene Cixous tells of her expected journey to Prague, "Promised Pragues. You dream of going. You cannot go. What would happen if you went?"[38] the result is the discovery that you have actually visited Venice before you go there for the first time. Readily reflecting on his two concetral concepts, Sorkin states:

> *An Urbanagram is one way to imagine a city; another is a building code. Indeed within every plan there lurks a set of principles, however general, that describe its hierarchies and preferences; that deploy its forms; and that resolve its conflicts. The purpose of the Urbanagram and codes is to articulate a theory and a practice of urban desirability. No dystopias on this bus please!*
>
> Michael Sorkin, *A City Nearby*[39]

"A City Nearby" is a document which maps the intentions and the products of a 1994 Summer studio taught by Michael Sorkin, at the Academy of Fine Arts in Vienna, where he is professor of urban design. The title represents the idea of familiarity which is at the heart of Sorkin's concept of creative geography, that the document is a study of creating cities which we all know of and could be nearby to the ones in which we live today, for the simple reasons that they are to be an amalgamation of our desires. This publication represents an interesting cross-point of Sorkin's work. Although it is strictly not his own work but that of his students, the interest lies in the reactions and translations which his students would necessarily need to make, in order to benefit from the (stylistic) freedom that his method insists upon, and for the hybrid state of the document. It tests out many of his ideas through applying the terminology of the Code into the collective design of a new city. Students are asked to produce their own codes. The results illustrated in the document show a level of intensity and collaboration. The premise for the project is clear, "To begin to conceive any city – however delightful – requires a certain fantasy of totality. Modernism went wrong by having only one."[40]

One of the most striking work methods encouraged in this studio appears to have been the idea of taking someone else's work, and reworking it, to take the qualities of it, which often remain hidden to the author, and to bring them to the surface through drawing over

---

[38]Helene Cixous, "Attacks of the Castle," in Leach, N. (ed.) *Rethinking Architecture* (London: Routledge, 1997) p 303.
[39]Michael Sorkin, *A City Nearby*, op.cit. p 8.
[40]Michael Sorkin, *ibid.*, Introduction, p 2.

someone else's drawing, or cut up and alter a model. This is a strong statement, both politically and methodically. What Sorkin states questions the issue of authorship, not responsibility, through saying that the integrity of the author is insignificant so long as through this sacrifice the qualities of the idea benefit the collective debate. Instead of finding different (synonymous) ways to describe urban desires, we must be equally intent on accepting conflicting ones as well.

[PAIR THREE]

The City and Propinquity

The study of viewpoints brings one closer to a subject one is working with, through encouraging one to repeatedly look, to study and record so as to be able to adopt a guise. It heightens the perception of the designer, as a means to allow for an informed response. Through acting out the role of the user one seeks an affinity with this person's situation. This becomes the hero-architect's cause, the cause masking inhibition. One is left open to a flood of impulses, instincts, which represent a pure architectonic experience as a direct consequence of the adoption of a particular view point. Finding the alternative stance however, is the task: the way to work, not how to work.

> *The question then arises from the above deductions: what is the relationship between propinquity and the exposure of our inner selves?*

Monuments, the grid and excessive travel caused through decentralisation are a few of the ordering proponents of how we conduct our city lives. Monuments serve as unconscious reminders of past events, "they're containers and institutionalisers for our fantasies of the past". [41] The grid, through its reductive grip, is inhibitive. Decentralisation is perhaps the greatest opponent of intimate space, blurring spaces into one another seen through the car window.

One of the interesting points about Sorkin's fascination with the extent to which our lives are watched today is that his plans evoke, more than other types of drawings used by his studio, the feeling of one watching the lives of the city-dwellers. We know from "See You in Disneyland" that surveillance troubles him. However, through the cut of the plan, the lids of the homes in his New York Shrooms are lifted away, and we become voyeurs of the urban experiment. In these instances, the plan displays the control that the drawing has – on

---

[41]Michael Sorkin, "The Urban Vibe," *Architectural Record* 06/98, p 71.

how we are allowed into these spaces, and how to exist within these walls. But a further reflection on the reversibility of voyeurism noted in PAIR ONE above might view the whole idea of watching as a productive gesture. There is much to be learned from one another's hidden lives, and perhaps projects such as the Shrooms, which grafts together new layers of skin, not on top of but within the gridiron, seek to direct us to finding a new sense of diversity through exposing previously separated parts of the grid to the next one; cutting across the fabric, it asks us to learn to look into other people's lives, watching how people might react to forms that free one from the grid. Whilst the watching is imaginary, what remains of interest is if we can translate the idea of architectural form as systems for taking pictures of the world beyond an enclosure, into urban terms: neighbourhoods which allow us to take pictures, and expose them, of our inner-worlds. The insecurity that this suggests is a matter for concern, given that our inner-worlds are our only remaining fixed points of reference. In the words of Sverre Fehn, "...our society takes too much in, we are fixated with the visual, there are no longer any limits with TV and telephones. It is no longer the same, to close the door and place yourself behind four walls and be entirely alone, to have a world which is untouched. It is completely unprotected, you are hunted by media and motifs, and the only building which is impermeable is the body..."[42]

Robert Harbison in his book, *"Eccentric Spaces"*, raises the concept of meaningful/meaningless cities. Although Harbison is concerned with the language that spaces speak to us of, when held against Sorkin's work, perhaps meaningful becomes that which is "helpful". Many of Sorkin's preoccupations are a direct result of how our cities, not all but many, have come to operate. So it is against the background of what might be deemed to be helpful not only for today, but for always, that one must discuss the work. Propinquity, the necessity of nearness and intimacy, is surely an apolitical desire; to avoid isolating spaces, causing the underlying politics of architectonic space to become a prevalent issue. Spaces are political. Yet the fact that we can build political constructs is difficult for most societies to accept. So for urban space to remain masked, a radical way to make them reappear as unpolitical is through making them useful to use, for them to work the way we want them to work. This can only come about through a continuation of conceiving radical projects, such as the Shrooms and the East New York Acupunctures, and eventually their realisation.

---

[42]Interview between the author and Sverre Fehn (Oslo 25 March, 1998). Taken from Franklin, Alexander *The Dialogic Line – the Temperament of the Work of Sverre Fehn,* Appendix A, p 5.

4] Exeunt:
Paper Politics, Paper Architecture,
Paper Omniscience

> *Of course, there is more than one way to be representational.*
> *The working drawing is representational largely in the way*
> *written words represent sounds, abstractly. But there is also*
> *an ancient tradition of directly representational drawing, in the*
> *pictorial sense. Like 20th-century art generally, architectural*
> *drawing has occupied many positions along the line stretched*
> *between the poles of abstraction and pictorialism. But archi-*
> *tectural drawings, rightly, are called architectural for reasons*
> *beyond the subject matter: their magic and force comes from*
> *their implicit relationship to the unbuilt. Thus one looks at*
> *these drawings at both levels: the drawing as artifact and the*
> *drawing as the representation of certain ideas about some*
> *architecture.*
>
> Michael Sorkin, *Exquisite Corpse*[43]

The remaining issue of point of view to be discussed is misrepresentation of a viewpoint. The obvious criticism of Sorkin's work is that
the conditions that he imagines are a necessity for us might be the
wrong conditions for some places. One can get caught up in the uni-
versality of codes, such as the idealism of Code [IV–13.4]: "No public
space may be unlinked. The public area of the City is to be continuous.," is very different in its tone to Code [III–5.5] "Every Hab shall
have a View of the moon." There is no room for control in the code,
[IV–9.5] "Although it may attenuate or transform the character of the
experience of passage through it, a gate shall, in no significant way,
impede passage in or out of the City: gates may not be closed." To a
certain extent we already live by certain codes, not necessarily as
laws but as moral codes. Should cities have their own codes, for
according to Sorkin in the preamble, the city is also a nation?

On paper the idea of the Code does free one's associations with
the city, which is Sorkin's intention. Christine Boyer speaks of the
need for guides through the city today, a "voice-over" between the
locations. Sorkin's Code then could be seen as the unspoken voice
of a utopic setting. So if we can learn to speak about and write about
the city in a liberated way, free of tenancy and localities falling apart,
the text will actually be paving the way for building these ideas. But
the very way that he avoids misrepresentation is through keeping
the text abstract: there are no drawings or diagrams, only a series of

---

[43]Michael Sorkin, *Exquisite Corpse*, p 36.

formulae. The text becomes a manifesto. It becomes many manifestoes, for with each Code, one's image of the city changes, becoming more complex, partly forgotten, partly hidden by the intricacy of the latest imperative. It is during the mental pauses between the codes that we find the wounds of this City. Between these gaps, we contruct our visions, our versions. Sorkin realises that, in the words of Bernard Cache, "attributing identity to a place leads to imitation".[44] The code does not change, unless we re-write it. But how we (mis)read it will keep it continually changing.

> *There is no way to perform architecture in a book. Words and drawings can only produce paper space and not the experience of real space. By definition, paper space is imaginary: it is an image...why should the paper space of a book or magazine replace an architectural space?*
> Bernhard Tschumi, *The Pleasure of Architecture*[45]

Tschumi in *"Architecture and Disjunction"* raises many such questions on spaces and mental transformations of how and what we perceive architecture to be, and perhaps the importance is to raise an awareness rather than to provide the solutions. This is what Sorkin does, he knows how to gather interest, and he knows many of the answers to the questions he asks. Urban Design had for many decades been a little touched subject for architects, and arguably, it still will remain in an uneasy relationship with the architectural profession for the very reason that no one knows what urbanism should be – an extension of architecture, or an independent field? A synthesis of the two would be the most beneficial to the city.

Many of the texts that I have come across whilst researching the whole issue of writing on architecture have only remained, tentatively, with architecture. To present architectonic qualities within the world of the page has been achieved by many new, and unthought of, formats. But to convey urbanism, not merely a story of a town or a city or a neighbourhood, but urbanism, this is something new.

Omniscience is a difficult term to apply to architecture, and in many senses it is the opposite of a viewpoint. To take a view is not only depictive of a movement into a viewing point, but also to place a limit, a boundary. Omniscience knows no boundaries, and hence the all-knowing hero architect feels at home acting as the total designer. It would appear that through adopting God's eye point from which to work, many simple confusions do occur, from the interchangibility of the layer, to one's memory of a place being jaded and corrupted by a similar drawing of a plan. Maps are to be lived

[44]Bernard Cache, *Earth Moves* (Cambridge, MA: MIT, 1995) p 14.
[45]Bernhard Tschumi, *Architecture and Disjunction* (Cambridge, MA: MIT, 1994) p 93.

in, not simply drawn on top of. But when we allow the grid to be imposed on us, one has to revert to this distance, so as to allow the distance from a place we know well to find a way back to knowing the city.

Sorkin's adaptation of the surrealist game, the Exquisite Corpse, is a potent metaphor for finding these voices. Assuming the city to be an entirety, each person's alterations, additions to and subtractions from the greater urban picture are all eating away at us: our spaces, our memories of them once, and our understanding of them now. This is not detrimental to the health of the city, for without realising it we are likely to find that we invariably can agree on various common points without much discussion. The Shoehaus project in Vienna of 1995 is itself a manifest Exquisite Corpse, saw seven architects working together; three attempts at the game, showed initially silence as each architect worked with the blinkers down, in solitude. Once dialogue later began, in the two latter schemes, it became apparent they were all looking for the same types of things, a mix of building typology and scale. Exquisite Corpses happen in the built world every moment. The issue is to view unpredictability as the key value that gives a place and the interventions a character, its own distinctive voice. Urbanism needs many voices, shouting at each other, for the myth of the collective voice, exists only insofar as the city is a mouthpiece for our disinterest in taking the city into our own hands and moulding it into an animated subject.

POSTSCRIPT

This dissertation is not an attempt to write two different types of text, although it is ordered around a way in which I came to view the subject of Sorkin's work. The concept of the pair was an attempt to differentiate between three different types of work, each of which is coupled with a dialogic counterweight.

One can either regard the pair as separate chapters within the text, or as indexes to the specifics of Sorkin's work. Thus one could read the pair first, and then return to the primary heading of the section, moving from the micro to the macro. Reading the text from start to finish, however, shows the overlapping nature of the three protagonists.

[PAIR ONE] is the relationship between the critic, and the politics of his observations and subsequent proposals.

[PAIR TWO] is the relationship between the author of the code (the encoder), and the "limits" of this view point and its political rhetoric.

[PAIR THREE] is the relationship between the urbanist and his imperatives, seeking propinquity through advocating collective responsibility.

Paul Gardiner

The Museum of the Museum

Gardiner's dissertation at face value is little more than a series of collected observations about museums, yet it is in the structure and arrangement of these observations that the argument and analytical power emerges. As Gardiner quotes from film director Peter Greenaway, "every exhibition has physical limits that define and shape its character." The extract reproduced here, concerning "The Museum/Memorial", offers a brief glimpse of this process at work.

Paul Gardiner

THE MUSEUM OF THE MUSEUM

FOREWORD

This study is entitled *The Museum of the Museum;* a self important name, you might think, which perhaps reflects its ambitions better than its content, although no more than any other museum, such as the *Museum of Childhood* or of *Mankind.*

> *'Still, it is nice to have a title which overcomes limits it is the
> task of the book it denotes to establish, in case someone
> should think that titles are only what works are called.'*
> AC Danto.[1]

Italo Calvino[2] showed aspects of the modern city by distilling and elaborating upon each to invent 55 *Invisible Cities.* Similarly this study hopes to construct a tale to better identify and illustrate the contemporary condition of the museum. It exists in two parallel texts; one describing an imaginary museum and its collection, and the second (which is rather more didactic) appending and annotating parts of the former. The Museum of the Museum is principally a collection of observations regarding architecture and the contemporary museum, related in the various parts of this paper, its contents and organisation.

> *'Every exhibition has physical limits that define and shape its
> character.'* Peter Greenaway.[3]

---

[1]Danto, AC (1981) <u>The Transfiguration of the Commonplace</u>. (Cambridge, MA: Harvard University Press,) Preface, p v.
[2]Calvino, Italo (1972) <u>Invisible Cities,</u> trans. Weaver, W. (New York: Harcourt Brace.)
[3]Greenaway, Peter (1993) <u>Some Organising Principles</u>, Wales Film Council, p 4.

The Museum of the Museum's limitations are set by time and the definition of its contents. It is open for only nine hours and might include everything. Sometimes it might even forget its limits and escape them, which is not always bad.

ITINERARY (ORIGINAL CONTENTS)

09.00   The Last Museum.
10.00   Museums and Order.
11.00   The Self-Conscious Museum.
12.00   The Museum/Memorial.
13.00   Lunchtime in the Museum of the Museum.
14.00   The Absent Museum.
15.00   The Fictional Museum.
16.00   Representing the Museum of the Museum:- What the writer concluded.
17.00   Outside of the Museum of the Museum.
        Bibliography

Notes for *The Last Museum*

09.00   *The Museum of the Museum* is the last museum. It is open for nine hours only, 09.00–18.00. No concessions. The morning will be spent describing the circumstances of the end of the museum, and looking at the reasons for the last museum being known as *The Museum of the Museum*. This afternoon is directed toward defining the characteristics of the last museum and its contents, and in this respect, we will come to form a brief for the last museum, to influence and shape its spaces.

[1]Macdonald, Shane & FYFE, Gordon (ed) (1996) *Theorizing Museums* (Oxford: Blackwell Publishers) p 1.

09.05   This text is written as a discussion of and a response to arguments which recognise the contradictions and eccentricities of the contemporary museum, and wonder over what might become of it.

09.07   Shane Macdonald summarizes all of these anxieties which surround the modern museum:- 'Bound up with much that is heralded to be nearing its end – stability and permanence, authenticity, grand narratives, the nation-state, and even history itself – their numbers are growing at an unprecedented rate... (and yet) museums face an unremitting questioning about whom they are for and what their role should be. Falling visitor numbers, failure to attract minorities, massive expenditure on art works, storage and conservation problems of ever-expanding collections (many of which are never displayed), and competition from the electronic media and other leisure pursuits, all threaten the future of the museum'.[1]

09.12   Curators, artists and academic writers all suspect that the museum building is no longer able to contain the new programme of the museum – although there is uncertainty over what that might actually be. Increasingly there is a feeling that the spaces of the museum are an anachronism and that, perhaps, the buildings of the contemporary museum will be remembered as the last generation of museums.

09.16   Between them, there is an agreement that the museum institution is in decline, toward an end, sometime soon. By six o'clock tonight the end might be overdue.

09.18   Consequently it seems that rather than correct or undo what has happened – it is too late for that – it would be kindest to encourage an end to the museum.

09.20   This museum is therefore the final museum, that is, the eccentricities of the contemporary museum followed to an extreme conclusion.

This room once contained models (at appropriate scales) of every museum that had been built or planned or conceived. They were displayed chronologically, beginning with the Treasury of the Athenians at Delphi, and certainly included a sectional model through the spaces of this museum. Now instead the room is filled by the museum, recorded in strata of miniature colonnades and escalators and pyramids that are legible only to an archaeologist. If you were to look through gaps, perhaps with a torch, you might make out the drum of Stuttgart's Staatsgalerie or recognise the folly of the Museum of Unlimited Growth.

[1] Viglus Zuichemus quoted in: YATES, Frances A. (1966) *The Art of Memory* (London: Routledge and Kegan Paul Ltd) p 130.
[2] Foucault, Michel (1970) *The Order of Things* (London: Tavistock Publications) p 55.

Calliope–Epic poetry
Clio-History
Euterpe–Lyrical poetry
Melpomene–Tragedy
Erato–Love poetry
Polyhymnia–Sacred poetry
Urania–Astronomy
Thalia–Comedy
Terpsichore–Choral dance and song

Microcosm; little world.
Macrocosm; the great world.

12.00   *The Memory Theatre* of Guillio Camillo, documented in his manuscript published in 1550 after his death, arranged a set of artefacts in space to represent and reveal all wisdom and knowledge of the cosmos, by means of relationships and associations between the parts of the theatre. His memory system was based upon the classical art of memory, the mnemonic system.

12.01   Mnemonic memory is a mechanism for recollection. Its invention is attributed to the poet Simonides, of Ceos. The orator makes an association between the significant moments of a narrative and a procession through the spaces of a real or imaginary building. The mnemonic system formalises remembrance in architectural terms.

12.02   For poets and rhetoricians, memory was the principle upon which knowledge was constructed and communicated, just as Mnemosyne is the mother of the muses. The muses represent the various forms of rhetoric.

12.04   'They say that this man has constructed a certain Amphitheatre, a work of wonderful skill, into which whoever is admitted as spectator will be able to discourse on any subject no less fluently than Cicero.' [1]

12.05   In her book *The Art of Memory*, Frances Yates reconstructs *The Memory Theatre* around the object of a Roman theatre as described by Vitruvius. The machine takes the number seven for its organising principle, seven tiers divided by seven gangways on seven columns, representing the planets, combinations of elements, nature, the arts, theology, the occult and human endeavour.

12.06   The theatre operated upon a hermeneutic conception that all creation could be summarised in a set of symbols, resemblances and likenesses that signify an essential truth beneath all things, established at the creation of the universe.

12.07   Michel Foucault elaborates:- 'in the sixteenth century, the fundamental supposition was that of a total system of correspondence (earth and sky, planets and faces, microcosm and macrocosm), and each particular similitude was then lodged within this overall relation'. [2]

12.09   Guillio Camillo retired to Milan, a pensioner of the Marchese del Vasto and the theatre was broken and lost. Guillio Camillo Delminio died in 1544.

12.10 Francis Bacon rejected the tradition of resemblance and association, and later René Descartes embraced the experimental methods of Newton. The Enlightenment of the 18th century introduced a system of knowledge that was now organised by measurement and comparison and observation. Voltaire openly advocated the Cartesian principle, that human development should be measured by scientific progress.

12.12 The Enlightenment thereby discarded the hermeneutic system. But the museum of the modern paradigm nevertheless still intended that its collection be representative of a universal order that was beyond its limits to measure. The museum came to symbolise a new spirit of rational progress.

12.13 In 1939 Le Corbusier published a proposition for *Musée à Croissance Illimitée, the Museum of Unlimited Growth*:-

'It grows one day from the centre... then develops by winding up its spirals according to its possibilities... This museum is under permanent construction: a mason and his helper, a game of framing, pole-types and beam types... It will not necessarily be a museum of fine art. In principle it is a museum of knowledge.'[3]

12.14 Le Corbusier had fifteen years previously written that 'the museum is bad because it does not tell the whole story' [4] and added 'let us have instead everything.'

12.15 It was, however, a misapprehension inherent within the museum, and a consequence of the modern paradigm of knowledge, that the mere accumulation of artefacts might make the museum somehow more truthful, and by extension that to possess all things would allow the comprehension of absolute truth.

12.16 The failed programme of Dada was meant to collapse the museum's sphere of influence, by making useful objects outside equivalent to artefacts in the museum environment. But in its denial of the premise of the museum, the Dadaist critique expanded the scope of what the museum considered to be worth collecting.

12.18 Instead the Dadaists have corrupted the museum in a manner they had not intended, by obesity. The institution's predicament became more and more one of excess.

12.19 As one observer noted:- 'another innovation in the design and running of contemporary museums is the broadening range of themes a museum can handle... the decorative arts, architecture, cars, ships, planes, photography, film, anthropology etc.' [5]

[3] Quoted in: Déotte, Jean-Louis (1995) 'The Museum as a Site of Passage from Modernity to Postmodernity.' In: DAVIDSON, Cynthia C. (ed) *Any Place* (London: Anyone Corporation, MIT Press) p 37.

[4] Quoted in: Davis, Douglas (1990) *The Museum Transformed* (New York: Cross River Press) p 122.

[5] Montaner, Josep & Oliveras, Jordi (1986) *The Museums of the Last Generation* (London: Academy Editions/St. Martin's Press) p 11.

Inside this room stands a model representing the Museum of the Museum as it was originally planned, before things became so complicated and the museum was expanded. It was built at such a grand scale that good children can walk inside, with some encouragement. Grown-ups remember a time when they were small enough to go into the model, and they wish they could almost still feel their fascination for the unusual objects they found there. It is a space to long for, inhabited in memory. But if they were to think back, those things might have been in a different museum, elsewhere. Now when children are asked by their fathers or aunts what they saw, blue-faced they finally exhale and answer.

nothing much"

Olivia Gordon

Word-robe: an Investigation of the Cupboard (. . . as prompted by Lucy)

Gordon's dissertation leads us on a journey from the humble wardrobe through themes of ordinariness, control, curiosity, intimacy, homeliness and the fold. The research is thorough yet wide ranging, and Gordon interrogates and questions texts creatively and brings her insights together in a rich and skilful way. The use of the figure of Lucy, from *The Lion, the Witch and the Wardrobe,* is a powerful device; adopted at first as a narrative to order an apparently disparate selection of ideas, eventually she emerges as a metaphor for the whole architectural process, from drawing to making to the unpredictability of occupancy. Originally presented as an extremely elegant interplay of format and typography, the text and page spreads reproduced here give an indication of the highly controlled, writerly and aesthetic nature of Gordon's final production.

Olivia Gordon

WORD-ROBE

an Investigation of the Cupboard (. . . as prompted by Lucy)

ORIGINAL CONTENTS

Chapter One: Following The Others

The aim for this dissertation piece is to use the famous extract from C.S. Lewis' *The Lion, the Witch and the Wardrobe*, where Lucy enters the cupboard and first discovers Narnia, as an index for a personal storage system. This will be used to house my own narrative on the theme of closet space, an individual 'wardrobe of words.'

My writing then, in inhabiting the 'fixed' text of C.S. Lewis' novel, uses the predetermined structure of the story to develop my own investigation on the theme of cupboards. In effect I aim to, like Lucy, enter the mundane space of the wardrobe and discover a "whole country"[1] within.

The methodology is similar to that used by Perec in his essay 'Think/Classify' where he explains, "The alphabet used to 'number' the various paragraphs of this text follows the order in which the letters of the alphabet appear in the French translation of the seventh story in Italo Calvino's *If On One Winter's Night a Traveller.*"[2] I, however, intend to use the words of my chosen extract, rather than letters, as a means of classification. In effect, the reading and writing between the confined lines of the text, a 'slotting between' as one would file objects away in a cupboard, becomes a means of generating a spacious place of creative investigation.

It is then from within this process of writing, where the method of classification is so obtuse that it questions the opposition of orderly classification versus random spontaneous thought, that the theme of the writing itself develops. This is namely an exploration of the nature of the space of the closet, both as a mechanism for control or categorisation but also as a place for the freedom of the imagination. And so, following Lucy's journey from exterior to interior, the discussion aims to investigate these alternate themes and then reflect on the implications that such a duality might have for the architect as designer and definer of space.

Chapter Four: The Cupboard And Control

"Nothing there!"[1] In many ways we are not surprised by Peter's reaction of seeing the room with a wardrobe in it and declaring it to be empty. The wardrobe is part of our expectation of a bedroom and we have already touched upon our blindness to our habitual surroundings. Highmore writes that it is "the everyday that receives our daily inattention."[2] However as the other children troop out, we read that Lucy hesitates. And this pause then becomes the space to consider the merging of the two separate discussions so far, our anaesthesia to the cupboard's perceived ordinariness and the designer's relationship to its function. Prompted therefore by Peter's assertion

---

[1] C.S. Lewis *The Lion, The Witch And The Wardrobe* (London: HarperCollins, 1950) p 63. "I suppose this whole country is in the wardrobe."

[2] Georges Perec *Species Of Spaces And Other Pieces* (London: Penguin Books, 1997) p 204.

[1] C.S. Lewis *The Lion, The Witch And The Wardrobe* (London: HarperCollins, 1950) p 12.

[2] Ben Highmore (ed.) *The Everyday Life Reader* (London: Routledge, 2002) p 21.

that the room is empty, the cupboard's 'nothingness' in terms of its design will be considered afresh. Focusing mainly on the fitted cupboards from the twentieth century to the present day, the discussion will reflect upon the extent to which the closet's anonymity has been used to impact the form of domestic design and the way we inhabit the surrounding space. In short, 'nothingness' is suggested to be a form of design control.

In the tightly designed spaces of post war housing the lynchpin upon which all other discussion hinged was the issue of space standards set down by the state. The size of the dwelling was therefore undoubtedly the most important factor in the new designs. As Glendinning and Muthesius, the authors of *Tower Block*, a comprehensive history on public housing, comment, "There were no fundamental scientific issues at stake; it was purely a quantitative matter."[3] The *New Metric Handbook*, in its chapter on domestic dwellings, assimilates this information on space requirements and here it lays out the minimum width of a corridor and staircase to be the measurement that is required for two people to carry a wardrobe up the stairs. Since, with The Parker Morris Report's abolition of the prescriptive sizes for individual rooms, space standards were allocated only for the overall dimensions of the dwelling, this presupposes that room sizes were determined from the remaining space after circulation had been accounted for. Followed through to its logical conclusion therefore, the handbook's recommendation determines the dimensions of the wardrobe to be the invisible measure at the crux of post war housing design. Thus the humble wardrobe becomes the principle tool for ordering domestic space.

However, this chapter was introduced as being not so much concerned with 'order' but more with 'control' and whilst it is obvious that the terms are to some extent interchangeable it is now necessary to clarify their separate definitions. For on one level, it seems that architecture will always be concerned with the concept of physical ordering, as Adrian Forty comments, "Architecture is in the business of producing order."[4] However in my mind 'control' has a more specific field of reference than 'order.' For 'control' to me is not associated primarily with the physical but more with the psychological. It implies a grasp that is subjective, an exerting of our will over another, rather than simply an objective proportionality. Therefore I would consider that the ordering of the dimensions of homes by the

[3] Miles Glendinning & Stefan Muthesius Tower Block, Modern Public Housing in England, Scotland, Wales and Northern Ireland (New Haven: Yale University Press, 1994) p 14.

[4] Adrian Forty *Words And Buildings. The Vocabulary of Modern Architecture* (London: Thames and Hudson, 2000) p 248.

wardrobe is harmless, if a little surprising, but the implication that the wardrobe becomes a mechanism used by the designer to control the inhabitant is more controversial. It is then with this suggestion in mind that I return to The Parker Morris Report of 1961. This prioritised not only an increased level of space designated for storage[5] but also made recommendations on its type, namely that clothes and kitchen cupboards should be in built as part of the design. Glendinning and Muthesius suggest that part of the underlying motivation for this new emphasis, although not overtly stated, was to induce tenants to keep their homes clean and tidy with all the moral overtones this encompassed. Joseph Amato, writing on the social pressure laid on the housewife in the 1950s and 1960s to maintain a spotless home, substantiates this with his comment that, "This attitude...was about realising the most utopian of enlightenment goals of cleaning up humanity, body and soul alike."[6] The placing of the recommendations for storage within The Parker Morris Report, alongside the promotion of other modern features such as constant hot water, electricity and internal bathrooms, is equally suggestive. For it is well documented that the advertising of the modern technical amenities to be incorporated into the new flats can be considered in part to have been a political tool for promoting to a sceptical public the appeal of high-rise living over detached cottages. In this way the flat was glamorised as part of the positive progress of modern living. The discovery therefore of the inclusion of in-built storage in the report among these more publicised amenities reveals the invisible cupboard to have played its part as a public persuasion device for political ends.

The reason however that the fitted cupboard had come to signify a style of modern living in British mass housing was due to a filtering down of Modernist design principles from the continent at the turn of the twentieth century, and it is to this era then that the discussion now turns. As such, Peter's declaration "Nothing there!", once taken out of context, could be mistaken for an extract from a Modernist design manifesto. Corbusier asserts a similar mentality in his *L'Art Décoratif D'aujourd'hui* where in criticising the overtly decorated furniture of the nineteenth century he states, "There has been a reaction to this obtrusive presence, and it is being rejected."[7] In

---

[5] "There is a strong demand for storage space within the flat, and we recommend that 15sq. ft. should always be provided in flats and maisonettes for 4 or more persons." From *The Ministry of Housing and Local Government Homes For Today And Tomorrow*, The Parker Morris Report (London: Her Majesty's Stationary Office, 1961) p 24.

[6] Joseph A. Amato *A History Of The Small And The Invisible, Dust* (London: University of California Press, 2000) p 111.

[7] Le Corbusier 'L'Art Décoratif D'aujourd'hui' from Max Risseladen (ed.) *Raumplan Versus Plan Libre* (New York: Rizzoli, 1988) p 143.

Chapter Seven: Folding Space

The introduction to *Architecture: In Fashion* reads, "To slip into the pocket, to hang on a rack, to hide in a closet ... is to locate the body in the spaces of fashion."[1] These actions are also however to locate fashion in the context of architecture, and more specifically the spaces of the closet. With this in mind then this final chapter intends to focus on the intermediary element that often forms the catalyst for our recognition, or experience, of closet space, that of our relationship to the objects or fashions that we place within them. The cupboard will be reviewed as a space of folding, both in terms of the status of the items that are stored away, but also regarding its mediation of our experience between closet and room. In this respect the discussion continues to parallel Lucy's journey into the closet's depths where she inhabits this transitory space between reality and fantasy. For whilst in Lucy's story the folds of the coats change into the branches of the Narnian fir trees, here the folding space of the cupboard will also be discussed as representing a place of change and creative transition. This specific reciprocal relationship between closet and room will then be used as point of literary transition in order to reflect on the closet's impact to the wider context of architectural fashions.

The assumed reaction to the placing of items in a cupboard is that it is an action that has everything to do with order and organisation. This aspect of the cupboard's function has already been touched upon in chapter four where the implication was that the ordering of one's possessions is a cathartic exercise which clears the mind as well as the home, in essence a 'tidy room, tidy mind' mentality. The previously mentioned *Sunday Times* article for example, linked the organisation of the laundry cupboard to the concept of the homely, expressing the belief that it is "as if by opening this fantasy linen cupboard we are reassured that all is right with the world."[2] Equally, the book of BBC television series Life Laundry works on the premise that storing items away tidily is an act which promotes clarity in all areas of life's decision making. Whilst this is to some extent true (most people feel that a tidy desk will help them work), the effect of storing items together in a confined space can equally be one of surreal juxtaposition, and as such fuel for the whimsical processes of the imagination, rather than circumscribed orderliness. Perec for instance, writes in his essay 'Think/Classify' that at the Great Exhibition of 1900, the division of the objects into logical cases for

---

[1] Deborah Fausch, Paulette Singley, Rodolphe El-Khoury, Zvi Efrat (eds.) *Architecture: In Fashion* (New York: Princeton Architectural Press, 1994) p 9.
[2] Victoria O'Brien, 'Clean Living' *The Sunday Times – Home* (Section 10) 13.04.03, p 12.

everyday life of which Colomina writes. For the subtle message is of one prying in the private 'closet' of domesticity, as we subconsciously form associations between this view and that into the interior of the adjacent cello cupboard. This feeling is capitulated by the hidden storage of the stairs into the dining room which makes this area seemingly unreachable to the viewer and therefore a deliberately private space with privileged access. There are other occasions too where Loos uses the placing of the cupboard to thicken the exterior walls, thus functioning as the mechanism of control that separates private interior from public exterior by turning our gaze in on itself and denying us reference points from the world outside. The cupboard is therefore seen to be an accomplice in Loos' intention to control inhabitation through 'the look.'

A similar relationship between control and anonymity, as has been discussed in various contexts, can also be seen in cupboard designs today. Therefore whereas other aspects of modern furniture design demand attention, a phenomenon Reyner Banham coined as "furniturisation,"[14] the cupboard has remained obscure, instead gaining desirability and status on account of its nothingness. As such the cupboard is pushed further within the depths of the wall and becomes a mask for the purging of one's possessions.

Minimalism's emphasis on invisible storage space so that the inhabitant is, superficially at least, liberated form their possessions in their own home provides the most obvious example, although a similar attitude to the cathartic clearing of one's possessions out of sight (and therefore out of mind) has filtered down into a plethora of home improvement books on the subject. To quote from just one of these, Elizabeth Hilliard writes, " Don't let your possessions take you over. Regain control of your life. Sweep away the detritus of decades and get back to the real you. Storage can help you do this, storage can provide solutions: it can give you perfect order."[15] It is interesting to apply Wigglesworth's view on the fetish in this context whereby she suggests that the fetish actually draws attention to that which it seeks to deny. So whilst the surface of the cupboard attempts to remain obscure and present a controlled exterior, it in fact arouses curiosity as its contents through its very nothingness. Who has not wanted to look inside the cupboards of a neat apartment, even more so a minimalist one? Perhaps in our desire for control a new design tactic is required, that of the ostentatious cupboard.

---

[14] Reyner Banham first used the expression in an exhibition catalogue for the Whitechapel gallery in the summer of 1970. From Alan Cummings 'Look At Me! Look At Me!' *A.D. Architecture And Furniture,* vol.72, no.4, July 2002.
[15] Elizabeth Hilliard *101 Simple Storage Solutions* (London: Kyle Cathie Ltd., 1998) p 9.

displays a wealth of in-built furniture. It is these interior fitments, which are mainly cupboards and closeted washing areas, that become the focus of the design; as Kenneth Frampton has explained, "It is probably correct to regard it as a large furnishing element rather than a house in the conventional sense."[11] In this respect the dominance of the fitted furniture translates the building into a highly articulated machine where every activity in relation to the life of the client becomes regulated through the design of interior features. In Wigglesworth's essay on the Maison de Verre this controlling tendency is interpreted as expressing control over the female in particular, where the surgery becomes a metaphor for the cleansing of the female attributes of the home. In general terms then the architect's favouring of the furnishings over the façade is evidence of a male desire to dominate over an area of traditionally female concern. More specifically, in re-interpreting this furniture in the guise of machinery apparatus, Wigglesworth suggests that they take on the nature of fetish objects in that they present an attractive surface that negates their true character. Therefore whilst the closeted washing area suggests concealment, it actually reveals the body through the perforations in the metal screens and therefore traps the female in the viewer's gaze. Furthermore, on seeing screen and body together, the female herself is also re-presented as she becomes part of the mechanics of the interior appliances, a tool therefore of the viewer's gaze and his masculine architecture.

The gaze as a mechanism of control is equally the subject of Beatriz Colomina's seminal essay 'The Split Wall: Domestic Voyeurism' where she seeks to uncover the hidden narratives in the architecture of Adolf Loos. Here she asks, "But can there be ... a detective story of detection itself of the controlling look, the look of control, the controlled look?"[12] An unnoticed trace however in her uncovering of this gaze of control in Loos' architecture is the role of the hidden in-built cupboard and it is on this I would like to focus, using one image that Colomina uses in her essay as a means of highlighting my suggestion.[13] The chosen image, that of the view from the music room to the dining room in the Moller House, shows a glass cabinet containing a cello. This closet, which reveals its contents, serves to inform the viewer of the room's function as a music room. More significantly however, its placing next to the opening to the dining room also intensifies the impression of the staging of

---

[11] Kenneth Frampton "Maison de Verre" *Perspecta 12: The Yale Architectural Journal* (1969) p 77.

[12] Beatriz Colomina (ed.) *Sexuality And Space* (New York: Princeton Architectural Press, 1992) p 74.

[13] This I consider to be further evidence of the wardrobe's 'nothingness' used as a mechanism of control.

comparison he heralds a new era of design with the proclamation, "This is the world of manufacture…we are looking for a standard and our concerns are far from the personal, the arbitrary, the fantastic, the eccentric; our interest is in the norm and we are creating type-objects."[8] 'Nothingness' was therefore a central tenet of Modernism where design tendencies, on both a physical and a psychological level, were founded in concepts of absence and anonymity. This encompassed both a stripping away of all superficial ornamentation which was not necessary to an object's function, as well as a rejection of the sentimental and personal to be replaced by standardised equipment to service human "type-needs."[9]

Erno Goldfinger's wardrobe's design as part of his 1923 competition entry for Austrian furniture makers Thonet provides a microcosm of these Modernist ideals and in this context serves as an introduction to its perceived controlling tendencies. In this respect, the wardrobe can be seen to display a total lack of extraneous decoration, and whilst never itself mass-produced, is understood to have been conceived independently of a specific interior, instead aiming to provide a standardised furniture type. In its utilitarian aesthetic therefore it bears an immediate comparison to the standardised travel trunks such as those manufactured by the company Innovation. Such wardrobe-trunks had been advocated by Corbusier in his articles for *L'Esprit Nouveau* magazine during the 1920s where he had used the whole series of them as images of exemplary objects. The text alongside these images reads, "The human-limb objects are responding to type-needs: chairs to sit on … machines to write with (yes indeed!), racks to file things in."[10] The reference to 'filing' is of particular interest in relation to Goldfinger's wardrobe where the most distinguishing feature are the vertical shelves to file away shirts in individual slots. Clothes are therefore viewed, not as expressions of individual taste, but as standardised equipment of which there is an optimum size and number. The other shelves in the wardrobe are equally prescriptive, with each shelf divided up into different length sections according to specific clothing types.

The controlling tendencies apparent in Goldfinger's closet design can be viewed on a larger scale in the fitted units of Chareau's design for the Maison de Verre in Paris. The house, which was built between 1929 and 31 as a home for the Dalsaces' and includes a surgery for Dr. Dalsaces' gynaecology practice on the ground floor,

---

[8] Le Corbusier 'L'Art Décoratif D'aujourd'hui' from Max Risseladen (ed.) *Raumplan Versus Plan Libre* (New York: Rizzoli, 1988) p 142.

[9] Le Corbusier 'L'Art Décoratif D'aujourd'hui from *Essential Le Corbusier: L'Esprit Nouveau Articles* (Oxford: Oxford Architectural Press, 1998) p 73.

[10] Le Corbusier 'L'Art Décoratif D'aujourd'hui from *Essential Le Corbusier: L'Esprit Nouveau Articles* (Oxford: Oxford Architectural Press, 1998) p 75.

display instead produced, "innumerable surprises."[3] He also suggests that in seeking to classify his own mental processes of classification he would have to speak instead "of flair, of inklings, of chance, of encounters that are fortuitous or prompted or fortuitously prompted ... and above all of montage."[4]

Ben Nicholson harnessed this concept, in his designs for the Telemon Cupboard as part of his *Appliance House* project, where he used the collaging of domestic appliances from manufacturers' catalogues as tool for surrealist creativity. The Telemon Cupboard is conventional in terms of its function as a place for storing objects for the inhabitant, the Kleptamon. However, the irrational element in his compulsive act of possessing is mirrored in the design process of the object, rendering the project as partial fantasy. The cupboard therefore develops from a mirrored bathroom cabinet juxtaposed with an entrance turnstile. Disassociated from their supporting structures and usual contexts, these disparate parts of become surreal and reveal their idiosyncrasies as functional appliances. The drawings equally play on notions of the cupboard's intent to both order and disorder as a means of pushing the design process. A series of measured working sections of the cupboard are therefore superimposed with unrelated collages of its possible contents. These "sorties into the imagination",[5] which ignore the drawings' scale and subvert their Cartesian properties, consequently transform the role of both cupboard and its image from functional to fictional.

The relationship between the cupboard and its contents has therefore been diagnosed to be both reciprocal and contradictory. For on the one hand, the cupboard is able to control the objects it houses, but on the other there is the ability of its contents to provoke un-controlled creativity. With this in mind then, the intention is now to focus on the folded item in the wardrobe as microcosm of the cupboard's dichotomy between order and disorder. Diller and Scofidio's *Bad Press, Housework Series* explores this theme in particular relation to the white dress shirt. As a background to the preoccupations of the project, they explain how at the beginning of the twentieth century the body became subjected to Taylorist analysis, with the aim of enhancing the efficiency, and therefore productivity, of the labour force. Such principles, transposed from the factory to the home, subjected the housewife's chores to the same scrutiny, including ironing that came to be guided by a similar drive for motion-economy. The creases of ironed shirt on the body have consequently become an unchallenged symbol of this drive for domestic efficiency. In this

---

[3] Georges Perec, *Species of Spaces and Other Pieces* (London: Penguin Books, 1997) p 193.
[4] Georges Perec, *Species of Spaces and Other Pieces* (London: Penguin Books, 1997) p 202.
[5] Ben Nicholson, *Appliance House* (Chicago: CIAU, 1990) p 51.

respect the whole lifecycle of the shirt, from production to worn item, is bound by codes of maximum efficiency ruled by the principle of minimums. The orthogonal lines of the folded shirt fit economically into orthogonal systems of storage, both in the factory, transport container, shop, domestic wardrobe and suitcase. As such, "The shirt is disciplined at every stage."[6] In response then, Bad Press aims to challenge this assumption and to free the task of ironing from the aesthetics of efficiency. A series of identical white shirts are instead folded into a series of irrational and dysfunctional shapes and the resulting starched contortions suggest the body held in a series of spasmodic poses from which it cannot act. As a whole the display, in contrast to its uniform and puritanical material, becomes an eccentric spectacle of mutations, surreal and hallucinatory.

Zvi Efrat has sought to explain Diller and Scofidio's Bad Press project with the comparison between Heidegger's approach to "two-fold-edness", an expression of the clear-cut dichotomies between concepts such as conceal/reveal and reside/dwell, and Deleuze's concept of the 'fold' that instead emphasises notions of change and mutability, "blindfoldedness"[7] and irregularity. Similarly, Henry Urbach in his essay 'Closets, Clothes, disClosure' writes about the graphic fold with reference to Deleuze's notion of the 'pli' or fold, as means of explaining his ideas on the 'ante-closet' as a space of changing. For to Urbach the Deleusian fold, understood as representing not a foreclosed space but an enclave, is suggestive of the space in front of the closet inhabited by its door swing. This ante-closet is not only situated at "a moment of graphic folding,"[8] with the dotted arcs of the door swing signifying its place on a drawing, but it is also an actual place where one undertakes the actions of folding and unfolding, as one changes outfits and so plays with perceived appearances. For Urbach then, the door swing as denoting the space of the ante-closet and the area where one changes, draws attention to possibility of the making and remaking of space with new identities that would contribute to informing a less rigid spatiality. In short the fold produces, rather than the sharp division of the crease or cut, a more blurred boundary, a thick edge.

And it as this expanded edge that I intend to start to draw my conclusions. For until this point, in seeking to follow Lucy's journey into the depths of the wardrobe, our own exploration has necessarily

---

[6] Deborah Fausch, Paulette Singley, Rodolphe El-Khoury, Zvi Efrat (eds.) *Architecture: In Fashion* (New York: Princeton Architectural Press, 1994) p 406.

[7] Deborah Fausch, Paulette Singley, Rodolphe El-Khoury, Zvi Efrat (eds.) *Architecture: In Fashion* (New York: Princeton Architectural Press, 1994) p 402.

[8] Henry Urbach, 'Closets, Clothes, Disclosure' in Duncan McCorquodale, Katerina Ruedi, Sarah Wigglesworth (eds.) *Desiring Practices, Architecture, Gender and the Interdisciplinary* (London: Black Dog 1996) p 261.

become increasingly introverted and focussed, as Lucy travelled from the wardrobe's exterior to interior. Looking back then, we can see that our discussion started with a view of the function of the wardrobe as a space among many in the overall context of the home and has completed its journey with a close inspection of a particular folded item of clothing, the white shirt. However, now that Lucy finds herself finally in more open space again, in the wood between the light of the lamp-post and the light of the wardrobe, our parallel discussion can now also broaden its perspective once again. It will then seek to shed some of its own light on the wider architectural implications for our new understandings of closet space and its relationship to the adjoining room. On the one hand there is a need for caution in making generalised references to 'the fold' in relation to architecture. For 'the fold' has become an expedient term to encompass various deconstructivist ambiguities about structure, skin and the marginalised with the convenient backing of philosophical theory. As such the fold has been often heralded as a new form for architecture, a new product which builds on notions of pliancy. The language of Claire Robinson's essay 'The Material Fold' is typical in this respect, "An admirable model for a crenellated building envelope – the fold – the border, the end, the beginning ... is one of material flux."[9] However on the other hand, the fold can also be viewed as signifying the process of architecture, the action of folding, and it is in this respect that I would consider the concept to bear a pertinent relationship to our understanding of the space of the wardrobe as signifying a point of change. Greg Lynn, in his essay 'Architectural Curvalinearity,' looks to culinary terminology to clarify the action of folding as one that blends separate ingredients smoothly without subsuming their separate identities. As such he comments, "the folded mixture is neither homogenous, like whipped cream, nor fragmented like chopped nuts, but smooth and heterogeneous."[10] For I would like to suggest that, in particular relation to our investigations into the space of the wardrobe, this folding of distinct entities has become apparent as the continuous thread in the narrative. For through these investigations the cupboard has been revealed to be a space of smooth transition, a space that encases a delicate blend of separate viewpoints and experiences. This is not just in the context of Lucy's fictitious journey, as a gateway into Narnia, nor simply as providing an area for changing, as Urbach has suggested but an object which itself bears the

---

[9] Claire Robinson, 'The Material Fold, Towards a Variable Narrative of Anomalous Topologies' *Architectural Design, Folding in Architecture*, vol. 102 (1993) p 64.
[10] Greg Lynn, 'Architectural Curvilinearity, The Folded, The Pliant And The Supple' *Architectural Design, Folding in Architecture*, vol. 102 (1993) p 8.

characteristics of change. Therefore these investigations have explored chapter by chapter the oscillations of closet space. As such, the wardrobe has been viewed both as a mundane object to be ignored and as the instigator for unexpected creative imaginings; equally it has shown itself to be, from the exterior, the ultimate symbol of domestic order and rationality, but one which houses in its interior a plethora of irrational experiences, those of curiosity and secrecy, fear and intimacy, as well as surrealist wonder and wit.

And therefore as Lynn suggests then, it is the processes of architecture that can be viewed as inhabiting this expanded edge of the fold, where the designer works within the confines of this fragile point of change between quantifiable drawing and uncontrollable inhabitation and weathering. Bachelard provides an analogy in this respect when he speaks of the half-open door as a metaphor for the realm of creative imagination. The architect can therefore be seen to reside, like Lucy, at the point of change, at the half-open door of possibility, and as such our understanding of the transitory space of the cupboard becomes a microcosm of the larger architectural debate where design is viewed as a process of transition between the two-dimensional drawing and the three-dimensional construction. And thus, as a result of this analogy, all the discussions of our smaller investigation on the particular space of the wardrobe become relevant to the larger debate about the processes of designed space at large. For from this perspective it can be seen that with each project the architect wrestles with similar issues to those which we have discussed in relation to the smaller space of the cupboard as he seeks to propose an architecture that, among other things, appeals to both the mind and the senses, is functional and yet not dogmatic, controlled but not controlling, curious but not self-consciously obtuse, intimate and yet not claustrophobic. And so it seems then that just as Lucy leaves her wardrobe and enters the unknown world of Narnia, there is also a point where the designer, in order to realise these aims in physical form, has to leave the comfortable dimensions of the drawing and embark on the new territory of the construction process. And in the knowledge of this, so I too, as a designer of this particular creative space of the wordrobe, now intend to leave this familiar collection of words hidden among the folds of the coats, and to continue reading uninterrupted, so as to find a new creative territory for my mind to wander within. For as the professor advises, "I don't think it will be any good trying to go back through the wardrobe, you won't get into Narnia again by that route ... Keep your eyes open. Bless me, what do they teach you at these schools?"[11]

[11] C.S. Lewis, The Lion, The Witch And The Wardrobe (London: HarperCollins, 1950) p 203.

Diploma Dissertation 2003
DG'03 Sarah Jackson

Olivia Gordon

wordrobe

An Investigation Of The Cupboard (*...as prompted by Lucy*)

wordrobe

A reading from C.S. Lewis
*The Lion, The Witch And The
Wardrobe* .....

"Of course it would be pretending" said Edmund. They had just finished their breakfast with the professor and were upstairs in the room he had set apart for them - a long, low room with two windows looking out in one direction and two in another. "It's very comforting, Ed," said Susan. "Let to one of us and to two or another. "It's very comforting, Ed," said Susan. "Let to one of us."

And as the mountains we're pretty well off. There's a window and lots of books."

"Not for me," said Peter. "I'm off. It's explore the house."

Everyone agreed to this and that was how the adventures began. It was the sort of house that you never seemed to come to the end of, and was full of unexpected places. The first few doors they tried led only into spare bedrooms, as everyone had expected that they would; but soon they came to a very long room full of pictures, and there they found a suit of armour; and after this was a room all hung with green, with a harp in one corner; and then came three steps down and five steps up, and then a little kind of upstairs hall and a door that led out on to a balcony; and then a whole series of rooms that led to each other and were lined with books - most of them very old books and some bigger than a bible in a church. And shortly afterwards they looked into a room that was quite empty except for one big wardrobe: the sort that has a looking-glass in the door. There was nothing else in the room at all except a dead bluebottle on the window-sill.

"Nothing there!" said Peter, and they all trooped out again - all except Lucy. She stayed behind because she thought it would be worthwhile trying the door of the wardrobe, even though she felt almost sure that it would be locked. To her surprise it opened quite easily, and two mothballs dropped out.

Looking into the inside, she saw several coats hanging up - mostly long fur coats. There was nothing Lucy liked so much as the smell and feel of fur. She immediately stepped into the wardrobe and got in among the coats and rubbed her face against them, leaving the door open of course, because she knew that it is very foolish to shut oneself into a wardrobe. Soon she went further in and found that there were a second row of coats hanging up behind the first one. It was almost quite dark in there and she kept her arms stretched out in front of her so as not bump her face into the back of the wardrobe. She took a step further in - then two or three steps - always expecting to feel the woodwork against the tips of her fingers. But she could not feel it.

"This is simply an enormous wardrobe!" thought Lucy, going still further in and pushing the soft folds of the coats aside to make room for her. Then she noticed something crunching under her feet. "I wonder is that more mothballs?" she thought, stooping down to feel it with her hand. But instead of feeling the hard, smooth wood of the floor of the wardrobe, she felt something soft and powdery and extremely cold. "This is very queer," she said and went on a step or two further.

Next moment she found that what was rubbing against her face and hands was no longer soft fur but something hard and rough and even prickly. "Why, it is just like the branches of trees!" exclaimed Lucy. And then she saw that there was a light ahead of her; not a few inches away where the back of the wardrobe should have been, but a long way off. Something soft and cold was falling on her. A moment later she found that she was standing in the middle of the wood at night-time with snow under her feet and snowflakes falling through the air.

contents

Chapter *Four*

The Cupboard And Control

"Nothing there?"

"Nothing there!"[1] In many ways we are not surprised by Peter s reaction of seeing the room with a wardrobe in it and declaring it to be empty. The wardrobe is part of our expectation of a bedroom and we have already touched upon our blindness to our habitual surroundings. Highmore writes that it is "the everyday that receives our daily inattention."[2] However as the other children troop out, we read that Lucy hesitates. And this pause then becomes the space to consider the merging of the two separate discussions so far, our anaesthesia to the cupboard s perceived ordinariness and the designer s relationship to its function. Prompted therefore by Peter s assertion that the room is empty, the cupboard s nothingness in terms of its design will be considered afresh. Focusing mainly on the fitted cupboards from the twentieth century to the present day, the discussion will reflect upon the extent to which the closet s anonymity has been used to impact the form of domestic design and the way we inhabit the surrounding space. In short, nothingness is suggested to be a form of design control.

In the tightly designed spaces of post war housing the lynchpin upon which all other discussion hinged was the issue of space standards set down by the state. The size of the dwelling was therefore undoubtedly the most important factor in the new designs. As Glendinning and Muthesius, the authors of *Tower Block*, a comprehensive history on public housing, comment, "There were no fundamental scientific issues at stake; it was purely a quantitative matter."[3] *The New Metric Handbook*, in its chapter on domestic dwellings, assimilates this information on space requirements and here it lays out the minimum width of a corridor and staircase to be the measurement that is required for two people to carry a wardrobe

up the stairs [11]. Since, with *The Parker Morris Report* s abolition of the prescriptive sizes for individual rooms, space standards were allocated only for the overall dimensions of the dwelling, this presupposes that room sizes were determined from the remaining space after circulation had been accounted for. Followed through to its logical conclusion therefore, the handbook s recommendation determines the dimensions of the wardrobe to be the invisible measure at the crux of post war housing design. Thus the humble wardrobe becomes the principle tool for ordering domestic space.

However, this chapter was introduced as being not so much concerned with order but more with control and whilst it is obvious that the terms are to some extent interchangeable it is now necessary to clarify their separate definitions. For on one level, it seems that architecture

12 Gordon Cullen, (drawings) for The Parker Morris Report, 1961

will always be concerned with the concept of physical ordering, as Adrian Forty comments, "Architecture is in the business of producing order."[4] However in my mind control has a more specific field of reference than order. For control to me is not associated primarily with the physical but more with the psychological. It implies a grasp that is subjective, an exerting of our will over another, rather than simply an objective proportionality. Therefore I would consider that the ordering of the dimensions of homes by the wardrobe is harmless, if a little surprising, but the implication that the wardrobe becomes a mechanism used by the designer to control the inhabitant is more controversial. It is then with this suggestion in mind that I return to *The Parker Morris Report* of 1961. This prioritised not only an increased level of space designated for storage[5] but also made recommendations on its type, namely that clothes and kitchen cupboards should be in built as part of the design. Glendinning and Muthesius suggest that part of the underlying motivation for this new emphasis, although not overtly stated, was to induce tenants to keep their homes clean and tidy with all the moral overtones this encompassed. Joseph Amato, writing on the social pressure laid on the housewife in the 50 s and 60 s to maintain a spotless home, substantiates this with his comment that, "This attitude... was about realising the most utopian of enlightenment goals of cleaning up humanity, body and soul alike."[6] The placing of the recommendations for storage within *The Parker Morris Report*, alongside the promotion of other modern features such as constant hot water, electricity and internal bathrooms, is equally suggestive [12]. For it is well documented that the advertising of the modern technical amenities to be incorporated into the new flats can be considered in part to have been a political tool for promoting to a sceptical public the appeal of high-rise living over detached cottages. In this way the flat was glamorised as part of the positive progress of modern living. The discovery therefore of the inclusion of in-built storage in the report among these more publicised amenities reveals the invisible cupboard to have played its part as a public persuasion device for political ends.

The reason however that the fitted cupboard had come to signify a style of modern living in British mass housing was due to a filtering down of Modernist design principles from the continent at the turn of the twentieth century, and it is to this era then that the discussion now turns. As such, Peter s declaration "Nothing there!", once taken out of context, could be mistaken for an extract from a Modernist design manifesto. Corbusier asserts a similar mentality in his *L Art Décoratif D aujourd hui* where in criticising the overtly decorated furniture of the nineteenth century he states, "There has been a reaction to this obtrusive presence, and it is being rejected."[7] In comparison he heralds a new era of design with the proclamation, "This is the world of manufacture... we are looking for a standard and our concerns are far from the personal, the arbitrary, the fantastic, the eccentric; our interest is in the norm and we are creating type-objects."[8] Nothingness was therefore a central tenet of Modernism where design tendencies, on both a physical and a psychological level, were founded in concepts of absence and anonymity. This encompassed both a stripping away of all superficial ornamentation which was not necessary to an object s function, as well as a rejection of the sentimental and personal to be replaced by standardised equipment to service human "type-needs."[9]

15 *Goldfinger s competition entry for Thesat*

Erno Goldfinger s wardrobe s design as part of his 1923 competition entry for Austrian furniture makers *Thonet* provides a microcosm of these Modernist ideals and in this context serves as an introduction to its perceived controlling tendencies [13]. In this respect, the wardrobe can be seen to display a total lack of extraneous decoration, and whilst never itself mass-produced, is understood to have been conceived independently of a specific interior, instead aiming to provide a standardised furniture type. In its utilitarian aesthetic therefore it bears an immediate comparison to the standardised travel trunks such as those manufactured by the company *Innovation*. Such wardrobe-trunks had been advocated by Corbusier in his articles for *L Esprit Nouveau* magazine during the 1920 s where he used had used the whole series of them as images of exemplary objects [14]. The text alongside these images reads, "The human-limb objects are responding to type-needs: chairs to sit on... machines to write with (yes indeed!), racks to file things in."[10] The reference to filing is of particular interest in relation to Goldfinger s wardrobe where the most distinguishing feature are the vertical shelves to file away shirts in individual slots. Clothes are therefore viewed, not as expressions of individual taste, but as standardised equipment of which there is an optimum size and number. The other shelves in the wardrobe are equally prescriptive, with each shelf divided up into different length sections according to specific clothing types.

The controlling tendencies apparent in Goldfinger s closet design can be viewed on a larger scale in the fitted units of Chareau s design for the *Maison de Verre* in Paris. The house, which was built between 1929 and 31 as a home for the Dalsaces and includes a surgery for Dr. Dalsaces gynaecology practice on the ground floor, displays a wealth of in-built furniture. It is these interior fitments, which are mainly cupboards and closeted washing areas, that become the focus of the design, as Kenneth Frampton has explained, 'It is probably correct to regard it as a large furnishing element rather than a house in the conventional sense."[1] In this respect the dominance of the fitted furniture translates the building into a highly articulated machine where every activity in relation to the life of the client becomes regulated through the design of interior features. In Wigglesworth s essay on the Maison de Verre this controlling tendency is interpreted as expressing control over the female in particular, where the surgery becomes a metaphor for the cleansing of the female attributes of the home. In general terms then the architect s favouring of the furnishings over the façade is evidence of a male desire to dominate over an area of traditionally female concern. More specifically, in re-interpreting this furniture in the guise of machinery apparatus, Wigglesworth suggests that they take on the nature of fetish objects in that they present an attractive surface that negates their true character. Therefore whilst the closeted washing area suggests concealment, it actually reveals the body through the perforations in the metal screens and therefore traps the female in the viewer s gaze [15]. Furthermore, on seeing screen and body together, the female herself is also re-presented as she becomes part of the mechanics of the interior appliances, a tool therefore of the viewer s gaze and his masculine architecture.

15 Washing Closet, Maison de Verre

16 View from Maids Room, Miller House

The gaze as a mechanism of control is equally the subject of Beatriz Colomina's seminal essay *The Split Wall: Domestic Voyeurism* where she seeks to uncover the hidden narratives in the architecture of Adolf Loos. Here she asks, "But can there be...a detective story of detection itself of the controlling look, the look of control, the controlled look?"[12] An unnoticed trace however in her uncovering of this gaze of control in Loos' architecture is the role of the hidden in-built cupboard and it is on this I would like to focus, using one image that Colomina uses in her essay as a means of highlighting my suggestion.[13] The chosen image, that of the view from the music room to the dining room in the Moller House, shows a glass cabinet containing a cello [16]. This closet, which reveals its contents, serves to inform the viewer of the room's function as a music room. More significantly however, its placing next to the opening to the dining room also intensifies the impression of the staging of everyday life of which Colomina writes. For the subtle message is of one prying in the private 'closet' of domesticity, as we subconsciously form associations between this view and that into the interior of the adjacent cello cupboard. This feeling is capitulated by the hidden storage of the stairs into the dining room which makes this area seemingly unreachable to the viewer and therefore a deliberately private space with privileged access. There are other occasions too where Loos uses the placing of the cupboard to thicken the exterior walls, thus functioning as the mechanism of control that separates private interior from public exterior by turning our gaze in on itself and denying us referencepoints from the world outside. The cupboard is therefore seen to be an accomplice in Loos' intention to control inhabitation through 'the look'.

A similar relationship between control and anonymity, as has been discussed in various contexts, can also be seen in cupboard designs today. Therefore whereas other aspects of modern furniture design demand attention, a phenomenon Reyner Banham coined as "furniturisation,"[14] the cupboard has remained obscure, instead gaining desirability and status on account of its nothingness. As such the cupboard is pushed further within the depths of the wall and becomes a mask for the purging of one's possessions. Minimalism's emphasis on invisible storage space so that the inhabitant is, superficially at least, liberated form their possessions in their own home provides the most obvious example, although a similar attitude to the cathartic clearing of one's possessions out of sight (and therefore out of mind) has filtered down into a plethora of home improvement books on the subject. To quote from just one of these, Elizabeth Hilliard writes, "Don't let your possessions take you over. Regain control of your life. Sweep away the detritus of decades and get back to the real you. Storage can help you do this, storage can provide solutions: it can give you perfect order."[15] It is interesting to apply Wigglesworth's view on the fetish in this context whereby she suggests that the fetish actually draws attention to that which it seeks to deny. So whilst the surface of the cupboard attempts to remain obscure and present a controlled exterior, it in fact arouses curiosity as its contents through its very nothingness. Who has not wanted to look inside the cupboards of a neat apartment, even more so a minimalist one? Perhaps in our desire for control a new design tactic is required, that of the ostentatious cupboard.

[*] *Shaker Millennial Laws*, from the Shakertown at Pleasant Hill, Lexington, Kentucky

[1] C.S. Lewis *The Lion, The Witch And The Wardrobe* (London: HarperCollins 1950) p.12

[2] Ben Highmore (ed.) *The Everyday Life Reader* (London: Routledge 2002) p.21

[3] Miles Glendinning & Stefan Muthesius *Tower Block; Modern Public Housing in England, Scotland, Wales and Northern Ireland* (New Haven: Yale University Press 1994) p.14

[4] Adrian Forty *Words And Buildings. The Vocabulary of Modern Architecture* (London: Thames and Hudson 2000) p.248

[5] "There is a strong demand for storage space within the flat, and we recommend that 15sq. ft. should always be provided in flats and maisonettes for 4 or more persons." From The Ministry of Housing and Local Government *Homes For Today And Tomorrow, The Parker Morris Report* (London: Her Majesty's Stationery Office 1961) p.24

[6] Joseph A. Amato *A History Of The Small And The Invisible, Dust* (London: University of California Press 2000) P.111

[7] Le Corbusier L. Art Decoratif D'aujourd'hui from Max Risselada (ed.) *Raumplan Versus Plan Libre* (New York: Rizzoli 1988) p.143

[8] Le Corbusier L. Art Decoratif D'aujourd'hui from Max Risselada (ed.) *Raumplan Versus Plan Libre* (New York: Rizzoli 1988) p.142

[9] Le Corbusier L. Art Decoratif D'aujourd'hui from *Essential Le Corbusier: L'Esprit Nouveau Articles* (Oxford: Oxford Architectural Press 1998) p.73

[10] Le Corbusier L. Art Decoratif D'aujourd'hui from *Essential Le Corbusier: L'Esprit Nouveau Articles* (Oxford: Oxford Architectural Press 1998) p.75

[11] Kenneth Frampton "Maison de Verre" Perspecta 12: The Yale Architectural Journal (1969) p.77

[12] Beatriz Colomina (ed.) *Sexuality And Space* (New York: Princeton Architectural Press 1992) p.74

[13] This I consider to be further evidence of the wardrobe's nothingness used as a mechanism of control.

[14] Reyner Banham first used the expression in an exhibition catalogue for the Whitechapel gallery in the summer of 1970. From Alan Cummings Look At Me! Look At Me! A.D. Architecture And Furniture vol.72 no.4 July 2002

[15] Elizabeth Hilliard *101 Simple Storage Solutions* (London: Kyle Cathie Ltd. 1998) p.9

Bibliography

Books

Adam, Peter *Eileen Gray, Architect And Designer* (New York: Thames and Hudson 2000)

Amato, Joseph *A History Of The Small And The Invisible, Dust* (London: University of California Press 2000)

Bachelard, Gaston *The Poetics Of Space* (Boston: Beacon Press 1969)

Beckworth, John & Twining, Robert *Clerks Of The Closet In The Royal Household, 500 Years of Service To The Crown* (Stroud/Gloucester: Alan Sutton Publishing 1991)

Bond, Simon *Secrets Of The Queen's Closet* (Southampton: Ashford Press Publishing 1986)

Cobs, Ian (ed.) *Louise Bourgeois* (Oxford: Museums of Modern Art Oxford 1995)

Christopher, Gwynedd, Joy (ed.) *Rachel Whiteread* (Edition in catalogue Haus). Philadelphia, Inmos 1995)

Colomina, Beatriz (ed.) *Sexuality and Space* (New York: Princeton Architectural Press 1992)

Constant, Caroline *Eileen Gray* (London: Phaidon 2000)

Diller, Elizabeth and Scofidio, Ricardo *Flesh, Architectural Probes* (New York: Princeton Architectural Press 1994)

Dawson, James & Stamp, *Queen Anne Gifthouse* (London: Architectural Association Publications 1983)

Edwards, Jane *The Cupboard In The Wall* (London: The Sheldon Press 1983)

Evans, Robin *Translations From Drawing To Building And Other Essays* (London: Architectural Association Publications 1997)

Enoch, Deborah & Bingley, *Padwin & El-Khoury, Kushyâfe & Eliot, Tri (eds.) Architecture: In Fashion* (New York: Princeton Architectural Press 1994)

Forty, Adrian *Words and Buildings: The Vocabulary Of Modern Architecture* (London: Thames and Hudson 2000)

Glendinning, Miles & Mathieson, *Stefan Tower Block, Modern Public Housing In England, Scotland, Wales And Northern Ireland* (New Haven: Yale University Press 1994)

Gunther, R.T. (ed.) *The Architecture Of Sir Roger Pratt* (Oxford: Oxford University Press 1928)

Hammond, M. *H.A. Ruff Everton* (London: Hamilton Adams and Co. 1935)

Harries, Karsten *The Ethical Function Of Architecture* (Cambridge, Massachusetts: MIT Press 1998)

Highmore, Ben (ed.) *The Everyday Life Reader* (London: Routledge 2002)

Illustrations

Robert Holford

The Blooming D'Or

This is perhaps the most unusual of dissertations presented in this book. Whereas most dissertations take the form of a printed object, Holford's was constructed in the form of a door, with various apertures, movements, texts, images and appendages. Conceived in part as an investigation of Derridean deconstruction, Holford's dissertation pays particular attention to the work of Jennifer Bloomer (hence the title word play). The whole rationale of the dissertation is as something to be experienced rather than read – the two illustrations reproduced here give some indication of that process.

Drawing on the linguistic play within Jennifer Bloomer's article "D'Or," Holford's dissertation is in the form of a door constructed within the studio of the architecture school. This installation contains elements that are physical manifestations of anagrams, palindromes, metaphors, similes, alliterations and other verbal forms relating to the sounds and functions of a door.

Michael Levey

The Charterhouse of Parkminster

A dissertation can often focus on a particular piece of local architecture to create a unique and original contribution to historical knowledge. In this case, Levey's meticulously researched study, complete with appropriate appendices material, has successfully addressed the hitherto largely untold history of the last working Carthusian monastery in England. In doing so, Levey investigates not only the history of the Charterhouse in terms of commissioning, design and construction but also its relation to Carthusian life as an everyday practice.

Michael Levey

THE CHARTERHOUSE OF PARKMINSTER

Acknowledgements

Thanks to:
Father Prior, Brother Simon, Dom Bruno Sullivan, Dom Thomas More and all at Parkminster for their generous help and hospitality.
David Robson, Julia Dwyer and Susanna Hagan at the University of Brighton.
John Warren RIBA.
All photographs and drawings by the author

ORIGINAL CONTENTS

Introduction
Chapter One: The dream of Saint Hugh
Chapter Two: Return of the Martyrs
Chapter Three: A Place for Contemplation
Chapter Four: A Cloistered Life
Conclusion
Appendix A: Saint Hugh of Lincoln
Appendix B: The Carthusian Timetable
Bibliography

Introduction

A little way from what was formerly the main route from London to the Sussex coast, a curious sight greets the observant driver. It is the Priory of Saint Hugh at Parkminster, the only working Charterhouse, or Carthusian monastery, in Great Britain. It is a vast structure (the Great Cloister alone encloses over a hectare), and probably the largest monastery in the Christian world. In terms of its scale and date, it has no peer in these isles. It was built in the late nineteenth century at the request of successive bishops of Southwark.

The aims of this dissertation are threefold: firstly, to examine the spiritual conditions and ecclesiastical and political events over several centuries which led to the birth of the Carthusian Order and the eventual building of Parkminster; secondly, to make a study of the Carthusian life and how the architecture of Parkminster reflects and encapsulates it; and thus to ascertain finally whether such a building merits greater attention than the footnotes in architectural and monastic history which it currently occupies.

The dissertation will be divided into four chapters, with a conclusion and appendices to follow.

Chapter One, 'The dream of Saint Hugh', will deal with the origins of the Carthusian Order. It will trade Saint Bruno's search for solitude, and the spiritual ideals which influenced him to found the mountain retreat of the Grande Chartreuse. It will then examine the development of the Carthusian architectural model and how this relates to the order's contemplative ideal.

Chapter Two, 'The return of the martyrs' will deal with the immediate spiritual and political conditions and events which brought Parkminster into being, setting to rest the persistent myth concerning French anti-clericalism.

Chapter Three, 'A place for contemplation' will recount the story of Parkminster's construction. It will then examine the actual design of Parkminster as an illustrated journey, from the gatehouse and guest rooms, through the communal and conventual buildings and finally to the Great Cloister and the individual cells. The building will be examined in terms of its relation to the standard Charterhouse model and to a French Charterhouse previously designed by the same architect.

Chapter Four, 'A cloistered life', consists of a brief history of Parkminster to the present day.

Chapter Three
A Place for Contemplation: the design and construction of Parkminster

Early in 1874, an architect was appointed to design the new Charterhouse. Clovis Normand, from Calais, was at that time busy with the rebuilding and extension of the Charterhouse of Notre-Dame-des-Prés at Montreuil near Boulogne, so he sent his son across the Channel to survey the site and draw up a schedule of materials.

Clay pits were dug on the site, and kilns set up to fire the bricks which would form the core of the masonry walls. The basic facing stone comes from Slinfold, some two miles west of Horsham. The freestone (fine-grained sandstone used for ashlar work) came from Bath, after local stone from Nuthurst was rejected and ground down for aggregate. The sandstone used for window and door surrounds was from Swanage. The only importation was the Belgian purple flagstone.

The bulk of the funding for the project came from the Grand Chartreuse – sales of their liqueur were now at their height, making them a wealthy order. Consequently, the influence of the mother house on Parkminster was great. Normand complained that he was forced to redesign the monastery nine times before construction began in September 1876. Some 700 workmen were employed on site, a mixture of English, French and German under two French foremen. An elaborate ceremony led by the Bishop of Southwark on 16 October, 1877, marked the laying of the foundation stone of the church, and more importantly, celebrated the return of the Carthusian order to England.

Construction was dogged by the removal of the main contractor, Messrs. Longman and Burge, in 1878; they refused to continue work as they were losing money, and their contract was terminated at considerable expense. Normand and the rector, Dom. Pascal Sené, took over supervision of the work. However, disagreements led to them both being removed: the latter was recalled to the Grand Chartreuse and replaced by Dom. Saturnin. The former was replaced by the presumably more malleable Mr. Crawley, who agreed to complete the work in accordance with Normand's final design. The monastery was completed in 1882, and dedicated to Saint Hugh, Bishop of Lincoln and Carthusian Prior, in 1883.

The sister-house: comparisons with the Charterhouse of Notre-Dame-des-Prés

It should be instructive to consider the Charterhouse of Notre-Dame-des-Prés at Montreuil-sur-Mer as a model for Parkminster. The first set of drawings show the original layout of the Charterhouse in plan, and an aerial perspective of the Charterhouse as it was in 1870, prior to its rebuilding by Clovis Normand.

Notre-Dame-des-Prés was founded in 1336 by Robert, Count of Auvergne and Boulogne, on the site of an existing chapel of the same name. A single house built according to Bruno's original prescriptions for the Grand Chartreuse, it was sited on the flanks of a steep hill – which these drawings unfortunately do little to show – above the Vallée de la Canche. This accounts for the elongation of the Great Cloister, and its asymmetric relationship to the church.

In 1791, the monastery and its possessions were seized by the revolutionary state, and the Carthusians forced to disperse. When the order bought back Notre-Dame-des-Prés in 1870, little remained but the conventual buildings and guest house. The Great Cloister was entirely destroyed: presumably no alternative use could be found for it but as a source of building material.

As is evidenced by the drawing of the rebuilt foundation, Normand followed the original layout very closely, even though little was left standing and none of it was retained. Evidently it makes sense to have the church in the same place, as much to avoid the bother of re-consecrating the ground as from any wish to preserve continuity with the original foundation. The position of the church and the fall of the site determine the position of the gatehouse in the same place as previously. Once again the elongation of the Great Cloister is subtended by the sloping ground, the foundation now being a double house, with twenty-four contemplatives' cells.

Since it was designed by the same architect only a few years earlier, Notre-Dame-des-Prés is undoubtedly the clearest precedent for Parkminster. Although the circumstances of the two buildings differ – geography aside, Parkminster was an entirely new and substantially larger foundation – the disparities between the two designs as much as their similarities give an indication as to the approach and priorities of the architect.

The plan of Parkminster is highly classicized. This is a trend easily identifiable in later French Charterhouses such as the one at Clermont which was studied by Viollet-le-Duc, and easily accomplished on Parkminster's extensive, flat site. At Montreuil this tendency is tempered by the conditions of the site and the existing layout. Although the main existing building at Parkminster, the house of Parknowle, has been retained, its difference is clearly articulated in the fact that the monastery's plan is skewed with respect to it.

The processional relationship of gatehouse to church in both Charterhouses is of little practical sense for a closed order; and although at Montreuil the architect may have been following the original layout, its repetition at Parkminster betrays a classical, beaux-arts wish for symmetry. The obedience courts, along with stables and vineyard, flank the approach to the gatehouse at Montreuil. At Parkminster where the site is not so constricted by the slope, one's approach is flanked by woods, the kitchen and obedience courts being instead on either side of the gatehouse behind the precinct wall.

A. Church.
B. Chapterhouse (library above).
C. Refectory.
D. Sacristy.
E. Brothers' Chapel.
F. Brothers' Chapter.
G. Procurator's Court.
H. Sacristan's court & chapels.
I. Great Cloister.
J. Guest House (Parknowle).
K. Pantry.
L. Kitchen.

M. Gatehouse.
N. Obediences.
O. Obedience Court.
P. Prior's Lodging.
Q. Novitiate Conference.
R. Stair to Library.

a-s , aa- ss. Monks' cells.
S. Monks' Cemetery.

Plan of Parkminster after J. Warren RIBA. Scale 1:2000.

All buildings at Montreuil save the conventual buildings and the cells in the great cloister have hipped mansard roofs with numerous dormer windows. The cells too have dormer windows but these sit on single pitch hipped roofs. At Parkminster, all buildings have lower pitched roofs with far fewer dormers, and all roofs are gabled save the apse of the church. Perhaps this simplification was Normand's concession to 'Englishness', though in truth the hipped mansard is as typical of Sussex as of the Pas de Calais. More likely it was a device used at Montreuil for differentiating between devotional buildings, which in a Charterhouse would include the Fathers' cells, and the 'secular' buildings; this device was discarded at Parkminster.

The entrance court at Montreuil is cloistered on one side only. Both this and the great cloister are not arcaded as at Parkminster, but are walled with paired Gothic windows and relieving arches above.

The church façade is similar in proportion to that of Parkminster, albeit on a smaller scale. Its higher angled gable and its pair of octagonal gothic spires make it rather more elegant than its Sussex counter-part. The church has an octagonal clocher or campanile over the nave. The clock tower at Parkminster sits at the far end of the church beyond the high altar and dominates the Great Cloister. Here it stands at the far corner of the claustrum minus, and is of more modest scale: its relationship with the clocher balances the asymmetrical relationship of church and cloister quite effectively.

As to the great cloister itself, the obvious similarity here, and a sensitive departure from beaux-arts classical rigour, is the varied relationship between cell, ambulatory and cloister which preserves the gardens' southerly orientation.

What the rebuilt Notre-Dame-des-Prés shows us is that although his library of forms was mostly that of the French Romanesque and early Gothic, Clovis Normand was essentially a classicising, beaux-arts architect. At Parkminster, a new house on a generous site, he was able to give full rein to this tendency, which had manifested itself at Montreuil but was modified by the conditions of the site. Perhaps to the modern eye, though, the more compact house is more architecturally satisfying; its mode is congruent with the locality, which Parkminster's is not; and its site-specific asymmetry makes it the less academic, more characterful, and maybe ultimately, more Carthusian of the two.

From Gatehouse to Cell: a narrative journey

Although its church spire is clearly visible from surrounding villages, the entrance to Parkminster is hidden from the road. A plain white sign opposite a small cottage which was the lodge of the Parknowle estate says simply, 'St. Hugh's Charterhouse.' The tarmac drive snakes its way through chestnut trees, brambles and shrubs, the

The Gatehouse, Parkminster.

undergrowth on either side rustling in summer with squirrels and
rabbits, and arrives at the gatehouse after some two hundred yards.

The gatehouse, though substantial, gives little hint as to the scale
of the foundation behind save the glimpse of the church's two

hundred foot spire. The great gate from the London Charterhouse sits in a Romanesque archway, with the orb of the Grand Chartreuse and the motto, 'stat crux dum volvitur orbis'[18] carved in low relief above the lintel. Above the arched gateway, to which flanking buttresses add the necessary weight of the Romanesque, are three aediculae, the central one containing a statue of the Virgin Mary. Above this a small dormer sits in the steep purple slate roof which is surmounted by an elegant, diagonally aligned cloche or campanile. The original iron bell-pull, though still in existence, has been superseded by an ordinary electric doorbell. Flanking the gateway on either side are arched and gabled aediculae containing on the left a statue of Saint John the Baptist, patron saint of the hermit, and on the right, the order's founder Saint Bruno.

To the left of the gatehouse is a small 'extern' chapel which was a later addition in 1939 to serve the needs of parishioners, and dedicated to Saint Roseline, a Carthusian nun. It is so named because the nave is outside the monastic precinct; it is separated from the chancel by a wrought-iron screen with a hatch through which offerings are passed and the sacrament administered. The rest of the range is the one of the priory's guest houses, with reception rooms on the ground floor and bedrooms above; these rooms are usually reserved for the monks' and donates' immediate families.

What strikes one immediately about the Gatehouse is its almost self-conscious Frenchness. This feeling is greatly accentuated once the gate is opened and we go into the entrance court. Perhaps it would be appropriate to call it a cour d'honneur, as it is impossible to escape the feeling, local building materials notwithstanding, that we have just passed through some portal with openings on both sides of the Channel. One moment you are in the heart of Sussex, the next, somewhere in the Pas de Calais.

The cour d'honneur is cloistered on all four sides, and planted with shrubs and fruit trees around its perimeter. The Romanesque arcading was originally open to the elements, however climatic pragmatism won out over aesthetic sensibility, as the vagaries of the British weather led to the simple stone arched being glazed over. This does lend the cloister a rather heavy, oppressive air; the grandeur of the court and its vegetation are viewed through thick, distorted glass, a slightly unsatisfactory experience.

Straight ahead, a cambered path of textured Staffordshire Blue paviors having replaced the original flagstones (which were

---

[18]'The cross is still, while the world revolves' has supposedly been a motto of the Carthusians since the late sixteenth century. This is remarkable since it was only in 1543 that Copernicus' *De revolutionibus orbium coelestium* first posited the theory that the earth revolved on an axis, and it was placed on the Vatican's list of banned books in 1610, remaining there until the early nineteenth century.

presumably too slippery when wet), is the façade of the church, which is faced in Bath freestone rather than the grey Slinfold stone around it. The shallow pediment over the round-arched door is surmounted by a statue of Saint Hugh. He is depicted in his guise as Bishop of Lincoln, with his swan at his feet.[19] The two towers, whose finials are orbs of the Chartreuse, attempt to deceive one into believing that they conceal a standard Romanesque basilica; unfortunately they lend the façade a rather unprepossessing squatness.

To the right of the cour d'honneur is the obedience court, which contains stores of building material and fuel, engineering shops, the bookbinding workshop and the now-defunct printing press, which came originally from Notre-Dame-des-Prés: Parkminster still publishes books, but they are printed elsewhere. Following the cour d'honneur round to the left, a flight of steps takes one down to the level of the kitchen court, and another flight back up again to the men's guest house, in the gaunt and now rather shabby house of Parknowle.[20] Inside, its air of faded grandeur reminds one of nothing so much as the more rambling and characterful sort of youth hostel.

Returning to the cour d'honneur, the cloister leads past the dishwasher's hatch and gives onto a small anteroom where the brothers and donates collect their food boxes. Handwritten notes left in the boxes are one of the primary means of communication between the brothers. This room gives on to a large and simply furnished kitchen: a passage straight ahead leads down to the stores on the western range of the kitchen court. At the southwest corner of the cour d'honneur, a flight of steps leads up to the left: these lead to the brothers' quarters and the prior's house, which has a private chapel and a substantial anteroom.

The prior's anteroom is not in itself a remarkable space – it resembles a truncated banqueting hall with its high collar-beam ceiling and clerestorey windows. However, it has great symbolic importance in terms of Parkminster's identity and its place within English Catholicism.

The anteroom has, among other relics contained in a rather unassuming glass-topped display cabinet, the seals of several English Charterhouses as well as the seal of the exiled community of Sheen Anglorum, and a stone from each of the English houses. Around the walls above head height, among numerous paintings and reproductions, are banners bearing the escutcheons of all the Charterhouses in the British Isles, including that of Parkminster. The inference is clear: this is emphatically not the house of an order in exile. Indeed,

---

[19]For further information on Hugh and his swan, see Appendix A.

[20]At the time of writing (September 1998) restoration work was about to begin with the aid of English Heritage.

it is quite the reverse: it is the house of an order returning from exile. One can see this notion of the return from exile further emphasized in the chapterhouse and its iconography.

Moving on from the corner of the cour d'honneur, the cloister turns into a passage between the pantry with its bread hatch, and the refectory, where communal meals are taken on Sundays and feast days. The refectory is divided into two parts, or the monks and brothers. Only the monks' refectory is still used as such. It is an austere space, with plain rendered walls and vaulting and simple wooden panelling, and a small stone pulpit built into the west wall. Flanking the refectory on its west side is a walled cloister which surrounds the Procurator's court, which consists of a garden laid out in the mediaeval manner. Once again, it is a pity that the openings are glazed over, that one does not feel a part of the space. At the corner of the cloister is a large stone sink; several are also dotted round the cour d'honneur and Great Cloister.

The Chapterhouse

At the northwest corner of the Procurator's court is a small, high-ceilinged antechamber. A noticeboard proclaims the day's offices, which saints' days are to be celebrated, and those people on whose behalf the monks are to intercede in their prayers that day. To the south is the chapterhouse. Like the relic chapel, this space is important not so much for its inherent qualities as for its contents. Some of its paintings (although they appear to be frescoes, they were painted on canvas in France by Antoine Sublet before being shipped to Parkminster) portray the execution and martyrdom of the Carthusians under Henry VIII. The iconographical programme serves to reinforce the link between Parkminster and the English Carthusians. Moreover, their grim realism and the power of the subject matter makes them by far the most convincing artwork in the house.

The altar, at the south end, is surmounted by a painting of the crucified Christ, and flanked by depictions of the first executions at Tyburn.

In the panel on the left, one father is about to be hanged, still in his Carthusian habit; the executioner makes the rope fast on the gallows beam above him. A second father has been cut down, and the bonds on his wrists are being cut. In the foreground, a third seems to be blessing his executioner. The vicar-general Thomas Cromwell, in a red ermine-trimmed robe and chains of office, directs the proceedings from astride a grey horse.

In the right panel, the last father, still conscious, is having his robes cut off while behind him, another has his entrails ripped from his body. In the foreground the first father, already dead and disembowelled, is about to be dismembered by the executioner's axe, while in the smoky background the fires are stoked which are to consume the martyrs' bodies. At the axeman's feet lie torn robes and a rosary, while above his head are two angels, carrying palm fronds. Paintings on the returning walls depict angels bearing mottoes: on the left, 'beati persecutionem patiuntur' – 'happy are they that endure persecution'; and on the right, 'mirabilis deus in sanctis' – 'how wonderful is God in his holiness'; as well as numerous Carthusian saints including Hugh of Lincoln.

At the north end, above the door to the Charterhouse, is shown the 'second slaughter' in which three more fathers were executed some six weeks later. Cromwell again directs the proceedings, his guards gazing almost casually at the gory scene. In the foreground one father has his robes torn off by the same executioner, who is speaking to a dark figure on the left and paying no attention to his victim. The father is bathed in a light emanating from behind a group of angels overhead, and is clearly still alive after hanging, his hand raised towards Cromwell in a gesture of forgiveness or defiance. Behind this, in the centre of the panel, a second Carthusian is disembowelled by two men, one of whom seems more interested in the dark figure, while the other seems to be demanding that he give attention to his grisly task. Further back, the severed head of the third martyr is displayed to the gathered public. The crowd are being restrained by guards armed with halberds, one of whom cannot resist a salacious peep at the scene behind him. At the bottom right of the painting, a young woman is consoled by her older companion. The young woman is possibly Lady Jane Dormer, sister of Sebastian Newdigate who was one of the three martyrs.

The panel on the returning wall at the north end of the chapterhouse depicts three scenes. In the top right panel, two Carthusians swing on a gallows on a hill: these are John Rochester and James Walworth, who were hanged at York after being exiled to the Hull Charterhouse.[21] A figure in the foreground waves his hat in farewell, seemingly mockingly.

In the lower half, ten Carthusians languish in gaol, of whom four are shackled to the wall, the others on the floor. The only light comes from the gaoler's torch at the open door; a shadowy figure behind him appears to be bringing a basket of provisions.

This was the final attempt by Henry to stamp out Carthusian resistance. He did not wish to create any more martyrs by public execution, and so ordered ten of the London Carthusians to be

---

[21]They are depicted here hanged by a rope around the neck, but Carthusian writings state that they were 'Hanged in Chains at York.' J.D. Lee, *Carthusians*, p 38.

starved to death in Newgate Prison. The figure bringing provisions is probably Margaret Clement, adopted daughter of Sir Thomas More, who bribed the gaoler to let her feed them: eventually the gaoler, fearing his own death if she were discovered, refused her access. One brother, William Horne, inexplicably survived the starvation long after the others and was finally executed at Tyburn on 4 August, 1540. He is shown lying disem-bowelled in the top left corner of the bay, the last of England's Carthusian martyrs.

Church and Chapels

Across the anteroom from the chapterhouse door is the south door of the church. Following the Carthusian model, the church is a simple, single-naved oratory with a polygonal chevet. The nave consists of four rectangular rib-vaulted bays, with a fifth comprising a gallery and porch. The door on the south side and a corresponding one leading into the sacristy separate the monks' choir from the chancel. Over the altar is a painting of Saint Hugh as Bishop of Lincoln, ascending into heaven. Above his head on either side are John the Baptist and Saint Bruno, and with them Hugh of Dié and Pope Urban II; below him, two angels spread out a scroll with an axonometric painting of Parkminster. The chancel is panelled, and carved with scenes from the life of Saint Peter. Christ presents him with the keys to the kingdom of heaven above the bishop's seat on the north side. The lay-brothers' choir is at the back of the church beyond a stone screen, where there are two subsidiary altars, dedicated on the left to John the Baptist, and on the right to Saint Bruno. Both monks' and lay brothers' choirs have stalls with simple misericordae; once again they are French, the work of a M. Buisine of Lille. The floor, as in all the main conventual and communal paces, is maple and oak parquetry, laid herringbone fashion in the middle of the floor, straight around the sides and where the floor is raised.

The most obvious feature of the church is its reverse orientation, its altar facing virtually due west. Possibly this could be put down to the unwillingness of a classicizing architect to depart from his processional design; yet I believe it has great significance for Christian architecture. That the Chapter of the Grand Chartreuse exercised a large measure of control over the design of Parkminster is clear enough from Normand's own account (see Chapter 2). The processional relationship of church to gatehouse has little or no significance for a Charterhouse; many early houses had gatehouses that were offset from or perpendicular to the church. If the Grand Chapter had felt that the liturgical significance of easterly orientation outweighed the architect's own preference, the orientation would assuredly have been reversed. It seems most likely, however, that the easterly orientation of Christian altars is a result of the taking over or imitation of non-Judaeo-Christian religous enclosures (such as the Mithraeum under St John Lateran in Rome). In such an enclosure, orientation to the rising sun is of paramount importance: and so Christian altars came to face east more by accident than by design.

Parkminster's church is a confusing paradox. Its arches and vaulting are Romanesque, and yet there is little of the feeling of weight inherent in that era's architecture. The clusters of columns are slender and insubstantial, and the rendered infill panels, scored to suggest Travertine or Istrian stonework, reflect the light harshly. There are hints of almost Mannerist playfulness in the capitals; each cluster differs dramatically from its counterpart on the opposite side, which may have been meant to temper the severity of the design but if anything accentuates it. Its simplicity of organization owes itself to Carthusian tradition, and yet design decisions seem to have been made without giving priority to the order's liturgical requirements. The clock tower is beyond the chevet, which means that in order for bells to be rung during a service, an extra clocher had to be placed above the monks' choir. If nothing else this violates the order's architectural principle of vilitas. Dom. Augustin Devaux chastises not only its lack of originality, but its lack of the rationality which he ascribes to Carthusian tradition:

> we find (at Parkminster) an anthology of antique forms,
> wanted only for their ornamental value.[22]

Leaving the church on its north side, one passes a stair on the left which leads to the sacristan's cell, and pausing briefly in the sacristy. This is a simple, square, low-vaulted room with head-height panelling and a modest altar. Through a door on the right, a top-lit corridor gives on to the devotional chapels which surround the sacristan's court, which is a planted counterpart to the procurator's court. Each of these thirteen square, vaulted rooms is dedicated to a different saint, whose altars take up much of the space inside. These are where the cloister monks say low mass, after Conventual Mass has been said in the church. They are usually attended by a novice. In most churches, whether monastic or not, subsidiary chapels would be part of the main body of the church, whether as 'radiant' chapels beyond the apse, as transept chapels, or taking up the aisles of a basilica. By segregating devotional chapels from the church, the Carthusian ideals of simplicity and privacy are preserved.

---

[22]Dom. Augustin Devaux, *L'architecture dans l'Ordre des Chartreux.* p 236. One suspects that Dom. Augustin never actually saw Parkminster, since he claims the Great Cloister to be four times larger than it actually is ('250 metres per side') and the church tower almost twice its true height ('about 100 metres'). Either that, or he is guilty of almost Biblical exaggeration.

The top-lit corridor leads into a lobby at its southeast corner. Stairs go up to the gallery of the church, while on the left is the brothers' chapel. This is also known as the family chapel, not because families are permitted to worship there, but because it is dedicated to the Holy Family. Nowadays, the cloister monks and brothers attend mass together in the main church: the brothers' chapel is only used once a week, when prayers are said in preparation for the weekly walk. It is a modest oratory, virtually identical to the refectory in form and decoration, but without a pulpit. The plastered walls, like those in the refectory, have an ethereal quality quite unlike the jarring 'stone-effect' render used in the main church. However, the air of almost Cistercian austerity found in the refectory is somewhat marred here by a weak altar, and above a statue of the Madonna and child which sits beneath a garish blue half-dome preposterously decorated with gold stars.

Exiting the brothers' chapel one turns and walks north along the western range of the cour d'honneur. In the northwest corner is a rather fine stone staircase leading to the brothers' accommodation above the obediences. These consist of single cells, virtually identical to the cubicula of the cloister monks' cells – of which a description will be given later – each with a small anteroom which gives on to the south-facing corridor. Other cells for brothers are to be found above the kitchen on the south side of the cour d'honneur.

The Great Cloister

Turning west, we pass between the sacristan's court on our left and the brothers' chapter – now redundant and used as a store for statuary and other artefacts – on our right, until we finally reach the glory of Parkminster, the Great Cloister. The main body of the cloister measures some 134 metres long on its north and south sides, and 115 metres on the east and west. The cloister garth which it encloses measures a little over one and a half hectares, making it the largest cloister garth in the world. Indeed it is so large that many of the brothers cycle round it rather than walk. There are thirty-six cells on the Great Cloister, of which five (including the prior's lodging) are on the extended southern range. Before considering the cells, two of the monastery's finest spaces, and one of its most curious, are to be found off the Great Cloister.

The novitiate conference room, the library and the relic chapel

The communal and conventual spaces at Parkminster remain largely as they were when first built. The novitiate conference room, though, has been altered and enhanced to produce a highly satisfying space. A few steps down from the extended southern range lead one into this rectangular room, also used for lectures and classes. At the request of the current Prior, who also happens to be the Novice Master, all the render has been removed from the walls and ceiling, exposing the rude, red clay bricks beneath. Made in a continental size of 250 × 100 × 80 mm, they form both the walls and the low vaults which span between steel I-beams. Their soft red glow is contrasted by the daylight filtering through the green of the prior's garden outside, and enhanced by the clay floor tiles. A marvellous round table with wrought-iron legs, made by one of the brothers and a local craftsman, sits around the circular steel column in the centre of the room.

Charterhouses were noted for the excellence of their libraries from the very early days, and Parkminster has one of the finest examples in any Charterhouse. The core of the original collection was purchased from King Victor-Emmanuel of Italy. The collection now numbers over forty thousand volumes, ranging from rare and ancient theological texts to modern history and fiction. Many books, including the annals of Parkminster and the pre-Reformation English Charterhouses, are kept in the house of Parknowle, with countless liturgical texts stored all over the monastery.

The main library is reached by a stair tucked between the chapter-house anteroom and the Great Cloister. It has a warmth conspicuously lacking elsewhere in the communal buildings, yet at the same time possesses a solemn, studious air. All the surfaces are simply yet effectively crafted in dark timber. The walls are entirely composed of bookshelves; further freestanding units have been added as the collection has increased. A timber gallery runs around above head height, enabling access to the highest shelves. The arched windows at gallery level become deep recesses or niches, white rendered and each furnished with a chair and small shelf for reading. Below this, a window lets light in to floor level: the illusion is created that the window sails right past the gallery, giving it a sense of impermanence.

The floor, once again, is of both straight and herringbone parquetry; the impressive ceiling is a dense forest of heavy wooden beams. The haunches of the main beams are exaggerated into triangular springings, white the tertiary beams are carved into dog's-tooth patterns.

Next door to the library is a curious and to modern eyes somewhat macabre space called the relic chapel; these were something of a fad in the nineteenth century.[23] Again it is a square, vaulted room,

---

[23]Dom. Bruno Sullivan remarks that 'that sort of thing was all the rage when this place was built.'

Library.

with an altar taking up a great deal of it, and cabinets and caskets all around containing the relics of saints; these are mostly single bones held in elaborate monstrances. The largest casket contains an effigy of, and below this the almost complete skeleton of, Saint Boniface. The most precious relic, though, is the stole of Saint Hugh of Lincoln, hung in a glass-fronted frame on the wall opposite the altar.

The siting of the library and its macabre companion is slightly disappointing. The time allowed to the cloister monks for private study means the library was and remains a crucial part of any

Charterhouse. The relic chapel has an important role in establishing firstly, Parkminster's place within what might be termed a continuum of divine mystery, and secondly, the house's link through the relic of its patron with the pre-Reformation Charterhouses of England. This being the case, why are Parkminster's library and relic chapel tucked away above the chapterhouse, and reached by a nondescript stair behind a couple of anonymous doors?

It might be argued that the monastic library does not have any ritual associated with it. In a secular world where daily religious ritual is increasingly absent or entirely non-existent, an act such as going to a public library has become imbued with institutional and private ritual significance. In a world based around a liturgical timetable, such a ritual becomes insignificant. On the other hand, it may be that there is a ritual of seclusion implied here, such that the monk must remain in a solitude analogous to that of his cell – although in practice there is rarely more than one person in the library at any one time, as most study takes place in the cell – and that the niche reading spaces, large enough for one reader only, are indicative of this. Perhaps, then, it is right that the library should be lofty and inaccessible. However the relic chapel has a clear liturgical and ritual significance: one would expect to find it by the sacristan's or procurator's court.

The cells

The cells for the cloister monks at Parkminster are two-storey houses. Those on the north and west ranges of the great cloister are built against, and form part of, the precinct wall and are each joined to the Great Cloister by an ambulatory running perpendicular to it. These cells are separated from each other by a gap of about 3 m. The gaps are crucial, and reflect a need to give tectonic expression to the individuality of the cells' inhabitants which far outweighs any question of material economy or fuel consumption. Along the south range, the cells are rotated to maintain a southern aspect to the gardens, and the ambulatories are parallel to the cloister.

The door into the ambulatory from the cloister has a sliding latch and a lock operable with a simple lifting key or *passe-partout*. This kind of door mechanism has been used in Charterhouses since the fifteenth century,[24] and can also be found on the east door of the church at Parkminster. By the door is the guichet through which food and drink are passed. It is not cranked as in many mediaeval houses, having instead a door on both sides of the wall. The brother delivering

---

[24]J.W. Gibbins, *op.cit.*, p 482.

food operates a bell-pull to one side of the door. The bell may also be sounded in addition to the church bell to call the cloister monk to conventual offices.

What follows is a general description of a typical cell, with the most common variations being noted. We now pass from the cloister into the ambulatory, which is a simple, well-proportioned space with white rendered walls and a red clay tile floor. The ceiling, above which is a lean-to slate roof, consists of short, stubby, dark wooden beams with joists spanning between them supporting timber boards. Three sash windows with dark wooden surrounds face onto the garden, except in some cells on the south range where a door out to the garden takes the place of the central window. At the end of the ambulatory, concrete steps (with a dormer rooflight above) lead up to the *Ave Maria*; there may or may not be a flight down to the lower floor. The stair has a simple, chunky but elegant timber handrail.

On the ground floor is a wood store, which has a door out to the garden except in those cells on the South range mentioned above; an open doorway leads through to the workshop, with tools, workbench and lathe – now rarely used – and a small room with a toilet at the back. The ground floor rooms have cobbled floors and whitewashed brick walls and ceilings. As in the novice conference room, the vaults span between steel I-beams.

Each monk is at liberty to do whatever he wishes with his garden. Accordingly, the nature of each garden is expressive of the individual monk's character. The more industrious grow vegetables; those less inclined to physical labour grow a few flowers and bushes, or let their gardens grow wild and unkempt.

The first floor living space comprises the Ave Maria and cubiculum. The entrance from the stair to the former is offset from the door through to the cubiculum, so that the monk must pass the fireplace with its statuette of the Madonna and Child on his way through the room. Both rooms have timber ceilings with exposed joists, bare floor-boards, and rendered walls with French windows.

The cubiculum serves as a room for study, eating, prayer and sleep. The latter two activities are circumscribed by a large cupboard along one wall. This contains a bed and a small private oratory as well as a door through to the shower. A traditional Carthusian device which originally had doors or curtains around the bed to preserve warmth, the cupboard is now largely symbolic of the greater degree of seclusion required for prayer and for sleep. Eating and study are accommodated by a table and a simple desk and bookshelf by the windows. The original design had no windows facing out of the precinct at all, giving emphasis to the introversion of Carthusian life. However, new windows facing outwards have been added since in what may be a dilution of the order's precepts but gives the cell an airiness it probably did not originally possess.

Cell 'L' and garden.

After many years' solitary prayer and contemplation, the Carthusian will be laid to rest in the cemetery. Parkminster's cemetery is a walled-off rectangular plot within the cloister garth, beneath the clock tower, and contains a crucifix carved in Burmese Teak by a Father Dapre. One of the avowed aims of the Carthusians is 'to make many saints, but publicize none'; the monk is buried, still in his habit, on a bare board and with an unmarked wooden cross.

> *A nameless wooden cross surmounts his grave: he is as unknown in death as he was in life*[25]

Conclusion

Having explored the origins of the Carthusian order and the development of the Charterhouse model, and subsequently analysed the origins and design of Parkminster as a reaction to this history and precedent, there are an number of conclusions to be drawn from this study.

First of all there is the setting to rest of the persistent myth that Parkminster was built as a house of refuge. There is no doubt that it

---

[25]J.D. Lee, *op.cit.*, p 43.

is a romantic idea, and it would enable one to bracket Parkminster with other foundations in the south of England, for example the convent chapel at Newhaven, which were built for precisely this purpose; and indeed with a whole sphere of architecture of exiles, from the Shakers to the builders of the Shri Swaminarayan. However, there are facts of history, material culture and architecture at Parkminster which disabuse this notion. Historically, there is the role of the three English bishops and their wish to bring the order back *from* exile for ecclesiastical and political reasons. There are the 'identifiers' at Parkminster: the relics and escutcheons of English Charterhouses; the paintings of the martyrs at Tyburn and York; and the stole of Saint Hugh. Finally there are the spaces, the chapterhouse, prior's anteroom and the relic chapel which house the identifiers.

How, then, did this myth come to be promulgated? Why is the gap of almost three decades between Parkminster's conception and the arrival of the exiles from Sélignac and Montreuil ignored? The centralization of the order, or rather the control over new foundations that has been exercised from the earliest days by the authorities of the Grand Chartreuse, might have led to the belief that the house must have been their idea. I believe, however, that the architecture itself is to blame for the myth's continuation. The fact that the architectural parti is entirely based on French Romanesque precedent gives the distinct impression that this is a branch of the order nostalgic for its old country, and which moreover has no connection whatever with the English Charterhouses. Writing in Pevsner's *Buildings of England* series, Ian Nairn excoriates Parkminster's design:

Cloister garth: the monks' cemetery.

> *Imported bodily from across the Channel, it represents the*
> *French Gothic revival at its weakest and harshest. The impres-*
> *sion of being in the outskirts of somewhere like Béthune or*
> *Arras is overwhelming.*[26]

It could be contended, in Normand's defence, that almost all English non-domestic architecture (at least in the limited sense in which Pevsner understood it) is in some way imported or derivative of foreign models; from the great Romanesque cathedrals to International Modernism and all points between. Nevertheless, it puzzles one why, in the first place, an English architect could not be found for this English Charterhouse. J.W. Gibbins argues that, because of the break in tradition occasioned by the Reformation,

> *it was assumed that continuity was lost and there was no*
> *local architect available with a deep understanding of the*
> *order's requirements.*[27]

This assumption may well have been made, but it was not a correct one. Many English architects would have been well aware of the London Charterhouse, which housed the famous public school until 1872, as well as Eugène Viollet-le-Duc's writings on French Charterhouses. Put simply, the Grand Chartreuse appointed Normand because he was already working for them at Montreuil, and as he was a little-known provincial architect, they could feel confident that he would devote himself to the design of Parkminster almost exclusively.

One might further contend that Parkminster tries too hard to be 'great <u>architecture.</u>' This should be qualified by saying that as an exercise in Romanesque revival it is, for the most part, a very competent piece of work, and one which offers a convincing version of the Carthusian model. Even Nairn concedes that the plan is 'magnificent',[28] and indeed, no-one could fail to be impressed by the classical vision of the Great Cloister, or moved by the monks' cemetery therein. Nonetheless, the church, and to a lesser extent the lesser conventual and communal buildings, excepting the library, are little more than pastiches. One might say that the spaces become more impressive as they become not only more intimate, but less self-consciously *architectural*. The serenity of the novitiate conference room, the reductive and mysterious cell ambulatories, the earnest simplicity of the cubicula, are a result of a wish to enclose space in a straightforward and robust manner. For the major spaces Normand had at his disposal a kit of parts lifted from *La Dictionnaire*

---

[26] Nairn/Pevsner, *The buildings of England: Sussex*, p 317.
[27] J.W. Gibbins, *op. cit.*, vol. II, p 550.
[28] Nairn/Pevsner, *op. cit.* p 317.

Raisonée; they are assembled with a reasonable degree of success. Where, on the other hand, he had to fulfil the planning strictures of the Carthusian model with only the basic surfaces of stone, brick, tile, plaster, mortar and wood, he succeeded admirably. One might almost say that where he attempted architecture, mere building resulted, and where he has simply built, he succeeded in creating architecture.

It might appear, then, that Parkminster merits no more attention in architectural history than it has hitherto received. It would be a pity, however, to ignore its uniqueness. Visiting Parkminster, it was both surprising and fascinating to find that its inhabitants were rarely what one would suppose members of a monastic community to be like. Here was not a body of men alike in thought, prayer and deed, but a collection of individuals. In particular the choir monks, who spend so much time in solitary prayer and contemplation, seemed as if their individual traits and idiosyncrasies must have been sharpened by their vocation. When this was suggested to the Vicar, Dom. Bruno Sullivan, he agreed wholeheartedly.

> *Of course we are individuals – and real tough old nuts, some*
> *of us! We each live and work and relate to God in a different*
> *way. You have to remember that when a man comes here as a*
> *novice, whether from the secular world or from another order,*
> *within a half hour of stepping through that gate he is alone in*
> *his cell with God. The biggest danger comes at that moment.*
> *And do you know what that danger is? They go up the wall,*
> *almost immediately, some of them! I have seen it happen.*

Western secular society, in other words capitalist society, tends more and more towards the glorification of the individual, this despite the vapid, often hypocritical commitment of politicians to the rather nebulous concept that is 'family values.' Even spiritual being is increasingly concerned with the understanding and improvement of self. Yet while the cult of the individual may be greatly liberating in some respects, in others it is destructive of social being, weakening vital support networks.

The trend from the collective to the individual has accelerated the growth of the single-person household. There are also building types which have for diverse reasons evolved or been resurgent in recent years, which rely not on communal living, but on individuals living with a common purpose or goal, for example foyer schemes, women's refuges and retreats. There is much more to be learned from the Charterhouse as a building type, in that it serves as an example of how a group of individuals can exist within a community, bound together by a common purpose which is of their own choosing. As the only working Charterhouse in Britain, Parkminster is therefore deserving of, and rewards, detailed study.

Yeoryia Manolopoulou

Drawing on Chance: Indeterminacy, Perception and Design
(PhD by Architectural Design)

A relatively new kind of dissertation is one which combines textual and design work to produce an integrated exploration of architecture. Pioneered at The Bartlett School of Architecture at UCL and other universities such as RMIT, these kinds of dissertation typically combine the methodological rigour and contextual awareness of the text-based PhD with the speculative and creative nature of the studio. Manolopoulou's dissertation explores the ways in which the slippery concept of chance might influence different ways in which architecture and buildings are designed. Part of a much larger 2 volume dissertation – containing a 50,000 text and substantial portfolio of design-based analyses and propositions – the extracts shown provide a brief glimpse of a comprehensive, powerful and intriguing study.

Yeoryia Manolopoulou

DRAWING ON CHANCE

Indeterminacy, Perception and Design

ORIGINAL CONTENTS

Volume 1: Notes

Title
Abstract
General Contents
Acknowledgements

Introduction
A Preliminary Work
B *Backward Looking*
C On *Film*
D *Viewing Instrument I*
E On *Glass*
F *Drawing Pier 40*
G Appendix

Volume II: Text

Title

General Contents
Contents of Volume II

Introduction

Odd Accidents

> *The considerate kindness of the Angel mollified me in no little*
> *measure; and, aided by the water with which he diluted my*
> *port more than once, I at length regained sufficient temper to*
> *listen to his very extraordinary discourse. I cannot pretend to*
> *recount all that he told me, but I gleaned from what he said*
> *that he was the genius who presided over the* contretemps *of*
> *mankind, and whose business it was to bring about* the odd
> accidents *which are continuously astonishing the sceptic.*
> [Edgar Allen Poe, *The Angel of the Odd*].

We never experience space without the intervention of accidents. Often these are small incidents, ordinary coincidences that we do not notice or remember. But sometimes accidents become unusually apparent and 'odd', disturbing our sense of logic and undercutting our assumptions about the world. Such accidents have triggered my curiosity about the strange 'power' of chance and a desire to understand its intimate relationship with how architectural space is experienced and produced. The activity around the dining table at a specific moment, the sound of the passing train, a reflection on the window, the sudden opening of the door, the sense of the evening storm, the rear garden's smell, all these orchestrate a spatiality that is based on chance factors and relationships as much as design. Accepting that chance is fundamental in how we experience space, I will argue that architects ought to explore its role as a productive element in design.

In the dominant architectural discourses and practices the issue of chance as a creative force is rather disregarded. In architectural writings aspects of it are implied through, for example, the discussion of computational systems, game theory or the argument for an 'architecture of events.' But chance as an issue alone is rarely considered thoroughly. In practice when architects acknowledge chance they usually do so in negative terms, referring to the failures or accidents in the realisation of their proposals. The idea that chance may be a positive element in the architectural process is barely pursued.

Chance influences the life of buildings, the ways in which they are perceived, occupied and aged. This fact is generally acknowledged. Yet, it has not yet been sufficiently reflected upon the process of architectural design itself. In this thesis I concentrate not on how chance affects buildings but on how chance should influence the way in which we design buildings. Chance, rather than being an intricate issue mainly encountered by the occupants of architecture, is here brought to the attention of designers.

To investigate the subject of spatiality and the role that chance plays in shaping it, it is necessary to consider a broader concept to which chance belongs, that of indeterminacy. The term indeterminacy here means the impossibility of determining in advance how designs will be understood, built and lived in. Artists have often employed chance as a creative tool and the principles of indeterminacy have long been considered in the fields of science and philosophy. Although indeterminacy has been considered in architecture, mainly in terms of function (for instance, flexibility of buildings), more fundamental aspects of the theme, yet to be fully explored, relate to the perception and representation of space. Based on the study of specific art projects and the production of individual design work, I firstly examine the theme of chance in perception and representation; I then explore the formulation of chance as a design tool.

My initial interest in the theme of chance was entirely intuitive. As I will show in the first pages of this volume, it emerged long before this research started in my design work. It was within design that the issue of chance came forth and I therefore decided that a closer inquiry into the meanings and implications of chance in architectural design would best be pursued in both drawn and textual form. Consequently, the course of this research developed through reading and writing on the one hand, and drawing and making on the other. Each procedure influenced the other: some design work initiated the theoretical research and challenged the scope of the text, while reading and writing influenced the development of design. But the activity which was mostly important in generating this process was the constant output of notes. As a result, the structure of the thesis reflects a three-way procedure. It consists of three interdependent components: the notes (Volume I), the design work (displayed) and the text (Volume II).

Volume I forms a condensed visual record of the research. It documents the practical course of the thesis focusing in particular on the formation of 'notes.' A note here is a short record made to help memory, an observation which is not necessarily written, a sketch, a diagram, a drawing, a photograph, a thought in visual or linguistic form for future use, a suggestion for something to be researched further, an interpretation or study of others' works, a question. Some of the notes have been extended into design work, some into text, many have remained unresolved.

More particularly, Volume I assembles extracts from three major notebooks (Notebooks I, II, III), some disconnected notes and key illustrations of the final design schemes in seven 'assemblages' of notes. Each assemblage corresponds to a separate theme. In it each note is accompanied with a caption that attempts to review and re-evaluate the work. The first assemblage, called Preliminary Work, functions as a visual introduction to the thesis. It refers to the earliest work, done between 1996 and 1997 while undertaking the MArch course at the Bartlett, UCL, that motivated my interest in chance. *Backward Looking* then describes a one-day project that marked more specifically the beginning of this PhD. On *Film,* mainly presenting extracts from Notebook I, uses Samuel Beckett's *Film* to explore the relationship between habits and accidents and the subject of self-perception. *Viewing Instrument I* derives from my interpretation of *Film* and investigates the subject of surrounding perception. It presents material from Notebooks I and II, the making of a viewing device and its findings. On *Glass* refers mainly to Notebook II and drawings that have originated from my investigation of Marcel Duchamp's *The Bride Stripped Bare by Her Bachelors, Even.* Finally, *Drawing Pier 40* presents extracts from Notebook III and additional visual material to describe a design proposal for Pier 40, New York, that employs chance operations. The Appendix summarises design work that was done during the course of this PhD but independent from it in a collaborative practice with Tessera. The work is mentioned because of its relevant aspects to the theme of indeterminacy.

Similar to how the notes have generated the projects and the text, Volume I suggests possible links among the three components of the thesis. The volume functions as a navigating tool for the reader: a reviewing catalogue for most of the displayed items and a directory for the text of Volume II. Most of the notes indicate their original source in the displayed work and a recommendation for reading relevant texts in Volume II. Volume I exposes the uncertainty of the design process, mistakes, weak points and failures of the research. This exposure is considered as a positive outcome.

The displayed work comprises notebooks, drawings, models, cards, photographs and slides. It presents On *Film, Viewing Instrument I,* On *Glass* and *Drawing Pier 40* in their full and original forms. The first two projects investigate the theme of spatiality and chance in perception, the second two in design. On *Film* and On *Glass* study the associated art works and use these as their 'sites' to be developed into drawing schemes. They have a narrative structure and most of their material is presented directly where it evolved, in the notebooks. Differently, *Viewing Instrument I* and *Drawing Pier 40* are presented through various media.

The subject of this research could not have been explored credibly without experimentation in practice. To suggest that chance can be employed as a design tool meant to directly test this proposition in design. The projects convey the message that it is necessary for architecture to accept chance as a central agent in the production of space and to explore it as a design tool. Yet they do not attempt to construct methodologies or exemplify modes of operation. None gives a single answer on exactly how chance affects perception and representation or on how it should be best used as a creative tool. But their assemblage into a body of work, that inquires the same theme from different viewpoints, scales and contexts, suggests that there is more than one answer. For although the projects have no obvious relationships among themselves and can function independently, they complement each other. Their presence in an assemblage aims to show that chance in architecture should be explored throughout all its stages, from a wide range of positions and in variable ways. Its use in design can either be intentional or incidental.

Volume II is a text, discussing first the subject of chance in perception, then in design. The text parallels the notes thematically, expressing similar content through different means. In Chapter 1 Beckett's *Film* linked with Jacques Lacan's theory of 'the split between the eye and the gaze' formulates the vehicle through which I investigate the role of chance in perception. I propose that while habits tend to 'screen' reality, forming our visual representations (images), accidents derive beyond the reach of optical vision and tend to rupture our defence against reality, puncturing these representations. The respective pairs of the eye and the gaze, vision and touch, and habits and accidents are interconnected. Next, through a study of chance-related techniques mainly in art, Chapters 2, 3 and 4 discuss the formulation of chance as a drawing tool. Chance in art can be an instructive model for architecture. For artists have explored the use of chance more explicitly and systematically than architects in order to specifically understand the role of indeterminacy in the perception and representation of space. Rather than presenting only prosperous modes of operation, chance in art shows a variety of both successful and failed attempts. Chapters 2 and 3 provide a comparison between several art processes and my definition of the drawing techniques of 'impulsive' and 'active' chance. Impulsive chance emerges from an individualistic creative process that is strongly linked with the unconscious. Active chance implies a collective manner of working that usually involves play and the social reality beyond the individual. Finally, in Chapter 4 I focus on a single art project, Duchamp's *The Bride Stripped Bare by Her Bachelors, Even*, to define the technique of 'measurable' chance. Duchamp's work is explored as a paradigm for architectural drawing that challenges the issue of chance in spatial representation. The drawing techniques of impulsive, active and measurable chance can be traced in architectural design as much as in art.

Volumes I and II have initially a sequential structure. However, they can be read in parallel to create non-linear readings. Such readings will reveal the links between the notes, the text and the design work.

To conduct research through projects means to work on a field where design and theory are mixed. I found that through the simultaneous preoccupation with design and text, projects are likely to embrace intuitive and intellectual activities in conversation. This has a significant value in research because it enables spontaneous ideas to suggest innovative outcomes and a more systematic intellectual process to test, affirm and sustain such impulses as factual or not. The notes, particularly, operate between drawing and writing and intersect both manners of working. They entail spontaneous action but also pose questions, tempting one's curiosity to understand and explore things through prolonged processes. The notes can be visited continuously in order to extract spare ideas, revise aspects of them or add completely new ones. They outline the most creative and open-ended area of the research, the area where chance and design mostly meet.

In the Conclusion I link the three components of the thesis to argue that the area where chance takes over design and control is often the area of transition from one medium or manner of working to an other. Accidents astonish us in presiding over the ways in which drawings are made, and buildings are constructed, perceived and occupied. The angel of the odd who brings about the accidents of our daily lives is also the angel of architecture. Chance can 'save' architecture from striving to determine the future of buildings, when its use in design cultivates indeterminacy and play.

Architecture is a product and a producer of both design and chance. Through my research, I have come to believe that by exploring the theme of chance in drawing, architects can more profoundly consider the non-optical accounts of space, the issue of inhabitation and the unpredictable lives of their buildings.

E On Glass

[...]
E03 This drawing sequence notionally occupies the site of the *Glass* itself. It describes the possibility of a momentary contact between

the Bachelors and the Bride. This contact is imagined through the demultiplied body of vision as it originates from the eye, the Occulist Witnesses on the Bachelors' panel (the red dot) and projects itself onto the Bride's panel (the blue cloud). A redrawing of the *Glass* occurs: the Bachelors' panel is drawn with the aid of measurable chance, the Bride's panel with the aid of impulsive chance.
[Notebook II, 01/02/03/04]
[Volume II, 2.1, 2.2, 4.1]
E04 The contact between the two panels is invisible. Therefore, it is drawn with the use of an arbitrary chance method: marking 81 points on a piece of tracing paper without looking. Firstly, I mark

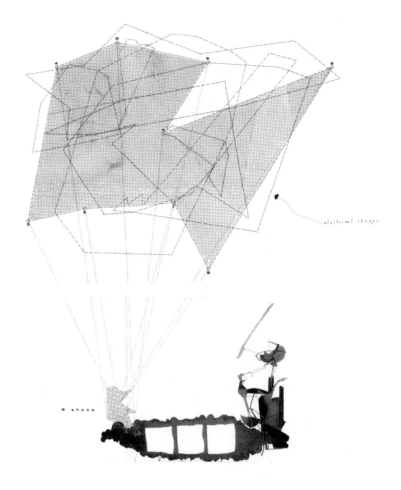

nine points (one point for each Bachelor), then I multiply each point nine times. Each set of nine points is outlined with a different colour pen. The dotted lines indicate the combined trajectory of the points as it traverses nine stages to form the demultiplied body of vision. The centre of this trajectory is the point marked in red.
[Notebook II, 06]
[...]
E07 The Bachelors' components rotate, spin, hinge and so on. Through their repetitive movements they generate a probabilistic mechanism of chance. The Bride swings in an unstable equilibrium. Her 'cinematic blossoming' recalls Eadweard Muybridge's *Dancing Girl—A Pirouette*. A, B and C indicate the viewpoints of three

synchronised cameras which simultaneously photograph the girl's 'enacted veil.'
[Notebook II, 13/14]
[Volume II, 4.5.1, 4.5.2]

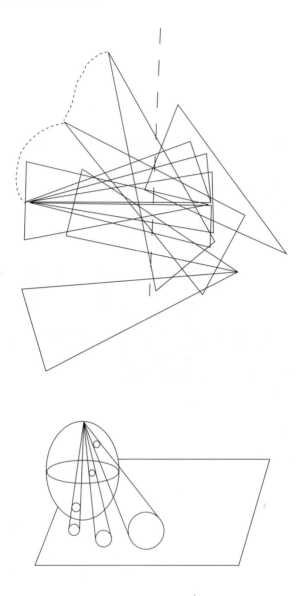

E08 The *Glass* exemplifies Henri Poincaré's machine of chance. The notes refer to how Duchamp and Poincaré's thoughts might be associated. Both men explored space in its triple form: visual, tactile and motor.
[Notebook II, 30]
[Volume II, 4.4.3, 4.6.2, 4.6.3]

E14 The gap between what the eye receives from external stimuli and what it projects with the aid of the hand on the screen is here linked with Lacan's schema of the eye and the gaze and Duchamps' definition of the 'art coefficient', the difference between the intention of an idea and its possible realisations. The *Glass* and Lacan's schema indicate the indeterminacy of spatial perception as an information-processing act that is largely affected by the complex physiological and psychological facts of vision.
[Displayed item]
[Volume II, 1.4.1, 1.4.3, 4.7.2, 4.7.3]

4.7   OBLIVION AND AWAKENING

4.7.1   Inattention and Oblivion: Infra-Thin

The *Glass* represents its events in the form of a painting, but it is also an architectural object. Making it and its associated works demanded Duchamp's physical engagement with materials and operations other than brushes and paint: glazing and metalwork, carpentry for the wooden rulers, drilling for the holes, tailoring for the nets and rubber caps. Its large size makes it analogous to a building element: a large window or a transparent wall. The viewer circulates around it, looks at and through it from various positions. It occupies a slice of space that cannot be physically inhabited but, in Duchamp's terms, may be seen as an *'inframince'* ('infra-thin') of this inhabitable space, the thinnest possible apparition of that space.
The *Glass* is only what he calls a 'possible.' Its creation takes place in the infra-thin:

The possible is
an infra-thin—

The possible implying
the becoming—the passage from
one to the other takes place
in the infra thin.
allegory on 'ing' [1]

The infra-thin is the passage between two conditions. It is also a shadow, a reflection from mirror or glass, and a paper-thin separation between two contacts or two very similar conditions of the same object that happens in the interval of a second. Duchamp writes:

... the shadow casters
work in the infra-thin
Sameness
similarity ...
In time the same object is not the
same after a 1 second interval [2]

The infra-thin is an ethereal quality that characterises the thinnest possible slice of space, reaching 'sameness', and the shortest possible duration in time, reaching synchronicity. In search for an explanation of the infra-thin Duchamp gave, not a single definition of the word, but a number of examples. He wrote that hollow papers, X-rays and light playing on surfaces belong in the infra-thin. He gave an arithmetical example too: in the infra-thin 70+40 does not make 110, but more than 110 and, as he must have meant, less than 111. The shadow casters, cut slices of smoke and gas, dandruff fallen onto paper wet with glue, slippery soap, all work in the infra-thin. The infra-thin is embedded in everyday experience and, as most of the examples indicate, relates less to sight than to the other senses:

just touching. While trying to place 1 plane surface
precisely on another plane surface
you pass through some infra thin moments—
The warmth of a seat (which has just
been left) is infra-thin

When the tobacco smoke smells also of the
mouth which exhales it, the 2 odors
marry by infra thin (olfactory
in thin)

---

[1]Duchamp, *Notes*, unpaginated.
[2][...] Duchamp, *Notes*, unpaginated.

> *Subway gates—The people*
> *who go through at the very moment*
> *infra thin—*
> *Velvet trousers—*
> *their whistling sound (in walking) by*
> *brushing of the 2 legs is an*
> *infra thin separation signaled*
> *by sound (it is <u>not</u>? an infra thin sound)* [3]

The infra-thin space is haptic, dominated by the sense of touch defined mainly by separation and contact. In the infra-thin space all the senses work as intermediary carriers of the sense of touch that signal its performance. Hearing the whistling sound signals the touching of the two legs; seeing light playing on surfaces signals the touching of light on surface and eye; seeing the reflection from a mirror signals the touching between the thing and its image; smelling or tasting two odours or flavours signals the touching of tobacco and breath. The infra-thin is touch as its takes place in five modes: the touch of sight, hearing, smell, taste *and* of touch.

Juhani Pallasmaa, writing about architecture and the senses, notes: 'The eyes want to collaborate with the other senses. All the senses, including vision, can be regarded as extensions of the sense of touch; the senses are specialisations of the skin. The senses define the interface between the skin and the world, the interface between the opaque interiority of the body and the exteriority of the world.' He adds: 'Vision reveals what the touch already knows. We could think of the sense of touch as the unconscious of vision.'[4]

The space of the infra-thin is nearly imperceptible. It exists between visibility and invisibility and signifies two often interwoven conditions: the psychological limitations of visibility (the unconscious of vision) and the physiological limitations of visibility (the insufficiency of human sight).

The infra-thin emerges in tiny details that usually quickly escape our attention and become forgotten. Infra-thin spaces involve habitual and automatic actions, and indifference and inattention because they are spaces that cannot be easily recognised visually and, thus, represented as such. For since it is difficult to see the infra-thin, it is also difficult to represent it. It is very hard for a drawing to capture the infra-thin and for geometry to calculate it. The absence of the infra-thin from our visual representations reinforces its oblivion. This is an oblivion of optical appearances, for we have the most intense memories of smell or taste experiences.

---

[3]Duchamp, *Notes*, unpaginated.
[4]Pallasmaa, p 29.

These tiny details of the infra-thin, the 'suspensions of perception' as Jonathan Crary calls them, have often been described in literature but their visual representation has been puzzling.[5] Duchamp sought ways to 'see' and represent the infra-thin. He searched for instruments that measure thinness instead of thickness and identified actions that might reach the infra-thin, including polishing, sanding, sliding, skating, rubbing, steaming, scratching, melting, breakage, burning, invisible weaving. Most importantly, his note on how to isolate the infra-thin started with the idea of 'cutting' (as noun and adjective). The cutting of the *Glass* that arrested the 9 Shots, of the glass plate that stopped the fall of the *3 Standard Stoppages*, of the photographic plate that momentarily paused the Draft Pistons, and of the shadow cast by the four-dimensional Bride, and the Poincaré cut of the *Glass* as the whole, all attempt to capture and visually represent the infra-thin.

The hidden spaces of the infra-thin are easily unnoticed or forgotten. Chance is the cut: it can rupture this ambiguous field to reveal a visual representation of it in the form of a sudden appearance.

4.7.2   Appearance and Apparition: Snapshot

Duchamp's sub-title and preface for the *Glass* give key explanations for the piece. *The Bride Stripped Bare by Her Bachelors, Even* is a 'delay in glass.' 'In the most general way possible', he writes, this delay expresses indecisiveness. Because a choice has to be made from a matrix of possibilities, from a succession of facts, 'capable of all the innumerable eccentricities.' The possibilities are indeterminate: they belong in a world where two fluid things are 'given', 'the waterfall' and 'the illuminating gas.' A choice out of these possibilities eventually forms an image, a possible glimpse of the infra-thin. The *Glass* presents a single appearance of a variable event, concealing innumerable others.[6] Duchamp chose aspects of this specific appearance with the calculus of chance.

The *Glass* shows an allegorical appearance of spatial perception and its indeterminacy. It is frozen in a 'delayed' configuration, a possible one out of many. This 'instantaneous state of rest' was illuminated on glass. The glass plate functioned like a photographic plate on which the image was arrested through a sequence of snapshots. This 'photographic' plate reflects what the eyes see when making an

---

[5]Crary's research on attention with regard to perception appears in his *Suspensions of Perception*.

[6]In Duchamp's words, the *Glass* is a 'hinge picture': 'as it opens out or folds back, physically and/or mentally, [it] shows us other vistas, other apparitions of the same elusive object.' Paz, p 94.

image, an 'extra-rapid exposure' of the processing facts of perception. Jean-François Lyotard writes: 'What the viewer sees on the *Glass*, is the eye and even the brain in the process of composing its objects, the images of these objects impressing the retina and the cortex according to laws of (de-)formation, which are their own and that organise the glass partition.... The *Glass*, being the film, lets us see the conditions of impression that reign on the inside of the optical box.'[7] He adds that 'the *Glass* was not only the film but also the recording apparatus with all its implied settings.'[8] I have tried to show that when Duchamp sought the non-retinal he set his recording apparatus to random mode.

If the *Glass* represents image formations in the process of visual perception in the optical chamber, this coincides with Lacan's screen between the eye and the object. Duchamp ruptured the screen of the picture plane to meet the gaze: with the apparatus of chance, he searched for the hidden and non-optical aspects of vision. Krauss argues that Duchamp's search for the non-retinal indicates the invisibility of the unconscious:

> If the mechanism of the *Large Glass* obeys Duchamp's dictum of 'going beyond' the retina, it does so not to achieve the condition of vision's transparency to itself – which is suggested by the model of classical perspective when applied to the *Glass* – but rather, quite obviously, to arrive at the threshold of desire-in-vision, which is to say to construct vision itself within the opacity of the organs and the invisibility of the unconscious.[9]

Elsewhere, Krauss argues that his preoccupation with *n*-dimensionality expresses, too, the problem of the invisibility of the unconscious just as his speculations on the infra-thin describe the invisible fold of the body's relation to itself.[10] But Duchamp's oeuvre concerns neither only *n*-dimensional geometries nor only invisibility, but both. The two accounts converge in his greater inquiry into the non-retinal, pursued through an understanding of chance: with the aid of his canned chance Duchamp saw aspects of a non-optical account of space, which he measured and drew.

In the realm of spatial perception and representation Poincaré's geometrical cuts, and conscious and unconscious optics, are interconnected. Virilio parallels the momentary absence of consciousness with the punctum, the absence of the point in the representation

---

[7]Lyotard, pp 169–70.
[8]Lyotard, p 180.
[9]Krauss, *Optical Unconscious*, p 125.
[10]Krauss, 'Where's Poppa?', p 459. [...]

of physical dimensions. Referring to Poincaré, he suggests, that since physical dimensions can be seen as slices in a continuum, absence of consciousness can be seen as a dimension of time that renews the experience of space and duration: 'this space is not defined as substantive or extensive; it is not primarily volume, mass, larger or smaller density, extension, nor longer, shorter, or bigger superficie. It is first and foremost *accidental* and *intensive*.'[11]

We tend to ignore the infra-thin, but the sudden appearance of chance can rupture our habits of perception and cause an awakening illumination of it.

4.7.3   Accident and Awakening: The Cracked Glass

In the process of creation, intention is an ambiguous factor and artists cannot express it fully. Their pure intention remains unexpressed and invisible even at the end of the work. The passage from the imagined (intention) to the projected (realisation) is a 'missing link.' Duchamp writes:

> The result of this [the artist's struggle] is a difference between the intention and its realisation, a difference which the artist is not aware of ... in the chain of reactions accompanying the creative act, a link is missing. This gap which represents the inability of the artist to express fully his intention; this difference between what he intended to realise and did realise, is the personal coefficient contained in the work. In other words, the personal 'art coefficient' is like an arithmetic relation between the unexpressed but intended and the unintentionally expressed.[12]

The 'art coefficient' indicates the difference between the intended idea and its possible realisations, a difference that exists in the infra-thin. Duchamp knew he could not fully control 'the passage in the infra-thin.' So he provoked deviations from the norm of his art production with the aid of chance. He sought the 'physical possible': 'the *possible* is only a *physical caustic* ... burning up all aesthetics or callistics.' He perhaps meant that the possible is in fact 'the real', that which in psychoanalytic terms we tend to ignore, forget or avoid but unavoidably encounter. The real may appear because of an accident: the 'apparent deformities of our little world' appear as accidents, distortions or confusions, 'until one finds the true point of view or sees them by means of a certain glass or mirror.'[13]

---

[11]Virilio, *Lost Dimension*, p 102. For a discussion of the accidental in relationship to space and time see the chapters 'Improbable Architecture' and 'Lost Dimension.'
[12]Duchamp, quoted in Watts, pp 40–1.
[13]Hamilton, quoted in Duchamp, *Bride Stripped Bare*, unpaginated.

The idea of replacing the canvas with glass occurred to Duchamp in 1913, when he used a piece of glass for a palette and noticed the texture of the colours from the other side. The blank space of the transparent planes is to be filled by chance, by whatever environment the *Glass* happens to be in. The depicted figures float in a sea of indecisiveness: reflections and shadows, passers-by, variable colours, the changing staging of other artworks, and so on. The reality of the surrounding space complements the Bride's and Bachelors' imaginary world and shifts the depth of the picture beyond its surface so that the vanishing point of the viewer's perception penetrates the picture plane and extends behind it. As Tomkins suggests, 'a painting on glass could be looked at and looked through at the same time, and the experience of looking was ambiguous, open-ended, and unfixed.'[14] Above all, the choice of glass for the material support of the Bride and the Bachelors meant weakness and fragility:

> – So here you are, Marcel, looking at your Large Glass.

> – Yes, and the more I look at it the more I like it. I like the cracks the way they fall. You remember how it happened in 1926, in Brooklyn? They put the two panels on top of each other, not knowing what they were carrying, and bounced for sixty miles into Connecticut, and that's the result! But the more I look at it the more I like the cracks: they are not like shattered glass. They have a shape. There is symmetry in the cracking, the two crackings are symmetrically arranged and there is more, almost an intention there, an extra – a curious intention that I am not responsible for, a ready-made intention, in other words, that I respect and love.[15]

The damage was discovered several years later when the *Glass* was unpacked. Duchamp welcomed, accepted and celebrated the accident. He said that the *Glass* was finished only after an intention, that was not his, had altered his work. He painstakingly assembled the broken pieces, and replaced two very shattered parts with new glass plates shaped to fit exactly. He was then surprised by a curious coincidence: the accidental cracks of the glass plates, when assembled, followed the lines defined by his 'canned chance' in the *Network of Stoppages*. Amused by the results of chance, he once asked: 'Do you think I should have made it on glass if I had not expected it to break?'[16] He then showed a sketch he had drawn prophesying the shape of the cracks, his *Network of Stoppages*. The Bride and

---

[14]Tomkins, p 125.
[15]Duchamp, *Writings,* p 127.
[16]Duchamp in Ford, p 139.

Bachelors were finally united by a real chance encounter.[17] The accidental cracks became a necessary addition to the piece, a real canned chance.

The *Glass* is an emblem of Lacan's screen between the geometral point and the source of light. It represents the split between the eye and the object, the viewer and the world. One can detect the Oculist Witnesses (who stand for the viewers of the *Glass*) when one's figure or the figure of another viewer is reflected on its silver lines. The Oculist Witnesses disappear when no one is reflected on their skin.[18] Similarly, the cracks almost vanish when no one casts a shadow on the back of the *Glass*. But the cracks show up intensely if light from the nearby window is blocked – by a viewer, for instance.

The *Glass* is perhaps the art work of the modern world that most traps the real. It was deliberately made from fragile material and the fabricated chance operations it embodies 'foresaw' the punctum of a genuine accident. The gaze eventually pierced Duchamp's representations and, since then, pierces the viewers' representations. The shimmering radiation of the cracks, the unexpected reflections and backgrounds, will always confuse us. The accident will indefinitely puncture our defence against the real. And we will always be rupturing the *Glass*'s screening of the real, for 'a work of art is dependent on the explosion made by the onlookers.'[19]

Conclusion

Drawing on Chance

Linking Lacan's series of seminars 'Of the Gaze as *Objet Petit a*' with Beckett's *Film*, I have tried to show how the relationship between the eye and the gaze, a fundamental condition of vision, determines our system of representations.[20] Representations are 'intelligent', selective, complex constructions based on interactive projections between subjects and objects, the eye and the gaze. Habits are linked with automatic processes that tend to screen the gaze. Accidents, on the other hand, identify with the unexpected punctum of the gaze and may pierce the screen of our representations. By the

---

[17]Two replicas were made with Duchamp's approval: one by Ulf Linda (housed at Moderna Museet, Stockholm), the other by Richard Hamilton (housed at the Tate Modern Gallery, London). Both have been shown in many exhibitions because the original is too fragile to travel. [...]

[18][...] De Duve, *Kant after Duchamp*, pp 401–13.

[19]Duchamp, quoted in Adcock, p 8.

[20][...] For the effect of his experience of psychoanalysis on [Beckett's] work see Steven Connor, 'Beckett and Bion', www.bbk.ac.uk/eh/eng/skc/beckbion (visited 17. 01. 02).

same token, habits of the eye and accidents of the gaze form inter-secting relationships that affect the perception and use of architec-tural space. Architecture needs to address this by understanding the meaning of chance and accepting its interdependence with design. Chance is a vital element of our experience of space, as vital as light. This suggests that architecture should not ignore:

1. The fact that architectural space is a physical and psychological con-struction, changeable and, to a great degree, unstable.
2. The limitations of visibility, which indicate the unconscious aspects of vision and the insufficiency of human sight.

The surrounding model of perception that I investigate with *Viewing Instrument I*, presented in Volume I, is opposed to the frontal spec-tatorial perception of space that has for long dominated spatial rep-resentation and design. It acknowledges all directions around the body as equally important in the construction of spatial perception and representation. It points to our invisible surroundings, the pres-ence of the gaze and of chance. Chance can expose invisible aspects of space; for this reason its exploration can drive architecture to a non-optical account of it.

If chance influences the perception and use of architectural space, this thesis proposes that architecture should value the implications of chance in the process of design. It argues that while architects have dabbled in aleatory manoeuvres, mainly in order to defy the functionalism, rationalism and aesthetics of modernism, architec-ture can benefit from more radical abandonments to chance. Chance should be one of architecture's main drawing tools.

The drawing techniques of impulsive, active and measurable chance do not construct didactic models or firm working method-ologies. None of the techniques is necessarily more effective than the others and the use of one does not exclude the exercise of oth-ers in the same project. Impulsive, active and measurable chance can coexist in a single creative operation, affecting different stages and aspects.

As the projects described in Volume II show, chance is usually seen as a 'revolutionary' means through which one overthrows or escapes traditional values. It is mainly favoured as an apparatus that can disrupt determinism and suppress habitual working modes. It is also favoured because it can cast doubt on the rules of Euclidean geometry, the Renaissance's model of perspective and proportional systems, and the notions of functionalism, rationalism and author-ship. However, although chance might aid escape from such formal or moral burdens, there is a danger in seeing chance as simply an antidote to other practices or beliefs. Rather than using chance as a tool against conventions, the use of chance in art and architecture should be explored in its own right.

Chance can trigger the mechanisms of imagination in playful and collaborative ways, and release spontaneity, humour and surprise. It can extend rather than eliminate aspects of modernism, such as functionalism and rationalism, to the function, logic and aesthetics of indeterminacy. I do not argue that chance-generated geometry should replace, say, the rules of Euclidean geometry, for this would be purely deterministic. Chance should not become an exclusive mode of operation but should complement other design mechanisms. Moreover, its benefits should not be necessarily identified with chaotic or unregulated constructions as opposed to neat and organised ones. As Duchamp shows, chance can have an internal logic that does not deny precision and order. The outcome of a controlled and rational process can be irregular or chancy, while that of an uncontrolled and accidental operation can be regular and ordered.

Duchamp knew he could not fully control 'the passage in the infra-thin', so accepted the outcomes of chance in his work. His projects are carriers of the idea of chance and its importance in the creative process. Beckett hoped, on the other hand, to fully control the production of *Film,* minimising the intervention of chance. Yet he, too, recognised that the difference between the directions of his script and their execution in *Film* was not only unavoidable but valuable. Unlike the *Glass, Film* was not supposed to involve chance, but did. There is always an art coefficient between intention and expression.[21]

The area where chance takes over design and control is often the transition from one medium to the next, of misinterpretations and gaps of translation. In architecture the gap between drawing and building, Robin Evans states, is a 'blind spot':

> because we can never be quite certain, before the event, how things will travel and what will happen to them on the way. We may, though ... try to take advantage of the situation by extending their journey, maintaining sufficient control in transit so that more remote destinations may be reached.... These destinations are ... merely potentialities that might be brought into existence through a given medium.[22]

---

[21]There are gaps between Beckett's first and second script for *Film*, the second script and its rendering into the final movie, Bacon's visual instinct for his *Painting* and the actual painting, the notations of Cage's *Fontana Mix* and each of its performances, Duchamp's *Glass* of 1924 and today's shattered and decayed *Glass*. These gaps indicate that the authors were not entirely in control. Within them the interference of chance with design is mostly active.

[22]Robin Evans, Translations from Drawing, p 182.

To reach 'more remote destinations', architects have to reconsider their means of expression and the representational tools they use. For architecture is available to perception, use and imagination through representation. Considering further the role and potential of architectural drawing, Evans notes the Western prejudice of favouring 'neatness as a sign of civilisation' and its counter-prejudice, a reaction to neatness which favours 'the unpremeditated and unregulated as signs of art and feeling.'[23] He disapproves of both but insists that the manner in which drawings emerge is significant, and suggests a study of architectural history that concentrates on the gap between drawing and building.[24] Such study might well illuminate with precision the role of chance in the making of architecture. It would most likely show that the insufficiency of architecture to fully determine its passage from imagining to drawing, drawing to building, and building to perceiving and occupying, has allowed chance to participate triumphantly and creatively in its formulation. The engaging questions of architecture's relation to built form, and to the perception and use of buildings, mostly occur in the failure of architecture to control this passage.

Drawing Pier 40, presented in Volume I, describes the gap between drawing and building: it represents neither the physical structure of the architecture nor its inhabitation. With the use of chance Pier 40 'draws' imaginary aspects of its future life. A success in 'drawing chance' is the result of playing the game from both sides: interchangeably, as designer and inhabitant. *Drawing Pier 40*, partly an undetermined proposal, considers how chance might operate during and after the design process. The element of indeterminacy in it exists precisely because design and inhabitation are not distinguished.

Architectural space is the product of a floating world of planned and unplanned actions, a flow of habits and accidents. Whether or not architects intend it, architecture is a producer of design and chance and a product of both. All drawing involves chance, but it can never abolish chance. Chance will always evoke change affecting all architecture. To bring together the last and first lines of Mallarmé's poem *Un coup de dés*:

> All Thought emits a Throw of the Dice [but] a throw of the
> dice will never abolish chance.

---

[23]Robin Evans, Translations from Drawing, p 185.
[24][...] Robin Evans, *Translations from Drawing*, p 186.

Anna Radcliffe

This Dream Upon the Water: the Representation of a City in Literature – Venice

Like Franklin, Radcliffe takes a large subject and investigates it through a very particular instance of that problematic. In this case, Radcliffe's concern with the way in which cities may be 'read' through perception and language is directed through the urban figure of Venice, more precisely, particular literary accounts of that city. As befits this kind of study, the referencing system and other forms of scholarly apparatus are exemplary in their deployment.

Anna Radcliffe

THIS DREAM UPON THE WATER

The Representation of a City in Literature – Venice

ORIGINAL CONTENTS

Acknowledgements

I would like to thank Judi, for believing in the interdisciplinary approach and for giving me the best support and guidance.
I would like to thank Andy, for listening to six months of Venice and still helping me out in the eleventh hour.
I would like to thank JCCS for ageing me 25 years in the space of 2 hours; a fine achievement as it has taken 5 years of architecture to do this previously.

Preface

> *The city must never be confused with the words that describe*
> *it. And yet between the one and the other there is a connection.*
> Italo Calvino, *Invisible Cities*[1]

The recognition that our understanding of anything is associated with the language we use to describe it for "meaning is not simply something 'expressed' or 'reflected' in language; it is actually *produced* by it",[2] is a commonly accepted concept in contemporary literary theory. This suggests that our experience of anything is socially based; thus any interpretation we make will be based on value-judgements which are derived from our social ideologies.[3]

In acknowledging that language is closely related to our social ideology, it is reasonable to assume that all literary texts are conditioned by a writer's previous influences and frames of cultural reference, and that all 'readings' are conditioned by a reader's preconceptions based on *their* frames of cultural reference. In other words, any 'reading' of a text is a combination of the already 'shaped' text and what we bring to it. Furthermore, that text is subject to successive reinscription and reinterpretation by different readers.

If these ideas are applied to the 'reading' of cities it follows that, if language is inseparable from what is described, the interpretation of a city confronts not only such issues as history, sociology, economics, demographics and morphology, but also the issue of the city's representation; this latter constitutes our *perception* of a city.

INTRODUCTION

This study explores some representations of the city in literature. To pretend to know, from the study of literary texts, the actual Paris of Baudelaire, or the London of Blake, Wordsworth or Eliot, is an arguably fatuous notion. Yet through reading, it is possible to understand how these cities were perceived by the writers who experienced them.[4] More specifically, the intention of this investigation is

---

[1]Calvino, Italo, *Invisible Cities* (Original English translation: San Diego, 1974) p 61.

[2]Eagleton, Terry, *Literary Theory: An Introduction* (Oxford, 1983; 2nd edition, Oxford, 1986) p 52.

[3]Eagleton promotes the concept of literature related to and as definite readings of social reality, using such language and phraseology as 'value-judgements'; 'social ideology' and 'frames of cultural reference.' See: *Ibid.*, pp 1–14. Note that the use of the expression, 'socially based', and similar, is Critical Literature phraseology. It seems to be similar to that which Historians would call 'culturally-based.'

[4]Sharpe, William, (ed.), *Unreal Cities* (Baltimore, 1990), p xi. A valuable text which assesses the influence of the modern city on poetry.

to look at how the image of one particular city, namely Venice, has influenced writers over the last two centuries.

The work will first of all focus on the *contrasting* ways that writers have – through different lenses of perception – characterised, or explored in words, that is, *textualised* Venice. Making reference to the history of Venice, the introductory chapter will chart the significant emergence of Venice as a *topos* for nineteenth century writers. After establishing this frame of reference, the subsequent chapters will explore three distinct and contrasting readings of Venice. In considering Dickens' *Pictures from Italy*, the second chapter will examine the impact of the strong pre-image of Venice on even the hardest of Victorian socio-moralistic journalists. The subject of the third chapter will be an evaluation of Thomas Mann's *Death in Venice* in relation to Plato's 'Ideal' and the theme of death. With Calvino's *Invisible Cities*, the fourth chapter shall take up the concept of the modernist city beyond all good and evil, and the indeterminate, fractured post-modernist city.

Following from these literature studies, there will be a concluding chapter in which, first, the texts are *compared* in order to discover whether there are any common responses or connections between the different representations evaluated. These underlying connections might be deemed an intertext. It is proposed that an examination of this intertext, as reflections or refractions of Venice, will be of particular value as an alternative method of grasping the ethos of a place.

Finally, the connection between myth and reality will be investigated, that is, the relevance of the literature study to the built actuality of the city. This will recognise the fine line between our perception of Venice in *fiction* and the real life *fact*.

Diane Wolfe-Levy has written an article for *Modern Fiction Studies* entitled "City Signs – Toward a Definition of Urban Literature."[5] According to her article, the notion of 'urban literature' was developed in the late 1960s, but its study, in her opinion, has not yet evolved. She writes, "Indeed, 'urban literature' may not yet exist." She continues by explaining:

> The study of urban literature seems natural at first. The city is the dominant ecological feature of modern western society; it is not unreasonable, then, to seek an expression and reflection of urbanism in literature. The very term, however, is treacherous. Its concision fosters a sense of concreteness.[6]

---

[5]Wolfe-Levy, Diane, "City Signs: Towards a Definition of Urban Literature", *Modern Fictional Studies*, Vol. 24, No. 1 (Spring, 1978) pp 65–73.
[6]*Ibid.*, p 65.

Wolfe-Levy poses the question; what exactly does the term 'urban literature' refer to? Is it literature "read in cities or written in cities?" Or is it "literature with an urban setting?" She suggests that urban literature could be identified as that where "setting takes precedence over character" or that "which translates the quantitative experience of the city; undistorted by moral judgements and comparisons with the natural world."[7]

Even a brief examination of the place of the city in the work of the three authors presented in this study will reveal that none of the texts can be included in Wolfe-Levy's genre of 'urban literature.' Whilst Dickens' account amounts to an experience *of* the city, it does not qualify because it is definitely not free from moral judgement and it remains a highly subjective vision. Experience *in* the city rather than experience *of* the city excludes *Death in Venice* since Mann uses the city as *background*, as an apocalyptic symbol. Calvino is also not free from moral judgement or comparison with the natural world. Furthermore, although *Invisible Cities* can be read as a substantive narrative of stories about the *city*, it is generally agreed that the cities in the work are symbolic and used as metaphor.

If the concept of value judgements related to social ideologies is now reintroduced, it surely follows that the place of a city in a text is always a reflection of the writer's frame of cultural reference. Therefore, if the text is an experience *in* the city – if it forms a background or is used as metaphor or symbol – this will in itself be a reflection of the writer's understanding or perception of the city. Alternatively, even if the literature is written as an experience *of* the city, the idea of the city will still be conditioned by a personal cultural reality, which will inevitably influence the writer's perception of the city. Sharpe and Wallock confirm this observation in *Visions of the Modern City*:

> The idea of the 'naked city' is itself a fiction compounded of our desires for unmediated vision and a conflicting cultural predisposition that identifies the 'naked' environment with violence, volatility, and a lack of order or control. The city we seek conditions the city we find.[8]

Hence, while all three texts evidently elude Wolfe-Levy's definition of 'urban literature', Dickens, Mann and Calvino have all undeniably written literature that explores the urban setting of Venice. Indeed, in defence of the proposed study, it is suggested that it is by virtue of the very fact that each work is subjective – the very fact that three unique texts can be compared and contrasted – that this process of

---

[7] *Ibid.*, pp 65–66.
[8] Wallock, Leonard; Sharpe, William (eds), *Visions of the Modern City* (Baltimore, 1987) p 9.

exploring the innate qualities of a city in literary representations can occur at all and be of any value.

DEATH IN VENICE

> *Linked to the new age of decadence and its literary references, Venice was seen as the new Byzantium, incarnating the myth/theme of death ... that dominated its final days, of destruction and the simultaneous extermination of ethical values by the sublime perfectionism of a damned generation. The years preceding World War One were distinguished by D'Annunzio and by a dream of political and ideological valour that sought an impossible return to oligarchic models. Byzantium became the key – take note here of the dual symbolism! – for decadent Venice and the new Venice: damned and 'ultimate' valour, on the one hand, and, on the other, adherence to the cultures of Vienna and Munich, to masterly skills and the trends set by the Wagnerian school.[9]*

Thomas Mann's 1912 novella, *Death in Venice*, is likely the best-known participant in "that ubiquitous trope of the nineteenth century",[10] which, consolidated by the Fall, couples death and Venice. It is Venice – both radiant and fatal – which will be explored here.

> *But of course! When one wanted to arrive overnight at the incomparable, the fabulous, the like-nothing-else-in-the-world, where was it one went? Why, obviously; he had intended to go there, whatever was he doing? A blunder. He made all haste to correct it, announcing his departure at once. Ten days after his arrival on the island a swift motorboat bore him and his luggage in the misty dawning back across the water to the naval station, where he landed only to pass over the landing-stage and on to the wet decks of a ship lying there with steam up for the passage to Venice.[11]*

Predestination:
As an escape from a literary impasse, Gustave Aschenbach, "Thomas Mann's quintessential German, North European, classical artist",[12]

---

[9]Romanelli, Giandomenico, "On Nineteenth Century Architecture of Venice" *Process*, No. 75 (October 1987) pp 101–102.

[10]Plant, Margaret, " 'Bereft of all but her loveliness': Change and Conservation in Nineteenth Century Venice", *Transition*, No. 33 (1990) p 13.

[11]Mann, Thomas, *Death in Venice*; Tristan; *Tonio Kroger* (English translation by Lowe-Porter, H.T., London, 1932) p 29.

[12]Tanner, Tony, *Venice Desired* (Oxford, 1992) p 353.

travels to find "a fresh scene, without associations."[13] After setting out, first for a small Adriatic island, Aschenbach realises that, in fact, it is Venice that was his "meant" destination. As Reed remarks, in *Death in Venice – Making and Unmaking a Master*, as the title of the book suggests, it soon becomes clear that his destination is, in some way, also his destiny.[14] This may be compared to Dickens' arrival by night, and likewise, embodies the concept of the unreal and the unexpected. The artist has now truly commenced his final journey.

Gustave Aschenbach, whose "forbears had all been offices, judges, departmental functionaries",[15] is a believer in discipline, detachment and application. Indeed, he is the "poet-spokesman of all those who labour at the edge of exhaustion; of the overburdened, of those who are already worn out but still hold themselves upright."[16] He rejects all emotion, inspiration or romantic notion of the artist:

> With rage the author here rejects the rejected, casts out the outcast – and the measure of his fury is the measure of all moral shilly-shallying. Explicitly he renounces the abyss, explicitly, he refuses the flabby humanitarianism of the phrase: tout comprendre, c'est tout pardonner.[17]

Tony Tanner briefly discusses *Death in Venice* in his book, *Venice Desired*. He notes that such a taut, uptight character, is "clearly ripe for cracking."[18] Indeed, the narrative states explicitly that Aschenbach is himself aware of "a growing fatigue which no one must suspect nor the finished product betray" and he is concerned that "feeling thus tyrannised avenged itself by leaving him, refusing from now on to carry and wing his art, and taking away with it all the ecstasy he had known in form and expression."[19] In fact, the first clear 'fissure' occurs before Aschenbach has even left his home town of Munich. Waiting at a tram stop at North Cemetery, he sees a stranger standing outside the mortuary chapel.

---

[13]Mann, Thomas, *Death in Venice; Tristan; Tonio Kroger* (English translation by Lowe-Porter, H.T., London, 1932) p 17.

[14]Reed suggests that from the beginning of the story, the recurrent series of patterns, themes and symbology, which may be taken to be fate, hint at Aschenbach's final destiny, whether these are consciously influenced by him or not. This idea is explored in particular detail in Reed's chapter, 'Destination, Destiny', which relates to Mann's 'Chapter Three.' Reed, J.J., *Death in Venice: Making and Unmaking a Master* (New York, 1994).

[15]Mann, Thomas, *Death in Venice; Tristan; Tonio Kroger* (English translation by Lowe-Porter, H.T., London, 1932) p 17.

[16]*Ibid.*, p 22.

[17]*Ibid.*, p 24.

[18]Tanner, Tony, *Venice Desired* (Oxford, 1992) p 353.

[19]Mann, Thomas, *Death in Venice; Tristan; Tonio Kroger* (English translation by Lowe-Porter, H.T., London, 1932) p 15.

> *He found the neighbourhood quite empty...Nothing stirred*
> *behind the hedge in the stone-mason's yard, where crosses,*
> *monuments, and commemorative tablets made a supernumer-*
> *atory and untenanted graveyard opposite the real one. The*
> *mortuary chapel, a structure in Byzantine style, stood facing it,*
> *silent in the gleam of the ebbing day. Its façade was adorned*
> *with Greek crosses and tinted hieratic designs, and displayed a*
> *symmetrically arranged selection of scriptural texts in gilded*
> *letters, all of them with a bearing upon the future life, such as:*
> *"They are entering into the House of the Lord" and "May the*
> *Light Everlasting shine upon them." Aschenbach beguiled*
> *some minutes of his waiting with reading these formulas and*
> *letting his mind's eye lose itself in their transparent mysticism.*
> *He was brought back to reality by the sight of a man standing*
> *in the portico, above the two apocalyptic beasts that guard the*
> *staircase, and something not quite usual in this man's appear-*
> *ance gave his thoughts a fresh turn.*[20]

The chapel's "Byzantine" structure and its apocalyptic beasts, the Greek façades, hieratic designs and scriptural texts in gilded letters are, as both Reed and Tanner affirm,[21] tacit pointers to the Byzantine architecture of Venice and the city emblem, the lion of St. Mark. Certainly, Tanner declares, "Aschenbach is already 'in' Venice, even if he does not yet know it."[22]

Moreover, it is commonly held that the unusual-looking, non-Bavarian stranger; with grimace, curled lips and distorted features, who appears to vanish, is the first of a number of harbingers of death.[23] This omen is emphasised by the cemetery chapel being the chosen setting for his appearance. Tanner considers that as Aschenbach regards these two premonitory figures of Venice and Death, unbeknown to him, this starts the cracking of his "Teutonic carapace."[24] "Whether his imagination had been stirred by the stranger's itinerant appearance, or whether some other physical or psychological influence was at work, he now became conscious, to his complete surprise, of an extraordinary expansion of his inner self, a kind of roving restlessness, a youthful craving for far-off places."[25]

---

[20] *Ibid.*, pp 10–11.

[21] Reed, J.J., *Death in Venice: Making and Unmaking a Master* (New York, 1994), p 32/Tanner, Tony, *Venice Desired* (Oxford, 1992) p 354.

[22] Tanner, Tony, *Venice Desired* (Oxford, 1992) p 354.

[23] Reed, J.J., *Death in Venice: Making and Unmaking a Master* (New York, 1994), p 32/Tanner, Tony, *Venice Desired* (Oxford, 1992) p 354.

[24] *Idem.*

[25] Mann, Thomas, *Death in Venice; Tristan; Tonio Kroger* (English translation by Lowe-Porter, H.T., London, 1932) p 12.

Desire projected itself visually: his fancy, not quite yet lulled since morning, imaged the marvels and terrors of the manifold earth. He saw. He beheld a landscape, a tropical marshland, beneath a reeking sky, steaming, monstrous, rank – a kind of primeval wilderness-world of islands, morasses and alluvial channels. Hairy palm-trunks rose near and far out of lush brakes of fern, out of bottoms of crass vegetation, fat, swollen, thick with incredible bloom. There were trees, misshapen as a dream, that dropped their naked roots straight through the air into the ground or into water that was stagnant and shadowy and glassy-green, where mammoth milk-white blossoms floated, and strange high-shouldered birds with curious bills stood gazing sidewise without sound or stir. Among the knotted joints of a bamboo thicket the eyes of a tiger gleamed – and he felt his heart throb with terror, yet longing inexplicable. Then the vision vanished.[26]

Indeed, Aschenbach will contract the real "primeval island-jungle" disease of Asiatic cholera, while in Venice. Moreover, it will be seen that the city, with its stagnant lagoon and heavy and foul air, will become something of a "primeval island-jungle" – or "labyrinth" – itself. "From the Aschenbach-Munich point of view, Venice is an oriental city where the East more than meets the West – rather, penetrates, suffuses, contaminates and undermines it."[27]

It is thus clear that these omens may hint, as the title does, at what is to come. For Reed however, Aschenbach's vision has deeper significance. It hints at the forces stirring within the artist. The suggestion already noted above, that "feeling ...(was) refusing from now on to carry and wing his art...", implies imbalance. The rank, luxurious jungle and the beast of prey lurking there, together with Aschenbach's own awareness of "an expansion of his inner self", represent, and therefore introduce, the concept of wilder primal impulses stirring in his subconscious.[28]

Chosen Path

On the journey to Venice, the theme of destiny continues, or, using Reed's analogy, it may be suggested that further "alien forces" guide Aschenbach along his "chosen" path.[29] For example, the sales pitch with which the ship's purser sells Aschenbach a ticket is overly

---

[26]*Ibid.*, p 13.
[27]Tanner, Tony, *Venice Desired* (Oxford, 1992) p 354.
[28]Reed, J.J., *Death in Venice: Making and Unmaking a Master* (New York, 1994) p 78.
[29]*Ibid.*, p 42.

persuasive. "His copious gesturings and empty phrases gave the odd impression that he feared the traveller might change his mind."[30] Furthermore, as in the scene of the mortuary chapel, the stage is empty except for Aschenbach; there are no more customers, although the purser calls for the next.

However, if voyaging to Venice is the 'right' path, Reed also notes that it is a dubious and disturbing one. Aschenbach feels "not quite normal...as though the world were suffering a dream like perspective which he might arrest by shutting it all out for a few minutes and then looking at it afresh. But instead he felt a floating sensation..."[31] As the ship moves away from the quay, he is on a literally unsteady element, which matches his current state of mind. Indeed, "Venice is itself half water...and in a phrase of Georg Simmel's, 'the ambiguous city'."[32] This forms the ideal site for the unexpected, unpredictable, uncontrolled revelations that will follow.

On arrival in Venice, Aschenbach is greeted by the "dazzling composition of fantastic architecture," seen when this "most improbable of cities" is approached from seaward.[33] However, Reed repeatedly emphasises that "beauty mixed with sordidness is the very grain of this novella."[34] Hence, the "elderly coxcomb", cosmeticized as a youth, who had danced and cavorted grotesquely during the journey, now repellently drunk, loses his false teeth as he importunes Aschenbach "Pray keep us in mind ..."[35] The narrative requests that the reader remembers this motif of "false youth."

The sinister, unlicensed gondolier, who insists on rowing an unwilling Aschenbach all the way to the Lido instead of to the vaporetto station represents a second death omen. According to Tanner, an "avatar of Charon",[36] the mythological ferryman of the dead. Furthermore, Aschenbach is secretly delighted as he steps into the gondola. "This singular conveyance, come down from ballad times, black as nothing else on earth except a coffin – what pictures it calls up of lawless, silent adventures in the plashing night; or even more, what visions of death itself, the bier and solemn rites and last soundless voyage!"[37]

---

[30]Mann, Thomas, *Death in Venice; Tristan; Tonio Kroger* (English translation by Lowe-Porter, H.T., London, 1932) p 30.
[31]Mann, Thomas, *Death in Venice; Tristan; Tonio Kroger* (English translation by Lowe-Porter, H.T., London, 1932) pp 31–32.
[32]Reed, J.J., *Death in Venice: Making and Unmaking a Master* (New York, 1994) p 43.
[33]Mann, Thomas, *Death in Venice; Tristan; Tonio Kroger* (English translation by Lowe-Porter, H.T., London, 1932) p 35.
[34]Reed, J.J., *Death in Venice: Making and Unmaking a Master* (New York, 1994) p 43.
[35]Mann, Thomas, *Death in Venice; Tristan; Tonio Kroger* (English translation by Lowe-Porter, H.T., London, 1932) pp 35–36.
[36]Tanner, Tony, *Venice Desired* (Oxford, 1992) p 355.
[37]Mann, Thomas, *Death in Venice; Tristan; Tonio Kroger* (English translation by Lowe-Porter, H.T., London, 1932) p 36.

As "the strange stillness of the water city seemed to take up the (row-ers) voices gently", Aschenbach leans back and gives himself to the "yielding element."[38] Thus begins, as Tanner summarises, "the entire demoralizing, dismantling, of all (Aschenbach's) Apollonian Germanic principles of discipline and control."[40]

Idyll

It is widely accepted that Thomas Mann's thinking was marked from an early stage, by Nietzsche's writings. In particular, *Death in Venice* was indebted to his first publication of 1872, *The Birth of Tragedy from the Spirit of Music*. Reed explains that the intention of this book was "to show the dynamic that underlay Greek tragedy."[41] In essence, this is the work which puts forth the idea of Nietzsche's famous oppositions – of formal control and primal impulse[42] – embodied in the mythological figures of Apollo and Dionysus. Nietzsche argues, that when these two opposing but complementary forces were held in equilibrium, they gave Greek tragedy its power. Likewise, balance between these two impulses is necessary for the production of art and, conversely, imbalance leads to crisis. Moreover, following Nietzsche's terms, it might be suggested that an Apollonian is only a Dyonisian, temporarily self-deceived.[43]

After the 'phenomena' of his journey, Aschenbach settles into the refined calm of the Lido's Hotel Excelsior. It is here that he first encounters the main instrument of his undoing, in the perfect form of the young Polish boy, Tadzio.

> *Aschenbach noticed with astonishment the lad's perfect*
> *beauty. His face recalled the noblest moment of Greek sculp-*
> *ture – pale, with sweet reserve, with clustering honey-*
> *coloured ringlets, the brow and nose descending in one line,*

---

[38]*Ibid.*, p 37.

[40]Tanner, Tony, *Venice Desired* (Oxford, 1992) p 355.

[41]Reed, J.J., *Death in Venice: Making and Unmaking a Master* (New York, 1994) p 76.

[42]"The moralist hates the primeval forest", wrote Nietzsche, taking it as a symbol for "the whole previous history of the mind and those of its possibilities that have not yet been drunk to the lees." Thus Aschenbach's vision of the jungle swamp discussed earlier, is psychological; a metaphor for his repressed impulses, as well as mythic; the place associated with the gods of those impulses, and also naturalistic; the source of the fateful disease he later contracts, cholera. Moreover, the tiger is a Dionysian animal; it drew the god's chariot and is a metaphor for primal and primitive. Reed, J.J., *Death in Venice: Making and Unmaking a Master* (New York, 1994) pp 76–79.

[43]Reed, J.J., *Death in Venice: Making and Unmaking a Master* (New York, 1994) gives a thorough account of the place of Nietzsche in Mann's works both generally and specifically in relation to Death in Venice.

the winning mouth, the expression of pure and godlike serenity.[44]

This initial classification of his appreciation of Tadzio's beauty safely within the realms of artistic appreciation ("Greek sculpture"), continues for some time. For example, soon after his arrival, Aschenbach attempts to leave Venice due to "malaise", which he blames on the oppressive sirocco weather. On his fated return (due to his luggage being sent to the wrong destination), his regrets at "the thought that he would never see Venice again",[45] thinly conceal the real reason that "leave-taking had been so hard", which he finally admits "was for Tadzio's sake."[46] Now, he observes Tadzio "almost constantly",[47] but he continues to see Tadzio in artistic terms. At one point, he feels the desire to write, in the Platonic belief that the boy's beauty can act as elevating inspiration. In fact, the notion of Plato's *Phaedrus* and the 'Ideal' flow through much of the novella in Aschenbach's thoughts as he attempts to justify his feelings towards Tadzio:

> *This lad should be in a sense his model, his style should follow the lines of this figure that seemed to him divine; he would snatch up this beauty into the realms of the mind, as once the eagle bore the Trojan shepherd aloft. Never had the pride of the word been so sweet to him, never had he known so well that Eros is in the word, as in those perilous and precious hours when he sat at his rude table, within the shade of the awning, his idol full in his view and the music of his voice in his ears, and fashioned his little essay after the model Tadzio's beauty set: that page and a half of choicest prose, so chaste, so lofty, so poignant with feeling, which would shortly be the wonder and admiration of the multitude.*[48]

However, after this page and a half, "he felt exhausted, he felt broken – conscience reproached him, as it were after a debauch."[49]

One evening Tadzio appears unexpectedly and finally responds to the continuous attention that Aschenbach pays him, with a smile. However, "Aschenbach received that smile and turned away with it as though entrusted with a fatal gift."[50] As Reed declares, the

---

[44]Mann, Thomas, *Death in Venice; Tristan; Tonio Kroger* (English translation by Lowe-Porter, H.T., London, 1932) p 43.

[45]*Ibid.*, pp 61–62.

[46]*Ibid.*, p 65.

[47]*Ibid.*, p 68.

[48]Mann, Thomas, *Death in Venice; Tristan; Tonio Kroger* (English translation by Lowe-Porter, H.T., London, 1932) p 75.

[49]*Idem.*

[50]Mann, Thomas, *Death in Venice; Tristan; Tonio Kroger* (English translation by Lowe-Porter, H.T., London, 1932) p 82.

openness of the smile drives Aschenbach into the open. With the posture of physical helplessness, Aschenbach leans back and whispers "I love you!"[51]

Pursuit

This act of declaring his love removes most of Aschenbach's scruples and now he begins to pursue Tadzio shamelessly: "After the idyll on the Lido, the city now comes into view more and more as the scene of pursuit and is itself morally dubious to match the foreground." Reed continues:

> From the start Venice has been a disorientating mixture: it is land surrounded, infiltrated, even threatened by water. Water is the "element" on whose brink "civilisation" is so precariously perched. It is the "yielding element" on which Aschenbach's weakening will was first shown up in the episode of the unlicensed gondolier; even further back, at the start of his journey to Venice, the "sensation of being afloat" made him feel "an irrational alarm" and disoriented him further as he strove to get a grip on increasingly bizarre experiences. Now his new and conniving gondoliers take him "gliding and swaying" – a forward motion at once unsteady and unhindered – through the "labyrinth" of canals where they are at home but he is, in every sense, lost. Likewise in the maze of bridges, alleyways, and "filthy culs-de-sac," under the oppressive heat and in the "stagnant malodorous air." There is still beauty, but it now comes paired with decrepitude or sordidness. There is the Oriental magnificence of St. Mark's Basilica with its glowing interior, but mingled with its heavy incense there is "the smell of the sick city", the chemicals being used against cholera. Lovely blossoms trail down crumbling walls and "Moorish windows (are) mirrored in the murky water"; the marble steps of a church dip below the surface of the dirty flood. Beggars and dealers feign and swindle.[52]

This is the city of unexpected oppositions and contradictory polarities. "This was Venice, this the fair frailty that fawned and that betrayed, half fairy-tale, half snare."[53]

[51]*Ibid.*, p 83.
[52]Reed, J.J., *Death in Venice: Making and Unmaking a Master* (New York, 1994) p 60.
[53]Mann, Thomas, *Death in Venice; Tristan; Tonio Kroger* (English translation by Lowe-Porter, H.T., London, 1932) p 89.

Indeed, the secret of the cholera which insinuates itself into the heart of Venice gives Aschenbach, who pursues it, a sense of complicity with the city, since it is comparable to the diseased passion which he conceals. "And all the while he kept doggedly on the traces of the disreputable secret the city kept hidden in its heart, just as he kept his own."[54] Moreover, here the text states explicitly all that has been implied; the disease has come from the "moist swamps of the delta of the Ganges ... bred in the mephitic air of that primeval jungle, among whose bamboo thickets the tiger crouches."[55] This is Aschenbach's Munich vision of "the primeval wilderness of islands" where he saw "the glinting eyes of the tiger." Hence, Venice is that wilderness of islands, "merely where the primeval has long been overlaid by a city civilisation."[56] Yet Aschenbach does not make this connection consciously, as the reader does, although he does recall "the vision of a white building with inscriptions on it."[57]

Reed argues that this paragraph stands as a bridge between realism and symbolism, for the following night Aschenbach has a fearful dream of a mythic orgy and finally succumbs to the power of Dionysus. The dream starts with howls and ends in a long drawn-out '*u*' sound. This is clearly the long '*u*' of the Polish vocative 'Tadziu!' that Aschenbach could not immediately make out at the beginning of the story. There is a "whirling rout of men and animals" and a cry of "The Stranger God!",[58] as Tadzio's name becomes the menadic cry of a Dionysian mob. Now, "Venice is notoriously a site where opposites begin to blur and distinctions fade"[59] and here, finally, after attempting to hold "his own god against this stranger who was sworn enemy to dignity and self control",[60] Aschenbach succumbs and joins the dance and shares the feast.

After the dream, Aschenbach has no scruples left and is concerned only with his own ageing appearance. By having himself rejuvenated by cosmetics, he thus re-enacts the spectacle of the "elderly coxcomb" that so repelled him on the journey to Venice. In his new guise, he renews his pursuit for Tadzio, and the scene of pursuit is, for the final time, the centre of Venice.

> *One afternoon he pursued his charmer deep into the stricken city's huddled heart. The labyrinthine little streets, squares,*

---

[54]*Ibid.*, p 91.
[55]*Ibid.*, pp 100–101.
[56]Reed, J.J., *Death in Venice: Making and Unmaking a Master* (New York, 1994) p 64.
[57]Mann, Thomas, *Death in Venice; Tristan; Tonio Kroger* (English translation by Lowe-Porter, H.T., London, 1932) p 104.
[58]*Ibid.*, p 106.
[59]Tanner, Tony, *Venice Desired* (Oxford, 1992) p 356.
[60]Mann, Thomas, *Death in Venice; Tristan; Tonio Kroger* (English translation by Lowe-Porter, H.T., London, 1932) p 107.

*canals and bridges, each one so like the next, at length quite
made him lose his bearings. He did not even know the points
of the compass ... he stole upon the footsteps of his unseemly
hope – and at the end found himself cheated. The Polish family crossed a small vaulted bridge, the height of whose archway hid them from his sight, and when he climbed it himself
they were nowhere to be seen. He hunted in three directions –
straight ahead, and on both sides the narrow, dirty quay – in
vain. Worn quite out and unnerved, he had to give over the
search.*[61]

Venice is, once again, the place of major disorientations and inexplicable disappearances. Furthermore, the city is not kind to
Aschenbach; it leaves him sweating and exhausted, gorging on the
overripe strawberries from which he finally contracts the cholera
which kills him.

*The street he was on opened out into a little square, one of
those charmed, forsaken spots he liked ... he sank down on
the steps of the well and leaned his head against its stone rim.
It was quiet here. Grass grew between the stones, and rubbish
lay about.*[62]

It seems that, as Aschenbach's adventure draws to a close, nature is
reclaiming the city again and he is merely becoming part of the
detritus left behind.

The conversation that follows, between Aschenbach and
Phaedrus, is crucial to the theme of the novella as Aschenbach
makes the claim that, by the very nature of artists, the difficulties of
living up to Plato's 'Ideal' are especially, even uniquely acute. He
concludes that there was no right path for him. Now this conclusion
has been drawn, Aschenbach's inevitable death, which follows, is
almost like a coda to the end of the novella. Predictably, it takes
place on the beach of the Lido as Aschenbach watches Tadzio for the
final time, before the Polish family's departure. There is no more
desperate pursuit. Instead, Aschenbach imagines Tadzio, his 'boy-
god', acting as a soul summoner, inviting him into the ocean. In this
way, he finds 'Death in Venice', which, once foreseen in Munich he
then set out, if unknowingly, to seek. As Tanner remarks, 'Mann is
not subtle, but it is a powerful image of a thing turning into its seem-
ing opposite in the city most tolerant, perhaps productive, of inver-
sions and reversibilities.'[63]

[61]Mann, Thomas, *Death in Venice; Tristan; Tonio Kroger* (English translation by Lowe-
Porter, H.T., London, 1932) pp 111–112.
[62]*Ibid.*, p 112.
[63]Tanner, Tony, *Venice Desired* (Oxford, 1992) p 359.

CONCLUSION: A REPRESENTATION OF VENICE

> *No intervention, no program for Venice is possible outside of*
> *an 'idea' of the city.....The idea of Venice is an exceptionally*
> *changeable one; it touches opposed polarities; it feeds contra-*
> *dictory mythologies. But all this is part of the city. No 'text'*
> *lives as much as a city also out of its interpretations, its*
> *images and its myths.*[64]

Three writers, with three different cultural frames of reference, came to Venice, in search of revelation:

Dickens came, from the nineteenth-century industrialised city, in search of the picturesque, and found the unexpected. Mann, in the guise of Aschenbach, came from the 'Apollonian nation',[65] in search of tolerance and respite, and found Dionysus. Calvino, in the guise of the Khan, came in search of a coherent, harmonious system underlying the 'invisible order' that sustains cities (or life). Through Polo's unique, ontologically ideal, 'first' city, he found a labyrinthine rebus composed of dialectic oppositions, dreams and contradictions.

It is clear, therefore, from these *contrasting* texts, that many cities exist within a single city. As literary texts are subject to successive rein-scription and reinterpretation[66] by different readers, so cities are subject to successive 'rewriting' by different societies who 'read' them. Multifarious social ideologies shape multivalent perceptions, for:

> *Every moment in society, no matter how slow or fast, deforms*
> *and readapts – or irreparably degrades – the urban fabric, its*
> *topography, its sociology, its institutional culture, and its mass*
> *culture or anthropology. We may believe that we are looking*
> *at one city. But there are many before us: those still undiscov-*
> *ered, still undefined and for which the diverse and contradic-*
> *tory 'instructions for use' are equally valid and equally applied*
> *by vast social groups.*[67]

Yet, it was proposed at the outset, that if these texts were compared, a common response or connection between the different representations, that is, an intertext, could be discovered. An examination of

[64]Cacciari, Massimo, "An Idea of Venice", *Casabella*, Vol. 53, No. 557 (May, 1989) pp 42–58; English summary: p 61.
[65]Nietzsche considered that Germany needed Dionysus more urgently than it needed Apollo. See: Reed, J.J., *Death in Venice: Making and Unmaking a Master* (New York, 1994) pp 76–79.
[66]Refer to Preface, with respect to this concept.
[67]Calvino, Italo, "The Gods of a City", *Harvard Architectural Review*, no. 4 (Spring, 1984) p 7.

this intertext, as reflections or refractions of Venice, would be of particular value as an alternative method of grasping the ethos of a place.[68] Overall, there is an implicit identity of a city in these readings. This common intertext, that forms the setting for these novels, and forms Cacciari's 'idea' of Venice, is that of the indeterminate, pluralistic, post-Nietzschean city. Venice is the ambiguous city, the dream city, the ultimate 'invisible city', the city that contains all other cities within it, the city floating on water, both supportive and subversive, which allows, even encourages, successive transfigurations from one state to another, for:

> ... stressing the need to keep in mind the process by which different cities using the same name follow one another and are superimposed, we must not forget that element which the city has perpetuated throughout its entire history, that element which has distinguished it from other cities and has given it meaning. Each city has an implicit program that must be found every time it is forgotten lest that city face extinction. The ancients represented the spirit of the city with just that bit of vagueness and precision that the operation requires, invoking the names of gods who had presided at its foundation. These names correspond either to personifications of vital attitudes of human behaviour that guarantee the real calling of the city or to personifications of environmental elements – a water course, a land form, a type of vegetation – that guarantee the persistence of the image of the city in its successive transformations as an aesthetic form as well as an emblem of ideal society. A city can go through catastrophes and dark ages, see different generations follow one another in its houses, see those houses change stone by stone, but at the right moment and in different forms it must find its gods once again.[69]

With the massive economic, commercial and financial power despoiled and traumatised, Venice mutated into an object for bitter remembrance and nostalgia of a legacy lost. The Venetian myth of death and decay, developed by outsiders' romantic notions and promoted in literature and other forms of representation, started to model the visitor's city. As a new ideology to overcome hardship, the Venetians, always adaptable and inventive, cultivated this image and turned towards that new enterprise of tourism. This industry

---

[68]See Introduction.
[69]Calvino, Italo, "The Gods of a City", *Harvard Architectural Review*, no. 4 (Spring, 1984) p 7.

has engendered and maintained, but now opposes and subverts any idea of a living city.

As an alternative to the current tourist monoculture, Massimo Cacciari, a prominent Venetian urban historian, proposes that Venice must be reinvented and reorganised. This might be possible, "not through Great Projects, but through different interventions, subjects and itineraries, which together would redefine Venice as a *capital city.*"[70]

With respect to "the monumental-artistic assets" of the city, in contrast to the approach of "containerising"; filling buildings with functions; Cacciari believes that "a building may be preserved for the one and only purpose of being seen and at last enjoyed, 'contemplated' ... this is the meaning of the [word] 'monument': a presence to listen to, study and inspect, in order to understand a story, an event, a living past – a presence that should not be reused, but rather *freed from use.*" The State authority, local culture, private collections and the patrimonies must be co-ordinated and reorganised, in order to realise this idea.[71]

Cacciari acknowledges that tourism will always be essential to Venice, but believes that the city must administer and regulate this function. Initiatives proposed include, organised tourist itineraries, in order to decongest exploded areas; promotion of medium-level tourist demand, such as international conferencing; provision of services for young people and, on the basis of a 'benefit-return strategy', taxation for tourist businesses, in order to divide the cost of preserving Venice more fairly amongst its citizens.[72]

To counterbalance the present exodus of non-tourist based pursuits. Cacciari proposes that strengthened research and university facilities must be located in the centre of the city. "Opportunities *implicit* in the city's given conditions, should be exploited", such as the creation of faculties dedicated to marine studies; architectural restoration and archival and library research.[73]

In order to prevent the centre of the city continuing to be isolated, Venice must be conceived as an "estuary city", consisting of linking elements and nuclei. Connecting with Mestre, this estuary city will form a "two-centre city ... stretched between inseparable, distinct polarities."[74]

---

[70]Cacciari, Massimo, "An Idea of Venice", *Casabella*, Vol. 53, No. 557 (May, 1989) pp 42–58; English summary: p 61.
[71]*Idem.*
[72]Cacciari, Massimo, "An Idea of Venice", *Casabella*, Vol. 53, No. 557 (May, 1989) pp 42–58; English summary: p 61.
[73]*Idem.*
[74]*Idem.*

A city can only 'live' if it is inhabited by natives as well as tourists. According to Cacciari, the contentious issue of the population exodus must be addressed by recognising the demands and requirements of the citizens, through providing facilities which enable Venetians to live and work in the heart of the city.[75]

The similarly contentious issue of physical safeguard, from pollution and high-tides alike, is "immensely complex." Cacciari recognises that pollution of the lagoon is discharged from a number of sources, primarily, industrial, urban (sewage), detergent and agriculture. The latter is considered to be the most significant, and it is proposed that an efficient de-pollution strategy must extend beyond the immediate surrounding coastline of Venice. With respect to the seaward defences, a global solution must be adopted, which includes consolidation of the entire coastline and the creation of seaward dams.[76]

In endeavouring to illustrate, even in this very delimited sense, some of the real issues that face modern Venice, it is hoped that the connection between fact and fiction; the relevance of the literature study to the built actuality of the city; can be recognised. For this city's position as transition point between oppositions, between east and west, nature and artifice, real and reflected, myth and reality, is Calvino's 'unique element', its singularity, its soul. Manifold diversity, which resists reduction to one meaning, must be exploited. It is clear that Venice can no longer exist as a homogenised, monocultural museum consecrated exclusively to tourism. Instead, it must be nurtured into a vibrant, rich and various city, which continuously resists decline, through its constant, chameleon metamorphoses. Venice must learn, once more, how to represent itself.

---

[75]*Idem*

[76]Cacciari, Massimo, "An Idea of Venice", *Casabella*, Vol. 53, No. 557 (May, 1989) pp 42–58; English summary: p 62.

E.J. Taylor

A Speculative Investigation into the Sacred and Aesthetic Principles of Alexander 'Greek' Thomson's Architecture, with particular reference to St Vincent Street Church

At times a dissertation delves into a relatively small area of research with extraordinary intensity and tenacity. Taking an architect who is very well known locally if not internationally (Alexander 'Greek' Thomson), Taylor's research uses historical, theoretical and drawn analysis to demonstrate how a particular theme (sacred and religious principles) was interwoven into building design and aesthetics. As with most of these dissertations, Taylor's submission is of publishable standard.

E. J. Taylor

A Speculative Investigation into
THE SACRED AND AESTHETIC PRINCIPLES OF ALEXANDER 'GREEK' THOMSON'S ARCHITECTURE
with particular reference to St Vincent Street Church

ORIGINAL CONTENTS

PREFACE

Alexander 'Greek' Thomson (1817–1875) is only now beginning to receive widespread recognition as Glasgow's other world-class architect. Significant portions of his work have been lost through war, neglect and institutionalised vandalism and the need to protect his remaining work for future generations is still a major concern despite the efforts of groups such as the Alexander Thomson Society.

Over the last 50 years appraisals of Thomson's architecture have tended towards a view of him as essentially a 'proto-modernist' perhaps born 50 years too early. Of these appraisals, Ronald McFadzean's *The Life and Work of Alexander Thomson* published in 1979 remains the standard and indispensable factual guide to the architect.

Over the last decade, however, a number of essays (such as several in the book, *'Greek' Thomson* published in 1994, edited by Gavin Stamp and Sam McKinstry) have begun to raise questions regarding the theoretical foundations of Thomson's architecture. From October 1993 to February 1997 over nine issues of the *Alexander Thomson Society Newsletter*, Sam McKinstry and Professor James Stevens Curl conducted a heated debate over the compelling question of whether or not St Vincent Street Church was designed as a 'mnemonic' of Solomon's Temple. The discourse between them raised valuable discussion of Thomson's religious beliefs and ideals. Yet still very little has been written on sacred and symbolic aspects of his work.

The following study is an attempt to build on previous work and particularly to explore how Thomson's religious faith and powerful intellect was manifest in his architecture. It is hoped that this study and all the other work being carried out to advance the appreciation of Thomson will help to ensure that his surviving buildings are treated with the respect and admiration that they deserve.

ACKNOWLEDGEMENTS

Without the following individuals and organisations this dissertation would not have been realised in its final state:
Page and Park Architects,
Gavin Stamp of the **Mackintosh School of Architecture** and Chairman of the **Alexander Thomson Society,**
George Kirton of **Glasgow City Council Property Services Department,** for allowing the use of photogrammetric survey drawings,
Alexander Stoddart,

Professor Keith Critchlow and **the Prince of Wales's Institute of Architecture**, for kindling an appreciation of the sacred and proportion in architecture.

AUTHOR'S DECLARATION

Whilst working at Page and Park Architect's, on a feasibility study for the long-term preservation of St Vincent Street Church, encouragement was given to begin exploring aspects of the church that went beyond an appraisal of the church based solely on historical facts and its physical substance. In addition to the permission to reproduce plans made whilst working on the study, the following is, in part, a development of ideas loosely discussed at the time, and not previously published.

INTRODUCTION

Towards the end of 1856, Alexander Thomson and his business partner of seven years, John Baird (2nd), amicably ended their formal relationship. Soon after this dissolution, Alexander went into partnership with his brother George, who had an open admiration for Alexander's talent in architecture. Seemingly the new partnership of 'A & G Thomson' freed Alexander to pursue his architectural gift without compromise. This turning point marked the beginning of the 'mature phase' in his work, the high plateau upon which he famously rejected the use of arches in his architecture and built all of his most admired buildings, which, during his lifetime, earned him the distinguishing epithet, 'Greek'. George looked after the partnership's administration and the process of seeing the work realised on site, whilst Alexander's genius was allowed to go into ferment.

There is a consistency of vision and character expressed in all of Alexander Thomson's work of 1856 onwards, that extends from his churches through to the warehouses. The idea that the essential characteristics of architecture, exemplified in man's temples and churches, erected to the glory of God, should be extended for use in all of man's structures, was a view expressed several times in the architectural literature of the mid nineteenth century, and would be consistent with Thomson's strong United Presbyterian faith.

However, it is the churches that perhaps best represent the highest expression of Thomson's ideals; in his own words:

> But however much a man may love his own house, there is a
> house which demands a still higher place in his regards – the
> house of his God. In every age since architecture began, its

highest efforts, aided by the sister arts of sculpture and paint-
ing, have been devoted to the service of the Deity.
(Haldane Lectures, II, 1874)

It is as the only surviving and functioning religious work carried out by Thomson that a large part of this dissertation has been devoted to an appraisal of St Vincent Street Church as an exemplar of his work and an embodiment of his intentions as an architect.

A greater understanding of Thomson is also strongly assisted by a thorough reading of the lectures delivered by him that have survived in written form. He was evidently an eloquent and compelling speaker, and his independent-minded views were boldly expressed. The most comprehensive account of his broad view on architecture, was delivered in a course of four lectures to the Haldane Academy in 1874, the year before his death. An analysis of these lectures has been attempted here, as an essential part of shedding light on the actual work.

THE SACRED AND AESTHETIC PRINCIPLES OF ST VINCENT STREET CHURCH

By looking into physical causes, our minds are opened and enlarged; and in this pursuit, whether we take or whether we lose our game, the chase is certainly of service.

(Edmund Burke, *A Philosophical Enquiry into the Sublime and Beautiful*, 1757. Quoted by D.R. Hay, *Proportion or the Geometric Principle of Beauty Analysed*, 1843)

The following study is partly an attempt to investigate the geometric proportions of St Vincent Street Church in the light of Thomson's views on aesthetics. Perhaps the strongest difference between the Haldane Lectures and the broader theoretical writing of Hay, is that Thomson's descriptions contain a greater element of the pictorial, and his language is coloured more strongly by his deep religious faith. It is apparent from Thomson's lectures that he saw aesthetics as an indivisible aspect of the divine. However it is clear that the evocation of images and connotations from the Bible and antiquity was also a source and aim of his imaginative genius. Therefore side by side with an aesthetic appraisal, speculation has been offered as to some of the 'allusive' aspects that are undoubtedly present in the church and from what thoughts they may have derived.

Background

During 1856, Alexander's brother and partner George, who was a member of the Gordon Street United Presbyterian Church, was

involved in discussions regarding the rehousing of the same congregation on another site. The site selected was at the junction of
Pitt Street and St Vincent Street and the firm of A. & G. Thomson
was chosen to design the new church. In February 1859, two years
after the plans by Alexander were given approval, the church was
opened for worship. (The hall was completed 1867–68.)

Within the city the church commands a prominent location, near
the top of a hill which falls steeply to the south towards the Clyde
and more gradually to the west; it is also embedded into the urban
grid that had been extended westwards onto the Blythswood Estate,
and so may be seen in part as a response to these conditions.

The plot of land chosen for the church was constrained on three
sides, by St. Vincent Street to the north, Pitt Street to the west, and a
service lane to the south. To the east, however, there may have been
some leeway in establishing the church's boundary. The immediately
adjacent site had not been developed and the land was also purchased. Upon this land a block of tenements (now demolished) was
erected a few years after the church also designed by Thomson.
Opposite the church, on the south west corner of the Pitt Street and
St Vincent Street there existed until 1982 a Unitarian church (1856) in
the form of a prostyle temple, designed by J.T. Rochead (1814–1878).

A variety of appraisals of St Vincent Street Church have been
made since its erection, as testament to its enduring, captivating
power. Previous studies have noted the church's imaginative composition and romantic-sublime pictorial qualities, as well as speculated on stylistic sources. The church's massing and elemental
organisation have been examined in a number of essays, not in iso-
lation but within a local and city-wide context.

The Solomonic Temple Debate

In addition to the architectonic and pictorial appraisals of the church
there has been some discussion of a symbolical, allusive dimension;
notably the dispute between Sam McKinstry and Professor James
Stevens Curl, through the medium of *The Alexander Thomson
Society Newsletter.*

Sam McKinstry in *The Alexander Thomson Society Newsletter*, No.
8, October 1993, opened what was to become a fascinating debate
between himself and Professor James Stevens Curl on whether St
Vincent Street Church was a 'mnemonic of Solomon's Temple' (in
Professor Curl's words) or not – the view held by McKinstry. In the
first article of the debate, for the purpose of his argument McKinstry
presumed that James Fleming's provocative statement on the church
– that, 'the Solomonic Temple appears to have had a similar arrangement' [ ] – was not attributable to Thomson. After a brief description

of Solomon's Temple as written in 1 Kings (the Good News Version), McKinstry surmises that, 'The resemblance is so basic that it could have arisen by chance rather than design'.

In the heat of the ensuing debate – over the course of seven subsequent Newsletters – their views become at times somewhat polarised, with McKinstry rhetorically questioning in Newsletter No. 13, 'for what conceivable reason would a man like Thomson want to hark back to the Temple?' And Professor Curl replying in the following Newsletter with the proposition, 'that Thomson's church is not only a mnemonic of the Lost Ideal, the Temple of Solomon, but tells us, loudly and clearly, that it IS the reconstructed Temple in Glasgow'.

During the riveting correspondence, however, a number of fascinating issues and areas for further investigation are raised. Such as the symbolism of the tower at St Vincent Street Church, the numerology of Freemasonry, as well as the great plinths upon which Thomson's churches are raised. By Newsletter No. 18, where the correspondence finally ends, neither protagonist concedes defeat, although both appear to agree that St Vincent Street Church is at least capable of 'embracing both Old and New Testament themes'.

Thomson's poetic vision was charged with images by artists such as David Roberts and John Martin (1789–1854), who combined epic subject matter with strong artistic vision. Martin brought apocalyptic scenes from the Old Testament to life in the most sublime compositions conceivable. His architectural backgrounds and tumultuous skies combined all Burke's ingredients for the sublime, such as terror, vastness, magnitude, magnificence and the infinite, together with a carefully managed light. Roberts is most noted for his radiant water-colours of evocative ruins in Egypt and the Holy Land, although he also painted some grand fantasies of historical events such as *The Israelites Leaving Egypt,* of 1829.

Many of the architectural qualities projected by Martin can be found in Thomson's work, such as the achievement of an 'artificial infinity' (Burke) through a horizontal repetition of parts, and the impression of and 'bigness', whatever the actual scale of the work. The buildings of Thomson may also have 'associative' similarities with Martin's paintings. For instance, if we were to accept Professor Curl's argument, a similarity in overall arrangement may perhaps be noted with St Vincent Street Church and Martin's depiction of Herod's Temple (the second reconstruction of Solomon's Temple) in his engraving *The Crucifixion,* of 1834, which was highly acclaimed at the time.

Thomson's use of the Ionic Order

A notable feature of the three United Presbyterian churches that Thomson designed in the late 1850s is that the Ionic Order is used in each to similar effect. The particular variant of the Ionic employed by Thomson is directly based on the Erechtheion at Athens. In the third Haldane lecture, he stated that, 'The most elegant example in the Ionic style is the Erectheion, rather a group than a single building ... one of the most charming compositions in existence'.

The unique composition of the Erechtheion would have shown Thomson how a classical design can also be picturesque, and yet it seems that this important lesson would not have been enough alone to justify such a purposeful and insistent use of the order in the churches.

Thomson's understanding of the Ionic volute seems to have been largely on aesthetic terms and consistent with his view on nature:

> *Then as to what it is meant to represent, I would say, that whatever the Creator meant to represent by all the spiral forms of nature the Greeks had the same purpose in view. It is a form found very frequently in nature ... But Mr. Ruskin regards this capital as an abominable thing, because it does not represent any natural object ... we should not regard nature as the source of art ... From whatever point of view we look at it there is a pleasing softness in the flow of the lines with ever-varying proportions of the volutes, as they appear more or less oval according to the position from which they are viewed. And these, with the other features of the thing, form a combination at once simple and complex. The simplicity of its form enables the mind to comprehend it easily; the complex of its beautiful lines causes the memory to dwell upon it with pleasing reflection.* (Haldane Lectures, III)

In an article in the *Builder* (May 20, 1854) entitled *The Entity of the Ionic Order and the Vitality of all the Orders*, Samuel Huggins expressed views very similar to those of Thomson. Huggins wrote on the Ionic order that,

> *There is something naturally pleasing in the ever-varying motion, wherever seen or however relatively situated, whether in the capital, the console, or the modillion; but in the capitals that grace the Erectheum we have an assemblage of curves that, from whatever point viewed is altogether unique, and which for harmony has perhaps never been equalled. The delightful combination of unity and variety in the geometrical or logarithmic spiral of its volutes, diversity of curvature and increment regulated by unit of law, joined to the motion and play of curves generally, constitute a total of linear and formal grace that no unprejudiced eye can behold without at least a pleasing interest.*

Like its elder sister, the Ionic disdains the "foreign aid of ornament;" in other words, it is independent of all imitations of natural organisation, whether of leaf or flower, and trusts to the beauty that is born of pure form; and as a harmony of form only, its capital is more purely a creation, and therefore a greater triumph of art-power than that of the Corinthian itself.

In addition to the strong aesthetic grounds given for the use of the Ionic order together with the flexibility of overall form suggested by the Erechtheion prototype, making it adaptable for modern usage, there may have been other 'associative' connotations in its ecclesiastical usage.

Henry William Inwood's *The Erechtheion at Athens* of 1827, the first publication devoted to a single Greek monument, attempted much more than just a description of that Greek temple. The 28 chapters of the volume are divided into four 'books' of continuous text: *Cadmeia, Homeros, Herodotus* and *Erechtheion.*

The first book began with a description of the Tabernacle of Moses, 'this first important instance of raising a temple'. Inwood went on to describe in some detail the events leading up to and the realisation of Solomon's Temple. Cadmus, a Phoenician commander, usually credited with introducing the use of letters into Greece, is also suggested by Inwood to have brought the Arts from Tyre to Thebes, around the time of Moses. Ion, the grandson of Erechtheus, was paralleled by Inwood in the manner of his birth, with Moses, both were placed in woven arks.

In the third book of Inwood's publication, *Homeros*, comparisons are made between the palaces of Homer's *Odyssey*, as well as the fable of the Cyclops, with Solomon's massive constructions. Inwood also discussed some of the rituals described in the Old Testament and how they prefigured equivalents in the New.

The importance of Inwood's work is two-fold in relation to Thomson, firstly because of its attempt to trace to a process of architectural evolution from Biblical sources, and secondly in its singling out of the Erechtheion as a culminative example.

Ten years after Inwood's work in 1837, the architect best known for the National Gallery in London, William Wilkins (1778–1839), published six essays in one volume, collectively entitled, *Prolusiones Architectonicae*; described by Dr. James Macauley as, 'possibly the most scholarly text of the nineteenth century' (in his essay in *'Greek' Thomson*).

As well as two descriptive essays on the history and construction of the 'Erechtheum,' the final assay, *the Temple at Jerusalem the type of Grecian Architecture*, continued a similar chronological theme to Inwood. At the outset Wilkins contended,

> *When we, therefore, institute a comparison between the Jewish temple and the sacred structures of Greece, we must expect to find a difference of arrangement, in conformity with the exigencies of the different and distinct rites of the two*

people. With these allowances, we shall find an intimate cor-
respondence of proportions, which will lead us to the conclu-
sion that both were constructed along similar principles; and
the necessary inference will follow, that the earlier examples
were the prototypes of those of later times constructed in dis-
tant countries.

Wilkins then went further than Inwood, however, in detailing one of the Doric temples at Paestum for *direct* comparison with the temple at Jerusalem. He concluded with plates illustrating the projected similarities and is, 'led to the inference that ... a mode of construct-ing temples was transmitted directly, and with little of the interme-diate assistance of a third state'.

After Wilkin's death, with the rise of the Gothic Revival, his opin-ions were given a critical, debunking reappraisal, with W.H. Leeds making a swipe in 1847. 'Infinitely better', Leeds remarked, 'if instead of labouring to convince us that the Temple of Solomon was a building of the Grecian Doric order, he had applied himself to more diligent and real artistic study at his own drawing board'.

Despite such criticisms, however, continuing as heir to Inwood and Wilkins's interpretations of biblical architecture, Edward Charles Hakewill (1816–1872), in 1850, published an unillustrated book enti-tled, *the Temple*. Edward, son of Henry Hakewill (also an architect) is not credited with any buildings of note, he was however articled, between 1831 and 1838, to Philip Hardwick, who built in a wide vari-ety of styles, but is mostly known for his classical work, such as the monumental Doric Propylaeum at Euston Station, of 1838 (demol-ished in 1962).

Hakewill's book, as a work entirely devoted to the subject addressed in only in part by Inwood and Wilkins, made several addi-tional steps in a bold attempt to canonise the suggestions of his predecessors. The book was widely reviewed at the time and was the subject of a generally favourable leader in *the Builder* (December 7, 1850).

Hakewill began in greater antiquity than either Inwood or Wilkins with a discussion of Noah's Ark. In the summing up of this introduc-tory chapter, Hakewill enthusiastically expounded the implications of the Ark:

We must acknowledge that this [Noah's Ark] was the great
prototype, not of the Jewish temples only, but of all the world,
who, in the early ages, acknowledged God. . . . And if we see,
as I think we shall not fail, that the Christian Temple was also
predicated in this type, and that the coming peculiarities of its
form were shewn in the successive developments of the
Tabernacle and Temple, how beautifully consistent with the
oneness of eternal truth is this revelation of the pattern of that

> *Temple, which, in every age, should be given to man, to be in itself as a fabric unmistakedly identified with the Church of God, the image of the body of Christ.*

In the book by Hakewill, as well as Inwood's, there are potential implications as to Thomson's use of the Erechtheion Ionic Order. In drawing comparison between the biblical archetype and various Greek temples, Hakewill stated, 'Striking as has been the general rule, I think this solitary instance [the Erechtheion] composed of exceptions still more striking'. He drew particular significance not only from the proportions but from the singular sacred aspects of the temple which was said to have housed relics of the gods. (The essential function of Solomon's Temple was as a repository for the Ark of the Covenant holding the Ten Commandments given to Moses by God.) Hakewill made a somewhat surprising dating of the first Erechtheion (which burnt down and was rebuilt in Pericles' reign – seen by Hakewill as another parallel with the turbulent history of the temple at Jerusalem) at about 1150 B.C. This was an unorthodox suggestion giving the temple a greater antiquity than usually attributed to it, and was picked up in *the Builder's* leader.

In the final chapter of *the Temple*, Hakewill speculated on the future relevance of the temple archetype (neither Inwood nor Wilkins went so far). He forecast another temple being built in anticipation of Christ's second coming:

> *And if the church architecture of this Dispensation, after having come to its perfection, has ceased, like the temple architecture, in its progressive growth, we may see and know, from this also, that the time is near for the preparation of that temple to which, as to His throne, Christ shall come in glory... For the temple and the throne must be first prepared.*

This sentiment may well have been shared by other Christians of progressive faith at a time when there was a movement urging worship in anticipation of a new Millennial age, as was strong amongst United Presbyterians. George Gilfillan (1813–78) a critic, essayist, lecturer and pulpit orator of the U.P. Church, in the *Bards of the Bible*, also expressed progressive views:

> *If no Pentecostal revival be sent – if the Church is to proceed at its present creeping and crippled rate – when, we ask, is its Millennium to dawn? Shall it ever? No alternative can we see but Jesus advenient and prayer and work done in this prospect, or despair.*
>
> *We have in the text anticipated objections which might be urged to our belief in a "Forerunner". Such a being would answer the same end with the Baptist. He would encourage*

*the friends and check the foes, till the hour for the Divine Man
would strike.*

If in sympathy with these views, could it be possible that Thomson
saw his churches as 'forerunners'? That the churches may in some
way be attempts to herald a new era?

Cyclopean Foundations

The massive masonry substructure of St Vincent Street Church has
been read differently by various commentators. Pragmatically it is
recognised as an architectural device to accommodate the hall,
ingeniously housed beneath the church, and thus make up the difference between the levels of north and south. This podium has
been seen to act as a stage for the upper parts of the church, and is
important compositionally as the bulk of the church diminishes
towards the sky.

The blocks of squared ashlar in the podium are bedded in a 'random' arrangement of various sizes. This, however, is an artistically
composed randomness, with the size of the stones subtly diminish-
ing higher up, adding to the sense of perspective, and the largest
stones are positioned near the pedestrian level where their full size
can be appreciated. Some of the blocks of stone are immense,
among the largest over nine feet long and almost three feet deep.
The sheer effort involved in the use of unusually large stones,
immensely difficult to transport and lift seems to suggest a deep religious sense of duty and devotion.

A full account of a lecture that Thomson read to the Glasgow
Architectural Society, entitled *On Masonry and how it may be
Improved*, appeared the following day in the *Herald* of 23rd February
1859. In it he argued for stones of a greater size and quality to be
used in the pursuit of endless duration, there being 'nothing more
humiliating or repugnant than decay'. He also remarked that,

> *In Assyria, in Egypt, in Greece, in Rome and even in the
> woody depths of Central America, we find recorded in stone
> and lime the particulars of a civilisation which still powerfully
> affects and influences our thoughts, although the peoples
> amongst whom it flourished have long since passed away;
> and in some instances left scarcely any other trace behind.
> There is nothing we cherish more fondly than "the longing
> after immortality"...*

The essential quality embodied in St Vincent Street Church's podium
is 'permanence'. This is the quality that Thomson devoted a large part
of the second Haldane Lecture to, as illustrated by the monuments of

Egypt. In the random arrangement of stones we may read the 'effect' or 'fact' of nature; and in terms of 'aesthetic faculty' it may represent the earlier stages of its understanding by man. In plan the proportion of the podium, as it covers the whole site, is an imperfect square. The character of the podium may be said to be successful on Burke's terms alone.

There may be another justification for the immense size of the stones in the church's podium, based on a biblical reading of them. King Solomon's great works, the temple and the House of the Forest of Lebanon are both described in the First Book of Kings as having massive blocks used in their foundations. With regard to the House of the Forest of Lebanon, it was written that, 'At the base were heavy stones, massive blocks, some ten and some eight cubits in size, and above were heavy stones dressed to measure, and cedar' (1 Kings ch.7, vs.10,11). Furthermore, in the New Testament building blocks are used in the analogy of a spiritual temple by Peter:

> *So come to him, our living Stone – the stone rejected by man but choice and precious in the sight of God. Come, and let yourselves be built as living stones, into a spiritual temple; to become a holy priesthood, to offer spiritual sacrifices acceptable to God through Jesus Christ. For it stands written: 'I lay in Zion a choice corner-stone of great worth. The man who has faith in it will not be put to shame'. The great worth of which it speaks is for you who have no faith, the stone which the builders rejected has become not only the corner stone, but also 'a stone to trip over, a rock to stumble against'. They fall when they disbelieve the word, such is their chosen lot.*
> (1 Peter ch. 2, vs. 4-8. Good News translation.)

A Synthesis of Old and New Testaments

Originally, there was no organ in the church (the present one was sympathetically added in 1904), and the large windows to the south would have been completely unobstructed. Beneath the windows in the pulpit and screen made of North American pine (moved forwards in accommodating the organ). This grand design seems to celebrate a transitional line, and is expressed as a ceremonial entrance to some inner sanctuary with two great portals flanking the pulpit, preceded by a series of steps and stages. Similar screens appeared in Thomson's other U.P. churches, Caledonia Road and Queen's Park. It seems that their symbolic purpose could be to commemorate the 'veil' across the inner shrine of Solomon's Temple which housed the Ark of the Covenant, superseded in the Christian church by the new covenant with God.

E.C. Hakewill in his book, *The Temple*, appealed that we should still 'mark the ancient boundary' and saw it as 'a universal symbolism which at no period has been changed: the heathen marked off the adytum from the naos, as the Jew did the Holy of Holies from the sanctuary, and as we do the chancel from the nave'.

Thomson himself in the Second Haldane noted a common sacred purpose between the Jewish temple and the sanctuary of a Greek temple, in serving to mark a distinction between common place behaviour and that expressive of adoration: 'But whether there was an image representing the majesty of God, or an ark containing the laws of God, it was found necessary to screen it from the vulgar gaze'.

Within the main body of the church, rising two levels from the upper ground floor to the clearstorey, a vertical, aspirational layering of meaning can be read, resting on the solid foundations already described. Supporting the gallery above, on the ground floor are six highly original cast iron columns, (two rows of three). Directly above, at the gallery level there are six more similar columns, supporting the clearstorey, yet they have modified capitals.

The ornamental components of the florid circular capitals appear to be the same above and below, yet the components of the capitals at ground floor point downwards and are cast in shadow by a deep rim, whilst the ones at gallery level are revealed and point upwards. It would appear that the capitals were conceived of as flowers that open in the light supplied by the larger windows at gallery level. This may have spiritual analogy as well as naturalistic.

Biblically *light* is used as a description of God's power, for light, invisible in itself, manifests everything. There are numerous biblical references to light. Jesus said, *'I am the light of the world,'* (John ch.8, vs. 12. Good News translation) and Paul in his Letter to the Ephesians (ch. 5, vs. 8. Good News translation) wrote,

> For though you were once all darkness, now as Christians you are light. Live like men who are at home in daylight, for where light is, there all goodness springs up, all justice and truth ...
> And so the hymn says:

> 'Awake, sleeper,
> rise from the dead,
> and Christ will shine upon you'.

A Mediator Between Heaven and Earth

What do we see here? A group of beautiful forms, so full of thought that they seem to think. They seem possessed of

some high, contemplative, rapturous kind of life altogether
different from any of the ordinary or natural sorts ... that
assemblage of angelic forms, that holy sisterhood standing as
mediators between earth and heaven, sending upwards the
prayers and praises of men, and drawing downwards the
approbation and blessing of the eternal gods.
(Haldane lectures, III, on the Acropolis of Athens)

The proportional study of St Vincent Street Church does not pretend to be a definitive analysis, it does however, hopefully illustrate a principled and deliberate use of some primary geometrical figures in plan, section and elevation, even if it seems certain that there are other layers of subtlety yet to be discovered.

The manifestation of certain proportional relationships in plan is inherent at each level because of the need for structural continuity from top to bottom. Thus the footprint of the clearstorey is super-imposed at each level, to differing degrees, with the proportions of the hall in the basement reflecting the walls of the clearstorey three levels above. The observance of significant proportions in the plans is most apparent in the areas covered by the clearstorey. The broader body of the church at ground level is only an approximate square.

In the study of the church's elevations, the podium is seen to act as a base for the establishment of certain proportional relationships, and takes up topographical differences of the site. The photograph illustrated above of c. 1890, shows how from the south, the 'zig-zag' band of small windows running along the top of the podium would have been visible at distance above the low buildings to the rear, and across a wide stretch of Glasgow. This band of windows has strong significance proportionally as the springing point of the perfect figure that implicitly but commandingly inscribes the church's Ionic portico. The figure discovered is the six pointed star or hexagram – shown in six of Hay's *seven elements of Geometric Beauty*. The figure has a wealth of symbolic connotations, it is widely recognisable as the 'Star of David' or sometimes 'Solomon's Seal', and has traditionally been seen to represent a mediation between heaven – the upward pointing triangle – and earth – the downward pointing triangle (*An Illustrated Encyclopaedia of Traditional Symbols*). Professor Curl's observation of the numeric significance of six columns is obviously given further support by the discovery of this figure.

The church's prostyle porticoes are derived from the east front of the Erechtheion at Athens, as has been noted. A book written by Claude Bragdon, *The Beautiful Necessity* of 1910, provides indirect corroboration of the proportions discovered in the north and south elevations of St Vincent Street Church, through his own short analy-sis of the Erectheion. In a chapter entitled 'Latent Geometry', he illustrated a diagram showing the 'application of the equilateral triangle to the Erechtheum at Athens'. With regard to the wider application of the equilateral triangle in architecture, he wrote that, 'It may be stated as a general rule that whenever three important points in any architectural composition coincide (approximately or exactly) with the three extremities of an equilateral triangle, it makes for beauty of proportion'.

The west elevation of St Vincent Street Church would appear to have been composed using primarily squares, derivative rectangles (such as the root-five) and forty five degree lines. The powerfully compressed entrance embedded into the plinth, is shown to have a dynamic relationship with the purely symbolical portal above it. Objections are anticipated that since these relationships are set up flatly in elevation, they would therefore not be read as drawn because of the way the clearstorey steps back. However it may be read from Hay and Thomson that a rational perception of these perfect but abstract proportional relationships would not be necessary for their appreciation, and a circular building, for example, is rarely seen as a circle. The degree to which Thomson wove the structure with proportional harmonies, may also have been an act of faith; in the fourth Haldane Lecture he noted in appreciation of the Greeks that, "The Gods see Everywhere".

The Tower

Not only do the porticoes appear to have been harmonised within a six pointed star but also the upper part of the tower seems to correspond with a repetition of the same figure. Implicit within the two interlocking stars are two Vesica Pisces, a smaller one within a larger one. These stretch from the centre of the clock to the top of the anthemion ornament. Held within the Vesica's are the four great portals of the tower, proclaiming themselves to the four corners of Glasgow. The evangelical message of the portals, and others used rhetorically elsewhere in the church, such as on the west elevation, seems clear; in the Gospel of John, Jesus says, *'I am the door: by me if any man enter in, he shall be saved and go in and out and find pasture'*. (John ch.10, vs. 9. King James translation).

The clocks immediately below the portals, celebrated in swathes of ornament, architecturally, and geometrically herald the portals, and may be read literally as the passage of time, and perhaps the succession of the Old Covenant with the New, or in prospect of a new Christian era. (The clocks were only installed in the tower in 1884, but they were almost certainly anticipated in the original design.)

The strikingly original 'T'-shaped windows and pairs of caryatid heads facing each other, beneath the clocks were the subject of intense debate between Sam McKinstry and Professor Curl. The windows were read by Professor Curl as representing the 'Tau' symbol of Freemasonry, whilst McKinstry thought a more likely reading of them would be as the early church's representation of the cross. McKinstry also noted that the paired heads seem to correspond with a description in the Book of Exodus of the cherubim that were placed, upon divine instruction, at either end of the 'mercy seat' (the cover of the holy Ark). The passage from the King James translation (Exodus ch. 25, vs. 18–22) reads:

> *"And thou shalt make two cherubims of gold, of beaten work shalt thou make them, in the two ends of the mercy seat. And make one cherub on the one end, and the other cherub on the other end ... And the cherubims shall stretch forth their wings on high, covering the mercy seat with their wings, and their faces shall look to one another ... And there I will meet with thee from above the mercy seat, from between the two cherubims which are upon the ark of the testimony..."*

In *the Alexander Thomson Society Newsletter* No. 17, Sam McKinstry interpreted the cherubims at St Vincent Street by echoing the New Testament lesson in Hebrews, writing that, 'The message is that the Presence betwixt the cherubim known to the children of Israel was indeed Christ, the fulfilment of the Old Testament'. McKinstry also noted that in measured drawings by A.L. Watson of 1940 a cross appeared in the glazing behind each pair of cherubim marking in elevation the point between them at which their gaze meets. Cherubim or angels are referred to elsewhere in the Bible and share the same significance: 'What are they all but ministrant spirits, sent out to serve, for the sake of those who are to inherit salvation?' (Hebrews ch. 2, vs. 14, Good News translation.)

An interesting implicit angular relationship has been discovered, relating the cherubim with the upper body of the church. If two lines are taken from the exact point at which the gaze of the cherubim meets, and are projected downwards in either north or south elevation towards the church they are found to intersect the antefixae, either side of the pediment at 30 and 60°, respectively; whilst in the west elevation there is an implicit right angled relationship with both of the portals at gallery level. So, in a sense, a harmonic umbrella is confered upon the church from 'between the cherubim', perhaps in prayerful hope of direct communication with God.

Flanking the portals of the tower are 'egg' shaped finials that begin to dissolve the tower and anticipate the perforated dome above. Also at this stage the tower becomes an octagon, before emerging as a cylinder above the portals. A little above the anthemion of the portals the continuity of the cylinder is interrupted by twelve squat columns. *Twelve* is a number of great biblical significance – the twelve stones taken out of Jordan, the Twelve Disciples, the twelve foundation stones of the New Jerusalem, or perhaps the Twelve Tribes of Israel, brought together to one by Christ. There is perhaps corroboration that Thomson was consciously seeking to invoke the attributes of *twelve,* in that the diameter of the cylinder approximates to twelve feet (12'44"), whilst the distance from the top of the tower's ultimate finial to the base of the cylinder approximates closely to 36 f (35'10"). The general arrangement of this upper part of the church may have been suggested to Thomson in the local example of St Georges Tron Church of 1807 by William Stark, which also has twelve columns supporting its perforated dome.

The culmination of the tower, however, has roused much speculation as to its pictorial derivations and meaning. Thomson's imagination may have been fired by images of Indian domes and stupas as published in books such as those by the Daniell brothers (*The Architecture, Antiquities, and Landscape Scenery of Hindoostan,* 1816) and James Fergusson's several works. The suggestion that the dome derived from a Glasgow policeman's helmet raises speculation of the dome as 'celestial helmet'. E. Baldwin Smith, in his book entitled *The Dome – a study in the history of ideas* of 1971 wrote that:

> *The one symbolic domical concept of great antiquity in the Near East which can be most definitely connected with Palestine and Christian writings is the idea of a celestial helmet... The lasting appeal of this particular domical shape and its direct link with Christianity came when its sky symbolism was combined with that of the piloi and the cosmic egg cult in the Dioskouri...the popularity of these ancient heroes, themselves born in an egg, came from their having become the intermediaries between men and gods, and the dispensers of immortality...their conoid bonnets, or helmets, surmounted by stars, became the common symbol of the cult and were identified with the cosmic egg...*

The most obvious Christian symbolic interpretation of the conoid dome, and the one most likely subscribed to by Thomson, is that of an egg symbolising rebirth. Thomson himself said in the final Haldane Lecture that, 'the form of the egg being beautiful in itself, and in having many pleasing associations, it is not wonderful that man should seek to reproduce it in his work'.

Sam McKinstry in *the Alexander Thomson Society Newsletter* No. 8, in his account of Solomon's temple, as described in the First Book of Kings, took the interpretative step of converting from cubits into metres. The precise measure of a cubit is an area of speculation, or at least it was in Thomson's day. Perhaps, however, more importantly in the biblical descriptions of buildings in terms of cubits, is the *numerical* values of the measurements, each of which may be held to have some meaning.

Biblical Measurements

The possible numerical significance of key dimensions in the upper reaches of the tower has been quoted above; another perhaps more remarkable sequence of measurements, however, is found to occur around the upper 'temple' part of the church itself. Measurements taken from the photogrammetric drawings, using the bottom step of the portico as the datum level reveal length and breadth measurements of 99'9" by 49'5", whilst a height from the underside of the cornice to this bottom step measures as 30'3". It may be recalled from the description in exodus, that Moses was instructed to make the court of the Tabernacle one hundred cubits long by fifty wide (Exodus ch. 27, vs. 18). In the opening pages of *The Erechtheion at Athens,* H.W. Inwood noted, regarding the Tabernacle, that:

> From the general description recorded by the ancient histori-
> ans and by Josephus is detailed the various interesting partic-
> ulars of this first important instance of raising a temple... The
> space enclosed Josephus called aethrium or artrium: it
> extended a hundred cubits, and was in width fifty.

The same dimensions are described again but for a different building further on in the Bible. In the account of the House of the Forest of Lebanon, it is written of Solomon that, 'He built the House of the Forest of Lebanon, a hundred cubits long, fifty broad and thirty high'. (1 Kings ch. 7, vs. 2 Good News translation.) It is commonly held that the primary purpose of the building was religious and judicial rather than domestic and Solomon was viewed as priest as well as king. If it is not coincidence, perhaps Thomson perceived an archetypal significance in the dimensions.

McFadzean in *The Life and Works of Alexander Thomson* suggested that Thomson had adopted the idea of the Gothic or Early Christian section, allowing him to express the church as a classical temple at clearstorey level, above the approximately square space that was necessary to house a big congregation. It may be noted, however, that the idea of a clearstorey is present in biblical descriptions of Solomon's Temple and the House of the Forest of Lebanon. James Fergusson, in *The Palaces of Nineveh and Persepolis Restored* of 1851, comparatively examined the similarities in arrangement of the Solomonic structures and those of Nineveh and

Persepolis (ruins of which had recently been discovered). He illustrated some alternative sectional diagrams, based on the descriptions of the House of the Forest of Lebanon that may be seen to have a basic generic similarity with St Vincent Street Church. Fergusson also noted that unlike the Temple of Solomon, the House of the Forest of Lebanon was built 'in the city itself, and surrounded apparently by the habitations of his subjects'; whereas the former was built outside the walls of Jerusalem.

Thomson may have had more reverence for the 'English foot' than we do for the modern metre which is solely based upon commodity. In the second Haldane Lecture, Thomson mentioned specific dimensions of the Great Pyramid, as '764 feet square at the base, and 480 feet high'. In 1859 John Taylor published a book entitled *The Great Pyramid, Why was it Built? and Who Built it?* In the course of his broad reaching analysis, he noted that,

> *A peculiar property of the English foot in connection with the measure of the base of the Great Pyramid is, that when we divide unity by 764 (the number of feet in the side of the base) the quotient gives the number of feet in the circumference of the Earth as it was measured in the latitude of the Great Pyramid. This may be deemed as nothing more than a numerical coincidence; but when we recollect that this foot alone expresses this relation, and that the measure by which it is expressed may possibly have had its origin at this time, and may even have been called into existence to denote this proportion, it seems a peculiarity which deserves notice ... one English foot bears the same ratio to the side of the Pyramid, that the circumference of the Earth bears to one hundred millions of English feet.*

CONCLUSIONS

Attempts to overtly associate St Vincent Street Church with any one biblical precedent seem unlikely both in terms of the often highly detailed descriptions given in the Bible and in recognition of Thomson's progressive faith. It does seem likely, however, that Thomson was aiming to manifest a modern version of the archetype common in the highest expressions of religious architecture, based on the sacred principles illumined by the most perfect examples of the past. It seems evident that he perceived all 'biblical architecture', from Noah's Ark to John's revelation of the New Jerusalem, to be various manifestations of the same divine blueprint.

Thomson perceived in the Greeks similar qualities to the Jews of the Old Testament, and in the remains of Grecian architecture he saw essences that were consistent with scriptural prototypes. The Greeks seem to have informed Thomson's imaginings on vanished Jewish architecture, but unlike perhaps some of his predecessors, he was not primarily interested in reproducing a correct biblical *style*. Rather Thomson was determined to find the *key* to designing works in a *co-creative duty*. His work may be seen as both Greek and biblical. He genuinely seems to have been working from 'within' rather than just mimicking external appearances. This was after all what he implored others to do.

In the present age with its suspicion of 'systems', the concept of an absolute in beauty may be uncomfortable. Mathematics has become associated with utility, mechanisation and economy, an aspect of the divine has been harnessed, but at what price? Thomson's liberated conception of proportion was something poetic, something that enabled him to see a divine pattern through all of nature. His belief in universal truths enabled Thomson to see ancient works of art being as relevant to the present as they ever were. He appears to have heard the voices of the ancients more strongly and warmly than many of those vocal in his own time. Not only may Thomson's architecture be said to have truly matched the Greeks in terms of 'art-power' but in the intellectual attainment embodied in his work Thomson is also surely deserved of the accolade 'Greek'.

ANALYTICAL DRAWINGS

The following study has been carried out using photogrammetric survey drawings of 1992 (Reproduced with the permission of George Kirton of Glasgow City Council Property Services Department), and from plans made whilst at Page and Park Architects of the church as it was in 1888 (so as not to pick up alterations made after Thomson's death). In addition a section has been constructed, reflecting information on the other drawings.

West Elevation Scale 1:250
APPLICATION OF THE EQUILATERAL TRIANGLE, THE SQUARE AND ROOT-
FIVE RECTANGLE

99'9"

30'3"

West Elevation Scale 1:250
SIGNIFICANT DIMENSIONS

Cross-Section looking South Scale 1:250
APPLICATION OF THE EQUILATERAL TRIANGLE AND SQUARE

Lower-Ground Plan c. 1888 Scale 1:250
APPLICATION OF THE VESICA PISCES AND GOLDEN RECTANGLE

Huw Williams

I'm Astounded By People Who Want To 'Know' The Universe When It's Hard Enough To Find Your Way Around Chinatown: an Essay in Unsymbolisation

Weighing several pounds, over a thousand pages in length with an extraordinary range of images, Williams' dissertation is clearly influenced by Koolhaas' magnum opus *S, M, L, XL*. It also contains, very importantly, a complex argument concerning the way in which social reality might be instilled in architectural and urban design. Although image copyright issues make this dissertation near impossible to publish here, a range of page layouts give some indication of the impressive intellectual and graphic effort.

Housing Texture

IN PART THIS REFLECTS THAT SUBURBAN SEMIS WERE LARGELY PRIVATELY OWNED, AND ALMOST WHOLLY SO AFTER THE PASSING OF THE RENT ACTS. TOWER BLOCK FLATS WERE RENTED AND DID NOT INSPIRE THE PROTECTIVE INSTINCTS THAT ARE EXPRESSED IN PRIDE OF OWNERSHIP..........TO CULTIVATE AND MAINTAIN HIS OWN GARDEN, TO DEFINE HIS OWN TERRITORY, AND TO OPEN HIS FRONT DOOR ARE ...

CAMERA CONTINUES TO PAN, EXAMINING TRAVIS' APARTMENT. IT IS ORIGINAL, TO SAY THE LEAST. A RATTY OLD MATTRESS IS THROWN AGAINST ONE WALL. THE FLOOR IS LITTERED WITH OLD NEWSPAPERS, WORN AND UNFOLDED STREET MAPS AND PORNOGRAPHY. THE PORNOGRAPHY IS OF THE SORT THAT LOOKS CHEAP BUT COSTS $10 A THROW – BLACK AND WHITE PHOTOGRAPHS OF NAKED WOMEN TIED AND GAGGED WITH LEATHER STRAPS AND CLOTHESLINES. THERE IS NO FURNITURE OTHER THAN A RICKETY CHAIR AND TABLE. A BEAT-UP PORTABLE TV RESTS ON AN UPRIGHT MELON CRATE. THE RED SILK MASS IN THE CORNER LOOKS LIKE A VIETNAMESE FLAG. INDECIPHERABLE WORDS, FIGURES, NUMBERS ARE SCRIBBLED ON THE PLAIN PLASTER WALLS. RAGGED BLACK WIRES DANGLE FROM THE WALL WHERE THE TELEPHONE ONCE HUNG.

INSIDE TRAVIS' APARTMENT, TRAVIS IS WAITING AT THE SMALL TABLE. ARE SOME NEW ITEMS ON THE TABLE: HIS GIANT ECONOM-SIZE BOTTLE OF VITAMINS, A GIANT BOTTLE OF ASPIRINS, A PINT OF APRICOT BRANDY, A PARTIAL LOAF OF CHEAP WHITE BREAD. ON THE WALL BEHIND THE TABLE HANG TWO MORE ITEMS: A GAS SIGN READING "ONE OF THESE DAYS I'M GONNA GET ORGANIZIZED" AND AN ORANGE-BLACK BUMPER STICKER FOR CHARLES PALANTINE.

TRAVIS HAS CLEANED UP HIS APARTMENT. EVERYTHING IS NEAT AND ORDERLY. THE MATTRESS IS BARE AND FLATTENED OUT, THE FLOOR IS SPOTLESS, THE CANS AND BOTTLES OF FOOD AND PILLS PUT OUT OF SIGHT. THE WALL IS STILL COVERED WITH PALANTINE PARAPHERNALIA BUT WHEN WE REACH THE DESK THERE ARE ONLY FOUR ITEMS THERE.

The mass media are turned a geography that contains the inverted depression of space. In addition, the television, although an intimate device, promises an increasing familiarity with the outside. Through its development the television has become more than just a thin in the corner. The advent of home shopping channels challenges the traditional distinctions between shop and home, and with the numerous combinations of media now on offer, there is also a growing indistinction between house and cinema. At this regard indicate that the on-off quality of the mass media can greatly transform to needs space where also steering remains spatial perception. Media inform us in a larger world. The global context in which we are placed, increasingly acting as a media centre, the house can also thus become a physical quality that will funnel liquidation our understanding of public and private so this way it is possible to counteract a situation in which, as Baudrillard has warned, "our houses are no longer aware of the drama of the outside world." For us to sustain an existential understanding of ourselves within a universe outside of our individual control, the house as a personalised corner of this space must address, and assert itself metaphorically, as a small tool navigating a vast sea. The combination of the house as a locus for heterogeneous concealment and a misconfirmation of the manifest core of the mass media, can offer a richer vision of the home, one that can take us beyond the idea of the fake house as a receptacle of tradition. Shots, or the modernist dwellings rigid self image as a simplistic spatial metaphor for up-to-the moment orbiting.

SEVERAL WEEKS LATER, THE FACE OF TRAVIS' APARTMENT HAS
CHANGED. THE LONG, BLANK WALL BEHIND THE TABLE IS NOW COVERED
WITH TACKED UP CHARTS, PICTURES, NEWSPAPER CLIPPINGS, MAPS.

TO LIVE IS TO LEAVE TRACES. IN THE INTERIOR THESE ARE EMPHA-
SISED. AN ABUNDANCE OF COVERS AND PROTECTORS, LINERS AND
CASES IS DEVISED, ON WHICH THE TRACES OF OBJECTS OF EVERY-
DAY USE ARE IMPRINTED. THE TRACES OF THE OCCUPANT ALSO
LEAVE THEIR IMPRESSION ON THE INTERIOR.

Index